Children's
Behavior

Children's Behavior

An Introduction to Research Studies

Henry Clay Lindgren
San Francisco State University

 Mayfield Publishing Company

Library of Congress Catalog Card Number: 74-33860
International Standard Book Number: 0-87484-317-0

Manufactured in the United States of America
Mayfield Publishing Company, 285 Hamilton Avenue
Palo Alto, California 94301

This book was set in Times Roman by Computer Typeset-
ting Services and was printed and bound by the George
Banta Company. Sponsoring editor was C. Lansing Hays,
Carole Norton supervised editing, and Alice Rosendall was
manuscript editor. Michelle Hogan supervised production,
and the book was designed by Nancy Sears. Cover photo
is by Tristram and Phoebe Dunn.

Contents

Preface

For the nonpsychologist and the psychologist alike, the study of children is an exciting and engaging activity, for in it we discover the past, present, and future. We learn something about our own childhood experiences, as well as about some of the factors that led us to become the persons we are today. We broaden and deepen our understanding of the children with whom we, as professionals and parents, are concerned. We may also discover some clues about how we can provide a better future, through improved human relationships, for the generations yet to come. The most valuable source of information lies in the findings of researchers, who use scientific methods to gather data and to build theories that give us a better understanding of the complexities of children's behavior.

This book consists of written textual material and selected reports of illustrative research studies, organized around major topics in child development. In writing and editing this book, I have kept in mind the interests and academic backgrounds of the students with whom I have worked at San Francisco State University and at universities in British Columbia, Italy, Brazil, and Lebanon. Not all of these students have had a "reading knowledge" of elementary statistics, and I have edited the research reports with this background in mind. Some technical terminology has been deleted and ellipsed (. . .) where the general sense of the author's message would not be affected. Interested readers can, of course, refer to the original text of the articles in the journals cited. A supplementary glossary has been included to assist the student who may not be familiar with some of the terms used in this book.

Whenever I assign the reading of a journal article to my students, I always urge them to read the summary first, as it gives a general idea of what the study is about. It often helps to read the author's discussion of his findings next, because it fills out the general picture of the study. The student should then read the entire article, first rapidly, without hesitating over difficult terms, and then in more detail and depth. I suggest the initial rapid overview because students often panic at an unfamiliar word or statistical symbol and never get on to the next sentence or paragraph, where the discussion usually clarifies the unfamiliar term within its context. I encourage students to guess at or to speculate about the meaning of a term or symbol, because when they look it up, they frequently find that they were at least close to its meaning. In any event, it is important to keep in mind that the significant factors in any study are its methods and its findings; the articles in this book were selected so that most students will have little difficulty understanding how the studies were done and what the investigators found. Additional clues as to what to look for are, of course, provided in my written commentaries.

Developing this book has been an interesting and rewarding experience for me in terms of my own growing understanding of children. I was helped in many ways with this enterprise by Fredi Lindgren, who served as editorial consultant and prepared the manuscript for the publisher. The copy editing of Alice Rosendall did much to make my writing clearer and smoother. I am also indebted for the comments and suggestions made by Patricia Keith-Spiegel and Dee L. Shepherd-Look of California State University, Northridge; Harry Munsinger of University of California, San Diego; and Fran Y. Fehlman of El Camino College. Most of all, I should like to express my appreciation for the cooperation of the scientific investigators who permitted their work to appear in this book.

Henry Clay Lindgren
San Francisco State University

1.
Research methods in child development

A century ago, when psychology was in its infancy, investigators were chiefly interested in what would today be called "pure science," or "basic research." The German psychologist Wilhelm Wundt and the generation of experimentalists who succeeded him were motivated by an abiding curiosity about the functioning of the nervous system and especially of the mind, but they were unconcerned about what practical value their findings might have. Although most of the American psychologists of that day followed the pure science tradition, others succumbed to the pragmatic spirit that has characterized American endeavors in all walks of life from the earliest pioneering days onward. This interest in practical, everyday experiences is reflected in the work of William James, who was interested in basic research but who also delivered his pragmatic *Talks to Teachers* in 1892, publishing them in 1899.

The academic, basic-research tradition, as originally espoused by the Wundt school of experimental psychology, continues to be strong on both sides of the Atlantic, but in America the pure-science approach is ameliorated by a culture that is still as pragmatic and practical as it was a hundred years ago. The American psychologist is therefore likely to lead a kind of double life—while he actively pursues knowl-edge for its own sake, he simultaneously works to develop the kind of understanding that will help to solve society's many problems and to improve the quality of human existence. While the academic psy-chologist may claim, especially when seeking a research grant, that his work is more relevant than it seems, the applied psychologist reviews the research literature produced by the academic psychologist, seeking concepts and techniques to help him treat the real-life prob-lems he encounters in his particular field of expertise.

The study of children and their behavior has attracted the aca-demic, basic-research psychologist as well as the problem-oriented applied psychologist. The research psychologist who wishes to under-stand human behavior by unraveling its puzzles may well decide to start with childhood, because this is where behavior begins. The applied psychologist, perhaps a clinician dealing with psychopathology in all age groups, reads research on child development to further his own understanding of how his patients' problems came into being. The study of children is a fascinating one, regardless of whether we are simply curious about the origins of behavior, or whether we are looking for clues to help us deal with the problems of adjusting to today's society.

If we are seeking information about how children think, solve problems, and become socialized, we can find more information in the research literature than we can if we are looking for clues to help us treat an adult or a community. A similar disparity exists if we are seeking information to help us make decisions concerning children. Urie Bronfenbrenner (1974) has commented ironically on this awkward gap between available information and that which is frequently sought. He reports that at various times in his career, government and private agencies have asked him for advice on matters concerning children. Their first questions were usually about what research has to say on the issues they were considering. As Bron-fenbrenner later observed, ". . . there was little I could tell them, at least in answer to the questions they were asking. I felt much better when they asked me for wisdom. Here I had quite a bit to say. But they interrupted me with an unfair question. They asked: 'What's your evidence?' Something happened that is rare in my experience: I had nothing to say."

Some of the questions Bronfenbrenner was asked by the policy-makers identify a few of the difficulties faced by modern psychologists who try to serve both science and social relevance.

How important is it for a child to be with its mother during the first three years of life?

How important is social class mix in group programs for children during the first three years of life?

Can fathers care for young children as effectively as mothers can?

What changes should be carried out in our schools to reduce rapidly rising rates of dropout, drug addiction, and vandalism?

Should parents be allowed to bring children to work?

How should housing developments be designed in order to enhance the psychological growth of the child?

As we consider these questions, it becomes clear that the exceedingly complex issues they raise have no simple answers. This is an important point, because scientific research, if properly designed and conducted, poses simple questions and obtains relatively simple answers. However, there are research studies whose findings are at least partially relevant to the issues raised by each of the preceding questions. No single study can provide a definitive answer to any question, but data gathered from a number of different studies may illuminate some of the variables that any policymaker should consider before making a decision.

Most of the relevant child-development studies are in the area of the personal-social dimension of childhood, concerning the child's growth as a person—the attitudes, values, feelings, and concepts that he develops in the context of his relationships with others. Inextricably involved in this dimension is the child's cognitive development—his ability to perceive, think, learn, and solve problems—an outcome of his interaction with his physical and social world. The techniques psychologists use to explore these dimensions of child development are illustrated in this section.

Patricia Marks Greenfield's article (1.1) examines the cognitive development of meaningful speech, using a research approach in which the techniques of naturalistic observation and some manipulation of variables are combined. Greenfield's only subject was her eight-and-one-half-month-old daughter, and the specific cognitive skill studied was the infant's learning to associate the sound of the word "Dada" with its referent, her father. Greenfield's approach and choice of subject have ample historical precedents. In the nineteenth century, the naturalist, Charles Darwin, and the physiologist, Wilhelm Thierry Preyer, independently kept diaries of the development of their sons. Jean Piaget (1932), who has played a leading role in studying cognitive and social development in children, also devoted much of his early work to recording observations of his own children's development.

As Greenfield points out, valid conclusions cannot be based upon the observation of a single subject, but her findings do suggest some general principles about how children learn to use language. Adults subconsciously use words abstractly when their referent objects are absent, but young children have to learn the meaning of words by first associating them with concrete objects. As their cognitive development progresses, they become able to use words in an abstract way—in the absence of the referents. Greenfield describes this as the process "whereby language becomes increasingly independent of external events" and eventually functions on a highly abstract level.

 Who is "Dada"? Some aspects of the semantic and phonological development of a child's first words

Patricia Marks Greenfield

When sound takes on meaning for the first time in the life of a child, a giant prototypic step in the development of his symbolic capacities has taken place. This step is surely worthy of careful scientific scrutiny. The present paper seeks first of all to describe the steps by which the author's child discovered the existence of meaning in sound and, second,

Reprinted from Report No. 041 253, Educational Resources Information Center (ERIC), U.S. Office of Education, 1970, with permission of the author. This article also appeared under the same title in *Language and Speech* 16 (1973): 14–43.

to describe the successive structurization and progressive refinement of this first word, as well as related lexical items.

THE DEVELOPMENT OF A WORD-REFERENT ASSOCIATION AND A PHONOLOGICAL CATEGORY

Lauren, a girl, produced "Dada" for her first word. We (her mother and father) started helping her to understand what these syllables meant at the point when they began to appear frequently as a spontaneous sound pattern. This point of spontaneous articulation was also identified by Allport (1924) as a first step in the development of language proper and a necessary preliminary to imitating the speech sounds of others.

In Stage I (Lauren was eight and a half months old), we successfully encouraged her to imitate the sound at will. Basically, we started by imitating *her*. This procedure seemed to provoke her to repeat her original sound. We would, of course, act pleased when she did this, but it seems that the important factor was learning that if *she* said a sound, *we* would say it. Indeed, Piaget (1962) has described this same phenomenon in great detail.

In Stage II we began to help Lauren learn what this sound pattern meant. First, we promoted an association between the person of her father and the word "Dada" by having him be the sole person to utter "Dada." This training lasted for three days. During the first two days, we kept track of the total frequency with which Lauren looked at her father when she said "Dada." Thus, visual attention, the orienting response, was our index of comprehension. This count was very difficult to make both because it interrupted our normal activities and because "Dada" was often repeated a number of times in an echoic series. The latter problem was met by counting each series of repetitions as a single occurrence of the word. We looked at the proportion of times *saying* "Dada" accompanied *looking at* "Dada," both when the sounds were said spontaneously and when they were said imitatively. These counts were crude, it must be remembered, but the results are interesting and suggestive.

On the first day, when Lauren said "Dada," both spontaneously and in imitation, she *failed to look* more often than she *looked* at her father. When Lauren imitated "Dada," she looked at her father three out of seven times. The absence of visual orientation was much more marked when the sound was said spontaneously: Lauren looked at her father only four out of twenty-two times. On the second day, the trend changed: Lauren looked at her father seven out of nine times when she imitated "Dada" and five out of nine times when she said it spontaneously. Thus the behaviour of looking seemed to indicate a quantitative shift toward referential psychological meaning of the phonemic entity "Dada." Lauren's pattern of attention indicated that word and action (if not thought) were drawing nearer one to the other.

Equally interesting, these data suggest that word was more closely tied to action, sound to meaning, when the utterance had an external source—that is to say, when it was spoken in imitation rather than spontaneously. I tentatively conclude that meaning is first imposed on sound from the outside and that spontaneous utterances only gradually take on meaning. If this description holds, then meaningful speech has not only a truly social origin but also a crucial period of complete dependence on other people's verbal behaviour. In this view, spontaneous utterances are, at the beginning, play with sound. This idea will be taken up again.

I return now to a chronological account of the study. For the next six days we shifted our instructional procedure: I would say "Dada" to signal to Lauren her father's forthcoming appearance. I would say "Dada" and her father would appear. On the third day, she once turned to look at a man other than her father when asked "Where is Dada?" (Dada was in fact there). In the light of the results of later testing, this occurrence is taken as an indication that the sound-meaning connection had not yet been completely formed. Two days later I tested Lauren's comprehension of the word systematically. This was accomplished by my saying different double syllables with father present and noting whether or not Lauren turned to look at him. At this point, Lauren was eight and three-quarter months old.

The first time we tested her, different combinations of the initial consonant phonemes /m/, /b/, /d/, and /f/ were tried with vowels /a/, /u/, and /ai/ to yield the combinations,[1] "Mama," "Baba," "Tata," "Bubu," "Dudu," and "Bye-bye." All sound entities containing the /a/ of "Dada" elicited an orientating response towards father, almost always

---

1. The spelling here, as for all other words, is that of common English orthography; its translation into a phonemic representation is simple if desired. Phonemic notation (/ . . . /) where it occurs, follows the system of Jakobson, Fant and Halle (1967).

with a spoken "repetition" on Lauren's part of the word "Dada." The only syllables without the /a/ were "Bye-bye" (/bai-bai/), "Bubu," and "Dudu"; none of these elicited the orienting response. "Dudu," the most similar of these to "Dada," did, however, bring forth a "Dada" from Lauren, although she did not turn to look at her father. The order of the stimuli and Lauren's responses to them are found in Table 1.

TABLE 1
TESTING PROCEDURE FOR COMPREHENSION OF "DADA"—FIRST DAY

Stimuli (in order of presentation)	No. of times presented	No. of times turned toward father
Dada	2	2
Mama	2	2
Bye-Bye	2	0
Baba	1	1
Dada	2	2
Tata	1	1
Bubu	1	0
Dudu	2 (or more)	0
Bubu	2 (or more)	0
Dada	2 (or more)	2 (or more)

The next day, the same pattern held at first, except that "Bye-Bye" caused Lauren to look toward her father one of the two times that it was said. Note that "Bye-bye," unlike "Bubu," does have a vowel sound in common with "Dada." As before, she looked towards her father when I said "Dada" but not when I said "Mama" (twice). The next trial utilized the double syllable "Papa," and she did not look at her father. After this, I called "Dada" and her father appeared from behind the door. Lauren laughed and we did this three more times. (The smile seemed to indicate the presence of a confirmed expectancy. I infer that the word "Dada" had made her expect her father to appear. This inference is partly based on Kagan's (1966) evidence and my own observations that the smile signifies subjective recognition of a cognitive accomplishment.) I now repeated a variety of double syllables, including "Gogo" and "Mama." She made no mistakes. I smiled when she correctly identified her "Dada." By the end of the testing session she was saying "Dada" as well as turning to look at him when "Dada" was said.

This description constitutes evidence that at least two processes occur in the genesis of the first meaningful word: (1) strengthening of the association between sound-pattern and thing, as evidenced by the increasing correlation between sound and orientating response and (2) a narrowing of the phonetic category that can elicit this response. The first process appeared primarily on the production side: in the beginning, "Dada" was said without meaning (first spontaneously, then in imitation); gradually it became a signal to look at father. The second process (perhaps overlapping the first, perhaps succeeding it, but in any case extending beyond it in time) took place on the comprehension side: not only "Dada" but also other double syllables functioned as a signal to look at father. Then the phonetic category constituting this signal narrowed down, finally to include only "Dada." Once these two processes—association and phonological categorization—were complete in the sense that "Dada," and only "Dada," would dependably elicit an orienting response from Lauren to her father, I began to study her categorization of referents. These two processes, the delineation of phonetic and of referential categories, comprise two of the components named by Brown (1958) in his description of "The Original Word Game."

REFERENTIAL CATEGORIZATION: THE GROWTH OF SEMANTIC MARKERS

In this part of the study, the question, in Fodor and Katz' (1963) terms, concerned the structure of Lauren's dictionary and how this structure was manifest in its initial entries. Fodor and Katz place this task outside the bounds of the semantic component of a general linguistic theory, although they specify the form which dictionary entries are to assume. In their theory, meaning is limited to what can be obtained from the *linguistic* context. The McNeills have also observed this constraint in dealing with the semantics of negation in the speech of a two-year-old Japanese girl (McNeill and McNeill, 1968). But, obviously in describing the origins of the semantic system, one begins at a point where there *is no* linguistic context. Indeed, there is no ready-made dictionary. One is forced, therefore, to look at verbal-extra-verbal relations if one is to understand or to analyze the semantic structure of a child's first meaningful utterance.

If one assumes that child language tends toward the adult model (an assumption fruitfully employed in Piaget's research and recent studies of syntactic development), then one can use the semantic markers found in the standard adult dictionary as a basis for the description of the child's system of meaning. According to linguistic intuition (my own) and the *Random House Dictionary of the English Language* (1966), "Father," of which "Dada" is the baby-talk form, has three principal semantic markers: male, parent, caretaker. Utilizing the McNeills' (1967) way of representing semantic dimensions, one can define a whole domain of related words in terms of the three dimensions implied by these markers. The three dimensions would be: male-female, parent-unrelated person, caretaker-non-caretaking person. Again, following the McNeills, I organize the dimensions into a cube and place relevant words at appropriate corners. (See Figure 1.)

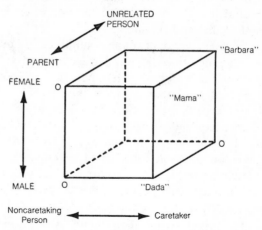

FIGURE 1

"DADA" AND RELATED WORDS LOCATED IN SEMANTIC SPACE

The cube indicates that there are three classes of referents which are semantically possible but non-existent in Lauren's world. These are indicated by zeros and consist of the following combinations of features: (1) non-caretaking male parent, (2) non-caretaking female parent, (3) unrelated male caretaker. (The remaining two corners represent existent classes of people but classes that did not yet have verbal labels at the time when this study ended. They are, in a sense, waste-basket categories and are as follows: (1) non-caretaking unrelated male, (2) non-caretaking unrelated female.)

Certain relationships may be easier to see if the terms under discussion are placed in a feature matrix. Once more I utilize the McNeills' mode of representing the semantic space and arrive at the matrix presented in Table 2.

TABLE 2
SEMANTIC FEATURES MATRIX FOR "DADA" AND RELATED WORDS

	"Dada"	*"Mama"*	*"Barbara"*
Male	+	−	−
Parent	+	+	−
Caretaker	+	+	+

Now, patterns of confusion will be utilized to study the construction of the above cube. Like the McNeills, I have looked at which terms replace others and have thus tried to determine whether and in what order the semantic dimensions emerge.

As soon as "Dada" was dependably established in Lauren's vocabulary in the manner described above, I tried to ascertain its semantic content by testing for generalization along the different dimensions described. It seemed clear that, initially, the meaning of "Dada" for Lauren was caretaker. The first piece of evidence for this conclusion was that when we tried to teach her "Mama" by associating my entrance with the word, she would often respond with "Dada." More convincing evidence, as it is on the comprehension rather than production side, was Lauren's orienting response to Barbara (her babysitter and member of our household), when a frequent male visitor asked "Where is Dada?" This test was done twice, both times with positive results, about three weeks after she had learned the referent for "Dada." She also turned to look at Barbara twice when I asked "Where is Dada?" (Her father was not present.) She did *not*, however, turn to look at any other man when asked "Where is Dada?" no matter how familiar these men were. I tried this test once each with two different men. Thus, "Dada" appeared to mark all caretakers and set them apart from non-caretakers. Clearly, the standard dimension of sex was absent—witness the extension of "Dada" to female caretakers; the parent-non-parent distinction was also missing, as Lauren's application of "Dada" to her babysitter indicates.

About a week after "Dada" was initially established, we started to try to establish "Mama" in the same way—by using it as a signal for my appearance, etc. Perhaps for this reason, Lauren appeared to have generalized "Dada" more to her babysitter than to her mother when tested about two weeks after the "Mama" training had begun.

It was predicted that once the word "Mama" was introduced into Lauren's semantic system, it would be generalized to Barbara. In other words, the opposition "Dada"–"Mama" would indicate the existence of a male–female distinction. Two days after the above test, Lauren's father asked about "Mama" with both her mother and her babysitter present; she turned to look at her babysitter. (She also looked at her and spontaneously said "Mama.") Thus, the predicted generalization did in fact occur. Why Lauren looked at her babysitter rather than her mother when *both* were present is a bit puzzling, however. At this point, then, the only missing distinction or dimension appeared to be the parent-non-parent one.[2]

Twelve days later, Lauren's father again tested to see if Lauren would orient toward Barbara at the word "Mama" when "Mama" was absent. This time the results were ambiguous. Two days later I tested to ascertain if this seeming reduction of generalization was due to the emergence of a separate word to denote Barbara. (We had not tried to teach her "Barbara," although Barbara had.) Indeed, Lauren did seem to know who "Barbara" was, again using an orienting response as the criterion of comprehension. This test was only made once, but the acquisition of "Barbara" was confirmed on subsequent occasions. Lauren responded either to "Barbara" or to "Baba." Her pronunciation, however, was invariably "Baba."

Two weeks after "Barbara" was first noticed as an item in Lauren's vocabulary of comprehension, she was observed to generalize this word to other women. When visiting a female friend, Lauren spontaneously looked at her and said "Baba." When I then asked "Where is Barbara?" she again turned to look at her. The reaction occurred more than once; at one point, she even seemed to say "Babwa" while looking at this lady. On a later occasion she seemed spontaneously to call yet another woman "Barbara."

An interesting sidelight on the matter of phonological categories—Lauren was already waving and saying "Bye-bye" at the time she was learning "Baba." At this point "Bye-bye" temporarily disappeared.

---

2. In concluding the presence of a male-female distinction, I am assuming that Barbara stopped being "Dada" when she started being "Mama."

It was as though "Bye-bye" and "Baba" were in the same phonemic class and therefore could not function as two different words. To the question "Could they not be homonyms?" the answer most likely is that homonyms can exist only where context sets them apart. But at this stage there is no linguistic context; there are only isolated words. Therefore, if homonyms are to be formed, it must be on the basis of distinctive situational contexts. It was unlikely, however, that the extra-linguistic contexts, that is the settings, for "Baba" and "Bye-bye" were actually in complementary distribution. For example, when Lauren and Barbara would part, Barbara's utterance "Bye-bye" would be situationally ambiguous. In any case, "Bye-bye" as a signal to wave did not return until a number of weeks later.

Presumably the appearance of "Barbara" meant that the third semantic dimension, parent—non-parent, had appeared, for this was the only distinction between "Mama" and "Baba." I hypothesized that "Baba" had three markers: non-parental female caretaker. The extension of "Barbara" to other women belies precisely this interpretation, however, because these other ladies were non-caretaking persons. An interpretation consistent with this fact is that, of all currently available terms, this word with its particular semantic markers came closest to fitting the class of non-parental non-caretaking females.

This account is consistent with Lauren's later generalization of "Dada." When she was in her twelfth month, she was observed to look at strange men and say "Dada." I further tested her extension of "Dada" to men in general by asking her about "Dada" in the presence of a fairly unfamiliar man when she was about eleven and three-quarter months old. She responded by turning towards him and saying "Dada" herself. A man like this was neither parent nor caretaker, yet at this point in time "Dada" was the only term in Lauren's lexicon to contain a "male" marker. The word "Baba," of course, could have been used with as much semantic accuracy as "Dada" to denote strange men, since it too contains one appropriate marker—non-parent. The fact that "Dada" was chosen instead is, however, consistent with the developmental priority of the male—female distinction over the parent—non-parent one. In fact, it is hard to see what Lauren's basis for making the parent—non-parent distinction could have been, although there are a variety of possible cues. Nevertheless, the fact that "Baba" and not "Mama," was the term generalized to strange women indicates the psychological reality of this parent—non-parent dimension.

The extension of "Dada" to all men is a common observation (for example, Piaget, 1962). Lauren's semantic development makes clear, however, that this is but one stage and certainly not the first, in the dynamic growth of a fairly complex classificatory system.

There is some evidence that the words "Mama" and "Baba" were confused after both were present. At least part of the confusion would seem to have had a phonological basis. At the age of eleven months, Lauren would say "Baba" in clear imitation of "Mama," thus indicating the absence of the nasal—oral distinction in speech. At this point, she probably confused /m/ and /b/ perceptually at least some of the time, thus sometimes failing to distinguish "Mama" from "Baba."[3] If so, then the parent—non-parent distinction was not totally established and "Mama" and "Baba" were used interchangeably to denote female care-takers. This hypothesis is consistent with the available evidence and explains why "Mama" was more than once applied to Lauren's babysitter rather than to her mother, who was also present. This lexical situation also makes sense in terms of Lauren's world, for Mama and Barbara did appear to be functionally interchangeable not only in terms of physical caretaking but also as far as Lauren's feelings were concerned.

By eleven and three-quarter months Lauren could say both "Baba" and "Mama" and seemed to apply them correctly. From eleven months on, it became increasingly difficult to elicit an orienting response with the words "Dada," "Mama," and "Baba." Lauren's boredom seemed to follow the mastery of a particular reference of a particular word. At this satiation point, her use of her words in *speech* appeared suddenly more advanced; this is a fairly subjective impression, however. This decrease in orienting behaviour, while making the study more difficult, is nevertheless in accord with the results of a Soviet experiment concerning the speech comprehension of children of this age: objects whose names are unknown will elicit a much stronger orienting response than others whose names are already familiar (Mallitskaya, 1960). That pattern agrees with the results reported here. Indeed, the internalization of the earliest word meanings appears to have occurred: it is now possible to "understand" a sound pattern without necessarily turning to look

---

3. The possibility of this hypothesis was later reinforced by Lauren's parallel confusion between "Nana" and "Dada" in her own speech. After having referred to bananas as "Nana" for some time, she suddenly started calling them "Dada." Like the phonemes /b/ and /m/ in "Baba" and Mama," /d/ and /n/ are identical save for the feature of nasality.

at its referent. It seems that once the predictive value of a word has been established by confirmatory events, it need not be re-tested each time the word appears. This is perhaps a first step towards the ability to make meaningful linguistic reference in the absence of a concrete, physical referent. This process, whereby language becomes increasingly independent of external events, will be carried even further when words come to be combined in sentences. At that point the semantic burden begins to shift from situational to linguistic context in both comprehension and speech. The combinatorial possibilities inherent in sentence formation yield that creative productivity which is the hallmark of the later freedom of language from external control. Thus, there is a striking developmental shift from outer to inner control of understanding and speaking.

A note on the relationship between comprehension and production. My observations extend those of Ruth Weir in *Language in the Crib* (1962) to a much earlier age, for Lauren always played a lot with the words she was learning, as well as with other sounds. I call it word "play" because external referents were absent. Much of this play did, in fact, occur in the crib. Where no external referent is present, one can assume that the word has no meaning *at that moment* for the very young child. The situation is psychologically the same as that described above wherein the child, before he has mastered a given word, utters it but does not look at a concrete referent. There, however, the referent is absent for the speaker although not absent in fact. This phenomenon of "meaningless" speech can be taken as evidence in favor of Vygotsky's (1962) notion that thought and speech develop in parallel streams and only gradually come together. The gradual coordination of saying with looking, described above, is striking evidence on this point. In applying Vygotsky's ideas about thought and speech to the stage of language development depicted here, I take comprehension to be the "thought" side of language. It is for this reason that I have studied semantic development mainly in terms of comprehension. For at an age when speech showed a playful quality and little consistent relation to the outside world, understanding proved to have a regular pattern. Comprehension and speech were for the most part still following separate, if parallel, paths. But it is plain that comprehension is carrying the burden of the child's linguistic competence at this time.

The preceding analysis is truly a tentative one. The findings certainly need to be confirmed with other vocabulary acquisitions and with other children. Perhaps this description, as much by its lacunae as by anything else, will suggest some problems in semantic and phonological development and some methods of attack.

SUMMARY

Head and eye orientation was used as an index of verbal comprehension in a study of earliest language acquisition. The development of the first association between sound and meaning and the later growth of semantic markers were observed in the author's own child between the ages of eight and a half and eleven and three-quarter months. There was evidence of a systematic internalization of meaning and a gradual coordination of comprehension and speaking. "Dada," the first word, and two later lexical items were found to be organized in terms of three gradually acquired semantic dimensions.

The article by James Kenneth Morrison (1.2) studies how children conceptualize moral issues. Moral development is both cognitive and social. When a child judges behavior, both his own and that of others, he uses logic appropriate to the cognitive level he has attained. His social development affects the highly abstract bases of moral judgment, which directly or indirectly involve both the child's self-image and his perceptions of the attitudes and feelings of others. During the preschool years, children see these abstractions in somewhat concrete terms, and judge misbehavior by the gross amount of damage or injury it causes. Piaget calls this early stage "objective," because children then focus primarily on the more outwardly visible aspects of behavior. As children grow older and learn to deal with more complex levels of abstraction, they see other, important dimensions of misbehavior—the circumstances surrounding the action, and the intentions of the individuals involved. When children perceive these dimensions, they are ready to enter the stage Piaget calls "subjective," wherein they consider the less obvious, subsurface aspects of behavior.

Morrison's investigation of moral judgment development in children compares the reactions of first and sixth graders to a videotape depicting the misbehavior of a boy called Joey. This "cross-sectional" study simultaneously examines two different stages of development. Morrison's subject samples were drawn from the same population of children and presumably differed only with respect to age and school grade, so we can assume that when his first graders become sixth graders, they will probably make moral judgments similar to those made by the six graders in the study. In a longitudinal study, the same children would be tested initially in the first grade and again in the sixth, but a cross-sectional study saves time and energy, and provides the investigator with an immediate test of his hypotheses.

This study uses other important techniques. In studies of this kind, the stimulus material that the children judge usually consists of brief anecdotes describing the misbehavior or misadventure of a child. In Morrison's study, the children both heard and saw illustrative incidents on videotaped presentations, which are more realistic than verbal anecdotes. The rating scales Morrison used to measure the children's opinions were also more sophisticated than those used in most studies of moral judgment. He used a conventional rating scale to assess the children's appraisal of the seriousness of Joey's observed behavior, but he also had the children complete two additional nonverbal tests in which they predicted how Joey would behave in circumstances where he faced other moral dilemmas. These additional measurements enabled Morrison to derive a highly reliable assessment of each subject's style of judgment.

The research method employed by Morrison fits the classic experimental design. The classic model calls for the investigator to test his hypothesis by setting up a situation in such a way that some of his subjects (the experimental group) are exposed to a certain condition or treatment. This condition or treatment, termed an *independent variable*, may produce an effect on the subjects that will appear in some noticeable form in their behavior. The extent to which the subjects' behavior has been changed, as a result of their exposure to the independent variable, becomes the *dependent variable*, because it *depends* on the independent variable. The amount of change produced by the independent variable can be determined by comparing the behavior of the experimental group with another group—the *control group*—consisting of subjects who were not exposed to the experimental treatment. The investigator may also compare the performance of the first group of subjects with that of other experimental groups who were exposed to variations of the independent variable.

The kind of independent variable we have described is also referred to as a stimulus (or S) variable, because the differences between the experimental and control treatments, as well as among various experimental treatments, are essentially differences in the kind or amount of stimulation to which the experimental and control groups are exposed. Characteristics of the persons or other organisms serving as subjects may also be employed as independent variables, in which case they are termed organism (or O) variables. In experimental child psychology, age and sex often serve as independent variables of this type.

Morrison used both types of independent variables. His S variables were the six videotaped sequences, each of which was seen by a different group of children, and his 0 variable was age. The dependent variables were the responses the children subsequently made to the three tests. The results confirmed hypotheses, based on Piaget's theories, that younger children make moral judgments largely on an "objective" basis, but older children tend to base their judgments on "subjective" criteria. Morrison's manipulation of S variables also demonstrated that older children, in contrast to younger children, are likely to be less judgmental and more optimistic in their evaluation of a misbehaving child, provided they are given sufficient information about him. In addition, older children are more inclined to take mitigating circumstances into account in making their appraisals.

 Developmental study of the person perception of young children

James Kenneth Morrison

Since Piaget (1932) formulated his theoretical views in *The Moral Judgment of the Child,* a vast amount of research has been done to elucidate the gradual development of the process of moral judgment making.

There are three principal objectives of the present study: (*a*) to establish the strong relationship between person judgment and moral judgment development; (*b*) to further study the effect of mitigating

Reprinted from the *Proceedings of the 81st Annual Convention of the American Psychological Association,* 8 (1973): 219–220, with permission of the author and the American Psychological Association. Copyright 1973 by the American Psychological Association.

circumstances on the person judgments of children (present technology—e.g., videotape equipment—enables one to control extraneous variables to such an extent that mitigating circumstances can be more clearly studied); (c) to avoid some of the artificiality of the previous moral judgment and person judgment studies. For example, Morrison (1971a, 1971b) has established that a multiple rating scale allows a child more latitude in his moral judgments and does not bias the child toward categorizing each story agent in both Piaget-type story pairs as "naughty," as is true of all previous moral judgment studies. In person judgment studies such as Asch's (1946) classical study, trait lists often induce a great amount of artificiality into the study (Luchins, 1948).

The hypotheses of the present study emerge directly from the three assumptions of this study: (a) Concerning the variable of *developmental differences over age,* it is predicted that the older more subjective Ss [subjects] (sixth graders) will make significantly more positive (good) global ratings and behavior predictions on all three dependent measures (Global Rating Scale; Behavior Prediction Test; Projective Film Test) over all five experimental conditions than will young more objective Ss (first graders). (b) Concerning the variable of *intentionality,* whereas the younger more objective Ss will not significantly differ among themselves from condition to condition, the older more subjective Ss will make significantly more positive global ratings and behavior predictions on all three dependent measures in the accidental conditions than in the intentional conditions. (c) Concerning the variable of *mitigating circumstance,* whereas the younger more objective Ss will not significantly differ from condition to condition as a result of being exposed to different mitigating circumstances, the older more subjective Ss will make significantly different global ratings and behavior predictions on the three dependent measures, with intentionality held constant, from circumstance to circumstance. Finally, younger and older Ss will not significantly differ in their responses on all three dependent measures in the minimum information condition.

METHOD

Subjects

One hundred forty-four middle-class male children from four different Roman Catholic elementary schools were used as Ss. First graders (objective) and sixth graders (subjective) were randomly assigned to each of six conditions, each condition containing 12 first graders and 12 sixth graders.

Stimulus items

The stimulus items consisted of six different videotape film packages. In each package the first two films depicted the film character Joey accidentally breaking a movie projector and then a wrist watch. These two films were identical in all five experimental conditions. The third film in each of these five conditions distinguished one condition from the other by combining different intentionality (Joey purposely or accidentally breaks 10 dishes) with different mitigating circumstances (Joey's father displays great anger toward his son; Joey's father makes a very unreasonable request). A final mitigating circumstance (Joey offers to do a favor for his father) is combined only with accidental damage, since to combine this circumstance with intentional damage would have been very confusing for the Ss, thus adding a confounding factor. The amount of damage in all experimental conditions is identical in all three of the films. The three stimulus films lasted a total of approximately 3 min. in the five experimental conditions. A sixth condition, a minimum information condition, was added in which Ss viewed 21 sec. of silent videotape film depicting Joey in more neutral scenes, showing neither good nor bad behavior.

Dependent measures

1. Global Rating Scale: a 7-point rating scale ranging from 1 (very, very bad) to 7 (very, very good). All Ss were sufficiently trained on the use of this scale before being exposed to the stimulus films.

   2. Behavior Prediction Test: a two-choice 20-item stick-figure test portraying Joey either in good (e.g., helpful or obedient behavior) or bad (messy, destructive, etc.) behavior. The S chooses one of two behaviors he feels would be typical of Joey, from what he knows of him in the stimulus films, in each of 20 item choices.

   3. Projective Film Test: five short videotape films, each lasting about 60 sec., each depicting Joey in the midst of some moral dilemma (e.g., Will Joey obey his father and watch his baby sister, or will he go out with his friend to see the big fire?). The S predicts what Joey will do from what he already knows about Joey from the stimulus films.

Procedure

After training Ss on the use and meaning of the Global Rating Scale, E [experimenter] had Ss watch three stimulus films on the television monitor without interruption. The Ss were tested in groups of three or four according to grade. Following exposure to the stimulus films, Ss then rated the film character on the 7-point rating scale. Then Ss made 20 behavior predictions of Joey using the Behavior Prediction Test booklet. Finally, Ss watched five projective films and predicted what Joey would do after each film. These responses were written down by the older children, but conveyed orally to E's assistants in the case of the younger children.

RESULTS

An analysis of the data, using analysis of variance and Pearson t tests, revealed, first, that older more subjective Ss (sixth graders) significantly differed from younger more objective Ss (first graders) over the experimental conditions on all three dependent measures. Whereas the older Ss in Condition B (favor plus accidental damage) viewed Joey as good, the other sixth graders in the other four experimental conditions (A: unreasonable request plus accidental damage; C: anger plus intentional damage; D: unreasonable request plus intentional damage; E: anger plus accidental damage) viewed Joey as not good, not bad, a more neutral rating. On the contrary, first graders in all experimental conditions on all dependent measures viewed Joey as bad, except in Condition E (anger plus accidental damage) on the global rating measure alone, where Joey was given a more neutral rating.

With regard to the variable of intentionality, older Ss differed significantly from younger Ss in that only the former differed consistently from condition to condition due to intentionality alone on the first two dependent measures (global ratings; Behavior Prediction Test). Older Ss made more positive ratings and predictions than did the younger Ss. The hypotheses regarding the effect of intentionality on person judgments related to the Projective Film Test were not so clearly confirmed for the older Ss.

With regard to the variable of mitigating circumstance, analysis of the data revealed strong evidence that older Ss focus more on mitigating circumstances than do younger Ss, although the latter at times seem to focus more on anger than do the older Ss. On two of the three dependent measures, the controls (sixth and first graders) did not differ from one another, as predicted. The younger Ss in the control condition tended to rate Joey as more positive (good) than did the older Ss. The younger Ss also rated Joey in a dramatically more significant positive direction in the minimum information condition than they did in any of the five experimental conditions.

DISCUSSION

Most of the hypotheses of the study were clearly confirmed. Even in a person judgment study, with the focus on the global person impressions of Ss, the theoretical postulates of Piaget (1932) regarding objective responsibility have been strongly validated. Older Ss focus more on intentionality than on damage in their person perceptions; younger Ss show the reverse tendency. This study provides the clearest evidence to date that older Ss use mitigating circumstances in assessing culpability more than do younger Ss, although the latter Ss focus more on the somewhat "dramatic" cue of anger, perhaps in the same way these Ss tend to focus on the somewhat dramatic cue of damage. When the mitigating circumstance is more subtle (e.g., unreasonable request) the younger Ss do not seem to use it in assessing culpability.

It is interesting to note that the younger Ss viewed Joey as significantly more "good" in the control condition than they did in the experimental conditions. This is probably explained by the fact that only in the control condition is damage not shown. And the damage cue is the one which in previous research seems to induce younger Ss to make "bad" ratings of the story agent. The significantly more positive ratings of Joey by the younger Ss in the control condition on all three dependent measures, as compared with the experimental conditions, attest to the fact that the younger Ss did know what they were doing and were not simply responding to *any* stimulus information in the same random fashion.

The results of this study validate the theoretical postulates of Piaget related to objective responsibility. Furthermore, the results clearly illustrate how moral judgment and person judgment can be viewed as quite similar cognitive processes in that the research in one area (moral judgment) provides postulates that are easily validated in the other area (person judgment), as this study attests. Finally, more evidence has been uncovered which points to the importance of mitigating circumstance in the assessment of culpability.

A great many questions regarding the nature of human development do not lend themselves to experimental investigation. We cannot, for example, conduct experimental studies using various methods of child-rearing—such as physical punishment or love-oriented disciplines—as independent variables, and school success as a dependent variable. Not only would it be impossible to control all relevant sources of variation that might confuse the results, but ethical and legal considerations would make such a study impossible. This question is worth researching, however, and it is possible to design studies to correlate parental punitivity with school marks and achievement test scores. Such studies generally show a negative correlation between punitivity and school success—that is, the more punitive the parents, the lower the children's achievement. The obvious conclusion is that severity of punishment causes lack of success, but further investigation shows that the obvious conclusion is greatly oversimplified, because parental punitivity is also correlated with the parents' economic and educational status, with lawbreaking, and with other factors. Poor marks are correlated not only with parental punitivity, but with children's truancy, difficulties in getting along with peers, attitudes toward school, and so forth. In the total perspective, punitivity and school failure are two tips of a very large, submerged behavioral iceberg, and it is difficult to say which of the tips more nearly represents the iceberg's weight and size.

Correlational studies can be extremely useful, especially in studies of personality traits, if we refuse to interpret correlations in narrowly causal terms. In longitudinal investigations, correlations measured at various points in time can tell us a great deal about the consistency of such traits as intelligence, dependency, aggressiveness, and so forth. Theories about the interaction of these variable traits with cognitive development, social development, and school success can also be tested using correlational techniques.

Beverly Brekke, John Williams, and Steven Harlow studied the relationship between conservation and reading readiness in children, using correlational research methods. Their study (article 1.3) is related to Piaget's stages of cognitive development, specifically to the stage during which the ability to conserve and the readiness to learn to read seem to coincide.

The Piagetian cognitive term *conservation* concerns not the preservation of ecological resources, but the preservation of a concept. The child who can conserve has learned to conceptualize the quantity or amount of a substance, and to retain, or "conserve," this concept of it even when he sees the substance changed in form and context. In testing for conservation, a child may be shown a cup of water, which is first poured into a tall, narrow receptacle, and then into a broad, flat plate. Younger children, who tend to confuse height, area, and volume, usually report that the quantity of the water is changed as a result of these manipulations. Older children are less likely to be disoriented by these alterations in appearance, and those who have acquired the cognitive concept of conservation report that the quantity is unchanged.

There is considerable debate among both behavioral scientists and laymen concerning the meaning and usefulness of IQ as a measure of intelligence. (IQ and its correlates will be further discussed in Section 9.) Although the work of Brekke, Williams, and Harlow reveals something about measured intelligence, the results of their study are not a final answer to the questions raised in the IQ controversy; their data do indicate, however, that a standardized intelligence test can be used as a fairly good indicator of listening comprehension, visual comprehension, and the other skills involved in reading readiness. It is interesting to note that the intelligence test used in the study apparently measured these latter skills better than it did the conservation tasks—evidence counter to the suggestion that conservation tasks may involve a more restricted range of traits than has been commonly assumed.

Conservation and reading readiness

Beverly W. Brekke,
John D. Williams, and
Steven D. Harlow

The question as to when a child is ready to learn to read has been the subject of extensive research and interpretation. Since the 1920's, the concept of reading readiness has represented a composite construct which includes the child's experiential background, as well as his physical, social, emotional, and intellectual maturation. Traditionally, schools have used various procedures to evaluate a child's readiness for reading. The three most prevalent measures of readiness are standardized reading readiness tests, intelligence tests (usually a group test), and informal assessment of the child by the kindergarten teacher. However, in recent years, Piaget's (5) formulations of cognitive development of children have presented opportunities for establishing additional objective criteria of readiness.

Piaget's theory (5) and experimentation have shown that the cognitive development of children occurs in predictable sequential stages: sensorimotor, preoperational, concrete operational, and formal operational. His studies have identified the characteristic thinking processes that comprise each stage. The time for beginning reading instruction usually coincides with the transition of the child's progression from the preoperational to the concrete operational stages.

The entrance to the concrete operations stage is marked by the child's acquisition of conservation of number and substance. The child's attainment of conservation indicates an ability to differentiate logical reality from perceptual cues. Piaget has described the attainment of conservation in terms of the three stages as (*a*) no conservation, (*b*) transitional, and (*c*) conservation.

Reprinted from the *Journal of Genetic Psychology,* 123 (1973): 133–138, with permission of the authors and The Journal Press. Copyright 1973 by The Journal Press.

155.4 H365h
C.1

Although numerous studies have been concerned with either conservation or reading readiness, there has been a paucity of previous research directly relating Piaget's findings on the child's cognitive development to selected factors involved in readiness for learning to read. This paucity is quite probably related to Piaget's own views on reading readiness (3, p. 30):

> So the concept of readiness is not bad but I am not sure that it can be applied to reading. Reading aptitude may not be related to mental age. There could easily be a difference of aptitude between children independent of mental age. But I can not state that as a fact because I have not studied it closely.

Almy (1) showed that conservers scored significantly higher on the *New York Tests of Reading Readiness* than did nonconservers. In a later study, Almy *et al.* (2) found a substantial correlation between conservation tasks of the concrete operational stage and progress in beginning reading. In a study relating the Piagetian tasks of conservation of continuous substance, discontinuous substance, number, length, and area, Lepper (4) found a low positive, but statistically significant, relationship of these tasks with the *Metropolitan Reading Readiness Tests.*

METHOD

The Ss included 81 first-grade students. Of these 81 students, 46 were male and 35 were female. The mean chronological age in months of the subjects was 77.3 with a range from 70 to 91. The mean mental age in months of the subjects was 80.3 with a range from 58 to 102. The 81 first-grade subjects in this study were enrolled in four classrooms in two schools considered to be representative of the Grand Forks, North Dakota, schools.

In the beginning of the school year, each S was administered the following tests on an individual basis: (*a*) *Gates-MacGinitie Reading Tests: Readiness Skills;* (*b*) *Primary Mental Abilities Test: Grades K-1;* and (*c*) Procedures of Conservation of Number and Substance with First-Grade Children.

Selected factors of reading readiness were measured by the *Gates-MacGinitie Reading Tests: Readiness Skills.* The skills tested were listening comprehension, auditory discrimination, visual discrimination, following directions, letter recognition, visual-motor coordination, auditory blending, and word recognition.

Intellectual ability was measured by the *Primary Mental Abilities Test: Grades K-1.* The four primary mental abilities measured were the following: Verbal Meaning, Number Facility, Perceptual Speed, and Spatial Relations. A total intelligence score is a composite of the four subtest ratings.

The Procedures of Conservation of Number and Substance with First-Grade Children were organized into five tasks to assess the child's acquisition of conservation and can be briefly described as follows:

Task I. Conservation of Inequality of Number with 17 white and 19 red wooden cubes. A transformation was made by pushing each set of cubes together into two groups.

Task II. Conservation of Equality of Number with two sets of 18 black and pink wooden cubes. A transformation was made by pushing the black blocks close together and stretching the pink blocks out in lines.

Task III. Conservation of Equality of Substance with two equal-sized play dough balls. One ball was transformed into a hot dog shape, with the second ball being unchanged.

Task IV. Conservation of Inequality of Substance with two unequal-sized balls. The smaller ball was transformed into a pancake shape. This was repeated with two additional unequal balls, and the larger ball was transformed into a pancake shape.

Task V. Conservation of Equality of Substance with two equal-sized balls. One ball was transformed into little pieces.

Each *S* was tested individually in a separate room. The mean procedure time for the group was 18 minutes with a range of 9 to 38 minutes. The mean procedure time for the children who successfully conserved on all five tasks was 15 minutes. All procedures were audiotaped and transcribed on record sheets for scoring.

For each task a conservation response was scored 1, and the total possible conservation score for each child was 5. Similarly for each task a reversibility response was scored 1, and the total possible reversibility score was 5. Both nonconservation and nonreversibility responses were scored zero. The child who succeeded on all five conservation tasks was defined as a conserver. All of the *S*s were divided into two groups. The first group consisted of conservers. The remaining *S*s were grouped together, and included both nonconservers and transitional conservers. No distinctions were made between the two categories.

RESULTS

Table 1 contains the means of the conservers ($N = 19$) and the nonconservers ($N = 62$) on the subtests of the *Gates-MacGinitie Readiness Skills.* Also included is the *F value* to test for the significance of the difference between conservers and nonconservers. . . .

TABLE 1
MEANS, CORRELATIONS, AND *F* VALUES FOR THE GATES-MacGINITIE READING TESTS: READINESS SKILLS BETWEEN CONSERVERS AND NONCONSERVERS

Variable	Conservers mean	Nonconservers mean	F Value
Listening comprehension	6.11	5.02	6.997**
Auditory discrimination	7.53	6.69	6.645*
Visual discrimination	7.11	5.55	12.981**
Following directions	7.26	6.23	5.317*
Letter recognition	7.63	6.71	10.478**
Visual-motor coordination	7.05	5.71	9.605**
Auditory blending	5.74	4.71	4.879*
Multivariate hypothesis			3.804**
($R = .517$)			

*Significant at the .05 level ($p < .05$).
**Significant at the .01 level ($p < .01$).

Table 1 shows rather conclusively that conservation is related to the readiness skills of the *Gates-MacGinitie Test.* In every case, the mean of the conserver is significantly higher than that of the nonconserver; in four subtests the significance reaches the .01 level, and in the other three subtests the significance reaches the .05 level. The multivariate hypothesis regarding the simultaneous consideration of all seven subtests also is significant at the .01 level.

While conservation has been shown to be positively related to reading readiness, it would be worthwhile to consider the amount of predictability due to conservation *independent* of intelligence. From Table 2 it can be seen that with the exception of visual-motor coordination, the contribution of conservation independent of intelligence to the prediction of the subtests of the *Gates-MacGinitie Readiness Skills* is slight.

TABLE 2
CORRELATIONS AND INDEPENDENT CONTRIBUTION OF CONSERVATION AND
INTELLIGENCE TO THE READING READINESS SUBTESTS

Variable	Correlation with intelligence	Correlation with conservation	Multiple correlation with intelligence and conservation	Independent contribution due to intelligence	Independent contribution due to conservation
Listening comprehension	.607	.285	.610	.2910	.0038
Auditory discrimination	.486	.279	.497	.1693	.0104
Visual discrimination	.392	.376	.463	.0726	.0603
Following directions	.521	.251	.524	.2120	.0036
Letter recognition	.347	.342	.415	.0552	.0518
Visual-motor coordination	.218	.329	.344	.0102	.0709
Auditory blending	.371	.241	.386	.0912	.0117

The higher predictability of conservation in regard to the subtest of visual-motor coordination is probably due to the similarity to the conservation tasks. A final correlation is of interest; the correlation between conservation and the intelligence test score was .38.

DISCUSSION

The correlations found between conservation and the reading readiness subtests were in the moderate range and, in general, were slightly less than the correlations between intelligence and the reading readiness subtests. From the point of view of predictability, the intelligence test score was more closely associated with reading readiness subtests than was conservation; in light of the moderate relationship ($r = .38$) between conservation and intelligence, it is clear that these two concepts are different.

Most primary teachers have only a general awareness of intelligence testing, but it would also seem that Piagetian principles have not been widely disseminated at the practitioner level. While the intelligence test ratings may be helpful in assessing readiness, a new focus of attention might also be placed on conservation. Conservation should be taken into account as an additional measure of readiness for beginning reading instruction. Attendant with this recommendation is the need to acquaint primary level teachers and reading specialists with Piagetian principles and ways of evaluating the child's operational level.

SUMMARY

Conservation has been found to be positively and moderately correlated with reading readiness, and only slightly less correlated with reading readiness than intelligence as measured by the *Primary Mental Abilities Test.* A moderate correlation also existed between conservation and intelligence. It was suggested that conservation would be worthy of attention by primary teachers as a predictor of the child's readiness for learning to read.

The three articles reprinted and discussed in this section exemplify the bifocal quality of child research, in that as each study examines a fundamental aspect of child development, both the research process and its practical applications are described. Greenfield's article is the most fundamental of the three studies, because it probes into the very beginnings of language learning and follows the cognitive development of meaningful linguistic references. These findings have practical value because discoveries about early semantic learning behavior may be useful in helping children with language problems or with other cognitive deficiencies. Greenfield's study is a contribution to our general understanding of cognitive development in children, and as such enables the practitioner, through his improved grasp of children's learning processes, to treat his patients more effectively.

The study by Morrison confirms the orderliness of children's moral development as noted by Piaget (1932) and by L. Kohlberg (1963). There are practical implications in these findings, because they indicate to the parent, the teacher, and anyone else who works with children what can reasonably be expected in the moral judgment of children at various ages and stages of development.

The article by Brekke, Williams, and Harlow examines the fundamental relationship between the development of conservation and the development of intellect. These findings are obviously relevant to the educational scene, because they assess the relative value of conservation and intelligence measurements as indicators of reading readiness.

Because common sense may suggest that reading readiness should be related to other dimensions of cognitive development, the layman might deem it a waste of time and money to conduct a study to verify this assumption. Much of the research conducted by psychologists and other scientists is in fact concerned with testing hypotheses that seem logically true. Although these assumptions are sometimes found to be faulty, the chief purpose of the behavioral scientist is not to challenge common sense assumptions but to discover how behavior and its processes are ordered and structured. If the investigator finds through scientific investigation that reading readiness and cognitive development are interrelated, as expected, he has learned something about cognitive development, as well as something about reading readiness. He can conclude with some certainty that conservation is not an isolated trait, but is actually a broad-gauge, general concept that is useful in describing cognitive development and in making predictions about children's behavior, not only in reading readiness, but in a variety of activities.

REFERENCES

Bronfenbrenner, U. "Developmental research, public policy, and the ecology of childhood." *Child Development,* 45 (1974): 1–5.

Kohlberg, L. "The development of children's orientations toward a moral order: I. Sequence in the development of moral thought." *Vita Humana,* 6 (1963): 11–33.

Piaget, J. *The Moral Judgment of the Child.* London: Kegan-Paul, 1932.

1.1

Allport, F. H. (1924). *Social Psychology* (Cambridge, Mass.).

Brown, R. (1958). *Words and Things* (Glencoe, Illinois).

Jakobson, R., Fant, C. G. and Halle, M. (1967). *Preliminaries to Speech Analysis: the Distinctive Features and Their Correlates* (Cambridge, Mass.).

Kagan, J. (1966). Three faces of continuity in development. Lecture presented at Syracuse University, Syracuse, New York.

Katz, J. J. and Fodor, J. A. (1964). The structure of a semantic theory. In J. A. Fodor and J. J. Katz (eds.), *The Structure of Language* (Englewood Cliffs, New Jersey), 479.

Mallitskaya, M. K. (1960). K metodike ispol'zoxaniya Kertinok dlya razvitiya ponimaniya rechi u detei v kontse pervogo in na otorom godu zhizri. (A method for using pictures to develop speech comprehension in children at the end of the first and in the second year of life). *Voprosy psikhol,* 122. In F. Smith and G. Miller (eds.). *The Genesis of Language: A Psycholinguistic Approach* (Cambridge, Mass.), 375 (abstract).

McNeill, D. and McNeill, N. B. (1967). A question in semantic development: What does a child mean when he says "no." In E. M. Zale (ed.), *Language and Language Behavior* (New York), 51.

Piaget, J. (1962). *Play, Dreams, and Imitation in Childhood* (New York).

The Random House Dictionary of the English Language: The Unabridged Edition (1966) (New York).

Vygotsky, L. S. (1962). *Thought and Language* (New York).

Weir, R. H. (1962). *Language in the Crib* (The Hague).

1.2

Asch, S. E. Forming impressions of personality. *Journal of Abnormal and Social Psychology,* 1946, **41,** 258–290.

Luchins, A. S. Forming impressions of personality: A critique. *Journal of Abnormal and Social Psychology,* 1948, **43,** 318–325.

Morrison, J. K. Moral judgment ratings and the self-image. Unpublished manuscript (pilot study), State University of New York at Albany, 1971. (a)

Morrison, J. K. The training of first-graders on the importance of intentionality in making moral judgments using a six-point rating scale. Unpublished master's thesis, State University of New York at Albany, 1971. (b)

Piaget, J. *The moral judgment of the child.* London: Kegan-Paul, 1932.

1.3

1. Almy, M. Young children's thinking and the teaching of reading. In W. Cutts (Ed.), *Teaching Young Children to Read: Proceedings of a Conference,* November 14–16, 1962. Bulletin no. 19, U.S. Department of Health, Education, and Welfare, Office of Education, Washington, D.C., 1964. Pp. 97–102.

2. Almy, M., Chittenden, E., & Miller, P. Young Children's Thinking. New York: Teachers Coll. Press, 1967.

3. Hall, E. A conversation with Jean Piaget and Barbel Inhelder. *Psychology Today,* 1970, **3,** 25–31, 54–56.

4. Lepper, R. E. A cross-cultural investigation of the relationships between the development of selected science-related concepts and social status and reading readiness of Negro and white first graders. *Diss. Abst.,* 1966, **26,** 4501.

5. Piaget, J. The Psychology of Intelligence, Totowa, N.J.: Littlefield, Adams, 1966.

2.
COGNITIVE
DEVELOPMENT

As a child grows and develops over a span of years, he undergoes impressive changes in physical appearance—be becomes taller and heavier, his "baby fat" is replaced by muscle tissue, and so forth. His relationships with other people also change, as he becomes less dependent and self-centered, and more independent and cooperative. But the change that evokes the greatest excitement from doting parents and admiring relatives is the development of his cognitive skills. His first word is eagerly awaited; his first sentence is a cause for celebration; and his ingenuous and ingenious use of word forms becomes part of the family lore. The cognitive growth manifested in these early verbalizations arouses the greatest interest among the child's family members, perhaps because it is cognition—our ability to perceive, analyze, recollect, and speculate—that makes us human. Although all the higher animals demonstrate some degree of cognitive ability, they are surpassed by man in this respect, for man alone is able to create and solve abstract, complex problems.

The various aspects of cognition—perception, language, intelligence, concept formation, and problem solving—have in one form or another constituted the major concerns of psychological investigators from the very beginning of the science of psychology. Interest in children's cognition has been motivated by three major concerns: first, a desire to learn about adult cognitive processes by studying their beginnings in childhood; second, an interest in understanding children for their own sake; and third, a search for more effective ways to teach children cognitive skills. Many researchers and theorists have devoted intensive study to children's cognition, but the figure who towers above them all is Jean Piaget, the Swiss psychologist whose tireless work at his Geneva institute over the last fifty years has earned him universal regard as the most influential thinker in the field of developmental psychology. Piaget first became interested in children's cognitive processes through noting the errors they make in attempting to solve problems. These observations led him to conclude that children's thinking processes are unlike those of adults, and he subsequently devoted his life to the study of how children apprehend, comprehend, and cope with their physical and social environment at various stages in their development.

Piaget (1970) calls the first stage of development, which ordinarily covers the first eighteen to twenty-four months of life, the *sensorimotor* period. During this period, the child is primarily occupied with discovering the physical attributes of his physical world. When he becomes able to move around and to explore his environment, and when he manipulates the objects within it, he learns that they have permanence, even when they are temporarily removed from his immediate vicinity or visual field. Although he becomes aware of relationships in time, space, and shapes, he is unable to deal with these relationships on a symbolic level.

The child's first spoken words are the most obvious indication of his transition from the sensorimotor period into the *preoperational thought* stage. The ability to verbalize is made possible by his having learned to conceptualize not only his environment, but his feelings and wishes as well. At first his thinking proceeds along very rigid lines—he can follow a sequence of events, but he cannot reverse them. He can express his own point of view, but he cannot apprehend the viewpoints of others. He is confused when the appearance of a substance is changed, such as when the contents of a cup are poured into a plate or a tall jar, or when a ball of clay is flattened or made into a sausage-shaped roll. Because he does not understand that a change in shape does not mean that the amount of the substance has changed, Piaget says that the child is unable to *conserve* quantity, a concept we discussed in Section 1.

Conservation is developed during the *concrete operations* period, which most children enter at about seven or eight years of age. During this stage of development, the child becomes better able to use logic and is less likely to be misled by appearances. He is able to make simple generalizations and abstractions, and he becomes increasingly aware of the thoughts and feelings of others. Moral concepts, however, are quite rigid and are attuned to the consequences of misdeeds, rather than to their causes.

The *formal operations* stage usually begins at about eleven or twelve years of age and extends for another two years. The child begins to think like an adult, to handle abstract relationships, to deal with hypothetical situations, and to understand the principles underlying probability. During this stage, concepts of morality and justice take into account the intentions of other people, as well as their overt actions.

According to Piaget, children in each stage of development build upon and extend the competencies acquired in the earlier stages; therefore they cannot "leapfrog" certain stages or substages, nor can development be accelerated by, for example, attempting to train a five-year-old to function at the formal operations level. The possibility of accelerating cognitive development has nevertheless intrigued American researchers, who tend to be environmentalists and to regard the human organism as much more plastic and malleable than do their European colleagues. Piaget's pronouncements have been taken by some American psychologists as a kind of challenge, and they have consequently designed experiments to determine whether cognitive development can be accelerated or reversed. Some of this research has been reviewed by Patrick C. Lee in the first article (2.1) included in this section. Lee is especially interested in the implications of this research for educational practice.

2.1

Cognitive development in young children

Patrick C. Lee,
assisted by E. Robert LaCrosse,
Frances Litman,
Daniel M. Ogilvie,
Susan S. Stodolsky, and
Burton L. White

Cognition implies a broad array of psychological and educational phenomena. However, for the sake of this review, we shall restrict ourselves to that part of cognition which is more properly called "concept learning." This is currently an area of great research interest, due to a combination of factors. First, of course, has been the importation of Piaget's theory over the last several years, and the invigorating effect this has had on an already active American interest. A second factor has been the maturing of "cognitive psychology" from its earlier roots in both the Gestalt and Learning Traditions. One of the primary signals of this maturity was Bruner, Goodnow, and Austin's book *A Study of Thinking*. A third contributing factor has been the great popular interest in accelerating the cognitive growth of children. This has grown out of an increasing awareness of the potential for intellectual growth possessed by children, and from an increasing concern that we have not been fully exploiting this potential. Central to this third factor is the renaissance in early childhood education which began in the 1960's and continued into the 1970's.

The single most influential figure in the field has been Jean Piaget, the Swiss epistemologist and psychologist. His primary focus has been on human ways of knowing and his outstanding contribution has been to trace the genesis of how we think and know from earliest childhood through adolescence. Most American researchers have concentrated on

A revised and updated version of Chapter 12, "Cognitive development in preschool children, pp. 230–240, from "The first six years of life," *Genetic Psychology Monographs*, 82 (1970): 161–266. Reprinted with permission of the author and his collaborators, and of The Journal Press. Earlier version copyright 1970 by The Journal Press.

the transition from the preoperational to the concrete operational stages of Piaget's theory. This transition takes place at 6 to 8 years of age, but researchers have generally used somewhat younger subjects because of their interest in the beginning phase of the transition or in trying to accelerate cognitive growth before its natural appearance in development.

REPLICATION STUDIES

Because of the great interest it has generated, one might almost believe that Piaget never studies anything but conservation. There is no question about the central role this construct plays in his theory, as evidenced by his assertion that "our contention is merely that conservation is a necessary condition for all rational activity" (24, p. 3). It should be no surprise, then, that researchers have moved heavily into the conservation issue, especially since there have been two outstanding criticisms of Piaget in this respect. First, his data often have not been reported fully, but rather in an illustrative, anecdotal form; and, second, he did not maintain a consistent procedure from subject to subject (2). Thus, there have been a number of English and American studies designated specifically to replicate Piaget's results in a more precise, quantitative manner.

For example, in a follow-up study to *The Growth of Logical Thinking* (14), Lovell (20) repeated 10 of the experiments on children and adolescents between 8 and 18 years of age. He found that the main stages of development of logical thinking proposed by Piaget were largely confirmed. Elkind (10) systematically investigated conservation of mass, weight, and volume in children and found that specific and general conservation abilities increased with age. He also found, as did Uzgiris (32), that conservation of mass (substance), weight, and volume developed in the sequence which Piaget had postulated. Elkind (10, 11) has also investigated discrimination, seriation, and numeration of size and dimensional differences in children, and again secured results in basic agreement with those of Piaget.

In general, the replication studies have tended to lower Piaget's age norms, but they have corroborated his *sequence* of stages. Approximately fifteen replication studies have been published over the last few years, but this line of research seems to be coming to a close. More recently American investigators have shifted their interest to the *acceleration* of cognitive growth. There seems to be general satisfaction that

Piaget's sequence of stages is sound, and a new fascination with the prospect of telescoping this sequence into the shortest possible age range.

ACCELERATION STUDIES

There have been a fair number of published studies over the past few years which have attempted to accelerate the appearance of conservation before its emergence in the natural course of development. Although most of the earlier studies were unsuccessful, some of the more recent ones have reported varying degrees of success (e.g., 4, 19, 26, 28, 30). The target variables in these studies have been an assortment of transitions that take place from preoperational to concrete operational thinking. Some of the variables studied have been number concept (35), conservation of weight (27, 28), and conservation of liquid and solid substance (19).

The significance of these acceleration studies, however, is found not in their number or variety, but in the methodological difficulties which researchers have encountered in this apparently simple procedure. These difficulties have particular significance for any early education program which purports to accelerate cognitive growth and to assess its own effectiveness. The problems lie specifically in the nature and conditions of criterion response—i.e., the child's performance *after* training—and in the nature of the training procedure itself.

Braine (2), for example, has found that, in using a *non*verbal criterion response, he gets evidence for the existence of certain logical operations one and a half to two years earlier than ordinarily expected. This fits the common finding by language researchers that verbal *comprehension* usually precedes verbal *production* in development. Yet most cognitive researchers have used verbal criterion responses as a means of assessing the effectiveness of their acceleration techniques. The upshot of this argument is that the "accelerators" may not have been training subjects in conceptual manipulations at all, but may simply have been providing the children with a basis for communicating skills which they already had on a verbal comprehension (or even totally nonverbal) level. At any rate, this is the most conservative evaluation of the work done on acceleration, and may represent a vindication of Piaget, who has been generally suspicious of acceleration procedures.

The question, however, is even more complicated when one considers that there are various kinds of verbal criterion responses. Children are generally able to predict conservation earlier than they are able to judge it. This means that before a modification in the material (e.g., clay or water) is made, children will assert conservation. But, once faced with the dramatic change in the shape of the material, they are often overwhelmed by perceptual input, and they lose conservation. Furthermore, when children are able to judge that the amount (or weight) of the material is the same in spite of perceived differences, they are often unable to provide a verbal rationale to support their judgment. What all this means is that acceleration research is susceptible to the same problems found in other kinds of research. Whether or not positive results are generated depends upon the criterion response used, and the *nature* of the criterion response is often dictated by the measure of the criterion response.

Much also depends upon the conditions under which the criterion response is elicited, or, in other words, on the kinds of tests used to see if training has been effective. Conservation is a logical operation, and should be conceived of as a cognitive principle. In this sense, it is supposed to apply to a number of different situations which vary in some respects, but which remain invariant in other respects. A very useful device for testing this notion has been to introduce a transfer test or test of generalization into the research design. To the degree that the characteristics of the generalized test differ from those of the training situation, fewer children pass the generalized test. Piaget would maintain that the only valid test of the existence of a genuine operation is to check for the presence of other operations contained in the same "grouping." For example, if one trained a child to grasp number and length, then a valid posttest would be to see whether or not he could conserve area, because these three conservations are all included in the same logical "grouping." This is a very rigorous posttest and Beilin (1), who tried it, was unable to achieve positive results. The problem with this kind of posttest is that it assumes that the underlying theoretical construct of "grouping" is valid. If the point of an experiment is to test an aspect of theory, then it is begging the question to assume beforehand that the theory is true. Any theory, no matter how elegant, must have some correspondence with external criteria.

A more reasonable posttest would probably be the generalization procedure mentioned above. Lee (19), for example, found that children trained in conservation were able to transfer their training to generalized posttest situations which differed in several respects from the training situation: different material (e.g., clay *vs.* water), different experimenter, and differing intervals of delay from training to posttest (one to seven days). Another kind of posttest would be to test the child under exactly or nearly the same conditions of the training procedure. This test, however, is too easy, and really doesn't demonstrate anything other than that the child can make the same response under the same conditions. Kohnstamm (17) has discussed this issue at some length and has opted for the posttest of medium difficulty.

The foregoing analysis has raised two questions which have direct relevance to education. First, can a teacher actually influence conceptual growth per se, or does he merely supply the child with a convenient set of verbal symbols? And, second, what represents a fair test of the effectiveness of a training procedure? Neither of these questions can be definitively answered at the present time, but they must be raised and considered if they are eventually to be answered.

TRAINING PROCEDURES

More important than the question of assessment, however, is the training procedure used to induce concept learning. A number of different procedures have been used in the acceleration research. Smedslund (27), for example, used reinforcement techniques. He has also used a questioning technique, as did Lee (19). This technique is designed to induce cognitive-perceptual conflict in the child as a means of enabling him to realize (through thinking) that things may not really be the way they appear. Bruner and his colleagues (4) used a screening technique to block perceptual input, while the child was given a verbal formulation to assist him in the conservation task. Although they found that this "saying before seeing" procedure elicited positive results, Lee (19) was unable to replicate their findings. Ojemann and Pritchett (21) used "guided experience" techniques by gradually exposing their subjects to problems of increasing difficulty. Sigel, Roeper, and Hooper (26) trained their subjects in Piagetian operations in the expectation that conservation of weight and substance would result.

For the most part, training procedures have been verbal or have at least contained a large verbal component. Again this raises the question as to whether verbal input actually influences concept learning or the child's ability to verbalize already present concepts. Bruner is very much in favor of using verbal techniques, maintaining that language encourages a child to substitute operational strategies for more primitive perceptual approaches. Piaget and his associates—e.g., Inhelder *et al.* (15)—argue that language is useless as an activation device, because a child cannot benefit from language until he has developed the prerequisite cognitive structure. There is currently no basis for finally deciding this argument, although the weight of the evidence seems to favor Piaget. Language has, however, demonstrated itself to be a formidable, if little understood, tool in the hands of the researcher and educator. Much more research is required if we are eventually to specify language functions and their relationships to concept learning. At the very least, verbal procedures *have* been successful in facilitating the communication of conceptual skills, and this is no mean accomplishment.

As is well known, one of the problems encountered by behavioral or social scientists is the multivariate nature of human beings. To the degree that experiments are controlled, they usually reduce the number of variables manipulated and/or measured. There has been a tradition of univariate experimentation among hard-nosed American researchers in the interests of precisely measuring the effect of manipulating one variable, while all others are carefully controlled. Of course, this procedure makes laboratory work somewhat remote from real life situations. Kohnstamm (17) has criticized the univariate approach for just this reason. His point is that most American researchers may be sacrificing not only external validity, but also positive results, for the sake of experimental rigor. Unlike the studies described above, Kohnstamm's approach to accelerating concept learning is multivariate and uncontrolled. He uses every conceivable technique, verbal and otherwise, to accelerate conceptualization, and then introduces an objective posttest as a check on the effectiveness of the all-out training procedures. He holds that this kind of "experimentation" has the greatest generalizability to the real educational process. In the school situation, when a teacher confronts the ignorance of a child, she uses whatever technique she can to move the child from ignorance to knowledge. For the most part, she is not interested in demonstrating the effectiveness of any particular technique, but she wants to get results. Afterwards, she introduces a "final exam" which is neutral and structured. In like manner, it is difficult to specify which independent variables Kohnstamm manipulates, but his techniques are verbal and they involve direct instruction. This is clearly in contradistinction to Piaget's ideas that verbal input cannot enhance cognitive development, and that the best teacher is one who subtly arranges the environment so the child can learn on his own. Yet Kohnstamm has achieved positive results in inducing classification skills in 5-year-old, "pre-operational" children.

This brief discussion has underscored three of the problems generated by experimental training procedures. Although no final answers can be given at this point, a reasonable expectation is that the most fruitful future work will have to confront these three issues:

(*a*) The relationship between language and conceptual growth or, more specifically, the value of verbal forms of training.

(*b*) The role of the adult: i.e., whether the teacher should directly instruct the child, or be an "environmental engineer," or manage some combination of the two.

(*c*) Orthodox *versus* eclectic training procedures. Is there a single best method of inducing conceptual growth or is there a battery of methods which have differential value according to the child, the teacher, and the learning situation?

IMPLICATIONS FOR EDUCATION

As anticipated in the above discussion, there have been great problems in translating Piaget's theory into educationally relevant procedures. Many of these problems have been discussed by Kohnstamm (17) and Sullivan (31). A milestone in this translation process was reached during the Cornell-Berkeley Conference of 1964, which was later published as *Piaget Rediscovered* (25). Although this conference stimulated a great deal of thought and speculation, its ultimate message seemed to be a polite but hopeful recognition that there is, indeed, a translation problem and that the profession may have to go beyond Piaget's prescriptions to make optimal use of his theory. The basic problem seems to be that Piaget is a genetic epistemologist and, as such, he is more interested in the natural growth of logical structures than in educational intervention. He does assign a role to the social environment in his theory, but his bias is toward the internal, proactive structuring on the part of the child himself.

Over the last few years, a significant controversy has emerged between two schools of thought, represented by Bruner (5, 7) on the one hand and by Piaget's Geneva-Montreal axis on the other. Very briefly, Bruner holds that intellectual structure exists in a given subject matter itself, and that the teacher must strive to communicate this structure on a level acceptable to the child. The most useful tool in this enterprise is language. Piaget, however, maintains that this structure emerges from the child's interaction with the physical and social aspects of his environment and that genuine conceptual growth advances only through his active manipulation of reality itself or his mental manipulation of representations of reality. The child actively constructs an epistemological model of the world as he transforms it in action and thought. The teacher, then, is not the primary agent of change, but is at best a helpmate to the child. To the degree that she actively instructs the child, especially when she uses language, she is informing the child's language "schemas," but not his concomitant conceptual "schemas." At best she may introduce a spuriously sophisticated quality to the child's thought, but she cannot actually accelerate the underlying operations. Operations are a function of maturation and child initiated experience. Clearly, then, Piaget's theory, when considered on its own terms, puts the *instructional* process at a distinct disadvantage. For a teacher to make use of his theory, it is probably necessary to remove oneself from Piaget's particular perspective, and look at it in a new way.

Piaget's perspective is not that of the educator or curriculum maker. Throughout his life he has been a dispassionate observer of child behavior and a sensitive diagnostician of children's level of thinking (22, 23). The fact of the matter is that he has little apparent interest in the pedagogical questions which are most germane to the educator. Kohnstamm's perspective is that of the teacher, one who sees his role as an accelerator of cognitive growth. Beyond the process of teaching, however, is the structural problem of curriculum formation. Lavatelli (18) has developed a Piaget-based curriculum which is designed to foster the acquisition of "schemas" in four-year-old, disadvantaged children. She has constructed a whole series of exercises from simple one-to-one correspondence problems (e.g., child has a bead for every one the teacher has) to fairly sophisticated class-inclusion problems (e.g., both bananas and apples belong to the class "fruit"). Kamii and her associates (29) have also developed a pre-school program based on Piaget's theory. Their curriculum includes a broad range of Piagetian derived topics, such as representation, physical knowledge, and various forms of logical knowledge: classification, seriation, number, and spatial and temporal relationships. Moreover, they have developed a number of ingenious pedagogical techniques which nicely bridge the gap between Piaget's theory on the one hand and teaching practice on the other.

Gagné (12) has also formulated a curriculum designed to teach conservation skills. He is a learning theorist and his approach has been to analyze the conservation task, and then to break it down into its prerequisite elements. His proposed curriculum, then, is based on a learning hierarchy—i.e., the child must learn or demonstrate a grasp of the elements before he can begin to combine them into higher order constructs. The ultimate goal is successively to combine and recombine until the ability to conserve is mastered. His cumulative learning model represents the imposition of a learning theory task analysis on Piagetian content.

These two approaches are representative of the two most vigorous movements in early childhood education today. Gagné's molecular analysis of the conservation task fits the programmed instruction model, while the work of Lavatelli and Kamii is closer to the experientially-oriented "open education" model. While research indicates that children can learn through programmed instruction, the experiential approach seems to be in closer correspondence with Piaget's description of the child's proactive ways of knowing.

CONCEPT LEARNING AND OTHER AREAS OF RESEARCH

As mentioned at the beginning of this chapter, concept learning is only a part of the total cognitive picture, albeit an undeniably large part. There are some researchers who have attempted to integrate concept learning with other aspects of cognition and their work deserves mention.

At the time of writing, for example, Charlesworth (8) was pulling together attentional and Piagetian constructs in his work on the functional properties of "surprise" in children and infants. His premise is that children are surprised by an event only because their existing conceptual schemas are unprepared for the event. The event jars the child's conceptual structure and causes him to focus his attention and curiosity on the event. Paying attention to a phenomenon increases the probability that the child will learn something about it. This learning, in turn, reorganizes the schema in the direction of further conceptual development. The proof of the pudding is that the child no longer demonstrates surprise with repeated presentation of the "novel" stimulus. By this time he has evidently satisfied himself that he knows enough about it, and is ready to go on to something else. As a corollary to his research, Charlesworth thinks that surprise is probably a good diagnostic indicator of the status of schema development. If the child, for example, is surprised by the fact that both bananas and apples are fruit, one should suspect that he has not yet mastered the concept of class-inclusion.

Jeffrey (16) has independently arrived at a similar conceptualization of the relationship between attention and concept learning. According to his "habituation" model, the child makes an orienting response (OR) to a novel object, similar to Charlesworth's notion of surprise and attention. Very quickly, however, the first OR habituates—i.e., the child tires of this response—and it is replaced in turn by second, third, and fourth OR's, each of which successively habituate. The child makes all the OR's which he considers necessary until his supply is exhausted. The point to all this is that each new OR takes in new information about the novel event, until the child has developed a schema which bears some correspondence to reality. Needless to say, the quality of the schema is limited by the child's level of maturation.

White has also developed a similar notion (33). He sees concept learning as a function of attending to regular cues which are imbedded in a mass of shifting, variable cues. In a given sequence of events the child looks for the common properties of each event and gradually excludes those properties which do not carry over from event to event. For this reason a child can, for example, call two apparently different objects "dogs," because he has learned to attend to the common cues possessed by all dogs. He has, in effect, learned the concept "dog." A breakdown of this functioning is indicated when a child refers to a large dog as a "horse." What is probably happening in this example is that the child is attending to the size of the dog at the expense of other cues.

Another area of cognition, which has attracted a great deal of research over the years is "Problem Solving." Unfortunately, however, at the time of writing this area was in a state of conceptual disarray. The reasons for this were nicely summarized by Duncan, who, after reviewing the research, concluded that "the field of problem solving is poorly integrated. The reason for this seems to be the use of a great variety of tasks to provide problems, the frequent use of unanalyzed and undimensionalized variables, the lack of agreed upon taxonomy and, to some extent, the failure to relate data to other data or theory" (9, p. 426).

Gagné (13), however, has recently been working on a learning theory analysis of problem solving as a way to clarify and make operational this troublesome phenomenon. He sees problem solving as being a special kind of concept learning for three reasons: first, solving a problem means more than learning a response to the problem. It means finding an answer to it, or, in other words, grasping the concept of solution. Second, in problem solving there is a sharp difference between the "learning phase" and the final performance phase. Just as the child constructs a concept out of successive OR's (c.f., Jeffrey), the end product is quite different from the means employed to get to the product. Third, solution of a problem is not specific to the given problem. It is based upon a grasp of the concept of the problem, and is, therefore, transferable to a class of tasks.

This brief discussion of the relationships between concept learning, attention, and problem solving has been included to give some idea of both the scope and the interlocking nature of cognitive activity. This is a most complicated area and a difficult one for the scientific researcher. As any educator can testify, it is as multivariate as thinking itself, and comes very close to the key of what it is to be human.

RECOMMENDATIONS

1. As has become apparent by now, one of the most difficult problems in this area is a terminological one. The field has long been using a set of terms without there being any consensus as to what these terms really mean. Gagné (13) has addressed himself to this problem in an attempt to redefine terms, such as concept, principle, and problem-solving. This is a good first step in a meaningful direction; the field ought to adopt a carefully defined and agreed upon set of terms.

2. As with many other areas of psychological research, the whole area of cognition is loosely integrated. We are in great need of a set of conceptual models which will draw together the disparate elements into a meaningful framework. Again, Gagné (12) has done yeoman work in this respect. His cumulative learning model incorporates concept learning, problem solving, S-R [stimulus-response] learning theory, and curriculum construction into a brilliantly articulated framework. He and others ought to continue this essential work of model building. Moreover, such models should incorporate longitudinal evidence so as better to describe specifically developmental parameters. White's (34) hierarchical model of learning processes is a good first step in this direction.

3. It is also recommended that the field continue to pursue the thorny issue of how language and concept learning are related. It is

highly probable that infants can think before they can talk, but there is also a great deal of evidence that, once language begins, it becomes a serious influence on thought. In fact, it may even be an externalized version of some properties of thought, just as thought internalizes many of the qualities of language. In any event, this can be a useful way of conceptualizing this apparent duality and may lead to some provocative research findings. This question is also central to the process of education, which uses language as one of its primary and most flexible tools.

4. The ongoing effort to translate Piaget's theory into educational terms should be continued. The most fruitful approach will probably be to adopt a specifically educational perspective on this problem, and proceed with the business of teacher training and curriculum construction. Piaget did not build an educational theory and we should not expect him or his associates to make educational prescriptions. That is the job of the educational profession.

5. There is considerably more to Piaget's theory than conservation and object permanence. The developmental periods of preconceptual thought (age 2 to 4) and intuitive thought (age 4 to 7) have largely been ignored as entities in themselves. Ironically, these are the years covered by early childhood education. In our rush to accelerate the child into concrete operational thought, we have forgotten the value of more primary thought styles. There are, of course, pragmatic reasons for this unbalanced emphasis, but we cannot afford to put aside several years of a child's early life in the interest of better preparing him for later years. This could be a dangerous and short-sighted practice.

6. There is a gap between ages 1 and 3 in the cognitive area as in most other areas of research. Since this is the period of transition from infancy to childhood, it is strongly recommended that meaningful research move into this age range. At the time of writing, language specialists seemed to be the only group taking this age range seriously (c.f., 3).

7. In the flurry of activity to accelerate cognitive development, we seem to have assumed that this is a desirable goal. Without answering this question one way or the other, we should consider if there is any point to acceleration procedures. This is a philosophical question, with moral, esthetic, and political overtones, and there are no readily available answers. But the question should be raised and should become and remain a high priority item on the agenda of educational philosophers.

Much early childhood learning concerns coping with the physical environment. Because the coping and perceiving skills are developmentally interrelated, it is easy to assume that all perceptual processes are learned. This is indeed true to a large extent, but considerable research shows that depth perception, at least in a rudimentary form, is innate. R. D. Walk and E. J. Gibson (1961) conducted the classic studies that suggest this conclusion. In these experiments, infants who had just entered the creeping stage were placed at the edge of a "visual cliff," a device consisting of a "crawlway" centered on a large sheet of plate glass positioned several feet above the floor of a large bin, or crate. On one side of the crawlway, the infant could see the checkerboard covering of the floor several feet below him; on the other side, he could see a similarly-covered shelf, which was placed directly under the glass, supporting it. Preliminary experiments using the young of animals showed that they stayed on the "safe" side of the crawlway and avoided the glass suspended over the floor. Six-month-old human infants exhibited the same behavior.

There is a possibility, of course, that the infants in Walk and Gibson's studies may have learned or discovered something about depth in their encounters with the physical world; but the experiments conducted by William Ball and Edward Tronick reported in article 2.2 question this explanation, as their subjects were only two to eleven weeks of age and could hardly have done much exploring of their environment. Ball and Tronick's subjects, regardless of age, reacted appropriately when approaching objects appeared likely either to collide with them or to pass them by. When a collision seemed to impend, they moved their heads back, stiffened, and even brought their arms toward their faces; and when a "miss" was in prospect, they merely followed the object with their eyes. These findings, like those of Walk and Gibson, are consistent with the theory that the basic elements of depth perception are innate.

Infant responses to impending collision: optical and real

William Ball and
Edward Tronick

The perception of an approaching object is of obvious significance to an organism. The approach is a complex spatiotemporal event. To apprehend its significance, the organism must detect object qualities, including relative distance and direction of approach, within a brief period of time. Moreover, if this apprehension is to occur more than once, the organism must act in a fashion appropriate to the event. Recently, Bower (1) found that infants respond to symmetrically looming shadows or to real approaching objects with an integrated response that consists of an initial widening of the eyes, a head withdrawal, and a raising of the arms. In addition, the stimulus presentation, particularly in the case of the real object, often produced upset and crying in the infants. Just as other species avoid looming shadows (2) or the deep side of a visual cliff (3), the infant's response reflects a capacity to respond appropriately to the distal stimulus.

The purpose of this research was to specify further the infant's initial perceptual capacities. The displacement of an object is specified optically by the transformation of a bounded segment of the optic array (4). The solidity and shape of the object are specified by the closed contour and by transformations of it that produce kinetic depth (4, 5). The path of approach is specified by the symmetrics or asymmetrics of an expanding bounded segment, and withdrawal is specified by its minification. In addition, collision is specified when the bounded segment fills 180° of the frontal visual field. The psychophysics of the infant's capacities requires the assessment of its response to these higher-order, event-specifying stimuli.

To make this assessment with shadow-casting techniques, 24 infants (eight infants, 2 to 5 weeks of age; eight infants, 5 to 8 weeks of age;

Reprinted from *Science*, 171 (1971): 818–820, with permission of the authors and the American Association for the Advancement of Science. Copyright 1971 by the American Association for the Advancement of Science.

and eight infants, 8 to 11 weeks of age) served as subjects. The apparatus (see Fig. 1) consisted of a 100-watt concentrated arc point-source lamp mounted at the end and below a 70-cm track. A Styrofoam cube (5 by 5 by 5 cm) was attached to a 51-cm rod suspended from the track. A motor-operated pulley system moved the rod along the track at a constant speed of 12 cm/sec. A second motor permitted rotation of the rod at a speed of ½ revolution per second. In addition, the point source could be displaced laterally relative to the track, so that the object moved either directly toward it or off to one side.

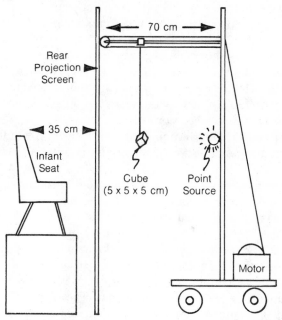

FIGURE 1

SHADOW-CASTING APPARATUS

The shadow caster was placed on one side of a rear projection screen (1.8 by 1.8 m). The infant was seated approximately 35 cm away from the opposite side of the screen in an infant chair. The chair had no head support or waistband and thus allowed free head, arm, and leg movements; but the infant was supported by an adult holding him around the waist. To the left of the infant, a television camera and microphone recorded the infant's responses to the various displays. The room itself was darkened except for the light from the point source, light from an overhead bulb, and light from a lamp on the floor to the infant's left. This combination of lights was intense enough for efficient operation of the television camera but was dim enough not to interfere with the clarity of the shadow transformations.

Movement of the static cube toward the point source (flat hit) produced a symmetrical growth in the shadow and the visual experience of an approaching object for an adult observer. Shifting the point source laterally produced an asymmetrically growing shadow that appeared to be an object coming toward an observer but on a miss path (flat miss). Movement of the cube away from the point source after an approach appeared to be an object moving away from the observer (flat recession). Rotation of the cube in front of the point source prior to and during its movement along the track resulted in the visual experience of a solid object. The rotating cube went through the same sequence as the static cube; that is, it was driven directly toward the point source (solid hit), toward the laterally shifted point source (solid miss), and away from the point source (solid recession).

A trial consisted of an approach followed by a withdrawal of the object from the point source. Two of the infants in each age group started with one of the four possible conditions. After three trials, if they were still alert and attentive, they continued through the other three conditions in a predetermined Latin square order.

In a second experiment, seven infants 3 to 6 weeks of age were exposed to a 30 by 30 cm object approaching on a collision or miss path (Fig. 2). Its rate of approach was 17 cm/sec. The object was hung from the shadow-casting apparatus and displayed in a three-sided visual corridor made of bamboo curtains. Its run was 75 cm in length and ended about 15 cm in front of the infant. The object was not rotated but remained frontal parallel to the infant seated at the end of the run, in the same fashion as in the shadow-casting procedure. Infants started with either hit or miss sequences in a balanced design across subjects. Three trials of each sequence were again attempted, and a video tape recording was made of the sessions.

Because the form of the infant's response is fundamental to the experiment, a qualitative description will be given before the quantitative results. Infants generally began the session slumped in the chair with their arms down. During a hit sequence, the infant moved his head back and away from the screen and brought his arms toward his face. This was the full avoidance response. Sometimes the infant finished by

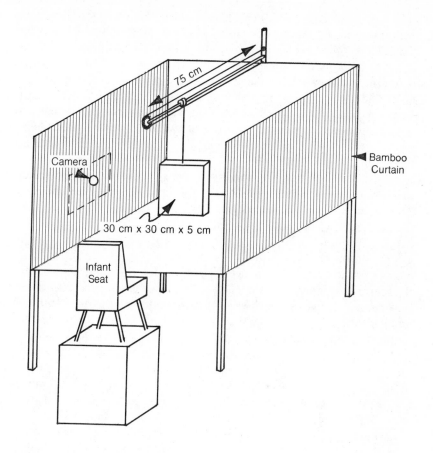

FIGURE 2
REAL OBJECT APPARATUS

facing toward the ceiling. The coming back of the head was usually observed only after the shadow had begun to fill the field or when the object came close. It was never observed before the transformation began. The person holding the infant often reported a "stiffening" of the infant's body during looming phases, followed by a relaxation during the recession phase. The response during the miss trials was dramatically different. There was commonly a slow turning of the head and eyes along the path of the shadow or object. The arms tended to come up, but the head did not come back as it did in hit trials, nor did the infant stiffen. Strikingly, visitors with no knowledge of the stimulus conditions, who observed the tapes, commented that the baby seemed to be either avoiding or following something in the respective conditions.

For the quantitative analysis, counts were made of the movement of the head backward, of the arms upward, and of the head tracking to the side; counts were also made of fussing (primarily vocalizations from low cries to wailing). Each of these events was scored and analyzed separately, and a combined measure of two out of three components produced a tracking or upset index. The quantitative results support the qualitative descriptions.

In the shadow-casting experiment, hit and miss trials were significantly different ($\chi^2 = 16.8, \ldots p < .001$) for the combined upset measure. The difference was accounted for by a significant difference between the movement of the head (movement backward versus tracking) in the two conditions ($\chi^2 = 82, \ldots p < .001$). There were no differences in any of the measures for the different age groups or for the solid as compared with the flat sequences. The recession trials did not produce the above components at all. The results in the case of the real object were similar. Hit versus miss was significantly different on the combined upset measures . . . ($p = .003$), and the difference was accounted for by the head-movement measure.

The qualitative and quantitative results support the interpretation that infants can detect object qualities of direction and relative depth of approach and collision for both real objects and their optical equivalent. Neither kinetic depth in the optical displays nor the real display appeared to produce a stronger response than the simple expansion pattern. It may be that the infants are unable to process all the information available simultaneously or that expansion alone is a sufficient elicitor of the response with or without additional information. The lack of age differences over the age range studied indicates that learning (either to detect the event or, in the shadow-casting case, to detect that it is *not* a real object) does not play a major role in the phenomenon.

SUMMARY

Twenty-four infants ranging in age from 2 to 11 weeks responded to symmetrically expanding shadows, which optically specify an approaching object, with an integrated avoidance response and upset. This response did not occur for asymmetrically expanding shadows nor for contracting shadows that specify an object on a miss path and a receding object. The response was observed in all the infants regardless of age, and the addition of kinetic depth information to the displays did not increase the intensity or likelihood of the response. In a second experiment, seven infants defensively reacted to the approach of a real object except when it was on a miss path.

When the child has entered the preoperational thought stage, observers become increasingly dependent on his verbal reports as indices of progress in cognitive development. It is easy to be deluded into thinking that language is essential to cognitive development. Although children who are deaf from birth do not develop linguistically as a typical child with normal hearing does, they nevertheless display normal cognitive development. Hans G. Furth surveyed the research literature that appeared between 1964 and 1969 and was unable to find any evidence showing that congenitally deaf children differ significantly from other children the same age in terms of the ability to learn rules, to encode and decode symbols and use them in logical ways, to recognize and remember designs and colors, and to identify and discriminate between similar but different figures (Furth, 1971). These findings raise awkward questions for those who insist that language competence is essential in cognitive functioning. There seems to be little doubt, however, that children of normal hearing quickly learn to use language as a tool to aid them in perceiving and coping with their environment. Apparently, a child makes use of whatever media are available to him.

Patricia Marks Greenfield (1970) has conducted a number of investigations showing that verbal symbols become embedded within the context of social experiences at a very early age. The experiment included in Section 1 describes how her eight-month-old daughter was first encouraged to produce a sound, then to attach a meaning to it, and finally to use the sound in a symbolic sense, away from the physical presence of its referent. This ability to use symbols independently of referents is an essential step in learning to use language as a cognitive—a thinking—tool.

The association of sounds with significant events occurs at an even earlier age. When her son was four months old, Greenfield conducted another series of experiments, which are reported in article 2.3. These experiments showed that the infant was more likely to respond appropriately with a smile to a game of peekaboo if the experimenter uttered the word "peekaboo!" The association was quickly acquired by the infant and was extended to other game situations of the peekaboo type. Verbalization, in other words, facilitated learning.

2.3 Playing peekaboo with a four-month-old: A study of the role of speech and nonspeech sounds in the formation of a visual schema

Patricia Marks Greenfield

The role of auditory signals, in general, and speech, in particular, in structuring the visual attention of a four-month-old baby was investigated by systematic study of my own baby in his natural surroundings. The question was whether sound in general and speech in particular would help the baby to segment continuous visual information by calling attention to critical points in a visual sequence. The visual sequences used in the study involved the disappearance and reappearance of objects or mother—the familiar peekaboo game played with inanimate things, as well as people.

A secondary purpose of the study was to ascertain whether patterns of response would differ according to whether the disappearing objects were human or inanimate. Trevarthen and Richards (10) have found that, from the beginning, infants respond very differently to people than they do to inanimate objects.

The peekaboo game would not be possible if it exceeded the visual capacities of the infants. Haynes, White, and Held (6) have shown, however, that by four months of age, the point at which this study began, infants adjust their visual accommodation quite precisely to the distance of the target. Nor would peekaboo be possible if an object ceased to exist for an infant when it disappeared. But Bower (2) has shown that when things disappear slowly and perspectively, they continue to exist for a seven-week-old baby for a duration of five seconds. By 12 weeks

Reprinted from *The Journal of Psychology*, 82 (1972): 287–298, with permission of the author and The Journal Press. Copyright 1972 by The Journal Press.

of age, babies have existence constancy for objects disappearing at rates even faster than those used in a peekaboo game. In peekaboo, disappearance is much shorter than five seconds. Thus, at 12 weeks of age, objects are sufficiently permanent for the normal peekaboo game.

Charlesworth (4) has very successfully used this game to study cognitive processes in babies from five months up. He showed that even the youngest babies develop clear-cut visual expectancies when objects reappear in a constant locale. But what does it mean to say that expectancies develop, if in a sense the expectancies are there from the outset in the form of existence concepts? The spatio-temporal characteristics of a particular game must be what the infant is learning from experience. In this present study, a hiding-reappearance game was used to determine what interactional conditions facilitate or impede the development of this type of learning.

It is known that newborns are selectively attentive to the frequency range of human vocalization [Eisenberg (5)]. Given its privileged position as a stimulus, can the human voice serve to make spatially coordinated information in another modality—vision—more distinctive for the infant?

Newborns possess a capacity for sound localization as well [Bronshtein and Petrova (3), Wertheimer (11), Semb and Lipsitt (9)]. Although the actualization of this capacity is initially constrained by information-processing limitation [Aronson and Tronick (1)], by the age of three months infants will orient to all visible sound sources [Piaget (8)]. When a four-month-old baby then orients to a sound emanating from a visually informative locus, can this experience help shape a pattern of visual attention? The question of this study is whether a sequence of such experience facilitates the growth of a visual expectancy.

These problems were investigated by comparing the baby's response to the reappearance phase of the hiding game under varying auditory conditions. In games where the disappearing object was inanimate, disappearance and reappearance were accomplished either in silence, accompanied by the object's own sound, or accompanied by mother's speech. When mother was the disappearing object, the same three conditions were used except that a nonspeech sound made by the mother replaced the sound of the inanimate object. Smiling when the object reappeared was used as an index of a confirmed expectancy. According to evidence from Kagan *et al.* (7), four months is an age when the smile functions to indicate assimilation of a visual stimulus to an emergent schema.

PROCEDURE

Study 1

The first study involved the typical sort of peekaboo game, in which I disappeared and reappeared. The baby's response to my reappearance was compared under two conditions: in one condition, the word "peekaboo," said with the bright intonation normal to the game, accompanied reappearance; in the other condition, I reappeared silently. Under both conditions, I made a sound ("ooh-ooh") to attract his attention before hiding. A series of 10 game sessions, each consisting of seven to 14 trials, was played in a number of different locales around the house. In each game session, the two reappearance conditions—"peekaboo" and silent—were represented an approximately equal number of times; in the average session, each of the two conditions was represented by five or six trials. Fatigue and boredom determined at what point to terminate a game session. The study began at 17 weeks and lasted until 19 weeks of age. Some ancillary sessions were held as late as 23 weeks of age. More than one game session took place in each locale over a period of days or weeks, so that it was possible to trace the development of a peekaboo schema in each of four different locales.

One locale was Matthew's crib, beneath which I would disappear while he was in it. This was the only one in which he had played peekaboo before the onset of the study; the three other hiding places were a large bathroom hamper, a bed, and a sofa. Locales for hiding around the house were thus sampled to a reasonable degree.

Reappearance consisted of popping my face up (or sideways, in the case of the hamper) into Matthew's visual field. The amount of time in hiding was not controlled. In this way I felt that I would obtain a "representative sampling" . . . of amount of time hidden while maintaining natural conditions. My experience has indicated that artificial timing constraints in infant experiments often destroy the phenomenon one wishes to study. Nevertheless, when simulated game conditions were timed in the laboratory, temporal characteristics turned out to be remarkably consistent: time spent hidden averaged 1.3 seconds; the range was from 1.2 to 1.4 seconds. Rate of disappearing averaged 41 cm/second; the range was from 38 to 42 cm/seconds. Thus, "natural" timing in disappearance-reappearance games turns out to be uniform without any experimental constraints.

As a more general point about methodology, it seems that two qualities of infant behavior make it necessary to develop systematic yet natural observation conditions; in comparison with adults, infant behavior is (*a*) much more sensitive to situational context and inner state, and (*b*) much less detachable from specific goals. These considerations are most important when one purports to study how commerce with the social or physical environment affects the growth of some aspect of development.

Although it is necessary to avoid arbitrariness in designing experimental conditions, it is also necessary to avoid "experimenter effects" which confound results. In the present case, an obvious source of such an effect could be the mother's smiling. Therefore, a conscious rule not to smile first but always to smile back when the baby smiled was initiated after the first game session. I thought that this rule would duplicate, in a systematic way, the naturally occurring contingency *vis-à-vis* smiling. Still, this procedure introduces the possibility that smiling is being operantly conditioned. This hypothesis will be evaluated later in the light of the actual results.

Study 2

This series of hiding games, begun after the main part of Study 1 when Matthew was 19 weeks old and continuing until 22 weeks of age, was designed to compare the effectiveness of speech and nonspeech auditory signals in structuring a response to the visual peekaboo game. A second complementary purpose was to see whether the pattern of response differed when an inanimate object, rather than a human being, disappeared and reappeared.

In this study, two parallel series of games were played with mother and with objects. In the object games, where three toys constituted the objects, experience with a given toy was the variable analogous to experience with a locale in the "mother" games. Thus, in both types of game the growth of a specific expectancy could be traced over time. During the object games, Matthew was always on the couch with me in front of it. The toy started in front of my face, disappeared downwards, and reappeared in front of my face. Thus, my presence was a constant stimulus in the object games. When the object game was simulated later in the laboratory its temporal conditions turned out to be extremely consistent and identical with those obtaining when the object was a person: disappearance occurred at an average rate of 41 cm/second; the range was

38 to 44 cm/seconds. The object stayed hidden an average of 1.3 seconds; time hidden ranged from 1.2 to 1.4 seconds.

Each game session consisted of nine peekaboo trials equally divided among three conditions. No condition was presented on two trials in a row. In addition to a speech and silent condition as in the first study, there was also a nonspeech sound condition. In game sessions where a toy was hidden, the speech signals were distinctive from those used when mother hid: "Hey, Matthew" to signal impending disappearance, and "Here it is" when the toy popped back. When mother hid under the nonspeech condition, the sound used to herald disappearance and reappearance was a sort of squeak, difficult to describe but often used with babies. This sound had in fact been a favorite for Matthew, but when tested before the study began, it no longer elicited a smile by itself. When a toy was hidden under the nonspeech sound condition, the toy's own sound—squeak or chime—signalled disappearance or reappearance. Under the silent condition, both mother and toy disappeared and reappeared in silence. This was a departure from the first study in which an orienting signal was given even under the silent condition. In both studies, however, a trial was not begun until Matthew focused visually on whatever was about to disappear.

In this study, two new hiding places were used when mother hid—a table and a chair in their normal locations in the house. Two game sessions took place at the table, one at the chair. For inanimate disappearance, locale was constant—the couch used in the first study—but the object itself was variable. One of two rubber squeakers, a deer, was already familiar; a duck squeaker and chime rattle were not. Altogether six sessions of inanimate disappearance took place. One was excluded from the data analysis because no smiles were elicited under any condition, probably because Matthew was tired.

RESULTS

Study 1

At first, speech constitutes a powerful cue in the peekaboo game with mother; her reappearance rarely elicits a smile without "peekaboo" marking the event. With increasing experience with the game in a given locale, however, the speech signal loses its privileged position, and the visual sequence alone suffices to elicit a consistent smiling response. Table 1 makes this pattern clear: in the first game in given locales,

TABLE 1
RESPONSE TO MOTHER'S REAPPEARANCE DURING GAME SESSIONS VARYING IN
FAMILIARITY OF LOCALE: STUDIES 1 AND 2

	First in given locale		*Second in same locale*		*Third in same locale*	
Reappearance marked by	*Smile*	*No smile*	*Smile*	*No smile*	*Smile*	*No smile*
Study 1[a]						
"Peekaboo"	17	2	11	1	4	0
Silence	6	11	6	6	3	0
Study 2[b]						
Human speech sounds ("peekaboo")	6	0	3	0		
Human nonspeech sounds	3	3	3	0		
Silence	0	6	3	0		

Game sessions

a Locales in Study 1 were as follows: First game session—hamper, sofa, bed; second session—hamper, sofa; third session—hamper.
b Locales in Study 2 were as follows: First game session—table, chair; second session—table.

silent reappearance elicits a smile only six out of 17 times, or 35% of the time. When the game is repeated in the same locales at a later date, silent reappearance elicits a smile 50% of the time; when it is repeated a third time at a still later date, silent reappearance elicits a smile 100% of the time. The results from the "peekaboo" condition are in sharp contrast; smiling occurs 17 out of 19 trials or 89% of the time the very first time the game is played in a given locale. This response remains constant: smiling occurs 11 out of 12 trials (92%) for the second game in a given place, four out of four trials (100%) for the third game in the same place. Whereas the difference between the "peekaboo" and silent conditions is large and statistically significant ($p < .01$, *one-tailed Fisher Test*) during the first session in a given locale, all differences evaporate by the third series of trials: the visual sequence alone elicits smiling on every trial, exactly as it does in combination with the "peekaboo" signal.

In the results presented thus far, experience is somewhat confounded with maturation, especially by the third game session in a given locale. In order to see whether experience can play an independent part, let us turn to the data collected on the second day of the study in the one locale where peekaboo had been played before the systematic investigation began. We may then compare these results with those collected at the same time in two new locales. In this comparison, we hold maturation constant while varying amount of game experience in a specific locale.

The second day of the study we played peekaboo by Matthew's crib, the place where he had previous peekaboo experience. Reappearance elicited a smile on five out of five "peekaboo" trials and five out of five silent trials. The day before and the day immediately following, games were played in two new locales—hamper and couch. The results obtained on silent trials in new hiding places were uniformly different from those obtained in the familiar hiding place. When I reappeared silently, smiling occurred one in five times at the hamper, one in seven times at the sofa. In sharp contrast, silent reappearance at the crib had elicited a smile on every trial, that is, five out of five times. (This result at the crib locale was replicated five days later.) In other words, experience can promote the development of the visual disappearance-reappearance schema at any chronological point within the one-month range tested in this study.

It is interesting that at this point in development, expectancies seem extremely specific. This fact emerges when one notes that performance fails to improve during a second game session when that session takes place in a *different* locale, whereas there is great improvement the second time when the game is played in the *same* locale. By the end of the month, either because of maturation or because of a learning-to-learn phenomenon, the initial game in a new locale (bed) elicits a much higher rate of smiling responses on silent trials (four out of six, or 67%) than was true at the beginning of the month (two out of 10, or 20%).

Thus, one can conclude, first, that the speech signal enables a consistent pattern of response to emerge earlier than is possible on the basis of visual cues alone. Second, experience that includes vocal articulation of the critical visual event promotes the future development of a consistent pattern of response in the absence of this auditory cue.

The inference is that the smile results from the confirmation of an emergent expectancy and that this consistent pattern of response therefore signifies the actualization in a specific instance of existence constancy. Some independent indication that the development of an expectancy constitutes the underlying process is furnished by more data collected one week after the last games reported thus far. In these two games, anticipatory smiles occurred on every trial at the alerting signal, so that recognitory smiles could no longer be scored. If prediction is the hallmark of an expectancy, then this anticipatory response constitutes extremely strong evidence for the reality of such a development.

The temporal patterning of the smile response would seem to offer the best evidence against reinforcement as an explanation of the results. Since I would smile back any time Matthew smiled, reinforcement in no way explains why, initially, he smiled only at the end of a trial (reappearance) and never at the beginning of a trial (before disappearance).

Study 2

The results of Study 2 replicate those of Study 1; Table 1 shows that the first time mother disappears and reappears in a particular place, reappearance elicits a smile when accompanied by "peekaboo." By the second game session in one of the same locales four days later, smiling occurs whether or not there is any sound to signal disappearance and reappearance. The nonspeech signal starts out exactly intermediate between speech and silence in eliciting a smiling response (three out of six trials, or 50% of the time). But experience either improves the effectiveness of the nonspeech signal or obviates the need for any auditory signal; during the second game in a given locale, smiling occurs on every trial in *every* condition.

The results of the parallel object-hiding games are displayed in Table 2 where three degrees of experience with game and object are distinguished. Degree of experience is a composite of two factors: (*a*) familiarity with an object before it was used in any hiding game, and (*b*) experience with an object in a game session. At all three levels of experience, speech-trials virtually always elicit a smile, silent trials never. Thus, Matthew never seems to learn what to expect from a hidden toy unless he is given some auditory cues. The visual schema seems harder to establish for things than for mother, and auditory cues become correspondingly more crucial in directing the pattern of visual attention.

As for nonspeech sounds, they gradually become more effective in structuring visual attention. In the first game with the unfamiliar toys (duck squeaker, chime rattle), the nonspeech sound condition elicited a smile on only one out of six trials (17%). In the games of intermediate familiarity (deer and duck squeakers), smiling occurred two out of six times (33%). In the games at the highest level of familiarity (second

| Disappearance and reappearance marked by: | Degrees of Experience | | | | | |
| | Level 1 (Initial game session with unfamiliar object) | | Level 2 (Initial game session with familiar object; second game with un-familiar object) | | Level 3 (Second game session with familiar object) | |
	Smile	No smile	Smile	No smile	Smile	No smile
Human speech sounds	5	1	6	0	3	0
Object sound	1	5	2	4	2	1
Silence	0	6	0	6	0	3

session familiar deer squeaker), smiling occurred in the object-sound condition two out of three times (67%). This trend toward the increasing effectiveness of nonspeech sounds is statistically significant at the .05 level when one considers the results both for "people" and for "thing" games (one-tailed Fisher Test).

In the object games, Matthew never smiled at my face alone (during the disappearance phase), but smiled only when face and object were visible together (reappearance). This pattern of response is inconsistent with a reinforcement explanation of the observed behavior, for "smiling back" as a reinforcer could occur at any point in an object game, not exclusively upon the object's reappearance.

Additional data would have been desirable, but Matthew refused to play any more. Since Charlesworth (4) has found persistence at a peekaboo game to be inversely related to the infant's ability to predict reappearance, this behavior constitutes additional evidence that reappearance had become predictable, that Matthew had indeed formed a visual schema.

In sum, the pattern of results is very striking and consistent for inanimate and animate objects. When Matthew starts to play a new game—that is, one involving a new locale or a new object—speech holds a very privileged position; it is the only condition that reliably elicits the recognitory smile. With experience, the sound of an inanimate object becomes almost as effective in producing this smile. Silent reappearance of an inanimate object never elicits a recognitory smile. As for games involving mother's disappearance and reappearance, nonspeech sounds are initially somewhat effective in eliciting the smile, although much less so than speech. After experience with the game in a given locale, Matthew shows consistent appreciation of my reappearance under all three conditions. At this point the visual event alone suffices to trigger an expectancy and to induce its confirmation.

DISCUSSION

The greater difficulty of establishing a disappearance-reappearance schema for things than for a person who is a mother may reflect strong general expectations about what happens to a mother or to any person in the baby's experience when she hides. This would be in line with a general conclusion of the two studies: the more unpredictable a visual sequence, the greater the role of auditory cues in delineating its critical points. Because I was the only person to play peekaboo with Matthew, we cannot distinguish a specific "mother" effect from a general "person" effect. The inanimate objects, by contrast, represented a sampling of different noise-making toys; generalization about inanimate objects therefore seems warranted.

A potential source of weakness in the studies was the failure to assess whether "peekaboo" and "here it is" would elicit a smile by themselves at the outset of the investigation. Even if they had, however, this fact could not explain why the silent and nonspeech conditions became equally effective in eliciting a smile after experience with a given visual sequence. The effectiveness of the silent condition in eliciting a recognitory smile the first time peekaboo was studied in the familiar crib locale shows that previous experience with a silent event is not a necessary requisite for the development of a purely visual schema, for there had been no silent hiding before the study began. While seeing that "peekaboo" trials are sufficient for the development of the hiding-reappearance expectancy, we do not know if the silent trials also made a contribution to this learning. But if the pattern of attention is the crucial aspect of learning a visual expectancy, then it makes sense to think that experiences in which attention is directed to the critical loci at the right times would be much more valuable in organizing a temporal pattern than would experience where attention might well be randomly or irrelevantly distributed, as on the silent trials.

If Bower (2) is correct in claiming that infants of this age have existence constancy at the outset, what does it mean to say that a child "learns" a simple hiding game in the course of certain kinds of experience? It must be the spatiotemporal pattern of this particular game that is being learned. In relation to timing, it is probably significant that many of the earliest games babies play have a strong rhythmic component, for example, "pat-a-cake." It is often this rhythmic component which seems to contribute most to the game-like quality of the interchange; rhythm comes to be a rule-of-the-game that the baby learns first. As for spatial learning, our results show that peekaboo is initially defined as a game-in-a-particular-place. Later, we have seen, Matthew's expectancy transcends the limits of any specific locale. It could well be that when the expectancy also transcends the limits of a specific temporal rhythm, the whole game loses its appeal for the baby.

If these results are valid, they suggest an important way in which caretakers can control and develop the deployment of an infant's visual attention through the use of sound. Sound can contribute informational redundancy *vis-à-vis* the visual event by encoding it in a second modality. Moreover, sound, under normal conditions, has two design characteristics—spatial localization and temporal organization—which may be important in guiding visual attention. The spatial localization of an ordinary auditory stimulus plus the omnidirectional capacity of human sound receptors means that visual attention can be guided to the informative locus. Temporal organization, on the other hand, brings with it the possibility of imposing points of articulation upon the relatively continuous flow of the visual world. It appears that a mother's speech, and probably speech in general, hold a privileged position among auditory stimuli in fulfilling these functions. Since the role of speech in the environment is a key source of subcultural variation in cognitive development, and since skillful deployment of attention may well be the crucial cognitive accomplishment in the first year of life, these phenomena could constitute the ontogenetic beginnings of an important relationship between language and attention. Many more infants must be studied if such developmental phenomena are to be fully understood.

SUMMARY

This study investigated the role of auditory signals in general, and speech in particular, in structuring the visual attention of a four-month-old baby.

The first study involved the typical sort of peekaboo game, in which mother disappeared and reappeared. The baby's response to reappearance was compared under two conditions: in one condition, the word "peekaboo," said with the bright intonation normal to the game, accompanied reappearance; in the other condition reappearance occurred in silence. The results showed, first, that the speech signal enables a consistent pattern of response to emerge earlier than is possible on the basis of visual cues alone. Second, experience that includes vocal articulation of the critical visual events promotes the future development of a consistent pattern of response in the absence of this auditory cue.

The second study was designed to compare the effectiveness of speech and nonspeech auditory signals in structuring a response to the visual peekaboo game. A second complementary purpose was to see whether the pattern of response differed when an inanimate object, rather than a human being, disappeared and reappeared. The pattern of results is very striking and consistent for inanimate and animate objects. In a novel hiding game—that is, one involving a new locale or a new object—speech holds a very privileged position; it is the only condition which reliably elicits the recognitory smile. With experience, the sound of an inanimate object becomes almost as effective in producing this smile. Silent reappearance of an inanimate object never elicits a recognitory smile. As for games involving mother's disappearance and reappearance, nonspeech sounds are initially somewhat effective in eliciting the smile, although much less so than speech. After experience with the game in a given locale, the baby shows consistent appreciation of mother's reappearance under all three conditions. At this point the visual event alone suffices to trigger an expectancy and to induce its confirmation.

It is quite possible that the willingness of parents to verbalize to their children has a significant effect on the children's cognitive development. A number of studies comparing life styles of middle-class and working-class homes indicate that members of middle-class families generate and use a great deal more language than do members of working-class families. Observations by S. R. Tulkin and J. Kagan (1972) showed that although their samples of middle- and working-class white mothers spent about the same amount of time with their ten-month-old daughters, the middle-class mothers were more inclined to talk to their daughters, to encourage them to vocalize, to imitate their daughters' vocalizations, and to comment on and praise their vocal efforts. The results of these studies are consistent with the general belief that middle-class people tend to deal with their environment in linguistic ways, but working-class people are more likely to deal with theirs in direct, physical ways.

The research by Mark Golden, Wagner Bridger, and Albert Montare described in article 2.4 suggests that these two different styles of coping—linguistic and physical—are learned at a very early age. This study compares the learning task performance of two samples of two-year-old boys. The mothers of one group of boys were college graduates and can be considered upper-middle-class; the mothers of the other group had no education beyond high school and can be considered working-class. The study clearly demonstrates the differences between the two life styles. The middle-class boys were considerably helped in learning associations when they were given verbal labels for unfamiliar objects, but the working-class boys were not. When verbal labels were not supplied, working-class boys had slightly greater success than middle-class boys, although the difference was not statistically significant.

Social class differences in the use of language as a tool for learning in two-year-old children

Mark Golden,
Wagner Bridger, and
Albert Montare

The present study of social class differences in the use of language as a tool for learning stems from two interrelated research findings: (*a*) SES differences in intellectual performance first manifest themselves somewhere between 18 and 36 months of age, when language becomes increasingly important for learning (Golden, Birns, Bridger, & Moss, 1971; Hindley, 1961; Knobloch & Pasamanick, 1960); and (*b*) a number

Reprinted from the *Proceedings of the 80th Annual Convention of the American Psychological Association, 7* (1972): 107–108, with permission of the authors and the American Psychological Association. Copyright 1972 by the American Psychological Association.

of investigators have shown that language can facilitate learning (Katz, 1963; Koltzova, 1960).

There are two ways in which social class differences in intellectual development may be facilitated by language: (*a*) parents with higher education may teach their children more verbal concepts and knowledge than less-educated parents; and (*b*) more highly educated, more verbal parents may rely more on language in teaching their children, and such children may be better able to use language as a tool for learning than children of less-educated, less verbal parents. On the basis of these considerations, the investigators hypothesized that there are no social class differences in learning on the sensorimotor or nonverbal level, but there are SES differences in learning ability on the verbal level. In order to test this hypothesis, children from different SES groups were presented with identical learning tasks, under verbal and nonverbal conditions.

This learning study is part of a larger longitudinal study, which is now in progress, of children from different social class groups during the third year of life, in order to see which factors account for the emergence of SES differences in intellectual development at this time. In the longitudinal study, children from two different SES groups are being compared on a number of different measures, including verbal and nonverbal learning. While there will be a total of 60 *S*s, 30 in each of two SES groups, the present paper reports the preliminary findings on 26 children from high-education families and 19 children from low-education families, or a total of 45 *S*s.

METHOD

White male 2-year-old children from the following two SES groups were included in the study: (*a*) high-education families: mother was a college graduate or more; father may or may not have been a college graduate; (*b*) low-education families: mother was a high school graduate or less; father was not a college graduate. The mother's education was the determining factor. Boys whose mothers were college graduates were compared with boys whose mothers had not gone beyond high school.

The *S*s were presented with identical learning tasks, under verbal and nonverbal conditions, with each *S* serving as his own control. The material to be learned was different but very similar under the two conditions. Under each condition the child was presented with five inverted boxes, on each of which was a different, relatively unfamiliar object. The learning task involved finding a reward under the correct object. Two sets of five objects were used, with one set under each condition. The first set included: a valve, caster, clip, switch, and lock. The second set included: a strainer, roller, level, pole-end, and opener. Both the sequences of conditions and materials were counter-balanced, so that half the Ss in each SES group were presented with the verbal condition first and half with the nonverbal condition first; half the Ss were presented with one set of five objects under one condition and half with the other set of five objects under the same condition. The learning tasks under each condition, which required about 20 min., were administered approximately a week apart, to reduce the effects of fatigue, loss of attention, or motivation.

Under the verbal condition, using the first set of five objects, E told S he was going to hide a reward (cookie, candy, or small trinket) under the "valve," which E pointed to. While pointing, E labeled the object: "This is a *valve.*" After allowing S to see where the reward was hidden for two demonstration trials, varying the position of the valve from one trial to the next and allowing S to find the reward, E then placed a screen in front of the five objects. Just before removing the screen, E said, "Don't forget, the cookie is under the *valve.*" The S was encouraged to search until he found the reward on each trial, but the label was not given in the presence of the objects. Only those trials on which S searched under the valve first were counted as correct, but he was allowed to search until he found the cookie and was rewarded on every trial. When the child searched under the correct object, E said, "It was under the valve." The position of the valve was varied from trial to trial. The criterion for learning each object was three successive correct trials. Once criterion for the first object had been reached, E said, "The cookie will not be under the valve anymore. From now on it will be under the *caster,*" which E pointed to. However, except for the first object, there were no demonstration trials. The same procedure was followed until S learned to search under each of the five objects, or until 30 trials had been administered.

Under the nonverbal condition, the procedure was the same, with two exceptions: (*a*) S was not told the name of the object; i.e., it was not labeled. The E merely said, "Find the cookie." Or when S looked under the correct object, E said, "You found the cookie." (*b*) When S reached the learning criterion of three correct successive trials, E shifted to the next object, without verbally informing S, so that the first postshift trial was actually a nonverbal cue informing S that the reward would now be under a different object. To summarize, the major difference between the two conditions was that under the verbal condition the correct object was labeled and S was verbally informed when a shift to a different object was made, whereas under the nonverbal condition the object was not labeled and information about the shift was provided when S discovered that the reward was under a new object. In order to make certain that Ss were not performing better under the verbal condition because of familiarity with the objects or their names, Ss were pretested to see whether they could identify the objects. The objects were placed in a row and E said, "Show me the valve," "Show me the caster," etc. If S correctly identified an object, a second trial was given later to make sure that the first response was not due to chance.

RESULTS

In terms of results, the high-education Ss learned a mean of 3.2 objects under the verbal condition and 1.3 objects under the nonverbal condition; the low-education Ss learned a mean of 1.5 objects under the verbal condition and 1.7 objects under the nonverbal condition. A two-way analysis of variance was computed with social class and learning conditions as the main effects and a repeated measures design for learning conditions. Two significant F ratios were found: (*a*) a significant F for the main effect of overall verbal learning compared to overall nonverbal learning . . . and (*b*) a significant F ratio for the Social Class × Learning Conditions interaction. . . . Both F ratios were significant at the $p < .01$ level of confidence. Further analysis indicated that, while there were no significant SES differences in learning under the nonverbal condition ($t = .97$), the high-education Ss did significantly better than the low-education Ss under the verbal-learning condition ($t = 2.99, \ldots p < .01$). Furthermore, whereas there were no significant differences in learning under verbal and nonverbal conditions for the low-education Ss ($t = -.72$), the high-education Ss did significantly better under the verbal- than under the nonverbal-learning condition ($t = 4.79, \ldots p < .001$).

The power of language to facilitate learning or influence behavior can be seen in the following findings. The Ss' performance was examined to see how many objects were learned without error under verbal and nonverbal conditions. Under the verbal condition, errorless learning occurred when a child responded correctly on three successive trials after a new object had been introduced. Under the nonverbal condition, errorless learning occurred when a child responded correctly on Trials 2, 3, and 4 after a new object has been introduced. Trial 1 was considered an information trial and did not count, since in contrast to the verbal condition, the shift to a new object was made without informing *S*. Under the verbal condition, 58% of the high-education *S*s learned one or more objects without error, whereas under the nonverbal condition only 4% of the high-education *S*s learned one or more objects without error. The reverse pattern was true for the low-education *S*s, where only 15% of the *S*s learned one or more objects without error under the verbal condition and 29% learned one or more objects without error under the nonverbal condition. Separate chi-squares were computed for proportion of errorless learning for high- and low-education *S*s under verbal and nonverbal conditions. The chi-square for the verbal-learning condition was 5.88, which was significant at the .02 level. The chi-square for the nonverbal-learning condition was 3.22, which fell short of the .05 level of significance.

CONCLUSIONS

The preliminary results on 45 *S*s confirm the hypotheses: while there were no significant SES differences in learning ability on the nonverbal or sensorimotor level, the high-education children did significantly better than the low-education children on the verbal level. This is the first direct evidence, which we know of, that middle-class children may be superior to lower-class children in their ability to use language as a tool for learning, which may partially explain why social class differences in intellectual development first manifest themselves between 18 and 36 months of age, when language enters the picture.

The results of this research suggest that the factors that are involved in the nonverbal task, such as attention, motivation, and perceptual discrimination abilities, do not differentiate between the SES groups. However, the ability to utilize the verbal instructions in the learning task does differentiate the SES groups. The results of the present study are also of interest for another reason. Whereas previous investigators (Katz, 1963; Koltzova, 1960) have shown that language can facilitate learning, the present study indicates that, at least for 2-year-old boys, language facilitates learning for middle-class but not for lower-class children.

The results of Golden, Bridger, and Montare's experiment are consistent with a study by C. Briggs and D. Elkind (1973), who compared five-year-olds who could read with children the same age who could not. Those able to read were more successful in dealing with Piagetian conservation tasks than were the nonreaders, evidence that the readers were cognitively more advanced. Significantly, the mothers of these early readers had more education than those of the nonreaders, and therefore probably had higher socioeconomic status (SES). Another indication of the emphasis placed on verbal activities by middle-class parents was the discovery that the fathers of the early readers spent more time reading to them than did the fathers of the nonreaders.

As the preceding studies suggest, the child's encounters with his environment, particularly with the stimuli it provides and the demands it makes upon him, determine the kind of progress he makes through the stages of cognitive development. A study of Mexican children, for example, showed that those who were members of potters' families and who had therefore worked a great deal with clay, were more advanced in the ability to conserve substance than were the other children in the study (Price-Williams, Gordon, and Ramirez, 1969). Another cross-cultural study concerning the development of logical thinking produced results suggesting that the emphasis a culture places on certain cognitive skills is an important determinant in their development. The children in the study by Crane Walker, E. P. Torrance, and Timothy S. Walker, article 2.5 in this section, were third and sixth graders in schools located in Delhi, India, and in a Minneapolis suburb. The children were asked to look at a picture of a boy who was neglecting his responsibilities and to generate as many guesses as they could about the probable cause of his behavior. The study shows a small difference between Indian and American third graders in the mean number of causal responses, but a large difference between the two groups of older children. American sixth graders suggested more than twice as many causal explanations as did their compatriot third graders, but Delhi sixth graders surprisingly offered fewer causal explanations than did Delhi third graders. The American results are consistent with Piagetian theory—older children are expected to be more sensitive than younger ones to antecedent events. The unexpected drop in causal responses for the Indian children elicits many speculative interpretations. The inference that Indian children do not mature cognitively between the third and sixth grade is inconsistent with established data and can therefore be rejected. A more reasonable explanation is that these children are able to discern causes and react to them in real-life situations, but are unable or unwilling to verbalize about them. Another explanation may be that the Indian culture is much less concerned with cause-and-effect relationships and instead stresses other aspects of behavior. These two explanations are not inconsistent with each other. The point to remember, however, is that the culture in which a child develops determines what is important or unimportant, and what children should learn or ignore. The influence of culture is pervasive and affects all aspects of cognitive development, a factor that is illustrated in a number of different ways by several of the articles in this book.

A cross-cultural study of the perception of situational causality

Crane Walker,
E. P. Torrance, and
Timothy S. Walker

The study of causality as perceived by children has been and is today, a matter of intense interest to many psychologists and educators. Substantial work has been done on children's perceptions of physical causality with regard to cloud movement, wind, dreams, flotation, equalibration, and other natural phenomena (Piaget, 1928, 1954, 1966; Michotte, 1963; Laurendeau & Pinard, 1962).

The developmental nature of the child's perception of physical causality has been well documented. Does an understanding of physical causality imply an equal level of understanding of situational causality? Does an understanding of why clouds move give the child insight into why people react in a given manner, or act in different ways under different circumstances? The developmental continuum might be quite different for these two types of perceptions.

Reprinted from the *Journal of Cross-cultural Psychology,* 2 (1971): 401–404, with permission of the authors and the publisher, Sage Publications, Inc.

The present study compares the perception of situational causality by children in two different elementary grades and in two different cultures. The third and sixth grades were chosen as representing two points on a developmental continuum. In studies of physical causality, significant differences have been found between these two age groups (Piaget, 1954, 1966; Laurendeau & Pinard, 1962).

India and the United States were chosen as representing distinctly different cultures, but having comparable educational systems. Cross-cultural differences had previously been found between these two countries by Torrance (1967) studying the fourth grade slump in creativity.

The work of Piaget and others gives strong support to the concept of the developmental nature of the perception of causality. Ausubel (1958) agrees with Piaget that children pass through gross qualitative stages in causal thinking. He states that children rarely appreciate antecedent-consequent relationships before the age of ten. The presence of developmental stages in the perception of physical causality appears to be firmly established by prior research.

The principal question to be taken up in the present study is whether cause-effect thinking, as related to situational causality, is perceived in the same manner as physical causality. It was hypothesized that developmental, cross-cultural, and sex differences would be found in the perception of situational causality.

METHOD

Subjects

The Ss were third and sixth grade children living in the United States and India. Three hundred and fifty-nine Ss were divided by grade, culture, and sex, thus generating eight groups. Indian Ss were drawn from seven elementary schools in Delhi, India. United States Ss were drawn from a suburban school in Minneapolis, Minnesota. None of these children could be regarded as disadvantaged economically or culturally.

Apparatus

The apparatus consisted of a polychromatic illustration of the nursery rhyme "Little Boy Blue." This stimulus material seemed to be familiar in both cultures and to elicit about the same number of responses in both cultures.

Procedure

The picture was shown to the children with the following instructions:

Guess Causes: In the space below, list as many things as you can which might have caused the action shown in the picture. You may use things that might have happened just before the event in the picture, or something that happened a long time ago that had an influence on the present event. Make as many guesses as you can. Don't be afraid to guess.

Responses are placed into five categories in the following manner:

Causal Responses—described actions or conditions which preceded or were concurrent with the depicted activity and were indicated as having produced one or more portions of the ongoing activity.

Phenomenistic Responses—had only a sequential relationship to the depicted activity.

Consequential Responses—described activity that was a result of or followed the depicted activity.

Descriptive Responses—indicated a quality or attribute of one of the children or things depicted, and this was not causally related to ongoing activity.

Other Responses—could not be classified within the other four classifications.

The first author scored all responses. A random sample of 75 *S*s' responses was drawn and these were scored by an independent judge using the above criteria. A coefficient of agreement of .84 was found.

Means for each category of response were computed and differences were tested by the Students' *t* test.

RESULTS

The total rate of responding was consistent from group to group. Mean number of total responses ranged from 4.92 for sixth grade United States males to 7.73 for sixth grade Indian females. There were no significant differences between third grade groups in total number of responses. Significant differences among some sixth grade groups were found, but only a small negative correlation (−.35) existed between total rate of responding and mean number of causal responses. Table 1 includes the number of *S*s and mean number of responses of all types for each group.

Sixth grade United States males gave the greatest mean number of causal responses (2.89) and sixth grade Indian females gave the fewest (.32). There was an increase in mean number of causal responses made

TABLE 1
MEAN NUMBER OF TOTAL RESPONSES AND CAUSAL RESPONSES

	Third grade				Sixth grade			
	United States		India		United States		India	
	Male	Female	Male	Female	Male	Female	Male	Female
Responses	(N = 49)	(N = 50)	(N = 50)	(N = 50)	(N = 36)	(N = 36)	(N = 42)	(N = 44)
Total (Mean)	5.20	5.22	5.02	5.04	4.92	6.06	6.50	7.73
Causal (Mean)	1.00	1.20	.58	.76	2.89	2.69	.62	.32

by sixth grade United States children. A decrease was found from the third grade to the sixth grade among Indian children. Table 1 shows the mean number of causal responses for all groups.

Students' t tests were calculated for all hypothesized differences, with significant values noted between the following groups: Third grade United States males and third grade Indian males ($t = 2.47$; $p < .01$), third grade United States females and third grade Indian females ($t = 2.34$; $p < .025$), sixth grade United States males and sixth grade Indian males ($t = 5.72$; $p < .005$), sixth grade Indian children and sixth grade United States children ($t = 10.89$; $p < .005$).

Students' t tests were also computed for sex differences within groups but no significant differences were found.

Within the United States sample, there was an increase between third and sixth grade in the perception of situational causality ($t = 5.96$; $p < .005$), but there was no such increase between third and sixth graders in India.

DISCUSSION

The results of the analysis of the perception of situational causality were not unidirectional. A developmental gradient was found for United States children, but not for Indian children. Perhaps children are not encouraged to look for causal relationships in a society that must accept hunger as a fact of daily life for a substantial portion of its people, whereas cows, monkeys, and rats forage freely for food while providing none.

A less speculative interpretation would hold that the perception of situational causality is a result of a learning process and that the attention given to this learning process is greater in the United States than in

India. Apparently, if instruction in this process is given in Indian schools, it is not given in grades three through six or at least it is not effective.

An explanation of the difference may derive from the different emphasis placed by the two educational systems on the originality of thought. One puzzling result of this study is the drop in the number of *causal* responses given by sixth grade Indian children from the number given by Indian third graders, while total responses are increasing. No satisfactory explanation of this finding is readily available within the data gathered.

SUMMARY

This study was designed to test developmental, cross-cultural, and sex differences in the perception of situational causality. Three hundred fifty-nine (359) Ss were divided by grade (third and sixth), culture (United States and Indian), and sex. It was hypothesized that developmental, cross-cultural, and sex differences would be found in the perception of situational causality. Ss were shown a picture depicting a Mother Goose nursery rhyme and were asked what might have caused the action shown in the picture. Responses were categorized as Causal, Phenomenistic, Consequential, Descriptive, or Other. Means were computed for each group and category and hypothesized differences were tested by means of the Student's t test. All cross-cultural differences were significant and developmental differences were found to be significant for United States children but not for children in the Indian culture.

In the final article (2.6) in this section, Seymour J. Friedland reports the results of his survey of elementary school children who were asked to identify how two individuals occupying common social roles resemble each other. The answers the children gave were consistent with Piaget's theory that younger children look on the world in highly specific, concrete ways, but older children are better able to generalize, abstract, and be aware of complexities and nuances. Like Piaget and other researchers in this field, Friedland had to use verbal criteria in assessing the competence of his subjects. Under this system of measurement, a child who said that a policeman on the crime squad and a policeman on the traffic squad are similar because they both enforce the law, was given full credit for understanding role functions. There is a question, however, of whether it is possible for a child to be aware of the role similarity of the two policemen and yet be unable to verbalize this awareness. We might further ask whether cognitive competence tests such as these actually measure a child's cognitive maturity, or do they measure his ability to find the right words to express what he understands?

The development of role concepts

Seymour J. Friedland

Role is sometimes considered as a class of behavioral expectations defined by a general or abstract set of functions or traits (e.g., the statement, "A policeman is someone who upholds the law"). In contrast, from a developmental point of view, it would be expected that a role concept, like any concept, would be realized in qualitatively different ways depending on the development status of the individual. Such developmentalists as Werner (15, 16), Piaget (14), and Bruner (3) have posited a sequence of concept development based on three general modes of functioning: (*a*) proceeding from concepts based on sensori-motor functioning, (*b*) those stemming from perceptual functioning, and (*c*) concepts characterized by abstract modes of functioning. The first two modalities, the sensori-motor and the perceptual, are characterized by a dependence on motor behavior and a strong tie to the concrete perceptual attributes presented by the immediate situation. The organization of experience in such a manner results in concepts that have as their primary content specific acts or perceptual details (e.g., the conceptualization of the role of a policeman as "Someone who shoots crooks," or as "Someone who wears a blue uniform"). The attainment of the third or abstract mode of thought results in "true concepts" not tied to the immediate situation; such abstract thought is ingredient in the ability to use and create general ideas about the world in a diverse and flexible manner. For example, the conceptualization of the role of a policeman as "Someone who

Reprinted from the *Journal of Genetic Psychology*, 122 (1973): 81–88, with permission of the author and The Journal Press. Copyright 1973 by The Journal Press.

upholds the law" would be seen as representative of this third, relatively abstract mode of thought. A role concept, from this point of view, is seen as a rule-like means of organization by which a person characterizes himself and others; as such, concepts of role would be expected to manifest a sequence of development paralleling concept development in general.

The concept of role has been used as an explanatory construct in such areas as social perception (1, 4, 5) and sex identification (2, 10, 11). Other studies (6, 7, 8, 9), influenced by the works of Piaget and G. H. Mead, have focused more specifically on the study of role behavior and development. These latter studies concentrated on the cognitive bases of role interaction, emphasizing the particular cognitive achievements necessary for role, or reciprocal interaction with others. The work of Feffer and Flavell stresses, as does the present study, the importance of viewing role behavior within the context of the overall cognitive functioning of the individual. However, relatively few studies have investigated specifically the development of role concepts; the present study was designed to address this question, as revealed in the ways in which children of different ages conceptualize specific occupational roles (e.g., policeman, scientist).

Qualitatively different modes of conceptualization can be revealed in a task requiring the individual to subsume a group of objects with diverse characteristics under a general class. In the present study, a modification of this general method was devised to be appropriate for young children and for the kinds of stimuli utilized. On a given trial, a child was presented verbally with two "objects" (i.e., proper names), and *told* that they belonged to the same general "class" (i.e., they shared the same general occupational role). The child was then told that the first person named engaged in some specific kind of activity, and that the second person named engaged in a second, different specific kind of activity. Both activities were appropriate to the particular occupational role they shared (e.g., two artists, one who paints, and one who makes statues). The child was then asked how the two people were alike. The purpose of this method was to force the child, in effect, to "define" an occupational role, when he could not simply rely on the role-name itself. In such a situation, one type of reason for the similarity may be based on those characteristics that reflect the individual's specific interactions with the objects, or on related perceptual characteristics of the objects. Such responses would be regarded as concrete-specific concepts. In contrast, responses based on general rules which are not tied to specific interactions with the objects, and which are not founded on purely perceptual attributes would be regarded as abstract concepts.

There is much evidence indicating that concept development in general is characterized by a progression from relatively concrete-specific concepts to relatively abstract concepts; it is expected that an examination of the development of role concepts will reveal a parallel developmental progression. Such a progression, if found, may be accounted for by specific environmental circumstances. For example, in role learning it may be that there is a strong environmental emphasis on concrete-specific classifications. Early in life children are taught roles by the specific behaviors and visible attributes associated with a role. The policeman is someone who "directs traffic and wears a blue uniform with a badge," rather than someone who "upholds the law." Piaget (13) has pointed to the child's attention to concrete specific consequences of acts, rather than to the intentions underlying them. If this is indeed the case, it is not surprising that a young child considers a role in terms other than general abstract goals and functions. The older child's increasing ability to use abstract functions and intentions allows for the eventual emergence of a role concept that transcends specific behaviors and perceptual details.

METHOD

Subjects

Groups of 10 boys and 10 girls each were drawn for the first (Group I), third (Group II), and sixth grade (Group III) of an elementary school in an upper-middle class suburb of Boston. The mean ages of the groups were 6.9 years, 8.9 years, and 11.9 years, respectively. The children were taken from their classrooms during the school days and seen individually by a female examiner.

Procedure

Each S was given the following general instruction:

> We'd like to see what you think about certain things. I am going to ask you some questions, and I would like you to tell me what you think. There are no right or wrong answers, it's what you think that is important. OK?

The following sample item was then read:

Dr. Smith and Dr. Johnson are both doctors. Dr. Smith puts casts on broken legs, Dr. Johnson operates on people's eyes. But how are they the same? How are they alike?

If the child responded that they were both men or both doctors he was asked "In what important way are they the same?" If his response was not an abstract function, he was told, "They both keep people healthy." The purpose of the sample item was to acquaint the subject with the task, and to break any set toward giving concrete responses or difference responses rather than similarities.

After the sample item all subjects were verbally given the following five role concept formation situations:

Policeman: "Mr. Jones and Mr. Thomas are both policemen. Mr. Jones goes after robbers, Mr. Thomas gives parking tickets. But how are they the same, how are they alike?"

Scientist: "Mr. Richards and Mr. Stevens are both scientists. Mr. Richards builds rocket ships, Mr. Stevens is trying to see how deep the ocean is. But how are they the same, how are they alike?"

Soldier: "Sergeant Davis and Sergeant Bennet are both soldiers. Sergeant Davis flies a plane, and Sergeant Bennet shoots a cannon. But how are they the same, how are they alike?"

Student: "Bill Adams and Jimmy Carlin are both students. Bill goes to school to play the piano, and Jimmy is finding out how to do math problems better. But how are they the same, how are they alike?"

Artist: "Mr. Evans and Mr. Gordon are both artists. Mr. Evans paints, and Mr. Gordon makes statues. But how are they the same, how are they alike?"

This same order was used for all children. If the child simply repeated the role title or said they were both men, he was asked, "Yes, but in what other way are they the same?" If the response was ambiguous, the child was told, "Tell me a little more about this." After all five role concept formation situations were administered, the child was told that he would be asked about some of the things he said. If the child's original similarity did not appear at the level of a general function, he was asked for an additional similarity. More specifically, the child was asked to deal again with the similarity of the two role figures, given the inapplicability of his original similarity. For example, if he had said that the policemen were alike because they "both shoot crooks," he would be asked how they would be alike if one did shoot crooks but the other policeman did not. The purpose of this procedure was to see if a pressed inquiry could elicit a higher level response.

Scoring

Each S's original response to each of the five role concept formation situations was assigned to one of the following three categories.

(a) Nonrelevant, Irrelevant response—Responses that do not provide a similarity, are irrelevant, or simply repeat the item information. Example: "I once saw an artist," "both policemen (no further elaboration)."

(b) Concrete Role Identification—Two types of responses fall in this category, those based on perceptual details, and those based on specific acts.

1. Perceptual detail—Response is based on some perceptual detail associated with role, may be a visual attribute associated with the person, or a physical characteristic of the environment in which that role is performed. Example: "They both wear a badge," "They both work in police headquarters."

2. Specific act—Response indicates a specific act that the role occupants engage in. In a sense, this kind of response is a single exemplification of the general role function. Example: "Both direct traffic," "Both take tests."

(c) General Role Functions—Response indicates the use of an abstract function or goal. Describes a general purpose or goal of a role. It is not an action but some purpose or function that can be true of a variety of actions. Example: "They enforce the law," "They try to add to what we know."

All responses were scored by two judges without knowledge of S's age. An examination of the reliability of the scoring indicated 80% agreement between judges. Differences between the two judges were arbitrated and agreement reached on the best category for a particular response. The most numerous category for a child was taken as the dominant type of role concept for that child.

RESULTS

Differences in type of role conceptualization were analyzed by means of a chi square (see Table 1). The age groups were found to differ significantly ($\chi^2 = 20.55$, $p < .001$).

The conceptualizations of children in the youngest group, Group I, fell primarily into the category of Concrete Role Identification, with

TABLE 1
DISTRIBUTION OF THREE AGE GROUPS FOR TYPE OF ROLE
CONCEPTUALIZATION

Type of role conceptualization	Age groups			Total
	I	II	III	
Nonrelevant	3	1	0	4
Concrete-identification	15	9	4	28
General role function	2	10	16	28
Total	20	20	20	60

Note: $\chi^2 = 20.55, \ldots, p < .001.$

few S's attaining conceptualizations qualifying as a General Role Function. This is in contrast to Groups II and III. In these two older groups, more than half of the children's responses fell into the highest category, General Role Function, the number being highest for the oldest group. For all groups, the number of children classified as primarily giving Nonrelevant responses was minimal.

Examination of the responses given in the inquiry conducted after the initial procedure indicated few changes in type of response. Only about 9% of the 300 responses changed category, and only four children changed in their dominant classification. In general, change occurred most in those cases where originally a Nonrelevant response was given. This small amount of change is taken as an indication that the initial responses were probably not attributable to a "set" toward concrete responding, nor to confusion as to the requirements of the task.

Additional analysis of the two sexes across all age groups indicated no significant differences due to sex. Although the size of the sample did not permit statistical analysis of differences attributable to sex at the various age levels, examination of the results did not reveal any major sex differences.

Results were examined for a possible effect of different role titles on the type of role conceptualization. Again, the size of the sample did not permit statistical analysis. In general, the student role had the highest frequency of conceptualization at the level of General Role Function. This role, and the role of the scientist to a lesser degree, contrasts with the roles of policeman, soldier, and artist; for these latter roles relatively few S's provided the higher conceptualization. The soldier and artist roles had the highest frequency of conceptualization at the Concrete Identification level. Additional differences related to role type appear when the effects of sex of subject are also included. Girls appear to reach a higher level of conceptualization than boys on the scientist and student roles, while boys appear to be superior to girls on the soldier role. The roles of policeman and artist do not indicate any major differences between the two sexes.

DISCUSSION

The examination of the development of children's conceptualization of various roles appears to parallel general conceptual development. That is, there appears to be a developmental progression from role concepts based on concrete-specific acts and details to those based on general abstract functions.

There has been some tendency to segregate the child's "social" development from those findings and approaches dealing with "cognitive" processes and events. Certainly, there are differences in the content of experiences that may make this a meaningful distinction. However, it is necessary to acknowledge that the means of knowing used by the child in experiencing and organizing the world of objects are also operative when applied to people and social events. There have been indications that the "cognitive" approach to "social" phenomena has been fruitful in other areas; for example, such an approach to the problems of impression-formation (e.g., 12) has provided a better understanding of the perception of, and processing of information about another. Similarly, it is felt that an examination of the development of role concepts will prove more fruitful than, for example, a view of role as a static entity which is "acquired" *in toto* at some given point during development.

The ability to integrate diverse information about another is dependent to a major degree on the availability of higher-order concepts for subsuming discrepant details. The economy of the attainment of a higher-level role concept is that it allows a diversity of behaviors occurring in a variety of contexts to be organized in a meaningful and consistent way, having a well-defined significance. For the child with a concrete-specific notion of a particular role, this economy of functioning is limited. Individuals are overly identified with specific role behaviors or perceptual attributes, and the ability to view role and role occupant as different does not exist for the young child. If one "catches crooks," then one must be a policeman, and *vice versa*. Thus, the ability to see an individual as an occupant of various roles, or one role as encompassing many kinds of behaviors is limited. Interaction with others, then, by necessity must be more rigid, and the organization of social experiences relatively less flexible.

There is some suggestion that the type of role conceptualization may be dependent on the particular role title. A factor here may be role relevance, and familiarity with the particular role. This is indicated by the generally higher-level responses of all subjects to the student role compared with other roles, and by the superior performance of boys compared with girls on the soldier role. The findings point to the possibility that further studies may isolate experiential factors that accelerate role concept development.

Many implications stem from differences in role conceptualizations. It can be expected that young children, who conceptualize roles at the Concrete-Identification level, will be less consistent in their perception of and response to role figures. These children may demonstrate less certainty in responding. Finally, children who conceptualize roles at the Concrete-Identification level may have more difficulty interrelating roles and thus more difficulty in understanding role relations or role reciprocity.

SUMMARY

Children's concepts of various social roles were examined in a task that required the child to indicate the similarity of two occupants of common social roles. Each occupant in the pair was described differently in terms of behaviors appropriate for a particular role. Children in the first, third, and sixth grades were studied. Findings indicated that children in the youngest group held role concepts based primarily on concrete actions, while role concepts of the older two groups were based on more abstract, general role functions. In addition, there is some suggestion that the level of role conceptualization is related to the relevance of the particular role.

Children and adults alike differ widely in how they perceive the world around them and how they classify these precepts in order to solve problems, satisfy social needs, and express themselves—but in the midst of all this confusing complexity, there is order. Piaget's work shows that children must deal in specific ways related to the world and its grossly obvious characteristics before they can move on to more complex, subtle, and abstract modes. The question of whether this process can be accelerated is still an open one. European psychologists, as we noted, maintain that children must develop at a more or less genetically determined pace, but American psychologists tend to believe that children are highly responsive to their environment and are more plastic than their European colleagues conceive them to be. The environmentalist concept of child development is supported to some degree by cross-cultural research showing that children's cognitive styles differ widely from one culture to another. These findings do not mean that cognitive development lacks order, but rather that this order is only partly determined by the child's neuro-muscular development, and that the pressures of the social environment, as expressed in the demands, expectations, and reinforcements of others, play a role of increasing importance each succeeding year during childhood and adolescence.

In interpreting research on cognitive development, it is tempting to equate a child's level of verbal ability with his general competence in solving problems, even though research with deaf children and with children who grow up in environments where language is not stressed, raises doubts about this questionable generalization. It may be that for children with normal hearing, verbal development is basic to all other aspects of cognitive development; but until we devise a full range of techniques for studying cognitive functioning without recourse to words, we cannot answer these questions.

REFERENCES

Briggs, C., and Elkind, D. "Cognitive development in early readers." *Developmental Psychology* 9 (1973): 279-280.

Furth, H. G. "Linguistic deficiency and thinking: Research with deaf subjects." *Psychological Bulletin* 76 (1971): 58-72.

Greenfield, P. M. *Who is "Dada"? Some aspects of the semantic and phological development of a child's first words.* Washington, D.C.: U.S. Department of Health, Education, and Welfare, National Center for Educational Research and Development (ERIC No. 041 253), 1970.

Piaget, J. "Piaget's theory." In *Carmichael's Manual of Child Psychology,* 3rd ed. Edited by P. H. Mussen. New York: John Wiley & Sons, 1970.

Price-Williams, D., Gordon, W., and Ramirez, M., III. "Skills and conservation: A study of pottery-making children." *Developmental psychology* 1 (1969): 769.

Tulkin, S. R. and Kagan, J. "Mother-child interaction in the first year of life." *Child Development* 43 (1972): 31-41.

Walk, R. D. and Gibson, E. J. "A comparative and analytical study of visual depth perceptions." *Psychological Monographs* 75 No. 15, 1961.

2.1

1. Beilin, H. Learning and operational convergence in logical thought development. *Journal of Experimental Child Psychology*, 1965, **2**, 317–339.

2. Braine, M. D. S. Piaget on reasoning: A methodological critique and alternative proposals. In W. Kessen and C. Kuhlman (Eds.). Thought in the young child. *Monographs of the Society for Research in Child Development*, 1962, **27**, 41–61.

3. Brown, R., & Bellugi, Ursula. Three processes in the child's acquisition of syntax. *Harvard Educational Review*, 1964, **34**, 133–151.

4. Bruner, J. S. The course of cognitive growth. *American Psychologist*, 1964, **19**, 1–15.

5. Bruner, J. S. *Toward a theory of instruction.* New York: W. W. Norton & Co., Inc., 1968.

6. Bruner, J. S., Goodnow, J. S., Austin, G. A. *A study of thinking.* New York: Wiley, 1956.

7. Bruner, J. S., Olver, Rose R., Greenfield, Patricia M., et al. *Studies in cognitive growth.* New York: Wiley, 1966.

8. Charlesworth, W. R., & Zahn, C. Reaction time as a measure of comprehension of the effects produced by rotation on objects. *Child Development*, 1966, **37**, 253–268.

9. Duncan, C. P. Recent research and human problem solving. *Psychological Bulletin*, 1959, **56**, 397–429.

10. Elkind, D. Children's discovery of the conservation of mass, weight, and volume: Piaget replication study. *Journal of Genetic Psychology*, 1961, **98**, 219–227.

11. Elkind, D. Discrimination, seriation, and numeration of size, and dimensional differences in young children: Piaget replication study IV. *Journal of Genetic Psychology*, 1964, **104**, 275–296.

12. Gagné, R. M. Contributions of learning to human development. Paper delivered at the American Association for the Advancement of Science, Washington, D.C., December, 1966.

13. Gagné, R. M. The learning of principles. In H. J. Klausmeier and C. W. Harris (Eds.). *Analysis of concept learning.* New York: Academic Press, 1966.

14. Inhelder, B., & Piaget, J. *The growth of logical thinking from childhood to adolescence.* New York: Basic Books, 1958.

15. Inhelder, B., Bovet, M., Sinclair, H., & Smock, C. D. On cognitive development. *American Psychologist*, 1966, **21**, 160–164.

16. Jeffrey, W. E. The orienting reflex and attention in cognitive development. Paper presented at Conference of the Society for Research in Child Development, New York, March, 1967.

17. Kohnstamm, G. A. Experiments on teaching Piagetian thought operations. Paper presented at the Conference on Guided Learning of the Educational Research Council of Greater Cleveland, Cleveland, Ohio, 1966.

18. Lavatelli, Celia S. A Piaget-derived model for compensatory pre-school education. In J. L. Frost (Ed.). *Early childhood education rediscovered.* New York: Holt, Rinehart and Winston, Inc., 1968, 530–544.

19. Lee, P. C. The activation and generalization of conservation of substance in children. Unpublished Doctoral Dissertation, Syracuse University, Syracuse, New York, 1966.

20. Lovell, K. A follow-up study of Inhelder and Piaget's "The growth of logical thinking." *British Journal of Psychology*, 1961, **52**, 143-153.

21. Ojemann, R. H., & Pritchett, K. Piaget and the role of guided experiences in human development. *Journal of Perceptual and Motor Skills*, 1963, **17**, 927-940.

22. Piaget, J. *Play, dreams, and imitation in childhood.* New York: Norton, 1951.

23. Piaget, J. *The origin of intelligence in children.* New York: International University Press, 1952.

24. Piaget, J. *The child's conception of number.* New York: Norton, 1965.

25. Ripple, R. E., & Rockcastle, V. N. (Eds.) *Piaget rediscovered: A report of the conference on cognitive studies and curriculum development, March, 1964.* Ithaca, N.Y.: School of Education, Cornell University, 1964.

26. Sigel, I. E., Roeper, A., & Hooper, F. H. A. A training procedure for acquisition of Piaget's conservation of quantity: A pilot study and its replication. *British Journal of Educational Psychology*, 1966, **36**, 301-311.

27. Smedslund, J. The acquisition of conservation of substance and weight in children. II. External reinforcement of conservation of weight and of the operations of addition and subtraction. *Scandinavian Journal of Psychology*, 1961, **2**, 71-84.

28. Smedslund, J. The acquisition of conservation of substance and weight in children. V. Practice in conflict situations without external reinforcement. *Scandinavian Journal of Psychology*, 1961, **2**, 156-160.

29. Sonquist, Hanne D., & Kamii, Constance, K. Applying some Piagetian concepts in the classroom for the disadvantaged. *Young Children*, 1967, **22**, 231-246.

30. Sullivan, E. V. Acquisition of conservation of substance through film modeling techniques. In Brison, D. W., & Sullivan, E. V. (Eds.) *Recent research on the acquisition of conservation of substance.* Ontario Institute for Studies in Education, Educational Research Series No. 2, 1967, 11-23.

31. Sullivan, E. V. Piaget and the school curriculum: A critical appraisal. *Ontario Institute for Studies in Education*, Bulletin No. 2, 1967.

32. Uzgiris, I. Situational generality of conservation. *Child Development*, 1964, **35**, 831-841.

33. White, S. H. Discrimination learning with everchanging positive and negative cues. *Journal of Experimental Child Psychology*, 1965, **2**, 154-162.

34. White, S. H. Evidence for a hierarchical arrangement of learning processes. In L. P. Lipsitt and C. C. Spiker (Eds.) *Advances in child behavior and development.* (Vol. 2) New York: Academic Press, 1965.

35. Wohwill, J. F., & Lowe, R. C. Experimental analysis of the development of the conservation of number. *Child Development*, 1962, **33**, 153-167.

2.2

1. Bower, T. G. R., personal communication.

2. Schiff, W., *Psychol. Monogr.* **79**, 1 (1965).

3. Gibson, E. J. and Walk, R., *Sci. Amer.* **202**, 64 (April 1960).

4. Gibson, J., *Vision Res.* **1**, 253 (1961).

5. Wallach, H. and O'Connell, D. M., *J. Exp. Psychol.* **45**, 207 (1953).

2.3

1. Aronson, E., & Tronick, E. Implications of infant research for developmental theory. In J. Eliot (Ed.), *Human Development and Cognitive Processes*. New York: Holt, Rinehart & Winston, 1971.

2. Bower, T. G. R. The development of object permanence: Some studies of existence constancy. *Percept. & Psychophys.*, 1967, **2**, 411–418.

3. Bronshtein, A. I., & Petrova, E. P. The auditory analyzer in young infants. In Y. Brackbill & G. G. Thompson (Eds.), *Behavior in Infancy and Early Childhood*. New York: Free Press, 1967. Pp. 163–172.

4. Charlesworth, W. R. Persistence of orienting and attending behavior in infants as a function of stimulus-locus uncertainty. *Child Devel.*, 1966, **37**, 473–491.

5. Eisenberg, R. B. Stimulus significance as a determinant of newborn responses to sound. Paper presented at the biennial meeting of the Society for Research in Child Development, New York, 1967.

6. Haynes, H., White, B. L., & Held, R. Visual accommodation in human infants. *Science*, 1965, **148**, 528–530.

7. Kagan, J., Henger, B. A., Hen-Tov, A., Lurne, J., & Lewis, M. Infants' differential reactions to familiar and distorted faces. *Child Devel.*, 1966, **37**, 519–532.

8. Piaget, J. The Origins of Intelligence in Children. New York: Internat. Universities Press, 1952.

9. Semb, G., & Lipsitt, L. Effects of acoustic stimulation on cessation and initiation of non-nutritive sucking in neonates. *J. Exper. Child Psychol.*, 1969, **6**, 585–597.

10. Trevarthen, C. B., & Richards, M. Development of communication and object-directed behavior in early infancy. Unpublished study, Center for Cognitive Studies, Harvard University, Cambridge, Massachusetts, 1968.

11. Wertheimer, M. Psychomotor coordination of auditory and visual space at birth. *Science*, 1967, **134**, 1962.

2.4

Golden, M., Birns, B., Bridger, W. H., & Moss, A. Social-class differentiation in cognitive development among black preschool children. *Child Development*, 1971, **42**, 37–45.

Hindley, C. B. Social class influences on the development of ability in the first five years. In, *Proceedings of the XIV International Congress of Applied Psychology*. Copenhagen: Munksgaard, 1961.

Katz, P. A. Effects of labels on children's perception and discrimination learning. *Journal of Experimental Psychology*, 1963, **66**, 423–428.

Knobloch, H., & Pasamanick, B. Environmental factors affecting human development before and after birth. *Pediatrics*, 1960, **26**, 210–218.

Koltzova, M. M. *Die Bildung der höheren Nerventätigkeit des Kindes. (The development of higher nervous activity in the child.)* Berlin: VEB Verlag, Volk und Gesundheit, 1960.

2.5

Ausubel, D. P. *Theory and problems of child development.* New York: Grune & Stratton, Inc., 1958.

Laurendeau, M., & Pinard, A. *Causal thinking in the child.* New York: International Universities Press, Inc., 1962.

Michotte, A. *The perception of causality.* New York: Basic Books, Inc., 1963.

Piaget, J. *The child's conception of physical causality.* New York: Harcourt, Brace & World, 1930.

Piaget, J. *The construction of reality in the child.* New York: Basic Books, Inc., 1954.

Piaget, J. *The child's conception of physical causality.* London: Routledge & Kegan Paul, Ltd., 1966.

Torrance, E. P. *Understanding the fourth grade slump in creative thinking.* U.S. Department of Health, Education, and Welfare, 1967.

2.6

1. Brim, O. The parent-child relation as a social system: I. Parent and child roles. *Child Devel.,* 1957, **28,** 343-364.

2. Brown, D. Sex-role preference in young children. *Psychol. Monog.,* 1957, **70,** No. 14 (Whole No. 421).

3. Bruner, J. On cognitive growth: I and II. In J. Bruner *et al.* (Eds.), *Studies in Cognitive Growth.* New York: Wiley, 1966.

4. Emmerich, W. Young children's discriminations of parent and child roles. *Child Devel.,* 1959, **30,** 403-419.

5. _____. Family role concepts of children ages six to ten. *Child Devel.,* 1961, **32,** 609-624.

6. Feffer, M. H. The cognitive implications of role taking behavior. *J. Personal.,* 1959, **27,** 152-168.

7. Feffer, M., & Gourevitch, V. Cognitive aspects of role taking in children. *J. Personal.,* 1960, **28,** 383-396.

8. Feffer, M., & Suchotliff, L. Decentering implications of social interaction. *J. Personal. & Soc. Psychol.,* 1966, **4,** 415-422.

9. Flavell, J. The Development of Role-Taking and Communication Skills in Children. New York: Wiley, 1968.

10. Hartley, R. Children's concepts of male and female roles. *Merrill-Palmer Quart.,* 1960, **6,** 83-91.

11. Kagan, J. Acquisition and significance of sex typing and sex role identity. In M. Hoffman & L. Hoffman (Eds.), *Review of Child Development Research.* New York: Russell Sage Foundation, 1964.

12. Kaplan, B., & Crockett, W. Developmental analysis in the problem of cognitive consistency. In R. Abelson *et al.* (Eds.), *Theories of Cognitive Consistency.* Chicago: Rand McNally, 1968.

13. Piaget, J. The Moral Judgment of the Child. New York: Free Press, 1965.

14. Piaget, J., & Inhelder, B. The Psychology of the Child. New York: Basic Books, 1969.

15. Werner, H. Process and achievement. *Harvard Educ. Rev.,* 1937, **7,** 353-368.

16. _____. Comparative Psychology of Mental Development. Chicago: Follett, 1948.

89

3.
Affective development

The commonsense division between thinking and feeling is reflected in the psychological distinction between cognitive and affective processes. Cognitive processes are concerned with perceiving, concept formation, and problem solving; affective processes include not only feelings and emotions, but attitudes, values, and psychological needs as well. Although the distinction appears to be an easy one to make, it is in fact difficult to draw any precise line between the two processes. What we perceive and think is largely determined by our attitudes and feelings, and our attitudes and feelings are based on what we perceive and think. The studies by Walker, Torrance, and Walker (2.5) and Golden, Bridger, and Montare (2.4) in the preceding section strongly suggest that attitudes and values from their parents' culture significantly influence children's cognitive style; and people continually make decisions and undertake courses of action for reasons that cannot be classified as either cognitive or affective, because both modes of behavior are so intimately involved.

Although we have suggested that affective aspects of behavior, like attitudes and values, are determined at least in part by the culture in which a child grows up, we should also recognize that within any given culture some of the differences that occur among children may

90

be genetically determined, at least to some degree. At birth and even *in utero* children differ in activity level, for pregnant women report marked differences in the frequency and intensity of movement their unborn babies exhibit. Some infants are active, others are passive; some are irritable, others are easily content; some enjoy being cuddled, others wiggle and squirm when held. These basic activity styles constitute what is termed *temperament,* an aspect of personality that has considerable influence on the kind of child, adolescent, and adult an infant eventually becomes.

Although some of the personality traits characterizing an individual's behavior from the preschool years onward are acquired or learned, temperament is generally considered to have physiological components and to be genetically determined. It is difficult to demonstrate this concept scientifically, but some studies suggest its validity. When I. I. Gottesman (1963) administered personality tests to high-school-age identical (monozygotic or MZ) and fraternal (dizygotic or DZ) twins of the same sex, he found that the MZ twins' scores showed considerably more similarity than did the scores of the DZ twins. Gottesman's results suggest that these pronounced similarities in personality must have been genetically determined, because MZ twins are believed to have identical genes. An earlier investigation by Newman, Freeman, and Holzinger (1937) produced similar findings.

In a study by L. Willerman and R. Plomin (1973), mothers were asked to rate both their activity levels as children and the activity levels of their own children; fathers rated their childhood activity levels. Correlations between mothers' activity levels and those of their children averaged .48; father-child correlations were .42. These significant correlations can be explained either genetically or in terms of the kind of environment parents create for their children, but when these findings are considered together with the results of the twin studies, the evidence strongly suggests a genetic interpretation.

How a child responds to his activity needs or drives may be very important in relation to his cognitive development. Some studies suggest that impulsive children, in contrast to reflective children, are more likely to make errors of judgment in cognitive tasks. Ruth L. Ault (1973) found that impulsive children asked less mature questions than did reflective children, when they played the game "Twenty Questions." It may be that the impulsive child is highly distractible, and when faced with a problem, does the first thing that comes to mind. Taking the time to think about the best course of action requires some awareness of the probable outcome of the action, including its effect upon others; the child who is able to exercise this necessary amount of self-control is therefore more psychologically mature than the child who acts impulsively.

The investigation conducted by Arthur F. Constantini and Kenneth L. Hoving (article 3.1) elucidates the relationship between cognitive development and the ability to control one's own behavior. The investigators measured children's ability to inhibit motor responses by having them walk a measured distance, first at their normal pace and then as slowly as they could. Cognitive inhibition was measured by having them delay their responses to easy questions. In contrast to adults, children find it difficult to slow down when walking or to refrain from blurting out an answer. The researchers' graphs show that seven-year-olds were much more successful in exercising self-restraint than were four-year-olds—further evidence that greater impulsivity indicates less maturity. Constantini and Hoving were also able to show that motor and cognitive inhibition are somewhat different. When institutionalized retarded children were given the same tasks, age but not IQ was found to be related to motor inhibition, while IQ but not age was related to cognitive inhibition.

3.1 The relationship of cognitive and motor response inhibition to age and IQ

Arthur F. Constantini and
Kenneth L. Hoving

There is increasing empirical evidence that the period between 5 and 7 years is one of major developmental importance. One process that has often been implicated in the dramatic changes that occur during this period is inhibition. White (9) suggests that before age 5 the child

Reprinted from the *Journal of Genetic Psychology*, 123 (1973): 309–319, with permission of the authors and The Journal Press. Copyright 1973 by The Journal Press.

solves problems according to an associative process; i.e., he simply emits those responses that have the strongest associative strength in his competitive response hierarchy. After age 7, the child functions at a cognitive level and is able to inhibit responses with strong associative strength and emit responses that are lower in the hierarchy. Kagan (2, 3) proposed a similar transition in his "reflective-impulsive" distinction with the emphasis on the older child's ability to inhibit his initial response and become more analytic. Luria (5, 6) also notes the importance of response inhibition which he views as a direct function of the development of the ability to regulate behavior with internalized speech. Proponents of the psychoanalytic approach (4) have viewed response inhibition as a component of the ego delay function which develops at about age 5 to 7. Although developmental psychologists working from different orientations have incorporated the concept of response inhibition in their positions, attempts to define response inhibition or to identify its parameters are rare. One possible definition is "the ability to delay or withhold a previously learned or preferred response."

The responses that are withheld or delayed have varied from study to study. For example, Luria's task (5, 6) of inhibiting the press of a trigger in response to various colored lights appears to involve withholding a motor response, whereas Kagan's (2, 3) task of selecting matching stimuli from a complex array involves the delay of responses that appear to be primarily cognitive in nature. If the responses to be inhibited are different, the factors that influence inhibition may also be different. The potential differences between the responses that have been inhibited have been neglected, with "response inhibition" serving as a vaguely defined term incorporating all forms. When an investigator has identified the type of response to be inhibited—e.g., motor inhibition—he has usually stopped there. For example, recent studies (7, 8) have measured motor inhibition, via instructions to walk slowly and draw a line slowly, and have correlated performance on these tasks with *IQ*. The findings from both studies suggest that motor inhibition and *IQ* are positively correlated. These findings do not offer any suggestions about the correlation between *IQ* and cognitive inhibition, or between cognitive inhibition and motor inhibition. If response inhibition is to assume an important role in our understanding of child development, it must be more clearly defined. The present study was undertaken to (*a*) test the hypothesis that response inhibition increases with age and (*b*) determine if the factors that influence the child's ability to inhibit vary with the nature of the response to be inhibited.

As previously noted many theories of child development assert that response inhibition increases as a function of age. Experiment I examined the development of response inhibition, as measured by two different tasks, across four ages. The tasks were designed to measure inhibition of different responses and the four age groups selected were within the transition age range noted by White (9).

EXPERIMENT I

METHOD

Subjects

The subjects were 80 children, 10 male and 10 female in each of four age groups. The mean age for each group was 4 years-5 months, 5 years-7 months, 6 years-6 months, and 7 years-5 months, respectively. The *standard deviation* was approximately three months in each age group. The children were from white middle-class families in a semiurban community. The children in school were age appropriate for grade level and were able to read numbers between one and 12. The 4-year-old group was drawn from a private nursery serving the area from which the school-age children came.

Apparatus and procedure

The *S*s were escorted into a mobile laboratory and shown a table upon which a number of small toys had been placed. The *S*s were instructed that they could win marbles by playing some games and later trade the marbles for toys. The more marbles the *S*s won the more toys they could select. Prior to testing all *S*s were required to label correctly which of two objects moved either fast or slow on three consecutive trials, in order to insure their understanding of the terms. Understanding of the term "wait" was also required of each *S*. The terms were uniformly understood by all *S*s. Two measures of response inhibition were employed:

a. Walk slowly task. The *S*s were instructed to walk a 6′ long by 6″ wide board at a normal pace. This was repeated three times to obtain a baseline measure of the *S*s' "normal" walking speed. Following these three trials, the Ss were given five trials on which they were instructed to walk the board as slowly as they could. On each of these trials Ss were given one marble for each five seconds it took to walk the board. The time was recorded from the point at which Ss stepped on the board until the point at which they stepped off, and this was used as a measure of motor response inhibition. After each trial the instructions to the S were "That was very good, but this time let's see if you can walk slower (or wait longer) because, remember, the more marbles you have, the more toys you get to pick."

    b. Matching task. The Ss were presented with stimulus cards that contained four line drawings of animals, two of which were identical. The Ss' task was to identify the two matching animals on each card. The Ss were given three baseline trials with no instructions regarding response inhibition, and then 10 inhibition trials. On the inhibition trials Ss were instructed to look at the stimulus, decide which two animals matched, and then to wait as long as they could before responding. The Ss were rewarded with one marble for each five seconds they waited before responding. On one block of five trials there was a clock on the table in front of the Ss. The clock had a 12″ by 12″ face with a sweep second hand, and the face was divided into one second intervals with each fifth second labeled in sequence from 1 to 12. The clock was started when Ss turned over the stimulus card and was stopped when Ss stated that they were ready to respond. Thus, on these trials, an S could tell exactly how many marbles he would win by responding at any given time. To insure that Ss understood the function of the clock they were required to tell the experimenter the number of marbles won on each trial. On a second block of five trials the instructions were the same, but the clock was not present. The inhibition trials with the clock were presented first to half the Ss, with the remaining Ss having the no-clock condition trials presented first. On all trials the time was recorded from the point at which S turned over the stimulus card until he signaled E that he wished to respond. This was used as a measure of cognitive response inhibition.

Results and discussion

The four age groups did not differ significantly in response inhibition on the three baseline trials of the walk-a-board task. The remaining analysis, therefore, did not incorporate the baseline data. Inhibition scores for the age groups on this task are presented in Figure 1.

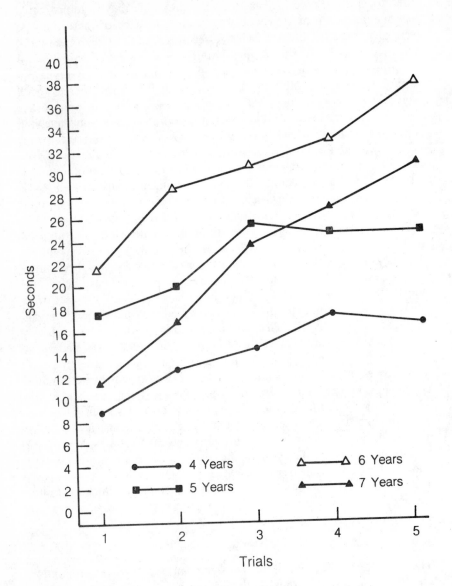

FIGURE 1

MEAN RESPONSE TIME ACROSS TRIALS FOR THE FOUR AGE GROUPS ON THE
WALK-A-BOARD TASK

3. Affective development

These data were analyzed with an analysis of variance procedure. The difference in response inhibition as a function of age was significant ... ($p < .05$). However, of the age comparisons only the difference between the four- and six-year-old children reached significance ... ($p < .05$). ... The sex of the Ss did not significantly influence response inhibition. The Age × Trials interaction was significant ... ($p < .01$). This interaction appears to be due to the marked improvement over trials for the 7-year-olds, whereas the 5-year-olds' performance leveled off by trial three. This is supported by the finding that the 4- and 7-year-olds did not significantly differ on trial one but did on trial five; whereas the 5- and 6-year-olds did not differ on trial one but did differ significantly on trial five.

The inhibition scores on the matching task for each age group are shown graphically in Figure 2. The difference in inhibition as a function of age was again significant ... ($p < .01$). There was also a significant difference in response inhibition in the three treatment conditions ... ($p < .01$). Ss responded significantly slower in the clock ... ($p < .01$) than they did during the baseline trials. Ss were also able to inhibit more effectively with a clock than without one ... ($p < .01$). This was true for all age groups except the 4-year-olds who did respond more slowly when the potential aid of the clock was available. ...

There was also a significant increase in response inhibition across trials ... ($p < .01$) with interaction of Trials × Age also being significant ... ($p < .05$). The 5- and 7-year-olds significantly increased their response inhibition across trials on both the clock and no-clock condition, the 4-year-olds did not demonstrate significant increased inhibition in either condition, and the 6-year-olds significantly increased in the no-clock condition, but not in the clock condition. The reason for the 6-year-olds not increasing inhibition across trials in the clock condition probably was due to ceiling effects as they delayed nearly the maximum interval on the first trial, and the task restrictions prevented additional improvement. There are no significant differences across trials or between ages on the baseline trials.

The results of Experiment I indicate that the board and matching tasks can be employed to measure inhibition. They yielded results that support the hypothesis that response inhibition increases as a function of age. It is important to note that the ability of children to inhibit increased with practice coupled with reinforcement on both tasks. This is true for the matching task for all age groups except the 6-year-olds

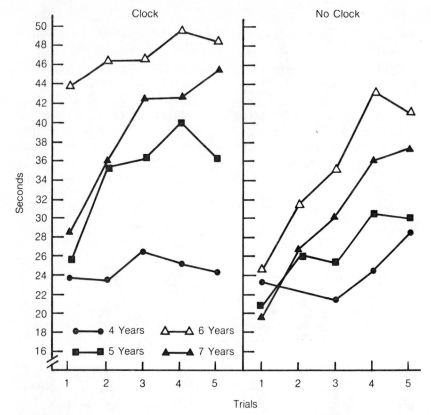

FIGURE 2

MEAN DELAY OF RESPONSE TIME FOR THE FOUR AGE GROUPS OBTAINED OVER THE INHIBITION TRIALS ON THE MATCHING TASK

in the clock condition and the 4-year-olds in both conditions. The 4-year-olds found it difficult to inhibit in this task and were apparently unable to use the clock to aid their inhibition. The results are interpreted to indicate that improvement in both motor and cognitive inhibition is possible with training. There was one age reversal in the data; the 6-year-old group demonstrated more inhibition on both the walk-a-board and the matching tasks than did the 7-year-old group. This finding is difficult to explain other than to suggest that sampling error may be involved. It is interesting to note that Kagan (1) also finds age reversals on the Matching Familiar Figures task.

3. Affective development

EXPERIMENT II

In the second experiment the two tasks were used with a population of retarded Ss in an attempt to separate the effects of age and IQ. Since the ability to walk slowly depends heavily upon motor inhibition, and delaying a response on the matching task depends more on cognitive inhibition, it was hypothesized that performance on these two tasks might be differentially affected by age and IQ.

METHOD

Subjects

The subjects were 48 white institutionalized retardates, half between the ages of 9 and 12 (mean age = 11 years 3 months) and half between the ages of 13 and 17 (mean age = 14 years 4 months). Half of each age group had IQs between 40 and 55 (mean IQ = 47), and half had IQs between 56 and 70 (mean IQ = 63). None of the children showed motor impairment. No attempt to balance the groups for sex was made, as the previous study revealed no sex differences. In the present study the younger group contained 23 males and one female, whereas the older group had 15 males and nine females.

Apparatus and procedure

The apparatus and procedures used were the same as in Experiment I.

Results and discussion

Figure 3 presents the inhibition scores for the four groups of Ss over five trials on the walk-a-board task.

There were no significant differences due to age or IQ on the three baseline trials; however, on the inhibition trials the older Ss performed significantly better . . . ($p < .05$) than did the younger Ss. Although the differences due to IQ appear of the same magnitude in Figure 3, the analysis reveals that this difference does not approach significance . . . ($p < .15$). There was a significant increase in motor inhibition across trials . . . ($p < .01$) with all four groups showing significant improvement between trials one and five.

Subjects responded differently in the baseline, clock, and no-clock conditions . . . ($p < .01$) with responses in both the clock . . . ($p < .01$) and

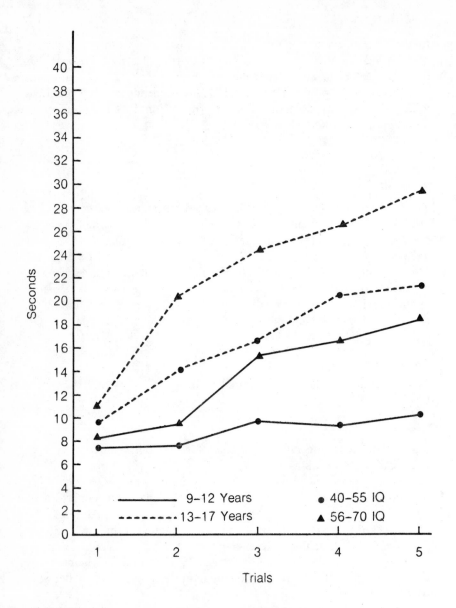

FIGURE 3

MEAN RESPONSE TIME FOR AGE AND *IQ* GROUPS OBTAINED OVER THE FIVE
INHIBITION TRIALS ON THE BOARD TASK

| 3. Affective development

no-clock conditions . . . ($p<.05$). Neither age nor *IQ* was responsible for difference in responding on the baseline trials. However, *S*s in the 56 to 70 *IQ* range were able to inhibit their responses significantly longer than low 40 to 55 *IQ* *S*s . . . ($p<.05$) across the three conditions. As is shown on Figure 4, this is largely due to the longer latencies of the higher *IQ*s when the clock was available to aid inhibition. The lower *IQ* children exhibited the same response latency whether a clock was present or not . . . ($p<.05$), whereas children in the 56 to 70 *IQ* range were able to inhibit longer when the clock was available . . . ($p<.05$).

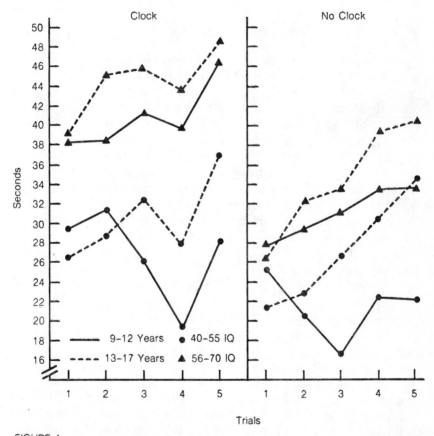

FIGURE 4

MEAN DELAY OF RESPONSE TIME FOR AGE AND IQ GROUPS OBTAINED OVER THE INHIBITION TRIALS ON THE MATCHING TASK

The implication is clear that the "brighter" children in this sample were able to use the clock to aid them in inhibiting their response, whereas the lower *IQ* children were not. When the clock was not available, there was no significant difference due to *IQ* or age. Age also did not significantly influence responding when the clock was present.

Responding did differ as a function of trials . . . ($p < .01$), but no readily interpretable trends are apparent. Age was found to interact with trials . . . ($p < .05$) which is probably due to the increase in inhibition across trials shown by the 13- to 17-year-olds in the no-clock condition.

DISCUSSION—EXPERIMENTS I AND II

Experiment I supported the hypothesis that both motor and cognitive response inhibition increases with age. Older children performed better on the board and matching tasks than did younger children. Whether prolonged training would increase response inhibition in the younger child, or if training on one task transfers to inhibition on other tasks are empirical questions that remain to be answered.

Experiment II was intended to test the hypothesis that cognitive and motor inhibition can be separated and are differentially affected by age and *IQ*. It is recognized that motor and cognitive behavior are not mutually exclusive and therefore cannot be measured independently, but it is also believed that the tasks used successfully measured behavior in which motor inhibition and cognitive inhibition were differentially important. If this assumption is valid, the data suggest that motor inhibition increases with age, while cognitive inhibition increases with *IQ* within the age and *IQ* range tested. Since cognitive abilities increase with age, it would be expected that older children would do better on both tasks than would younger children, which experiment I demonstrated.

In summary, response inhibition plays an important role in child development theories and it is an integral part of our society's child rearing practices. Almost as soon as children begin to respond, they are taught to inhibit particular responses. Thus, response inhibition is too important a term to be vaguely defined. It is proposed that response inhibition be defined as "The ability to delay or withhold a previously learned or preferred response," and that the determinants of, and influences on, response inhibition be investigated in relation to the type of response that is to be inhibited.

SUMMARY

The relationship of age and *IQ* to response inhibition in children was investigated in two experiments. Two tasks were employed: a "walk slowly" task designed to measure motor inhibition and a simple matching task designed to measure cognitive inhibition. In Experiment I, the *S*s were 20 "normal" children at ages 4, 5, 6, and 7 years of age. Response inhibition was found to increase with age. In Experiment II, the *S*s were 48 institutionalized retardates, half between the ages of 8 to 12 and half between the ages of 13 to 17. Half of each age group had *IQ*s between 40 and 55, and half had *IQ*s between 56 and 70. Motor response inhibition varied as a function of age but not *IQ*, while cognitive inhibition varied as a function of *IQ* but not age.

We usually think of anxiety as inhibiting, rather than facilitating, performance of tasks, and a great deal of research with school children confirms this impression. In adults, as well as in children, evaluation by others is a prime source of anxiety, whether the evaluation consists of a paper-and-pencil examination or of delivering a prepared report before an audience. As we are all well aware, the general effect of anxiety is to interfere with such cognitive processes as problem solving and information recall. Highly anxious children are routinely found to have more than the average number of problems in learning and retention. K. T. Hill and S. B. Sarason (1966) found that elementary school children who scored high on the Test Anxiety Scale for Children scored lower on intelligence tests and school achievement tests than did children who rated low in anxiety.

What we often overlook, however, is that too little anxiety is as detrimental as too much. The child who is apathetic and passive is just as likely to do poorly on classroom tasks and in other complex situations as is the child who is unconcerned about both the needs or feelings of others and his own intellectual and social development. The relationship between concerned arousal—anxiety—and achievement is not a simple one, as the child who is unconcerned is as likely to fail as the child who is overconcerned.

Perhaps we have in the past been preoccupied with the problems of the overanxious child because we have learned to be preoccupied with anxiety. Our urbanized, industrialized culture generates a great deal of anxiety in both children and adults. The effects of too much stress are evident in the psychologists' waiting rooms, in the divorce courts, and in the sales of tranquilizers. School personnel have become so highly sensitized to stress reactions in children that the child who wants intensely to succeed but cannot do so is quickly noticed, while the child who is simply unconcerned and passive is overlooked.[1] Linking anxiety with difficulties in school may be caused by the middle-class bias of school personnel in our culture. Research with children from other social and cultural settings suggests that the relationship between anxiety and difficulties in school may not be an obvious one. In a study of Navaho first graders, E. R. Oetting and N. G. Dinges (1971) found that those who were believed by their teachers to be adapting very well in the school setting, actually scored higher on objective scales of anxiety than did those who appeared to be adapting poorly. The concept of anxiety as an adjustment facilitator also appears in a study by Sheldon and Eleanor Glueck (1950), comparing delinquent and nondelinquent youngsters living in poorer areas of Boston. The investigators found that the nondelinquents, who were making better progress in school, reported more anxieties and emotional problems than did the delinquents.

Article 3.2 by Henry Clay Lindgren and Maria Jorgiza Mello also raises questions about the relationship between school success and anxiety-related problems of adjustment. Brazilian elementary schools provided the setting for the study, which compared the adjustments of overachievers and underachievers. Overachievers were defined as children who scored below the median on intelligence tests and above the median on school marks; underachievers were children who scored above the median on intelligence tests and below the median on school marks. Contrary to what would ordinarily be expected, the overachievers reported more anxieties and made poorer scores than the underachievers on all scales of a Portuguese version of the Bell Adjustment Inventory. The authors speculated that these findings might reflect a cultural bias against school achievement. In other words, if most of the children in the community subscribe to an antiachievement norm, the child who achieves contrary to the norm usually suffers in terms of worsened peer relationships.

---

1. Our tendency to overlook the unconcerned and passive child may reflect the fact that we have a number of techniques—psychotherapy and reassurance, for example—to deal with the anxiety of children, but relatively few that enable us to deal with their apathy.

3.2 Emotional problems of over- and underachieving children in a Brazilian elementary school

*Henry Clay Lindgren and
Maria Jorgiza Mello*

This study grew out of a project for developing instruments that could be used to study emotional problems associated with underachievement in Brazilian schools. The assumption underlying the study was that in Brazil, as in the United States and elsewhere, emotional and social adjustment is a significant negative factor in school success. Researchers have found, for example, that underachievement in school work is more likely to be associated with adjustment problems than is satisfactory or high achievement (2, 3, 9, 14, 15), and that adjustment problems interfere with academic success (1, 6, 10, 12, 13). It was hypothesized that a survey of the problems of Brazilian school children would show that underachievers have more problems than overachievers.

METHOD

The sample selected for study consisted of two fourth-year elementary classes located in a São Paulo school that draws most of its pupils from upper-lower-class and lower-middle-class families. The father of the modal child in the sample had received some secondary education (about the equivalent of junior-high school), and the mother had received some primary education. Previously the children had taken two forms of an experimental intelligence test, described more fully by Lindgren and Guedes (7). From each class, the authors selected a group of overachievers who scored below the median of their class on the combined scores of the two intelligence tests and above the median of the school marks assigned by their teacher. Conversely, underachievers were children who scored above the median of their class on intelligence, but below the median of school marks. One class consisted of 34 children, including eight overachievers (three boys and five girls) and seven underachievers (five boys and two girls). The other class consisted of 48 children, including eight overachievers (two boys and six girls) and seven underachievers (three boys and four girls). Inasmuch as there were no significant differences in the educational level of the parents of the overachievers and of the underachievers, it was assumed that (for all intents and purposes) the two groups could be considered as approximately equal with regard to this variable and probably also with respect to socioeconomic status.

Two instruments were used to gather data on emotional problems. One was a 106-item[1] version of the Bell Adjustment Inventory for adolescents that had been translated into Portuguese and adapted for use with children in the preadolescent stage of development and at that social-class level. This test was selected partly because of the availability of a Portuguese version and partly because its four subscales permit classification of problems in terms of home, health, social, and emotional adjustment. It was recognized, however, that the obvious nature of most of the Bell Adjustment Inventory items might permit or encourage conscious or unconscious faking. Therefore, a second instrument was constructed to serve as a partial control. It was a 30-item sentence-completion test (SCT). It was hoped that, in addition to serving as a check on the results obtained with the Bell Adjustment Inventory, it would provide further information on the problems and personality factors associated with over- and underachievement.

The Bell Adjustment Inventory was scored in accord with the key provided with the original scale and thus produced scores correlated positively with adjustment. The SCT was scored by classifying sentence completions in one of four ways: as "aggressive" (or "hostile"), as "accepting," as "anxious," or as "neutral" (or otherwise unclassifiable)—following a method used by Lindgren and Lindgren (8) in classifying the sentence completions of teachers and school administrators in Canada and California. The rationale of the method was based on a formulation by Karen Horney (5), who has suggested that human needs relative to the environment may be classified in three ways: against (hostile), toward (accepting), and away from (fearful or anxious).

---

1. Two of the items turned out to be unscorable. Results are based on the remaining 104 items.

SCT responses were classifed independently by three judges. The means of interjudge correlations were as follows: aggressive hostile, .51; accepting, .81; and anxious, .58. The lower correlations for aggressive-hostile and anxiety very likely were affected by restriction in range, inasmuch as the means of each judge's mean scores for the three categories were aggressive-hostile, 2.8; accepting, 14.9; and anxious, 4.9. The statistics reported in Tables 1 and 2 are based on the summed scores of the judges' ratings.

The correlations between the part scores of the Bell Adjustment Inventory and SCT are presented in Table 1. The intercorrelations of the Bell scales are high and positive, as is characteristic of questionnaires of this type. The correlations between the part scores of the SCT and those of the Bell also tend in the expected direction. This is especially true of the SCT Anxiety scale, which scale is negatively and significantly correlated with all but one of the scales of the Bell Adjustment Inventory. As expected, the SCT Acceptance score is positively correlated with the four scales and with the total score of the Bell, although only the correlations with the Home Adjustment and with the Health Adjustment scales

TABLE 1

CORRELATIONS AMONG PART SCORES OF A PORTUGUESE VERSION OF THE ADJUSTMENT INVENTORY AND PART SCORES OF A SENTENCE-COMPLETION TEST FOR 82 BRAZILIAN ELEMENTARY-SCHOOL CHILDREN

Scale	1	2	3	Scale 4	5	6	7
The Adjustment Inventory							
1. Home adjustment							
2. Health adjustment	.61***						
3. Social adjustment	.62***	.41***					
4. Emotional adjustment	.67***	.58***	.65***				
5. Total score							
Sentence-Completion Test							
6. Aggressive-hostile	.06	.00	.09	−.03	.00		
7. Acceptance	.36***	.25*	.15	.12	.20	−.44***	
8. Anxiety	−.30**	−31**	−.24*	−.20	−.35***	.02	−.48***

*** p<.001.
** p<.01.
* p<.05.

are statistically significant. However, the Aggressive-Hostile score appears to have little relationship with the scales on the Bell. The intercorrelations among the three scales of the SCT are also in the expected direction. The Aggressive-Hostile and the Anxiety scales appear to be relatively independent of each other, but each is correlated negatively with the Acceptance scales.

RESULTS

The comparison of mean scores of over- and underachievers, as shown in Table 2, lends no support to the hypothesis and, in fact, suggests that the reverse of the hypothesis may be more tenable. Overachievers have lower mean scores (signifying a greater number of problems of adjustment) on all scales of the Bell Adjustment Inventory, and the differences between the mean scores of the Health Adjustment, Emotional Adjustment, and the total are significant at the five per cent level of confidence. Furthermore, overachievers score higher than underachievers on the Aggressive-Hostile and Anxiety scales of the SCT and lower on the Acceptance scale, although the differences do not approach the same level of confidence.

TABLE 2
DIFFERENCES BETWEEN OVERACHIEVERS AND UNDERACHIEVERS ON THE ADJUSTMENT INVENTORY AND A SENTENCE-COMPLETION TEST

Scale	Overachievers	Underachievers	Difference
The Adjustment Inventory			
Home adjustment	15.38	17.20	1.82
Health adjustment	18.36	22.36	4.00*
Social adjustment	10.12	11.78	1.66
Emotional adjustment	13.00	18.08	5.08*
Total adjustment	57.35	68.70	11.35*
Sentence-Completion Test			
Aggressive-hostile	8.50	7.07	1.43
Acceptance	41.40	46.55	5.15
Anxiety	15.76	14.20	1.56

*$p < .05$.

An analysis of the responses made by over- and underachievers by sex shows that overachieving girls have more problems of adjustment than do overachieving boys. On 58 per cent of the items on the Bell, overachieving boys have poorer responses than underachieving boys; whereas on 75 per cent of the items overachieving girls have poorer responses than underachieving girls. On the items that discriminate between over- and underachievers of each sex at the 10 per cent level, overachieving boys have poorer responses than do underachieving boys on only nine out of 20 items, whereas overachieving girls have poorer responses than do underachieving girls on 14 out of 16 items. The area of greatest difficulty for members of both sexes, with reference to items discriminating at the 10 per cent level or better, is that of Health Adjustment, with psychosomatic problems (respiratory ailments, digestive upsets, and the like) predominating.

DISCUSSION

Because the sample used in this study is limited to two classes of students in a single school, the results reported cannot of course be generalized to other Brazilian school children. Nevertheless, results that are the direct opposite of the findings of studies conducted elsewhere deserve some kind of explanation.

One interpretation is that the overachievers had fewer problems than the underachievers, but were more honest in reporting them. To some extent this possibility is contradicted by the moderate but significant correlations between scores on the Bell and scores on parts of the SCT which, as a projective test, might be expected to be less affected by faking.

Another interpretation is that the overachievers have more problems than the underachievers, but they are the kind of problem that does not interfere with school achievement and may encourage achievement or stem from superior achievement. To some degree, such an interpretation is consistent with the findings of Sheldon and Eleanor Glueck (4). They found that a sample of 500 nondelinquents tended to report more emotional problems than a matched sample of delinquents. Inasmuch as the nondelinquents in the Gluecks' study were making better progress in school than the delinquents, one would assume that an analysis of their data would show a positive correlation between the number of emotional problems reported and school success. A further resemblance between their study and the present one is the fact that the populations from which the samples were drawn were in the low socioeconomic category.

Still another and possibly related interpretation is that (perhaps) in Brazil school success does not occupy as central a position as it does in the United States. For North American children, adjustment to school and its problems is a "key" adjustment. The child who succeeds in school is functioning more consistently with respect to the values and expectations of his culture than the child who does poorly; hence in the United States the relationship between emotional problems and school success tends to be a reciprocal one. The child who has problems in school tends to have other problems as well, and problems that occur outside of school create or aggravate problems in the classroom. The authors' observations suggest the possibility that in Brazil there may be a cultural norm, probably more characteristic of lower-class children, that is characterized by attitudes of agreeableness (acceptance), low levels of hostility and anxiety, and the lack of an aggressive drive to achieve and compete academically. If these observations are valid it follows that the lower-class child who strives academically and is competitive (*a*) deviates from well-established norms and (*b*) is likely to experience internal and external disturbances of a psychological nature: that is, he is likely to have more anxieties and to experience poorer relations with his peers than does the child who conforms to the norm.

This hypothesis rests, of course, on a slender base: the results of a study conducted in two classes in one Brazilian school. However, if further research supports the hypothesis, it may have important implications for those who plan educational programs in underdeveloped countries. One of these implications is this: It is not safe to assume that the expansion of the educational program will be accompanied by a corresponding increase in school attendance and in educational achievement. The fact that people are eager to possess the advantages that accrue to members of more developed societies should not be taken to mean that they wish to pay, or are aware that they must pay, the price for such advantages: a price that is measured in terms of more years of school and of more intense study. Even the eagerness to pay this price must be accompanied by a willingness to develop an entire new set of attitudes and values oriented toward self-improvement through education.

The results presented in this study, tenuous though they may be, suggest a need to be cautious about translating to other cultures concepts that are fundamental to the interpretation of human behavior in North American contexts. In North America, it is a fairly good operating principle to assume that low achievers generally have more problems of emotional and social adjustment than do achievers; and the success of counseling programs and school mental-health programs is based in part on the validity of that assumption (11, 16). But the results of this study suggest that such an assumption may not be valid in Brazilian schools. Indeed, the results suggest that attempts to promote higher levels of school achievement on the part of Brazilian school children, at least among the lower socioeconomic groups, may result in an *increase* in the number or in the extent of emotional problems. This does not mean that attempts to raise the educational level of these groups should be abandoned on that account, but it does mean that those who attempt to extend the years of school attendance and to improve educational achievement should be alerted to the possibility of an increased number of mental-health problems and should be prepared to cope with them.

SUMMARY

A Portuguese version of Bell's Adjustment Inventory and a 30-item sentence-completion test were used to measure the problems of adjustment of 16 overachievers and 14 underachievers in two fourth-year elementary classes in São Paulo, Brazil. Contrary to an hypothesis that had been based on studies of North American school children, overachievers tend to report significantly more problems of adjustment than do underachievers, particularly in the Health Adjustment and in the Emotional Adjustment areas of the Bell Inventory. This difference between over- and underachievers is more marked for girls than it is for boys. It is suggested that cultural differences may explain the unexpected results, and that such differences should be taken into account by those who plan expanded educational programs for underdeveloped countries.

Several studies have found antiachievement values to be prevalent in societies where ties with tradition are strong, as well as in working class groups. The overachieving child in a working-class community is often rejected by his peers and is treated much the same way as the "rate-breaker" in manufacturing plants who is ostracized and harassed by his fellow workers because he produces more than the norm. Individuals who exceed production norms have been found to have an unusually high degree of *the need to achieve* or *n Ach* (D. C. McClelland, 1961). McClelland and his coworkers measured *n Ach* by asking subjects to look at pictures of the type used in the Thematic Apperception Test (TAT) and to say who the individuals in the picture are, what they are doing, what led up to the events portrayed, and what the outcome will be. Subjects who are strongly motivated to achieve tell stories that depict individuals attempting to achieve, often against difficult odds. Children who strive for academic success are also likely to score high on *n Ach*. Studies by S. H. Honor and J. R. Vane (1972), for example, showed that TAT measures of *n Ach* identified 100% of the high school boys who were high achievers and 96% of those who were low achievers.

Achievement motivation appears to be associated with many attitudes and behavior styles that are also related to success. For example, persons scoring high in *n Ach* usually say that whether an individual succeeds or not depends on whether he is willing to try hard and persevere, but persons scoring low in *n Ach* are likely to say that success is a matter of luck. These life views may explain why individuals with high *n Ach* tend to persist in trying to solve perplexing problems, and why individuals with low *n Ach* either do not attempt the problems or attack them impulsively with random efforts.

Studies comparing children from different socioeconomic classes generally find that middle-class children tend to score high on measures of achievement motivation, children from slum areas score low, and children from working-class homes score between the two. In her study of Hawaiian children (Article 3.3), Toni Falbo not only found the usual relationship between socioeconomic level and achievement motivation, but she also was able to identify achievement striving in five-year-olds. Falbo's article has several interesting features, one of which is her ingenious measure for achievement motivation: she had the children take an orally administered forced-choice test after they heard a story in which a child completed (or did not complete) a puzzle. Her data also suggest that achievement motivation may be higher for females than for males in the Hawaiian culture, a finding that is consistent with other research on child-rearing practices among Hawaiians. Falbo also noted that the teachers were inclined to adopt a child's explanation for his successful striving—if the child explained his success as the result of trying hard, the teachers usually used the same explanation.

 ## The attributional explanation of academic performance by kindergarteners and their teachers

Toni Falbo

The development of achievement motivation has received considerable attention. Recently, Weiner (1972) and his associates devised a cognitive-developmental model of achievement motivation within the framework of attribution theory. As such, this model concerns a person's explanation of outcomes, or his understanding of the causes of outcomes. Weiner and Kukla (1970) proposed that certain tendencies in these explanations, which they call attributional tendencies, are related to high and low achievement in adults. This paper presents an attempt to discover if such attributional tendencies occur in young children. More specifically, the experiments described here were designed to determine if 5-yr.-olds possess the understanding of causation that conforms to the Weiner, Frieze, Kukla, Reed, Rest, and Rosenbaum (1971) achievement model. Furthermore, this paper presents a study of the similarities between the attributional explanations of 5-yr.-olds and their teachers.

METHOD

Subjects

The sample included 28 5-yr.-old children who were enrolled in the same kindergarten class in Honolulu, Hawaii. These children were predom-

Reprinted from the *Proceedings of the 81st Annual Convention of the American Psychological Association,* 8 (1973): 123–124, with permission of the author and the American Psychological Association. Copyright 1973 by the American Psychological Association.

inantly of part-Hawaiian ancestry and spoke Hawaiian-Creole, a non-standard form of English. The sample also included 4 female teachers, ages 24–48, who were involved in teaching the 28 children of the sample.

Procedure

A story concerning a 5-yr.-old child was written in Hawaiian-Creole. It was tape-recorded while being read by a native speaker. There were four versions of the story: two outcomes (positive/negative) and two sexes for the main character. The outcome concerned the successful or unsuccessful completion of a puzzle.

Each child listened to the taped story once. Half the children heard the positive outcome, half the negative. The Ss were randomly assigned to outcome groups. The experiment took place within the classroom as a learning center activity.

Each child was asked to explain why the main character completed (or left incomplete) the puzzle by making choices between pairs of alternatives. Each child was given six paired comparison choices representing the six possible combinations of the four dimensions of the Weiner et al. (1971) model: task difficulty, luck, ability, and effort. The order of presentation of these six alternatives was systematically varied.

Each teacher was given 28 questionnaires. Each questionnaire was devoted to an individual child and his puzzle performance. The child's puzzle performance was presented as a number derived from the observation of children's actual puzzle behavior within the classroom. This number, called the puzzle score, reflected the number of puzzles completed by each child minus the number left unfinished. The teachers were given 17 rating scales based upon the Weiner et al. (1971) dimensions of achievement behavior. In terms of these dimensions, the teachers were supposed to explain the child's puzzle performance.

Other measures. The WPSSI, an IQ test, was administered to each child in his home during the summer before school began. An SES measure was also available. Half the children belonged to families receiving welfare benefits; half were middle-class.

RESULTS AND DISCUSSION

Children's attributions

The attributional choices were scored as the number of times each attributional dimension was chosen when presented in paired comparison form. Even though paired comparison data are nonindependent, the use of analysis of variance here is justified if certain restrictions are made in interpreting the data.

Significant sex differences were found in the children's attributional choices. Males were more likely to use luck as an explanation than were females . . . ($p < .05$). This sex difference is contradictory to McMahon's (1972) finding that females use luck as an explanation of their behavior more often than do males. There are two possible explanations for this contradiction. First, McMahon's Ss were older, the youngest group being 12-yr.-olds. Second, it is possible that Hawaiian culture was responsible for this reversal. Indeed, Mays, Gallimore, Howard, and Heighton (1968) reported that Hawaiian parents gave their sons less responsible chores and more freedom than they gave their daughters.

A significant difference in the children's attributional explanations of positive and negative outcomes was also found. Ability attributions were made more often when the outcomes were positive than when the outcomes were negative . . . ($p < .05$). This result indicates that 5-yr.-olds are more likely to say someone is "smart" after he completes a task than are they to say someone is "stupid" after he leaves a task unfinished. Similar results were reported by Frieze and Weiner (1971).

A significant SES difference was also found. Middle-class children were significantly more likely to choose "try hard" as an explanation for an outcome than were the welfare children . . . ($p < .05$). This finding is perhaps the most striking of all. Weiner and Kukla (1970) found that high achievers explain outcomes in terms of both their ability (such as "I'm smart") and effort (such as "I tried hard"); while low achievers only use the concept of ability in explaining their outcomes. The inclusion of effort in the high achievers' attributional tendencies means that when they experience failure, they have the redeeming explanation "I didn't work hard enough." This effort attribution provides high achievers with an explanation of their outcomes that keeps them working. Low achievers, however, rely on ability attributions so that when failure occurs their explanation is "I'm not capable." Unfortunately, an ability attribution such as this discourages further effort. Thus, the finding that middle-class children choose "try hard" more often than welfare children means that this cognitive safety valve of effort attributions is already present in the attributional tendencies of middle-class, but not lower-class kindergarteners.

IQ had no relation to the attributional choices of the children ...
($p < .10$).

Teachers' questionnaire

The results of the teachers' questionnaire were a little less straightforward. The 17 items of the questionnaire were summed over the 4 teachers. The teachers' responses were significantly related to the SES and IQ of the children. The puzzle score of middle-class children was viewed by the teachers as more "typical" of the child's behavior in general ... ($p < .05$), and as dependent upon the child's "native intelligence" ... ($p < .01$). The puzzle score of welfare children evoked an effort explanation from the teachers ... ($p < .05$). Overall IQ was also related to the teacher questionnaire. Children with higher scores had their puzzle performance explained more often by "native intelligence" ... ($p < .05$) and regarded as more "typical" of their general classroom behavior ... ($p < .05$). The puzzle score of children with lower IQs more often evoked the explanation of an "ability deficit" ... ($p < .05$), "difficult puzzles" ... ($p < .05$), and "work hard" ... ($p < .05$).

The configuration of the SES and IQ results provides some support for the validity of the Weiner et al. (1971) conceptualization of achievement motivation. For example, Weiner et al. proposed that the ability dimension represented a stable attribute about the person. The SES and IQ differences found in the teacher questionnaire repeatedly paired the items "native intelligence" and "typical of the child's behavior." Thus, in the minds of the teachers, ability, as represented by intelligence, is seen as a stable characteristic of children.

No significant interactions between SES and IQ were found.

In order to study the relationship between the teachers' use of attributional dimensions and their students' use of these same dimensions, the children's attributional choices were used to predict the teachers' ratings. That is, the children's choices for task difficulty, luck, ability, and effort were ranked within each category as high or low and these variables were used as independent variables in an analysis of variance in which the teacher ratings served as dependent variables. The children's task and ability choices failed to predict the teachers' ratings. Their luck and effort choices, however, were significantly related.

Those children who emphasized effort and those children who did not emphasize luck were seen by teachers as (a) having a "special knack" for puzzles ... ($p < .05$), (b) choosing either "easy" or "difficult" puzzles

. . . ($p < .05$), (c) showing greater improvement in classroom behavior . . . ($p < .05$), and (d) switching to another puzzle after they had completed one . . . ($p < .01$).

Therefore, considerable agreement in attributional explanations was found between teachers and their students. If a child emphasized effort, and not luck, the teachers also emphasized effort in their explanations of the child's behavior.

Thus, the usefulness of Weiner and his associates' attributional model of achievement motivation has been demonstrated with 5-yr.-old children. Weiner and Kukla (1970) argued that one's attributional tendencies are crucial factors in triggering achievement behavior. If this is the case and if attribution patterns are present in children at the onset of kindergarten, as these data indicate, then one must look into the preschool years for the genesis of at least some attributional tendencies.

The earlier research of McClelland and his associates (1955) showed that children rating high in achievement motivation often had parents who expected them to help around the home and to perform self-care tasks without help at a relatively early age. Such training seems to foster a higher than average degree of independence. Teachers' attitudes appear to have a similar effect on children. B. I. Fagot (1973) observed that preschool children were more interested in doing tasks and worked on them longer when they received little direction from their teachers. The teachers of these children tended to criticize infrequently and to show little physical affection. Experiences such as these teach the independent child to be his own reinforcer. The more dependent child tends to look to adults for reinforcement and reassurance, but the independent child finds sufficient reinforcement in the satisfaction he gets from the successful completion of tasks. D. J. Reschly and A. Mittman (1973) conducted an experiment in which seventh-graders, mostly from lower-class homes, carried out several tasks; as a form of reinforcement, they were permitted to award themselves as many points as they wished. Students who rated high on self-esteem, as measured by the Coopersmith Self-Esteem Inventory, gave themselves more reinforcement than did those whose self-esteem scores were average or low.

One of the more interesting ways of measuring self-esteem is a technique developed by Barbara H. Long and her coworkers. The subject is shown a series of pages each containing six circles in a horizontal line, and is asked to use the circles as positions for symbols representing himself and five other persons. The closer to the left, or beginning, end of the row the subject places the self-symbol, the higher his self-esteem score. Conversely, unsuccessful or unhappy persons tend to place symbols at the end of the row, at the right. When the test is given in Israel, the positions are reversed, because Hebrew is written from right to left. This nonverbal measure of self-esteem has the advantage of being useful in cross-cultural research. Barbara H. Long and Edmund H. Henderson, whose survey is Article 3.4 in this section, reported that children who attend higher-status schools in several countries tend to score higher on this measure of self-esteem than do children in schools that are more cross-sectional. The investigators also noted a tendency—especially strong among girls—for the children with high self-esteem to identify with their mothers.

3.4 Measuring esteem across cultures

Barbara H. Long and
Edmund H. Henderson

Ziller, Hagey, Smith, and Long (1969) described a nonverbal measure of esteem which has been used in a number of studies with American *S*s (summarized in Long, Henderson, & Ziller, 1970). In this task, *S* places symbols representing self and five other persons in a row of circles. A higher score for esteem is assigned to a placement of the self to the left (beginning) of the row. [Reliability coefficients] in the .80s have been reported, and evidence for [the method's] validity includes tendencies to place negative persons (unhappy, unsuccessful) in low positions, and positive relations between esteem and status, whether sociometric, academic, socioeconomic, or noninstitutionalized.

Reprinted from the *Proceedings of the 79th Annual Convention of the American Psychological Association* 6 (1971): 255–256, with permission of the authors and the American Psychological Association. Copyright 1971 by the American Psychological Association.

| 3. Affective development

Carlson (1970) has recently criticized this measure of esteem, suggesting that (*a*) it fails to distinguish between level and source of self-esteem, (*b*) it has a masculine bias, and (*c*) it has a cultural bias—i.e., it is most suitable for adult males in "white America."

The purpose of this paper is to present certain data which seem relevant to Carlson's third point—cultural bias. This criticism would seem best met by positive empirical findings supportive of reliability and validity among groups other than Americans. In harmony with Triandis's (Triandis, Vassiliou, Tanaka, & Shanmugam, 1971) concept of "subjective culture," the data from eight groups were examined with an eye toward assessing the "meaning" of this measure within each group. It was reasoned that if *S*s responded reliably and meaningfully to this task, doubt would be thrown on Carlson's charge of cultural bias, and positive support would be gained for cross-cultural reliability and validity.

METHOD

Subjects

The *S*s consisted of eight samples of 50 boys and 50 girls aged 10–14 (median age 12; 96% of sample aged 11–13), all enrolled in school, in the following settings: (*a*) Barbados, (*b*) England, (*c*) English Canada, (*d*) France, (*e*) French Canada, (*f*) India, (*g*) Israel, (*h*) Thailand. In each case, permission was obtained to carry out the study in a suitable school or schools (where pupils seems to represent families typical of the area). The *S*s were an unselected sample of children of the proper age who attended school on testing day. Data from 100 United States *S*s of the same age are included for purposes of comparison.

Procedure

The Self-Social Symbols Tasks, which includes six esteem items, was administered to all *S*s in groups in their native language. The original version (English) was used for the groups in Barbados, England, and English Canada. A French translation was used for the French and French Canadian groups, a Hebrew version for the Israeli group, and a Thai and Telugu version, respectively, for the groups from Thailand and India. The tests were administered by *E*s who resided in the locale and who were fluent in the language. All tests were scored under the auspices of the authors. Scores ranged from 1–6 for each item, and were summed over the six items.

RESULTS

Split-half reliability coefficients corrected for length are shown in Table 1. These ranged from .76 (India) to .91 (Barbados).

TABLE 1
RELIABILITY COEFFICIENTS AND CORRELATIONS BETWEEN ESTEEM AND IDENTIFICATION WITH MOTHER AMONG NINE GROUPS

		Esteem vs. identification mother		
Groups	*Reliability*	*Both sexes*	*Boys*	*Girls*
Barbados	.91	.45***	.48***	.43***
England	.85	.28**	.24*	.32**
English Canada	.88	*ns*	*ns*	.25*
France	.87	.17*	*ns*	.28**
French Canada	.84	.28***	*ns*	.35**
India	.76	.45***	.52***	*ns*
Israel	.84	.36***	.27*	.45***
Thailand	.89	*ns*	*ns*	.27*
United States	.80	.23**	*ns*	.26*

Note: $N = 100$ in each group; $*p = .05$ (one-tailed); $**p = .025$; $***p = .005$.

Placement of "unsuccessful person." Placement of the "unsuccessful person" by each group and chi-squares comparing obtained frequencies with a rectangular distribution are shown in Table 2. A preponderance of Ss in each group, with the exception of Israel, placed the "unsuccessful person" to the right (unfavorable) end of the row. Chi-squares were significant in each case.

Reverse hierarchy for Israel. Most Israeli Ss placed the "unsuccessful person" toward the left. It appeared that a reverse hierarchy was operating; therefore, a different scoring system (higher scores to the right) was used for this group. Additional findings supporting this scoring include a positive relation ($r = .66$) between the new scores and the absolute difference (in circles) between self and negative persons (found also among American Ss with regular scoring) and the relations reported below for group differences and identification with mother.

Group differences. Group differences within single settings were found for Canada, India, and Israel. Higher esteem was hypothesized for higher status groups—English Canadians, "in-school" Indians, and residents of kibbutzim in Israel. The Canadian comparison involved the

TABLE 2
PLACEMENT OF "UNSUCCESSFUL PERSON" BY VARIOUS GROUPS

Group	Positions in row						$\chi^{2\ a}$
	A	B	C	D	E	F	
Barbados	6	5	6	3	16	64	54.1
England	6	3	5	13	12	61	46.1
English Canada	5	4	9	18	8	56	29.1
France	3	8	8	23	21	36	20.0
French Canada	2	3	10	12	22	51	39.8
India	4	1	0	4	9	74	83.5
Israel	40	16	15	11	7	5	18.4
Thailand	14	4	3	9	5	63	53.4
United States	3	3	3	15	17	53	43.7

Note: Positions appear as in the task itself—that is, Position A is furthest left; Position F, furthest right, etc. Entries in cells represent number of Ss placing the "unsuccessful person" in each position. Total Ns vary somewhat due to S error.

a Chi-squares were computed comparing the obtained data with an even distribution over the six categories. All were significant at the .005 level.

groups described above (means for English Canadian and French Canadians were 23.4 and 20.5, respectively; . . . ($p < .01$).

The comparison for India contrasted the sample described above and a second group of 51 of similar age (tested by V. E. Reddy, who kindly shared his data with the present authors) who did not attend school (means for in school = 28.1 and out of school = 22.1; $t = 6.15$, $p = .001$).

The comparison for Israel was between about half the sample who resided in kibbutzim (collective agricultural communities) and the other half who lived in moshava (more traditional agricultural communities). (Means for revised scoring were $K = 20.3$, $M = 16.8$, $F = 8.7$, $p < .01$.)

School placement. For three groups—Barbados, England, France—information about placement in school (more or less selective schools in Barbados and France; higher or lower sections on the basis of achievement in England) was available. Higher esteem was again hypothesized for higher status positions. This was found to a significant degree for Barbados, England, and for the French boys (but not the girls). The means for Barbados selective schools ($N = 20$) = 25.8 and unselective schools $(N=80)=20.6$ $(t=2.44, p=.01)$. The means for French boys' selective school $(N=10)=27.6$ and unselective school $(N=40)=20.8$ $(t=2.48, p=.05)$. For the English sample, a correlation of .19 $(N=100, p=.05$, one-tailed test) was found between esteem and placement.

Identification with mother. In all groups, either for girls or boys or both, a positive relation (see Table 1) was found between esteem and identification with mother, as measured in two items in the Self-Social Symbols Tasks (distance in circles between self and mother). This relation had been found earlier among five samples of American children (see Long et al., 1970).

DISCUSSION

The findings related to reliability show that Ss are not responding randomly to the task. Despite the limited length of the test (six items), responses are consistent, thus suggesting that measurement is reasonably accurate.

Placement of the "unsuccessful person" to the right among all groups but Israel supports that hierarchy of value from right to left which is the basic theoretical assumption of this task. A very likely explanation for the reverse hierarchy among Israelis is that it is a function of habits related to reading and writing, which in Hebrew begins on the right. If such be the case, stable directional patterns of language use must be considered a prerequisite for a valid response on this measure. Lack of findings supporting validity among American preschool children upholds this idea.

The findings for both group differences and school placement are similar to those made earlier with American Ss and offer additional support for a positive relation between social status and esteem. The findings related to identification with mother may also be related to status. According to Ausubel (1958), the "satellite" who identifies with parents thereby gains in status.

Altogether, the findings of this study show strong similarities across cultures and do not differ substantially from those found earlier with American Ss. These findings in general would seem to support the usefulness of this measure among diverse cultural groups.

Because the affective development of children is a broad topic, we have had to be selective in choosing the papers to include in this section. We have focused primarily on the aspects related to competence, effectiveness, and control that some personality psychologists call *ego strength.* A child's affective development is intimately involved in other aspects of his life, especially his relationships with others. When we study child-peer relationships, we will examine aggressive behavior and the development of moral values, both of which are related to affective development. Attitudes and values are also very important in social-class and ethnic differences, which we will discuss in Section 7.

REFERENCES

Ault, R. L. "Problem-solving strategies of reflective, impulsive, fast-accurate and slow-inaccurate children." *Child Development* 44 (1973): 259-266.

Fagot, B. I. "Influence of teacher behavior in the preschool." *Developmental Psychology* 9 (1973): 198-206.

Glueck, S. and Glueck, E. *Unravelling Juvenile Delinquency.* New York: Commonwealth Fund, 1950.

Gottesman, I. I. "Heritability of personality: A demonstration." *Psychological Monographs* 77 No. 9 (Whole No. 572), 1963.

Hill, K. T. and Sarason, S. B. "A further longitudinal study of the relation of test anxiety and defensiveness to test and school performance over the elementary school years." *Monograph of Society for Research in Child Development* 31 (1966): 1-76.

Honor, S. H. and Vane, J. R. "Comparison of Thematic Apperception Test and questionnaire methods to obtain achievement attitudes of high-school boys." *Journal of Clinical Psychology* 28 (1972): 81-83.

McClelland, D. C. *Studies in Motivation.* New York: Appleton-Century-Crofts, Inc., 1955.

McClelland, D. C. *The Achieving Society.* Princeton: Van Nostrand, 1961.

Newman, H. H., Freeman, F. N., and Holzinger, K. J. *Twins.* Chicago: University of Chicago Press, 1937.

Oetting, E. R. and Dinges, N. G. "An anxiety and mood scale for young Navaho children." *American Psychological Association Experimental Publication System* 12 (June, 1971): Ms. No. 472-35.

Reschly, D. J. and Mittman, A. "The relationship of self-esteem status and task ambiguity to the self-reinforcement behavior of children." *Developmental Psychology* 9 (1973): 16-19.

Willerman, L. and Plomin, R. "Activity level in children and their parents." *Child Development* 44 (1973): 854-858.

3.1

1. Kagan, J. Developmental studies in reflection and analysis. In A. H. Kidd & J. L. Rivoire (Eds.), *Perceptual Development in Children.* New York: Internat. Univ. Press, 1966.

2. ———. Reflection-impulsivity: The generality and dynamics of conceptual tempo. *J. Abn. Psychol.*, 1966, **71**, 17–24.

3. ———. Biological aspects of inhibition systems. *Amer. J. Dis. Child.*, 1967, **114**, 507–512.

4. Levine, M., Spivak, G., & Wight, B. The inhibition process: Some further data. *J. Consult. Psychol.*, 1959, **23**, 306–312.

5. Luria, A. R. Verbal regulation of behavior. In M. A. B. Brazier (Ed.), *The Central Nervous System and Behavior* (3rd Macy Conference). New York: Macy Foundation, 1960. Pp. 359–423.

6. ———. The Role of Speech in the Regulation of Normal and Abnormal Behavior. New York: Liveright, 1961.

7. Maccoby, E., Dowley, E., Hagan, J. W., & Dergman, R. Activity level and intellectual functioning in normal preschool children. *Child Devel.*, 1965, **36**, 711–770.

8. Massari, D., Hayweiser, L., & Meyer, W. Activity level and intellectual functioning in deprived preschool children. *Devel. Psychol.*, 1969, **1**, 286–290.

9. White, S. H. Evidence for a hierarchical arrangement of learning processes. In L. P. Lipsitt & C. C. Spiker (Eds.), *Advances in Child Development and Behavior* (Vol. 2). New York: Academic Press, 1965.

3.2

1. Armstrong, R. D. Reading success and personal growth. *Reading Teach.*, 1958, **126**, 19–23.

2. Easton, J. Some personality traits of underachieving and achieving high school students of superior ability. *Bull. Maritime Psychol. Assoc.*, 1959, **8**, 34–39.

3. Fliegler, L. A. Understanding the underachieving gifted child. *Psychol. Rep.*, 1957, **3**, 533–536.

4. Glueck, S., & Glueck, E. Unravelling Juvenile Delinquency. New York: Commonwealth Fund, 1950.

5. Horney, K. Our Inner Conflicts. New York: Norton, 1945.

6. Kitano, H. J. L. Refusals and illegibilities in the spelling errors of maladjusted children. *J. Educ. Psychol.*, 1959, **50**, 129–131.

7. Lindgren, H. C., & Guedes, H. de A. Social status, intelligence, and educational achievement among elementary and secondary students in São Paulo, Brazil. *J. Soc. Psychol.*, 1963, **60**, 9–14.

8. Lindgren, H. C., & Lindgren, F. Expressed attitudes of American and Canadian teachers toward authority. *Psychol. Rep.*, 1960, **7**, 51–54.

9. Morrow, W. R., & Wilson, R. C. Family relationships of bright high-achieving and underachieving high school boys. *Child Devel.*, 1961, **32**, 501–510.

10. Richardson, H. M., & Surko, E. F. WISC scores and status in reading and arithmetic of delinquent children. *J. Genet. Psychol.*, 1956, **89**, 251–262.

11. Rothney, J. W. M. Guidance Practices and Results. New York: Harper, 1958.

12. Salzinger, K. Academic achievement in a group of mentally disturbed adolescents in a residential treatment setting. *J. Genet. Psychol.*, 1957, **90**, 239–253.

13. Semler, I. J. Relationships among several measures of pupil adjustment. *J. Educ. Psychol.*, 1960, **51**, 60–64.

14. Shaw, M. C., Edson, K., & Bell, H. M. The self-concept of bright underachieving high school students as revealed by an adjective check list. *Person. Guid. J.*, 1960, **39**, 193-196.

15. Shaw, M. C., & Grubb, J. Hostility and able high school under-achievers. *J. Couns. Psychol.*, 1958, **5**, 263-266.

16. Trione, V. One hundred eighty cases: A follow-up by a rural school psychologist. *Calif. J. Educ. Res.*, 1958, **9**, 86-90.

3.3

Frieze, I., & Weiner, B. Cue utilization and attributional judgments for success and failure. *Journal of Personality*, in press.

Mays, M., Gallimore, R., Howard, A., & Heighton, R. H. A qualitative analysis of family development. In R. Gallimore & A. Howard (Eds.), *Studies in a Hawaiian community*. Honolulu: Bernice P. Bishop Museum, 1968.

McMahon, I. D. Sex differences in expectancy of success as a function of task. Paper presented at the meeting of the Eastern Psychological Association, Boston, April 1972.

Weiner, B. *Theories of motivation: From mechanism to cognition.* Chicago: Markham Publishers, 1972.

Weiner, B., Frieze, I., Kukla, A., Reed, L., Rest, S., Rosenbaum, R. M. Perceiving the causes of success and failure. In E. E. Jones, D. E. Kanouse, H. H. Kelley, R. E. Nisbett, S. Valins, & B. Weiner (Eds.), *Attribution: Perceiving the causes of behavior.* Morristown, N.J.: General Learning Press, 1971.

Weiner, B., & Kukla, A. An attributional analysis of achievement motivation. *Journal of Personality and Social Psychology*, 1970, **15**, 1-20.

3.4

Ausubel, D. P. *Theory and problems of child development.* New York: Grune & Stratton, 1958.

Carlson, R. On the structure of self esteem: Comments on Ziller's formulation. *Journal of Consulting and Clinical Psychology*, 1970, **34**, 264-268.

Long, B. H., Henderson, E. H., & Ziller, R. C. Manual for the self-social symbols tasks and the children's self-social constructs tests. Unpublished manuscript, Goucher College, 1970.

Triandis, H. C., Vassiliou, V. N., Tanaka, Y., & Shanmugam, A. V. *The analysis of subjective culture.* New York: Wiley, 1971.

Ziller, R. C., Hagey, J., Smith, M. D., & Long, B. H. Self-esteem: A self-social construct. *Journal of Consulting and Clinical Psychology*, 1969, **33**, 84-95.

4.
Social
development

Students of personality have long been aware that certain traits seem to cluster together. The research we discussed and presented in Section 3 shows that self-esteem, independence, and achievement motivation tend to be associated with one another. Children who score high on tests of these dimensions tend to see their lives as controlled by themselves, rather than by external forces. J. B. Rotter (1966) was one of the first investigators to develop *locus of control* measures which enable psychologists to determine the extent of an individual's perception of himself as internally or externally controlled. Internally controlled persons perceive a relationship between their behavior and the amount and kind of reinforcement they receive, but externally controlled persons, seeing little of this relationship, perceive their experiences as caused by luck, fate, or powerful other persons. The self-reinforcing child would therefore be classified as internally controlled; the child who looks to others for reinforcement and who is passive or dependent, would be classified as externally controlled.

For most children, locus of control shifts with age. M. Lifschutz (1973) found that there was a significant increase from age nine to age fourteen in the willingness of Israeli and American children to accept credit for their successes and to take the blame for their failures.

126

As might be expected, locus of control scores are also related to measures of social maturity and emotional adjustment. B. K. Bryant (1974) found that the sixth-grade boys in his study who perceived themselves as externally controlled exhibited more behavior problems than those who were internally controlled. The externally controlled boys were more likely to express fear of the teacher and to feel that she blamed them, created difficulties for them, and expected too much of them. The teachers expressed disappointment in the performance of the externally controlled boys and reported that these boys seemed confused, were unconcerned about the teachers' needs and goals, and were generally unsupportive.

A number of studies report that locus of control is related to social-class differences. M. W. Stephens and P. Delys (1973) conducted interviews with children enrolled in largely middle-class nursery schools and in Head Start classes. The interviews were designed to determine the children's control expectancies. The questions—for example, "What makes Mother smile?"—could be answered in terms of some behavior of the child, such as "When I help her with the dishes," or in terms of some external event, such as "When Daddy comes home." The middle-class children were more likely to express internal control expectancies. No differences were found between the black children and the white children. Other research by Stephens and Delys showed that children in a Montessori school made the greatest gain in internal-control scores during the school year, followed by children in parent cooperative nursery schools. The smallest gain reported was for children in a highly structured preschool. Another study, which compared structured with open-classroom schools, showed greater gains for the latter. The authors interpreted their results as suggesting that less structured programs may encourage internal control development more than highly structures schools do.

The paper we have chosen to illustrate locus of control research and to introduce another aspect of social development is a study by Stephen Nowicki, Jr., and Jarvis Barnes (article 4.1). These investigators administered questionnaires to eight groups of inner-city teenagers before and after a week's stay at a special summer camp, where the program of activities involved the campers in working together to accomplish common goals. The results showed that youngsters can be moved toward greater internal control, even in this brief span of time. The authors explain the change as an outcome of a camp program that enabled the boys to see the connection between their behavior and the reinforcing contingencies of their environment.

4.1 Effects of a structured camp experience on locus of control orientation

Stephen Nowicki, Jr., and
Jarvis Barnes

Children from the inner-city area often encounter an environment that is confusing and bewildering. Within this sort of environmental chaos it is virtually impossible to delineate what, at best, are cloudy behavioral contingencies. Children in this situation may see little relationship between how they behave and the reinforcements (rewards or punishments) they receive for their behavior. They may perceive events as being unpredictable and beyond their control and may as a result feel helpless or powerless to do anything constructive about their condition. Individual differences in how much control an individual perceives that he has over his reinforcements have been related to various correlates via a dimension that is called internal-external locus of control (6, 7, 11, 12). Those individuals who perceive a connection between their behavior and the resultant reinforcement received are called "internally controlled." Those individuals who perceive little or no connection between their behavior and the resultant reinforcement but rather see reinforcement due to luck, fate, or powerful others, are called "externally controlled."

Studies using adult measures of locus of control have found internality to be positively related to a number of variables, such as achievement motivation (3), number of activities engaged in (2), level of aspiration (12), and information seeking (5). On the whole, internality has been taken to be a more positive orientation than externality (12). A number of studies involving locus of control in children have also found this dimension to have wide predictive utility (1, 9). Internality was found

Reprinted from the *Journal of Genetic Psychology*, 122 (1973): 247–252, with permission of the authors and The Journal Press. Copyright 1973 by The Journal Press.

to be positively related to such variables as popularity (8), achievement (9), delay of gratification (13), and academic motivation (4).

Since the locus of control dimension seems to have substantial predictive power, and there is a socially relevant need to find out how to change the belief systems of inner-city youngsters, the main purpose of the present study was to investigate the effects of a highly structured camp experience on the locus of control orientations of predominately Negro inner-city teenage youngsters. It was predicted that a structured camp experience which makes clearer the connection between a youngster's behavior and the resultant reinforcement should have the effect of making the students perceive themselves to be more in control of events and thus more internal. If this is true, then the longer the camp experience, the more internal the youngsters should become.

METHOD

Subjects

The students who participated in the camp experience were seventh, eighth, and ninth graders from Title 1 schools in the city of Atlanta. Students were chosen by their high school counselors, who, in turn, were instructed to select youngsters who might benefit from an outdoor structured camp experience. During the summer these numbers were supplemented by canvassing done by community school directors. The modal age of the youngsters was 13. Ninety-five percent of the 261 participating male students were Negro, while five percent were white.

Procedure

The Nowicki-Strickland scale is a paper and pencil measure consisting of 40 questions which are answered yes or no. The yes-no rather than the forced choice format was used to make the task easier for younger and lower social class youngsters. The items sample a variety of situations (If you find a four leaf clover, do you believe it will bring you good luck?) and persons (Most of the time do you think your parents listen to what you have to say?). This wide sampling yields a measure of a generalized expectancy of reinforcement, which parallels in children an adult measure of the locus of control developed by Rotter (12). Reliability estimates are satisfactory at all grade levels tested ($N = 1732$, grades three through 12, test-retest reliabilities from .67 to .79). Considerable evidence of construct validity is presented elsewhere (8, 9, 14, 15). The camping agenda provided five and one-half days of outdoor education and camping experience (from Monday morning to Saturday afternoon). There were seven individual weekly sessions with a special session on the eighth week in which selected students from the first seven weeks were invited back. The campers during the first seven sessions spent five and one-half days at the camp site with a camp-out experience coming on Thursday night. There were about 60 campers for each of the first four weekly sessions and 30 for each of the last four weekly sessions. This numerical arrangement was made necessary by the fact that the camp site had to be shared with another agency from the fifth week on. For the first four weeks the students were divided into three groups which stayed at three separate cottages, each with its own two counselors. There was spirited competition among the three groups or "tribes." From the fifth week on, the camp was shared with youngsters from another agency, and the camp youngsters stayed in one cottage.

The schedule for the campers was organized around such activities as camp craft, fishing, swimming, arts and crafts, canoeing, conservation classes, and nature study. There was some free time for the youngsters to follow their own pursuits. However, the overall attitude of the program was to emphasize structured working together to accomplish goals. To accomplish this, a number of conservation projects, among other tasks, were completed by groups of campers. Campers were reinforced socially at every opportunity. For example, Friday evening was a high point of the camp program when an "Indian ceremony" was conducted. At this ceremony both the youngsters and the staff dressed in homemade Indian garb, and each student was individually introduced into "brave-hood" by a counselor who gave him an Indian name (for example, Tall Oak) and recounted an *actual* deed showing how the student deserved to become a brave (such as paddling a canoe over one mile).

The students were tested twice for each weekly session. The first testing session took place during Monday morning in the gymnasium on the high school grounds from which the students left for the camp site. The students were assured that their responses would be kept secret and that it was very important that they answer the questions just the way they felt. The Nowicki-Strickland locus of control scale for children (9) was then handed out and the students were instructed that the examiner would read each question aloud, and that they should check the "Yes" place if they felt the answer to the statement was Yes or mostly Yes, or the "No" place if they felt the answer to the question was No or mostly No. Each of the 40 questions was then read aloud to equate testing time and assure understanding. The second testing was held five and one-half days later on Saturday morning in the dining hall of the camp. The procedure was similar to that of the first testing session.

Results

Table 1 presents the results the t tests computed for each weekly session, as well as the overall t test for all eight weeks. The results show complete support for the major hypothesis. Indeed, the students became more internal ($t = 5.93, \ldots p < .005$). The only week which showed any score in the external direction was the sixth one.

As predicted, an analysis of the Nowicki-Strickland scores for those youngsters ($n = 27$) who returned for the extra week's session indicated that scores continued to become more internal with more time spent at camp ($F = 21.56; \ldots p = <.001$).

Further analysis of the specific items showed that significant changes in an internal direction had occurred in 10 of the items ($p < .05$). These items were quite general, ranging from "Do you feel that when good things happen they happen because of hard work?" to "Are some kids just born lucky?"

TABLE 1
SUMMARY OF t TESTS FOR PRE- AND POST-NOWICKI-STRICKLAND LOCUS OF CONTROL SCORES FOR EACH WEEKLY SESSION

Week	N	Pretest	Posttest	t
1	28	16.67	15.28	2.43
2	35	16.22	15.25	1.52**
3	54	17.27	15.37	4.34
4	54	16.27	14.88	2.76****
5	31	18.22	17.54	1.10***
6	27	17.03	17.11	.13
7	32	16.31	14.12	2.05*
8	30	13.70	12.63	2.04*
Total	261	16.48	15.25	5.93****

*Significant at .05; **Significant at .01; ***Significant at .005; ****Significant at .0005.

Discussion

The statistical results indicated that the camping experience had a definite effect on the campers in terms of locus of control changes. These changes were found with a general measure of locus of control on items that were *not* specific to the camping experience itself. It is suggested that the camping experience made the youngsters feel more in control of events and better able to see the connection between their behavior and the results of their behavior in terms of reinforcement. The most significant finding was that the trend toward a more internal perception of control was not only maintained in the group of youngsters who returned for the extra session, but was continued. Whether it was the additional time, the fact that relationships between the staff and the youngsters were allowed to deepen, or some combination of these and other factors, these youngsters seemed to benefit, in terms of their locus of control, from the longer camp experience. The continued trend toward internality in the group that returned suggests that the changes were not due to errors of measurement or chance but reflect effects of the camp program. It is interesting to note that the final mean score for campers who experienced two weeks of camp was similar to that of white males in the standardization sample for the Nowicki-Strickland scale (9).

The least amount of change in the internal direction came during the fifth and sixth week sessions. This corresponds to the time when the camp began to share the site with youngsters from another agency. The fact that the emphasis of the other agency was not focused on clarifying the behavior consequence relationship may have had a negative effect on the camp project.

The results of this study, though, must only be taken as suggestive and generalized with care for a number of reasons, not the least of which is the lack of a control group and the lack of experimental control of procedures in the camp program. The former came as a result of scheduling difficulties and the inability to get teenage inner-city youngsters to volunteer to sit down for two sessions a week and take tests. Test results gathered the following fall on black high school students ($n=25$) indicated that scores became more external on retesting but not significantly so. The latter, the lack of experimental control of camp procedures, could be handled by adopting experimental designs used in applied behavior modification projects (10, 16). Future projects should seek to combine an experimental manipulation with controls.

SUMMARY

Inner-city teenagers ($n=261$) experienced a structured camp program for a week. It was predicted and found that this experience led to a change toward internality, in the locus of control orientation of these youngsters. The trend toward internality continued in a group of youngsters ($n=27$) who returned for an additional week. Item analyses revealed the specific items on which the changes occurred and indicated that a rather general change of orientation had occurred. The results were discussed in terms of social learning theory and suggestions were made to improve future programs of this sort.

There is a continuing controversy among developmental and social psychologists about how the learning of social behavior takes place. Psychologists adhering to the operant conditioning approach of B. F. Skinner would explain the attitude changes of the youngsters at the camp in terms of reinforcement, as Nowicki and Barnes did. It is also possible, however, to explain the changes as having resulted from the campers' exposure to a new set of adult models. Such an explanation would be consistent with the social learning theory developed and elaborated by Albert Bandura (1969), who believes that reinforcement alone is possible only if the behavior to be reinforced is already in the learner's repertoire. Therefore, if a new response is to be acquired, it will probably be picked up through the learner's imitating other people.

The two points of view are not really contradictory, although they have generated many arguments. Bandura does not reject reinforcement, which he says can have a facilitating effect, and which can enter the picture in many ways—for example, through the child's self-reinforcing feeling of satisfaction when he realizes he has acceptably imitated the model's behavior. Skinner accepts the precept that self-reinforcement may take place, but he and his followers are little concerned about it. Instead, they are interested in how reinforcement can be applied and manipulated by the experimenter. Unless variables can be controlled and manipulated by the experimenter, the experiment is neither replicable nor scientific; it is obviously impractical, therefore, to conduct experiments in which the independent variable —reinforcement—is controlled by the subject.

Imitation also attracts little attention from the Skinnerians, who are relatively unconcerned about how a response happens to be in a learner's repertoire; they are interested in response reinforcement only as a means to get the subject to acquire new ways of behaving. The disagreement between the two schools of thought is more about what is significant in learning than it is about fundamental processes, although Bandura thinks that social learning is much more complex than the Skinnerians conceive it to be.

A disagreement about what is significant may, however, have important consequences in how we deal with children. Both approaches have value for parents and teachers, whom Skinnerians are likely to tell, "Stop worrying about misbehavior; just be sure to reinforce the responses that will lead to the kind of positive behavior you want the child to display." Bandura's followers are likely to say, "You can't continually hover over a child, waiting for him to do something positive so that you can reinforce him. The best course of action is to expose him to a good model—you, for example—a model who will consistently display the kind of behavior you want to see in him."

The rationale of the Skinnerians underlies experiments and demonstrations in which the clever manipulations of reinforcement schedules cause misbehaving children to abandon disruptive and unproductive behavior forms and to spend increasing amounts of time in behavior that is prosocial and self-fulfilling. Bandura-type social learning experiments, like those of Mary B. Harris (4.4), follow a form in which the willingness of children to share the prizes they have won is influenced by the generosity of a model.

Both approaches have their value for teachers and parents, of course. The work of the Skinnerians provides us with techniques that can be used to ameliorate problem behavior, while social learning research supports the axiom that "honesty is the best policy" in dealing with children, who are much more attentive to what we do than to what we say; and if they turn out to be neither better nor more effective than we are, perhaps we should not be surprised: we have only ourselves to blame.

Bandura's position, incidentally, has been fairly well supported by research findings. In a classical study conducted by Bandura and F. J. McDonald (1963), children saw and heard an adult model express views on the seriousness of a misdemeanor that were contrary to a point of view the children themselves had expressed earlier. Some of the children were reinforced by the experimenter for changing their views to match the model's, and others were not. Still other children saw no model but were reinforced for changing their views. Test items administered subsequent to the experiment indicated that exposure to the model had a significant effect on the children's views, but that reinforcement had little effect, regardless of whether the children saw the model or not.

Studies such as Bandura and McDonald's have not, however, stilled the controversy. Some psychologists claim that making responses similar to those of a model is in itself reinforcing, and experiments have been conducted to substantiate this theory. Gerald B. Adams and Norman H. Hamm, who have contributed the second article (4.2) in this section, discuss both the controversy and the studies supporting the different interpretations of what happens in social learning situations. The second part of their paper reports an experiment in which kindergarten children were either reinforced or not reinforced for performing a simple task, after which they saw a film of an adult model who behaved aggressively to a Bobo doll (a life-sized rubber clown doll with a weighted base, which enables it to return to an upright position after it has been knocked over). Because their results showed that reinforcement prior to viewing the aggressive model led the children to display more aggression, the authors support the view that imitation may in itself be reinforcing. The dependent variable in this study was the amount of aggressiveness, imitative and otherwise, that each child subsequently displayed when he was left alone in a playroom containing a Bobo doll and some other toys.

4.2

A partial test of the "contiguity" and "generalized imitation" theories of the social modeling process

Gerald R. Adams and
Norman H. Hamm

While a great deal is known about the variables that control the imitative process, several different explanations have been offered to account for the phenomenon. Of these, two seem to stand out in the recent research literature. Bandura (3, 4) maintains that imitation learning is most adequately accounted for by a contiguity theory of learning. He proposes that imitation learning occurs when an observer witnesses some chain of modeled responses which are then acquired by the observer through contiguous association of sensory, perceptual, and symbolic responses that possess cue properties. At some later date, these cue properties are capable of eliciting similar model-like responses by the observer. In contrast to Bandura's position, Baer and Sherman (1) and Baer, Peterson, and Sherman (2) maintain that similarity of responding is a rewarding dimension. When the observer matches the modeling stimuli and is consistently rewarded, behavioral similarity acquires secondary reinforcing properties. Hence, a child will perform precise imitation responses because of their reward value.

Evidence has been provided by Baer and Sherman (1) in support of their operant approach to imitation learning. These investigators exposed children to a nodding, mouthing, talking, and bar-pressing puppet. In an instrumental conditioning situation, all imitative responses except bar-pressing were socially reinforced by verbalizations from the puppet. The imitation of the bar-pressing responses, which were never reinforced, were found to increase in frequency when reinforcement followed the nodding, mouthing, and talking responses. The increase in imitative bar-pressing was taken to indicate that a generalized similarity of responding between puppet and child could be a reinforcing stimulus dimension in control of the child's behavior. More recently,

Reprinted from the *Journal of Genetic Psychology*, 123 (1973): 145–154, with permission of the authors and The Journal Press. Copyright 1973 by The Journal Press.

Parton and Fouts (13) found that children would maximize similarity in a situation in which similarity was contingent on pressing the light which matched one lit by the *E*.

In contrast to Baer and Sherman's view, Bandura, Ross, and Ross (7) suggest that acquisition of matching responses may take place through a process of contiguity, while reinforcement of model influences primarily the performance of imitation learning. To verify this contention, Bandura (4) attempted to separate the learning and performance effects of reinforcement. Children observed a film-mediated model that performed unique physical and verbal aggressive behavior. Three treatment conditions were established, model-rewarded, model-punished, and a no-consequence group. The models were either rewarded, punished, or received no consequence, respectively, for their aggressive behavior. A postexposure test revealed that the model-rewarded group imitated more different classes of responses, followed by the no-consequence group, and then the model-punished group. Following the first three treatment conditions and test for imitative behavior, children in all three groups were offered attractive incentives that were contingent on the reproduction of the model's unique responses. The results of the second performance measure showed that the introduction of a positive incentive removed the initial differences among the three treatment conditions; whereas the model-reward group's imitation was significantly greater than the model-punished and no-consequence group on the first performance measure, the introduction of positive incentives which were contingent upon reproducing the model's responses removed the initial differences between the groups.

As a further test of the theory, Bandura and Barab (5) conducted some preliminary studies to test the contiguity and reinforcement theories of imitation. First, a high level of imitative responses was established in retarded children by the reinforcement of matching responses. Second, these same children were reinforced for matching the behavior of the first *E* but not for the second *E* who modeled a number of responses during the same session. In the third stage of the experiment the reinforcing model demonstrated three sets of responses: (*a*) 20 of the original rewarded responses, (*b*) five nonrewarded and unrelated motor responses interspersed among rewarded modeled responses, and (*c*) a second set of five nonrewarded responses which made them more distinguishable. To increase the discriminability of this last group, all five responses were modeled one after the other.

Five children completed the three-phase program. Two of the children formed a discrimination between the models, never imitating the nonrewarded E, thus providing some supportive evidence for contiguity (discrimination) theory. However, during the third phase, Bandura and Barab reported that the children initially exhibited a tendency toward "generalized imitation"—imitating both rewarded and nonrewarded Es. Bandura proposes that the generalized imitation effect was due to the inability of the Ss to discriminate initially between reinforced and nonreinforced response classes. Thus, the Ss imitated every response that was modeled.

The following quotation perhaps presents Bandura's most cogent indictment of reinforcement theory (4, p. 589):

". . . reinforcement theories of imitation fail to explain the learning of matching responses when the observer does not perform the model's responses during the process of acquisition, and for which reinforcers are not delivered either to the model or to the observer."

However, he may be short-sighted in falsely restricting this deficiency of reinforcement theory to the immediate experimental condition. He fails to examine the S's prior history of reinforcement for imitative behavior and neglects the possibility that imitative behavior may become functionally autonomous. Therefore, the purpose of this study was to test the second criticism—reinforcement theories fail to explain the acquisition of matching responses when reinforcement is not delivered either to the model or to the observer—by controlling the S's immediate history of reinforcement for imitation.

METHOD

Subjects

The Ss were 36 Caucasian kindergarteners from a school located in an upper-lower- to lower-middle-class neighborhood in Omaha, Nebraska. The experimental (reward) and control (nonreward) groups consisted of nine boys and nine girls each. The mean age of the Ss was 65 months.

Apparatus

A 9- by 27-foot research trailer, located near the children's classroom, was used to conduct the experiment. The trailer consisted of two rooms with a one-way mirror. The smaller of the two rooms was designated as the reward-control room. This room contained a small table and two chairs. Placed on the table was an electrical panel box with two rows of lights. The top row of lights was controlled by the E with switches located on the back side of the panel box. The S controlled the bottom row of lights by using push-button switches located directly under each of the three lights. Some small rewards (marbles and trinkets) were placed within reach of the $E,$ but hidden from the immediate view of the $S.$ Also located in the room was a video tape recorder, a television, and a cassette recorder.

The larger room was called the experimental playroom. It contained a Bobo doll, some balls, a mallet and pegboard, a cap gun, cars, toy kitchen utensils, plastic animals, a fire engine, a baseball bat, and an assortment of dolls. This array of toys was similar to those used in Bandura's (4) experimental surprise playroom.

Experimental design and procedure

The experimental modeling used was a derivation of that used by Nelson, Gelfand, and Hartmann (12). The Ss were taken one at a time by the E from the classroom to the reward-control room. The S and a male E were seated at the table with the electrical panel box. The reinforcement of the experimental group was contingent upon matching the responses of the $E.$ The imitative response required was the matching of the same positioned light in the S's row as that which was lit in the E's row. Each time the S matched the E's responses he was rewarded with physical (trinkets and marbles) and verbal ("That's good," "Fine," "Well done") reinforcers. Each S in the experimental group was run until he completed 10 reinforced trials.

The control group performed the same task as the experimental group, with the exception that any imitative responses exhibited were not reinforced. This group was run for a total of 10 consecutive trials regardless of the number of imitative responses exhibited.

The S was then asked to watch on television an adult male model physically and verbally attack a Bobo doll for three minutes. Three distinctive behaviors were exhibited accompanied by highly aggressive verbalizations. These model responses were for the most part those used by Nelson et $al.$ (12). The model kicked the Bobo doll and said, "Out of my way, Bobo"; the model pushed the Bobo doll down, sat on it, and while punching it in the nose said, "Pow, right in the nose"; finally, the model knocked the Bobo down with a mallet while he said, "Sockeroo, stay down." This sequence of unique responses was repeated five times.

Imitating model's aggression: Test I. The *S* was taken into the experimental playroom. The second *E* then joined the first *E* in the reward-control room. The *S* was left in the room alone for eight minutes. After approximately four minutes, the first *E* returned to assure the *S* he was not alone in the trailer. In addition, the *E* told the *S* he would return again with some refreshments and that the *S* was to continue playing with the toys until then.

The first and second *E* served as judges who recorded the matching responses through the one-way mirror. Interrater reliability was established by having the judges score the *S*s independently. Every 15 seconds for eight minutes the judges checked the number of responses that occurred in the following five behavioral categories from Nelson *et al.* (12): (*a*) *imitative physical aggression:* kicking Bobo, sitting on the Bobo and punching him in the nose, hitting Bobo with a mallet; (*b*) *imitative verbal aggression:* "Out of my way, Bobo," "Pow, right in the nose," "Sockeroo, stay down"; (*c*) *partial imitation:* sitting on Bobo but not punching him in the nose, throwing the Bobo down; (*d*) nonimitative aggression: shooting cap gun, aggressing Bobo in ways not demonstrated by the model; and (*e*) *nonaggressive play:* any other play behavior, including standing or sitting with or without toys.

Retention of model's aggression: Test II. The final phase of the experimental procedure consisted of the *E* returning with some attractive refreshments (pretty pictures and juice treats) to the experimental playroom. The *E* asked the *S* to show what the television model did, rewarding him immediately after each imitative response. If the *S* merely verbalized the model's responses, the *E* asked for a demonstration of his behavior (motor and verbal). The judge behind the one-way mirror then recorded the number of matching responses that fit the first two categories of the five previously described.

RESULTS

Before the frequency ratings were subjected to data analysis, interrater reliability was determined for each of the five behavioral categories. Of the 36 *S*s in the experiment, eight *S*s were used to check reliability. For these eight *S*s, two raters were present; one rater was aware of the *S*'s treatment condition, while the second *E* was not. The *reliability coefficients* were (*a*) physical aggression ($r = .98$); (*b*) verbal aggression

$(r=1.00)$; (c) partial aggression $(r=.99)$; (d) nonimitative aggression $(r=.92)$; and (e) nonaggressive play $(r=.98)$.

A χ^2 technique was employed because of the lack of interval data necessary for the use of parametric tests. An overall χ^2 test was completed for each analysis. Binomial tests were then used to make specific comparisons as dictated by the experimental design.

Control versus experimental imitation on test I. Figure 1 contains the mean frequency rating for the control and experimental groups on the five categories of behavior. Figure 1 shows that the experimental group responded with slightly more physical, verbal, and nonimitative responses than the control group. Also, children in both groups manifested more nonaggressive behavior than physical, partial, and nonimitative behavior.

A χ^2 test was performed to identify overall differences between the experimental and control groups on the five rating categories, and a

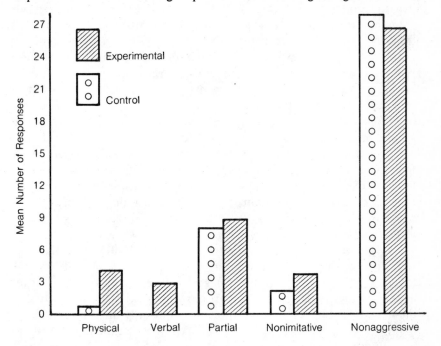

FIGURE 1

MEAN NUMBER OF IMITATIVE, NONIMITATIVE, AND NONAGGRESSIVE PLAY RESPONSES

series of binomial tests were used to examine various group differences. The χ^2 test [showed significant differences]: physical aggression ($p < .001$), verbal aggression ($p < .001$), and nonimitative aggression ($p < .008$).

Control versus experimental retention of imitation on test II. A second χ^2 test examined the retention of physical and verbal aggression when Ss were rewarded for correct imitative responses. Only the first two rating categories were used, since they were the only two modeled on television by the adult. The χ^2 was found to be nonsignificant ... ($p < .80$). However, it should be noted that the difference was in the predicted direction: the experimental group exhibited 31 instances of physical aggression and 17 instances of verbal aggression, as compared to 23 and eight instances, respectively, for the control group.

Practice effects. A χ^2 was completed to determine if there was an increase or decrease in imitation during the first test session. This statistical test was divided into two parts. The first analysis contrasted the experimental group's frequency scores during the first 16 rating periods with the last 16 periods. The second analysis examined the control's frequency ratings in like manner. The test results were nonsignificant ... ($p < .30$) for the experimental group and significant for the control group ... ($p < .02$). While individual comparisons by the binomial test on the control group data revealed no behavioral categories in which significant practice effects occurred, there was a nonsignificant decrease of 79 to 44 partial imitative responses, while the frequency of responding for the other four categories remained relatively constant across trials.

Imitative responses as a function of sex and treatment condition. A final χ^2 analysis examined the frequency of imitative responses as a function of sex and treatment condition. The four reinforcement conditions were (*a*) female (reinforced) experimental group; (*b*) male (reinforced) experimental group; (*c*) female (nonreinforced) control group; and (*d*) male (nonreinforced) control group.

A χ^2 test yielded a significant value ... ($p < .001$). Binomial tests were then completed on each rating category if a χ^2 for that row was found to be significant. All five categories were found to be significant at the .01 level. Individual comparisons (binomial tests) revealed that the male experimental group exhibited significantly more responses ... (p .001) on all five rating categories than the female experimental group, indicating that the experimental male Ss were, in general, more active in the free play situation. Furthermore, the male control group responded with significantly more nonimitative aggression ... ($p < .01$) than the female control group, while the differences between the sexes on the remaining four categories were nonsignificant.

DISCUSSION

The results of this study support the hypothesis that imitation learning is enhanced by prior reinforcement for matching the responses of a model. The χ^2 test revealed that the experimental (reinforced) group emitted significantly more physical, verbal, and nonimitative aggression than the control (nonreinforced) group as a result of prior reinforcement for imitative responses. These results provide further evidence for the position that similarity of responding acquires a reinforcing value through a conditioning procedure (1, 2, 10, 11). A closer examination of an S's prior history of reinforcement for imitative behavior is necessary before one takes the criticism seriously that reinforcement theories fail to explain the learning of imitation when reinforcement is not delivered to the model or to the observer.

As previously mentioned, Bandura maintains that the cognitive equivalent of learned imitative behavior may be acquired during a modeling process but not exhibited in a motoric form unless an incentive is present. In the context of the present study, it might be expected in Test I that the experimental group would emit significantly more imitative aggression than the control group; however, according to Bandura (4) these differences should disappear under an incentive-to-imitate condition. The present study is consistent with Bandura's earlier finding. While the experimental group emitted significantly more imitation in the free play situation (Test I) than the control group, the introduction of an incentive-to-imitate condition (Test II) diminished the significant difference originally found in Test I. Apparently, prior history of reinforcement for imitation does affect the level of imitative behavior emitted in a situation where neither the model nor the observer is reinforced; however, prior reinforcement does not appear to influence the amount of *learning* when Ss are measured for imitation under an incentive to imitate condition.

From reinforcement theory, it was expected that the effects of secondary reinforcement, and hence imitation behavior, would diminish across trials, reflecting an extinction effect. However, such an effect did not occur; the results for the experimental group demonstrated that responding during the first 16 trials did not decrease significantly. Such a result might provide negative evidence for the "generalized imitation" view of modeling processes. However, the apparent absence of extinction may be due to a disinhibitory effect. That is, upon entering the playroom the novelty of the situation may have served to inhibit aggressive behavior; subsequently, as the novelty of the situation diminished, Ss may have become less inhibited as they adapted to the situation. Hollenberg and Sperry (9) completed a doll play aggression study which provides some support for the preceding explanation. An examination of their control (nonpunished) group revealed that aggressive responses increased from session to session, and that this steady increase in aggressive responding may be interpreted in terms of weakening of inhibitions. Perhaps, in the present study, no change in aggressive responding occurred across trials because any extinction may have been countered by a disinhibition of aggressive behavior.

Sex of S was found to be an important variable in the present study. As previously mentioned, the results clearly demonstrated that the control males exhibited significantly more nonimitative aggression than the control females. However, the sexes did not differ significantly on the remaining four rating categories of behavior. This last finding questions, in part, Bandura, Ross, and Ross's suggestion that males exhibit significantly more total aggression than females. Perhaps the hypothesis that males are more susceptible than females to aggressive modeling needs further testing.

An analysis of the experimental group data demonstrated that males exhibited significantly higher response frequencies on all five rating categories than did the females. At face value, such a result suggests that male children, in general, are more active in a playroom setting than females. However, interpretation of the preceding results may be difficult, since both the E and television model were males. Sex of model effects have been noted in the literature. For example, Bandura et al. (6, 8) found that males exhibit more aggression following exposure to an aggressive male model than do female Ss. Conversely, female Ss exposed to a female model perform considerably more imitative aggression than do the male Ss. Therefore, the male Ss in the present study may have imitated more because historically they have been more frequently reinforced by an adult male to act aggressively.

It might also be noted that the notion that girls are prone to imitate verbal aggression (3), while boys are more likely to imitate physical aggression was not supported. It was found that the control male Ss and control female Ss did not emit significantly more verbal or physical aggression. However, as previously mentioned, the male control group did emit significantly more nonimitative aggression than the control female group. Hence, it might be noted that differential imitation of verbal and physical aggression by males and females might appear at a later stage of development in children.

SUMMARY

Imitative behavior was studied with the use of 36 kindergarten children who were either reinforced or not reinforced for imitative behavior prior to observing a male model exhibit aggressive behaviors. The children were tested for imitative aggressive behaviors in an eight-minute free-play situation, by means of a five-category rating scale. The results revealed that the reinforced group emitted significantly more physical, verbal, and nonimitative aggression than the nonreinforced group. A second test examined the retention of the model's aggressive behavior under an incentive condition. The incentive condition diminished the initial differences found in the first test, revealing a nonsignificant difference between the reinforced and nonreinforced groups. Hence, the study provided support for both the "contiguity" and "generalized imitation" theories of social modeling.

Adams and Hamm's use of filmed aggressiveness reminds us that children are exposed to a great deal of televised violence. The prevalence of such programs has seriously concerned experts and leaders in law enforcement, psychiatry, child care, and social welfare, because extensive exposure to these programs would seem to encourage children to be aggressive and destructive, and to create a social climate characterized by lawlessness and interpersonal violence. Although some research studies do suggest a relationship between watching violent programs on television and aggressive tendencies, the findings are not clear cut. A longitudinal study by L. D. Eron *et al.* (1972) found some connection between preference for violent television programs at age nine and aggressiveness ten years later, but the relationship existed only for males, and there were puzzling inconsistencies in the results. S. Feshbach and R. D. Singer (1971) found that watching televised violence actually reduced aggressiveness in preadolescent boys. However, a great deal of research employing methods like those of Adams and Hamm strongly suggests that what children and adults see in films or on television has a significant effect on their subsequent behavior (J. H. Bryan and T. Schwartz, 1971).

One consistent finding in aggression research is that boys are consistently more hostile and destructive than girls. In article 4.3, Ann McIntyre reports on her observations of direct and indirect aggression in both verbal and physical forms, in the preschoolers she studied. McIntyre was interested in how the sexes differ with respect to expression of aggressiveness. With boys, increased social activity led to decreased physical aggression and increased verbal aggression. Verbal expression of aggression apparently served as an outlet for the boys' aggression, for the more frequently they aggressed verbally, the less frequently they aggressed physically. With girls, social interaction and aggression of all types were positively correlated, although their overall rate of physical aggression was much lower than the boys' rate. McIntyre's finding that one way to control boys' physical aggressiveness is to increase their social activity, has practical value for people who work with children.

4.3 Sex differences in children's aggression

Ann McIntyre

Murphy's (1937) study demonstrated a relationship between social interaction and aggression in preschoolers but failed to find sex a relevant variable; though sex differences in aggression have been occasionally reported elsewhere in the literature, there have been few attempts to clarify them. Comparing verbal and physical modes of aggression, Durrett (1959) found girls more verbally aggressive than boys. In Feshbach's (1969) study, adolescent girls were more indirectly aggressive than boys, suggesting the importance of a style dimension. However, none of these studies included dominance or noncompliance under the rubric of ag-

4. Social development

gression. This omission seems to be important, since these forms of aggression are more culturally acceptable in females than are the more explicit aggressions.

The present study investigated whether sex differences in frequency of aggression among preschool children are related to differences in rates of social interaction, and whether girls manifest aggression in different ways than boys do. Included was the consideration of differences in the *style* dimension—contrasting the active, direct aspect of aggression with the more passive, indirect aspect (e.g., bossiness vs. noncompliance, or scolding vs. teasing)—and differences in *mode* of expression, i.e., physical vs. verbal.

METHOD

Subjects

Twenty-seven *S*s (CA = 2 yr. 9 mo. to 4 yr. 2 mo.; 14 boys, 13 girls) enrolled in two preschool programs were observed. Families of the *S*s [subjects] in both programs were predominantly middle class; both programs were interracial.

Social activity rate (SAR) and aggressive behavior rates. The SAR and aggressive behavior rates were independently established by two *O*s [observers] for each *S* on the basis of 10 5-min. observations over separate 2-wk. periods.

For SAR, the frequency of both verbal and nonverbal events with peers or adults was recorded. The inter-*O* reliability for SAR, recorded simultaneously by two *O*s on a nonstudy sample, was .88 (Pearson *r*). An event was credited each time *S* had a new opportunity to interact with another person, whether or not *S* initiated the event (adapted from Stevenson & Stevenson, 1960).

Aggressive behavior rates for each *S* were established for four classes of behavior: direct physical aggression, indirect physical aggression, direct verbal aggression, and indirect verbal aggression. The inter-*O* reliabilities for aggressive behavior classes, recorded simultaneously by two *O*s on a nonstudy sample, ranged from .77 to .93 (Pearson *r*).

RESULTS

Aggression and SAR. Significantly more boys than girls had high rates of social interacting when *S*s were ranked according to their SAR scores

(Mann-Whitney $U=41$, $z=2.43$, $p<.01$). Aggressive behaviors were categorized as physical (P-Agg), verbal (V-Agg), direct (D-Agg), and indirect (In-Agg). Pearson r correlations between SAR and aggression rates are shown in Table 1. For the total sample, all types of aggression were significantly and positively correlated with social activity, supporting Murphy's (1937) finding. The same pattern was true for the subsample of girls. However, only V-Agg was positively correlated with SAR for boys. P-Agg, D-Agg, and In-Agg were all significantly but negatively correlated with SAR for boys.

TABLE 1
CORRELATIONS OF SOCIAL ACTIVITY AND AGGRESSION RATES

Group	Tot-Agg	P-Agg	V-Agg	D-Agg	In-Agg
Boys	−.69**	−.76**	.72**	−.73**	−.76**
Girls	.72**	.62*	.74**	.60*	.85**
All Ss	.52**	.32*	.64**	.50**	.50**

*$p<.05$.
**$p<.01$.

Components of aggression. The Pearson r correlations between aggression behavior frequencies are shown in Table 2. All significant correlations were positive. While all categories of aggression were significantly intercorrelated for girls, among boys, V-Agg was not correlated with any of the other categories of aggression, although P-Agg, D-Agg, and In-Agg were significantly correlated with each other. The assumption that In-Agg is related to more explicit forms of aggression is consistently supported in the case of girls. In-Agg was clearly related to P-Agg and D-Agg for boys, but not to V-Agg, results which partially support this assumption.

TABLE 2
INTERCORRELATIONS OF AGGRESSION CATEGORIES

Agg types	All Ss			Boys			Girls		
	V-Agg	D-Agg	In-Agg	V-Agg	D-Agg	In-Agg	V-Agg	D-Agg	In-Agg
P-Agg	.64*	.91*	.74*	−.36	.99*	.99*	.83*	.93*	.73*
V-Agg		.88*	.80*		−.32	−.37		.89*	.82*
D-Agg			.74*			.99*			.72*

*$p<.01$.

Modality and style. The *Mann-Whitney U statistic* was used to test for sex differences on each category of aggression by ranking Ss according to the frequencies with which they manifested the specific kinds of aggression. Boys were high on P-Agg significantly more often than girls ... ($p < .003$), but there were no significant differences for V-Agg, D-Agg, or In-Agg. Within-group comparisons on modality were made by classifying each S according to whether P-Agg exceeded V-Agg or V-Agg exceeded P-Agg. All girls using P-Agg and V-Agg differentially (12 of 13 Ss) used V-Agg preferentially ($\chi^2 = 10.08$, $p < .01$). Nine boys used P-Agg preferentially and five boys used more V-Agg, a nonsignificant difference. Similar comparisons were made for style, with all boys using D-Agg preferentially ($\chi^2 = 12.07$, $p < .001$) and 12 of the 13 girls using more D-Agg than In-Agg ($\chi^2 = 7.69$, $p < .01$).

DISCUSSION

Upon first analysis, Murphy's (1937) conclusion that there is a relationship between the frequencies of social activity and aggression is supported by the present findings. However, more detailed analyses of the data suggest that the direction of this relationship depends on the quantity and quality of aggression expressed. Verbal aggression, of similar frequency in boys and girls, was positively correlated with social activity in both sexes. For boys (among whom there were many more high physical aggressors than in the girls' group), physical aggression was negatively correlated with social activity, while for girls—who seldom used high rates of physical aggression—the correlation between social activity and physical aggression was positive. The possibility that this directional difference might be a simple sex difference is contradicted by the fact that inspection of the data revealed two discriminable patterns of boys' aggression. High social activity was associated with high verbal aggression but low physical aggression for one subgroup, while another group was marked by low social activity associated with low verbal aggression but high physical aggression. (The number of Ss was too small to apply statistical tests to these patterns.) In other words, a subgroup of boys showed a pattern like the girls', suggesting that the direction of the social interaction-aggression relationship depends primarily on the modality and relative frequency of aggression rather than on the sex of the aggressor.

Why is physical aggression inversely related to social activity while the relation of verbal aggression to social activity is positive? It seems possible that aggressing physically keeps others away from you, while verbal aggression does not. This is a directional hypothesis that cannot be tested by the current data, although it has some face validity. This hypothesis is limited to the effects of physical aggression on interpersonal interactions. It should also be noted that the interpersonal nature of these interactions was objectively defined here; they might or might not be subjectively experienced as interpersonal situations by the *S*s themselves.

There was a striking sex difference in the use of the physical modality for aggressive expression. Girls used physical aggression so much less than boys that the aggression of girls was predominantly verbal. For both sexes, aggression was predominantly direct in style. This latter finding is not consistent with Feshbach's (1969) and suggests that, at least for preschoolers, modality differences, not style differences, explain the aggression differences between boys and girls. An alternative explanation for the discrepancies between the Feshbach findings and those of this study may be the differences in the ways indirect aggression was defined; i.e., the inclusion of noncompliance under indirect aggression here may have increased the total amount of indirect aggression for boys more than for girls, obscuring real differences. (This hypothesis could not be tested because of the way the data were originally recorded.) Another alternative reason for the discrepancy may be that the aggressions observed occurred under quite different circumstances. Feshbach observed aggression occurring in a single, contrived situation that provided little opportunity for physical aggression, whereas the present study observed aggressions over many spontaneous situations.

One obvious way to reduce aggressiveness in children is to get them to substitute prosocial for antisocial behavior. A child who is engaged in sharing, cooperating, and reassuring forms of behavior cannot at the same time behave in aggressive or destructive ways. Research reviewed by J. H. Bryan and T. Schwartz (1971) shows that the filmed behavior of models can be used to produce behavior in subjects that is characterized by courage and self-sacrifice, or by aggression. Other experiments also show that exposing children to a live model behaving in prosocial, altruistic ways encourages similar behavior. The study in this section by Mary B. Harris (article 4.4) demonstrates this principle. Her results also show that although the observation of a generous model encourages generosity in children, they are much more likely to share with others if the model shares with them.

4.4 Models, norms, and sharing

Mary B. Harris

In the past several years, many research studies have attempted to investigate some of the factors mediating altruistic behaviors. In particular, the effects of observing a model upon children's subsequent sharing have been investigated in several recent studies (Bryan & London, 1970; Bryan & Walbek, 1970a, 1970b; Harris, 1970; Hartup & Coates, 1967; Midlarsky & Bryan, 1967; Rosenhan & White, 1967). Neither direct nor vicarious reinforcement appears necessary for the elicitation of such sharing, as in many of these studies the children shared under conditions in which they believed their generosity to be unknown. Moreover, it has been shown that the effect of a model's actual deeds is far greater than that of his verbal comments (Bryan & Walbek, 1970a).

One explanation for the effect of observing a generous model is that seeing the model reminds the child of the appropriateness of an internalized norm of social responsibility (Berkowitz & Daniels, 1963) or of giving (Leeds, 1963). Some evidence that children do indeed hold such a norm is suggested by the report of Bryan & Walbek (1970a, b) that children do indeed verbally report that sharing is desirable and recommend it to other children. However, the evidence does not exist, as Berkowitz & Daniels (1963) have postulated, that increased salience of this norm is the factor responsible for the increase in generosity following exposure to an altruistic model. The research by Bryan and Walbek (1970a, b) indicates in fact that neither the model's verbalizations nor the subject's own preachings were significantly correlated with his donations, although both might be expected to correlate with salience

Reprinted from Report No. ED 046 512, Educational Resources Information Center (ERIC), U.S. Office of Education, 1970, with permission of the author.

of the social responsibility norm. The present study attempted more directly to assess whether or not increased salience of this norm is indeed responsible for the facilitating effect of observing an altruistic model, by assessing indirectly through a questionnaire the salience of sharing for the child. If salience is indeed the mediating factor, one would expect it to be correlated both with the model's behavior and with the child's subsequent generosity.

Another possible interpretation of the modeling effect on altruism is that true generosity is not involved; rather, what occurs is a very specific imitation of the modeled behavior, which can be explained in terms of demand characteristics of the experiment, learning the rules of the game, or simply an innate or learned tendency for children to imitate adults. Very few of the studies on sharing, with the exception of one by Midlarsky and Bryan (1967), which did find some generalized altruism, have attempted to investigate the generality of the sharing response. Most studies, moreover, have permitted the subject only a dichotomous choice of whether or not to share, which makes it difficult to assess more subtle modeling effects. A previous study by the author (Harris, 1970) which provided children the option of sharing with either charity or the model while unobserved indicated that, although amount of sharing was unaffected by whether the child had previously been the recipient or observer of sharing, he tended to imitate the model's behavior in determining whether and with whom he shared. These results are consistent with both a social norm interpretation and a specific imitation explanation of sharing. The fact that subjects receiving chips from the model were subsequently no more generous than those who merely observed her share made it possible, however, to reject the idea that a reciprocity norm (Gouldner, 1960) was affecting sharing in this instance. The present study attempted to assess whether or not the child is simply imitating the model's specific response or demonstrating a more generalized altruism by replicating the alternatives of the Harris (1970) experiment with the addition of an unappealing charity to which the model donated.

Third and fifth grade children were exposed to a model who shared with either a Mental Health charity container, with the child, or not at all. Their own subsequent sharing with the model, Mental Health, the presumably more appealing Toys for Tots charity, or no one, was observed, unknown to the subjects. It was predicted that generalized imitation of altruism would indeed occur, such that children who had seen the model share with Mental Health would indeed be more likely to share with Toys for Tots than those who had not.

The specific hypotheses of the study were therefore as follows:

1) Salience of the social responsibility norm, as measured by the child's first spontaneous mention of sharing on a questionnaire, will be greater in the conditions in which the model shares than in a control condition.

2) Salience of the social responsibility norm will be greater for children who share than for those who do not.

3) Children in the model-shares-with charity (MSC) condition will share more chips with Mental Health than those in the other conditions.

4) Children in the MSC condition will share more chips with Toys for Tots than those in the other conditions.

5) Children in the model-shares-with-subject (MSS) condition will share more chips with the model than those in the other conditions.

6) The total number of chips shared will be greater in both experimental conditions than in the control (no sharing) condition.

7) As previous studies have consistently found, fifth grade children will share more chips than third grade children.

METHOD

The procedures and apparatus of the study were very similar to those used by Harris (1970).

Subjects, model, and experimenter

The subjects were 156 third and fifth grade boys and girls from two Albuquerque public schools. A young woman served as the model (M). She was identified by different names and dressed in different clothes, so that the subjects would not identify her as the same person each time. A female graduate student experienced in dealing with children served as the E.

Equipment and apparatus

The study was conducted in a trailer parked on the school grounds. The apparatus, identified as a game, consisted of a yellow box with large red and green signal lights, 9 smaller lights which flashed in random patterns, and a chute through which marbles were dispensed. The signal lights indicated whose turn it was and the smaller lights marked the individual trials. Both sets of lights and the marble dispenser were operated by remote control from another room in the trailer. Marbles dispensed in the first part of the game were pink and those in the second part were green.

The apparatus was positioned on a table in front of a one-way mirror, so that *E* could observe the apparatus, *S,* and *M* from the adjoining room. Four small glass jars to collect the chips won by *M* and *S* in Parts I and II of the study rested on the table, along with a cylindrical box labeled Mental Health and a rectangular box covered with pictures of appealing children and labeled Toys for Tots.

Procedure

The details of the procedure are described more fully in Harris (1970). *S*s were run individually by *E*, who explained to *S* and *M* that she was testing a new game, in which each of them could win marbles when his signal lights were on. They were informed that their marbles could be traded in for prizes later on and that the person who won the most marbles could share, if he chose, with the other person, with Mental Health, or with some poor children who did not have many toys. *E* then left the room to turn on the apparatus and "do some work."

During this phase of the experiment (Part I) *M* won by far the most marbles and either gave five marbles to the subject, shared five marbles with Mental Health, or kept all her marbles. In all conditions the number of marbles won by *M* and *S* was arranged so that *S* always ended up with 15 marbles and *M* with 20.

Immediately after *M* had shared or not, *E* returned, showed *S* and *M* how to deposit their jars of marbles in opaque bags, and informed them that they would now be playing the game again, this time for green marbles, exchangeable for different prizes. *E* reminded them that the one winning the most marbles could share and asked them to notify her after the game was all over and they had put away their marbles. During this time, *M* remarked that she was in a hurry and hoped it wouldn't take long, to provide a rationale for her later abrupt departure.

After *E* had left the room, *S* and *M* received marbles on the same predetermined schedule in all conditions, one in which *S* received 25 marbles and *M* only three. After *M*'s last trial, when *S* had one more turn, she looked at her watch and rushed off, asking *S* to please put away her marbles and apologize to *E*. All *S*s continued gathering their marbles for the last trial and put them away before notifying *E* that they were through.

After reentering the room and hearing *S*'s explanations of *M*'s departure, *E* then asked a predetermined series of questions. The *E* began with asking whether *S* had enjoyed the game and whether he thought *M* had enjoyed it and if other adults and children would enjoy it. The four crucial questions, embedded in the middle of the interviews, were, "Did you understand the rules?" "Can you tell me what they were?" "Do you remember what you could do with the marbles?" and "What were you supposed to do with the marbles?" Other questions about the lights and patterns followed; *S*s were asked if they had guessed that the patterns were controlled by a computer and were asked to try to help think of a name for the game. The purpose of the latter sequence of questions was to divert the *S* from the idea of sharing (never mentioned by *E*), so that if he did later discuss the experiment with others, it would not be mentioned. All *S*s were requested very strongly not to mention the project to others who had not yet had a turn and were told that a man would come to pick up their marbles and bring them their prizes after everyone had played the game.

RESULTS

The mean number of marbles shared with Mental Health (MH), Toys for Tots (TT) and the model (M) in the different conditions are shown in Table 1.

An *analysis of variance* across all twelve groups revealed significant differences in the number of marbles shared with Mental Health . . . ($p < .02$) . . . and with the model . . . ($p < .001$) . . . , as well as in the total number of marbles shared . . . ($p < .001$) . . . , with the differences in the number of marbles shared with Toys for Tots reaching only a borderline significance level . . . ($p < .10$) . . . Collapsing across age/sex categories, the three experimental conditions differed on the measures of donations to Mental Health, the model, and total sharing at the $p < .001$ level and on donations to Toys for Tots at the $p < .01$ level.

Mann-Whitney U tests were conducted between pairs of experimental conditions on the measures of total marbles shared, marbles shared with *M*, marbles shared with MH, marbles shared with TT, and marbles shared with MH + TT. On all measures but marbles shared

TABLE 1
MEAN NUMBERS OF CHIPS SHARED

		Third grade boys	Third grade girls	Fifth grade boys	Fifth grade girls
Condition: Model shares with charity					
Shared with: children	MH*	.69	.92	1.46	1.54
	TT	.23	1.23	1.23	2.62
	M	.00	.92	1.46	1.15
	Total	.92	3.07	4.15	5.30
Condition: Model shares with subject					
Shared with:	MH	.46	.15	.54	1.00
	TT	.46	.15	.62	2.23
	M	3.30	3.61	6.15	5.38
	Total	4.23	3.92	7.31	8.62
Condition: Model refuses to share (control condition)					
Shared with:	MH	.38	.07	.30	.15
	TT	.23	.07	.69	.15
	M	0	.00	.15	.46
	Total	.61	.15	1.15	.77

*MH—Mental Health
TT—Toys for Tots
M—Model

with TT, Ss in the control group shared significantly fewer marbles than Ss in either of the two experimental conditions at the $p < .04$ level or beyond, using two-tailed tests; however the MSS group differed from the control condition on the measure of chips shared with TT at only the $p < .06$ level, two-tailed. Comparisons of the two experimental conditions revealed that Ss in the MSC condition shared significantly more marbles with MH and with MH + TT than Ss in the MSS condition, although not significantly more with TT; Ss in the MSS condition shared significantly more marbles with the model and also a significantly greater total number of marbles than Ss in the MSC condition.

On all four measures of sharing (including total marbles shared), Mann-Whitney U tests revealed that fifth grade children shared significantly more marbles than third grade children at the $p < .03$ level or beyond. No significant sex differences on any of the measures were found.

Inspection of the questionnaire data revealed that most Ss who mentioned sharing did so in response to the question, "Do you remember what you could do with the marbles?" Therefore, the data were trichotomized by whether the S mentioned sharing before that question, during or after it, or not at all.

The numbers of Ss in each category who did and did not share are presented in Table 2.

TABLE 2
MENTION OF SHARING BY SUBJECTS WHO DID AND DID NOT SHARE

	Shared	Did not share
Before question 8	26	14
Question 8 or after	35	54
No mention	10	17

$\chi^2 = 8.29$, $p < .02$

Chi-square tests revealed that the number of Ss who mentioned sharing at each point did not differ significantly for the three experimental conditions, although the relationship did reach a borderline level of significance . . . ($p < .10$). The relationship between mention of sharing and actual sharing was significant at the $p < .02$ level.

DISCUSSION

The data clearly support the hypothesis of a very strong effect of observing a model upon subsequent sharing. Ss who observed a model refuse to share gave fewer marbles to the model and to both charities than Ss who either observed a model share with Mental Health or received marbles from her. A more specific modeling effect was also observed, in that Ss in the Model-shares-with-subject condition subsequently shared more with her than Ss in the Model-shares-with-charity condition, and Ss in the MSC condition subsequently shared more with MH and with MH+TT than Ss in the MSS condition. The difference in marbles given to TT, although in the predicted direction, did not reach statistical significance, however, failing to confirm Hypothesis 4 and suggesting again the specificity of the imitative response. Nevertheless, the fact that the control group shared less on *all* measures indicates that there was indeed some generalized imitation of altruism rather than simply direct imitation.

The questionnaire data indicate tentative support for the hypothesis that salience of the norm of altruism does mediate sharing. There was a tendency for Ss observing a generous model to mention sharing earlier, although it did not reach statistical significance, and Ss who shared were subsequently more likely to spontaneously mention sharing than those who did not. It is possible, of course, that it is the act of sharing which makes the social responsibility norm more salient to the child, rather than vice versa, as the interview was administered after the chance to share rather than before, so as not to affect the subject's sharing.

In opposition to previous results (Harris, 1970), the data do provide some support for the notion of a reciprocity norm as affecting altruism, since subjects in the MSS group were subsequently more generous than Ss in the MSC group. Thus it seems possible that more than one social norm may serve to mediate sharing.

The effects of modeled behavior on sharing would appear from this study to be both specific and generalized. It is clear that not only is general altruism imitated, so that subjects observing a generous model share more even with those to whom the model does not donate but that specific details of with whom one shares are also imitated. The role of norms in mediating this sharing is not completely clear, but the evidence is in favor of the interpretation that increased salience of a norm of altruism and possibly of a norm of reciprocity may indeed mediate the modeling effect.

SUMMARY

To investigate the effect of modeling on altruism, 156 third and fifth grade children were exposed to a model who either shared with them, gave to a charity, or refused to share. The test apparatus, identified as a game, consisted of a box with signal lights and a chute through which marbles were dispensed. Subjects and the model played the game twice. The first time the model won and disposed of prize marbles in one of three ways. The second time the subject won and was free to dispose of or save prize marbles. The subjects' subsequent sharing with the model, sharing with Mental Health or a Toys for Tots charity, or their refusal to share was observed through a one-way mirror in the test van. Subjects also responded to a questionnaire designed to assess the salience of a norm of altruism. Both specific and generalized imitation of altruism were found and salience of sharing appeared to be strongly related to actual sharing and weakly related to experimental conditions.

Other investigations also indicate that models who behave in positive ways toward children are more likely to be imitated than those who do not. One set of experiments made clever use of dioramas and pictures that portrayed people or animals involved in distressful situations (M. R. Yarrow *et al.*, 1973). In one experimental treatment, preschool children who saw an adult model react to a diorama scene in helpful and supportive ways were later given an opportunity to express similar behavior. One diorama portrayed a monkey reaching for a banana. The model said, "Oh, Mr. Monkey, you must be hungry. You can't reach your food. I'll help you. Here's your banana. Now you won't be hungry." The child was then shown a second diorama, which portrayed a similar scene. If the child behaved appropriately, the model said that the monkey was now feeling better because the child had helped him to get his food. Other children participated in training sessions where a pair of adults showed the children pictures of people or animals in distress. One of the adults commented sympathetically on the depicted problems and told what she would do if she were there; the other adult expressed approval. The models in the experiment visited the children's nursery school during a two-week period prior to the experiment for five one-half-hour sessions. On those occasions half of the models behaved in a supportive and sympathetic way with the children, and the other half maintained a cool detachment. Two weeks after the training sessions, each child participated in a "real-life" situation in which a basket of buttons and spools "accidentally" fell off a table. Observers noted whether a subject child voluntarily picked up the spilled objects. A short time later, the child was invited to play with a year-old baby who was in a playpen. While playing with the baby, the child could see that some of its toys had fallen out of the playpen, and once again observers noted whether the child retrieved the toys. An analysis of the children's behavior in these test situations showed that those children who had seen the nurturant and supportive adult model in the training sessions were more likely to give help than were either the children who had been exposed to the cool and distant model, or those who were in a control group and therefore received no training at all. Such studies show that children are more likely to imitate models who have rewarded or reinforced them, rather than models with whom they have had little or no positive interaction.

We began this section with a discussion of locus of control, thus continuing the study of ego strength we started in Section 3. As children develop and become more mature they tend to see control as located within themselves rather than as external. The success they have in coping with their physical and social environment undoubtedly has a reinforcing effect in developing the attitudes essential to internalizing locus of control, but it is also likely that imitation is a powerful force. If their models act in ways that indicate they believe themselves to be in control of and responsible for their own actions, the children who imitate them will be inclined to develop similar life views. Children can learn less mature attitudes and patterns of behavior from models who behave in an immature manner, as the research on aggression shows. Some models have more influence than others; Several studies, including the one by Harris (4.4), indicate that the model who has the power to reward is the one whom children are most likely to imitate.

For young children, the models most often imitated are likely to be their parents. During the middle-childhood years, most children continue to imitate their parents' attitudes and behavior, although the increasing power and prestige of the peer group may provide influential peer models. The way in which parents influence their children's behavior will be examined in the next section, and peer influence will be discussed in Section 6.

REFERENCES

Bandura, A. "Social-learning theory of identificatory processes." In *Handbook of Socialization Theory and Research*, edited by D. A. Goslin. Chicago: Rand McNally, 1969.

Bandura, A. and McDonald, F. J. "The influence of social reinforcement and the behavior of models in shaping children's moral judgments." *Journal of Abnormal and Social Psychology* 67 (1963): 274–281.

Bryan, J. H. and Schwartz, T. "Effects of film material upon children's behavior." *Psychological Bulletin* 75 (1971): 50–59.

Bryant, B. K. "Locus of control related to teacher-child interperceptual experiences." *Child Development* 45 (1974): 157–164.

Eron, L. D., Huesmann, L. R., Lefkowitz, M. M., and Walder, L. O. "Does television violence cause aggression?" *American Psychologist* 27 (1972): 253-263.

Feshbach, S. and Singer, R. D. *Television and Aggression.* San Francisco: Jossey-Bass, 1971.

Lifschutz, M. "Internal-external locus-of-control dimension as a function of age and socialization milieu." *Child Development* 44 (1973): 538-546.

Rotter, J. B. "Generalized expectancies for internal versus external control of reinforcement." *Psychological Monographs* 80 No. 1 (Whole No. 609), 1966.

Stephens, M. W. and Delys, P. "External control expectancies among disadvantaged children at preschool age." *Child Development* 44 (1973): 670-674.

Yarrow, M. R., Scott, P. M., and Waxler, C. Z. "Learning concern for others." *Developmental Psychology* 8 (1973): 240-260.

4.1

1. Bialer, I. Conceptualization of success and failure in mentally retarded and normal children. *J. Personal.*, 1961, **29**, 303-320.

2. Brown, J. C., & Strickland, B. R. Belief in internal-external control of reinforcement and participation in college activities. A paper presented at the Southeastern Psychological Association Meeting, Tomsville, Kentucky, 1970.

3. Cardi, M. An examination of internal versus external control in relation to academic failures. Unpublished Master's thesis, Ohio State University, Columbus, 1962.

4. Crandall, V. C., Katkovsky, W., & Crandall, V. J. Children's beliefs in their own control of reinforcements in intellectual-academic achievement situations. *Child Devel.*, 1965, **36**, 91-109.

5. Davis, W. L., & Phares, E. J. Internal-external control as a determinant of information-seeking in a social influence situation. *J. Personal.*, 1967, **35**, 547-561.

6. James, W. H. Internal versus external control of reinforcement as a basic variable in learning theory. Unpublished Doctoral dissertation, Ohio State University, Columbus, 1957.

7. Lefcourt, H. M. Internal versus external control of reinforcement: A review. *Psychol. Bull.*, 1966, **65**, 206-220.

8. Nowicki, S., & Roundtree, J. Correlates of locus of control in secondary school age students. *Devel. Psychol.*, 1971, **4**, 479.

9. Nowicki, S., & Strickland, B. R. A locus of control scale for children. Paper to be presented at the American Psychological Association meeting, Washington, D.C., 1971.

10. O'Leary, K. D., Becker, W. C., Evans, M. B. & Saudargas, R. A. A token reinforcement program in a public school: A replication and systematic analysis. *J. Appl. Behav. Anal.*, 1970, in press.

11. Phares, E. J. Expectancy changes in skill and chance situations. *J. Abn. & Soc. Psychol.*, 1957, **54**, 339-342.

12. Rotter, J. B. Generalized expectancies for internal versus external control of reinforcement. *Psychol. Monog.*, 1966, **80**, 1-28.

13. Strickland, B. R. The relationships of awareness to verbal conditioning and extinction. *J. Personal.*, 1970, **38**, 364-378.

14. _____. Delay of gratification as a function of race of experimenter. *J. Personal. & Soc. Psychol.*, 1971, in press.

15. Strickland, B. R., & Nowicki, S. Behavioral correlates of the Nowicki-Strickland locus of control scale for children. A paper presented at the American Psychological Association meeting, Washington, D.C., 1971.

16. Zimmerman, E. H., & Zimmerman, J. The alteration of behavior in a special classroom situation. *J. Exper. Anal. Behav.*, 1962, **5**, 59–60.

4.2

1. Baer, D. M., & Sherman, J. A. Reinforcement control of generalized imitation in young children. *J. Exper. Child Psychol.*, 1964, **1**, 37–49.

2. Baer, D. M., Peterson, R. F., & Sherman, J. A. The development of imitation by reinforcing behavioral similarity to a model. *J. Exper. Anal. Behav.*, 1967, **10**, 405–416.

3. Bandura, A. Social learning through imitation. *Nebraska Sympos. on Motiv.*, 1962, **10**, 211–269.

4. _____. Influence on models' reinforcement contingencies on the acquisition of imitative responses. *J. Personal. & Soc. Psychol.*, 1965, **1**, 589–595.

5. Bandura, A., & Barab, P. G. Conditions governing nonreinforced imitation. *Devel. Psychol.*, in press.

6. Bandura, A., Ross, D., & Ross, S. A. Transmission of aggression through imitation of aggressive models. *J. Abn. & Soc. Psychol.*, 1961, **63**, 575–582.

7. _____. Imitation of film-mediated aggressive models. *J. Abn. & Soc. Psychol.*, 1963, **66**, 3–11.

8. _____. Vicarious reinforcement and imitative learning. *J. Abn. & Soc. Psychol.*, 1963, **67**, 601–607.

9. Hollenberg, E., & Sperry, M. Some antecedents of aggression and effects of frustration in doll play. *Personality*, 1951, **1**, 32–43.

10. Mowrer, O. H. Learning Theory and the Symbolic Processes. New York: Wiley, 1960.

11. Mowrer, O. H. Learning Theory and Behavior. New York: Wiley, 1960.

12. Nelson, J. D., Gelfand, D. M., & Hartmann, D. P. Children's aggression following competition and exposure to an aggressive model. *Child Devel.*, 1969, **40**, 1085–1097.

13. Parton, D. A., & Fouts, G. T. Effects of stimulus-response similarity and dissimilarity on children's matching performance. *J. Exper. Child Psychol.*, 1969, **8**, 461–468.

4.3

Durrett, M. E. The relationship of early infant regulation and later behavior in play interviews. *Child Development*, 1959, **30**, 211–216.

Feshbach, N. D. Sex differences in children's modes of aggressive responses toward outsiders. *Merrill-Palmer Quarterly*, 1969, **15**, 249–258.

Murphy, L. *Social behavior and child personality.* New York: Columbia University Press, 1937.

Stevenson, H. W., & Stevenson, N. G. Social interaction in an interracial nursery school. *Genetic Psychology Monographs*, 1960, **61**, 37–75.

4.4

Berkowitz, L., & Daniels, L. Responsibility and dependency. *Journal of Abnormal and Social Psychology*, 1963, **66**, 429–436.

Bryan, J. H., & London, P. Altruistic behavior by children. *Psychological Bulletin*, 1970, **73**, 200–211.

Bryan, J. H., & Walbek, N. H. Preaching and practicing self-sacrifice: Children's actions and reactions. *Child Development*, 1970, **41**, 329–353.

Bryan, J. H., & Walbek, N. H. Determinants of conformity: The impact of words, deeds, and power upon children's altruistic behavior. Unpublished manuscript, Northwestern University, 1970b.

Gouldner, A. W. The norm of reciprocity: A preliminary statement. *American Sociological Review*, 1960, **25**, 161–178.

Harris, M. B. Reciprocity and generosity: Some determinants of sharing in children. *Child Development*, 1970, **41**, 313–328.

Hartup, W. W., & Coates, B. Imitation of peers as a function of reinforcement from the peer group and the rewardingness of the model. *Child Development*, 1967, **38**, 1003–1016.

Leeds, R. Altruism and the norm of giving. *Merrill-Palmer Quarterly*, 1963, **9**, 229–240.

Midlarsky, E., & Bryan, J. H. Training charity in children. *Journal of Personality and Social Psychology*, 1967, **5**, 408–415.

Rosenhan, D., & White, G. M. Observation and rehearsal as determinants of prosocial behavior. *Journal of Personality and Social Psychology*, 1967, **5**, 424–431.

5.
PARENT-CHILD RELATIONSHIPS

There was little place for love in the mechanistic theories of psychology that developed in the early part of this century. Although J. B. Watson and J. J. B. Morgan (1917) included love as one of the three basic emotional reactions of infants, experimental psychologists saw love as less obviously related to survival than the other two emotions, fear and rage, and consequently less important. It is possible that this view resulted from the greater ease with which fear and rage, as opposed to love, can be manipulated in experimental settings. Whatever the reason, love was virtually ignored by psychological researchers during the first half of the century; C. N. Cofer and M. H. Appley (1964) mention it in their authoritative survey of motivation only in connection with their discussion of Maslow, Fromm, and other members of the humanistic school of psychology. Even the psychoanalytic theorists of that period seemed uninterested in love, and wrote instead of drives, cathexes, and transference.

It was H. F. Harlow, an experimental psychologist at the University of Wisconsin's primate laboratory, who made love psychologically respectable. Harlow's presidential address at the 1958 American Psychological Association convention was entitled "The nature of love" and concerned the attraction of infant macaque, or rhesus, monkeys for their mothers. Harlow has an irrepressible sense of humor coupled with a dramatic flair, and we might suspect him of using the word "love" (instead of "attachment" or "attraction") in order to needle other experimental psychologists, who continued to consider motivation only in extremely narrow terms. Harlow's shafts of wit also struck the Freudians, who were appalled at the suggestion that experiments with monkeys might provide information relevant to the emotional attachment between human infants and their mothers. However, in spite of the outrageous puns and ironic asides that characterize Harlow's research reports, a review of his investigations during the last two decades makes it clear that he takes his work very seriously, and that he considers the emotional attachment of the infant monkey for its mother to be a variable that, like hunger, thirst, or any other motivational state, can be manipulated experimentally.

Infant monkeys normally spend most of their first few months of life clinging to their mothers. If an infant becomes separated from its mother, it shows obvious signs of distress and makes every effort to find her. A skeptical behaviorist might attempt to explain this behavior in elementary survival terms, such as the mother is a source of nourishment, but Harlow's research demonstrates that hunger is not the only motive, nor even the main one. When infant monkeys were separated from their mothers and permitted to choose between a wire-frame surrogate, or substitute, mother with a nipple attached to a source of milk, and a terry-cloth surrogate mother without either food or nipple, the infants clung to the terry-cloth mother and sought the wire mother only when they were hungry. It is clear that the motive to cling to something soft and furry was dominant and that no amount of food reward could get the infant monkeys to prefer the wire mother.

Although the infants found the cloth surrogate mother more reassuring than the wire surrogate when they were frightened, the cloth surrogate proved to be a very inadequate substitute for their real mothers. Infants who were permanently separated from their mothers and who had access only to cloth surrogates behaved inadequately and ineptly in social situations when they reached adolescence and adulthood, and were especially awkward in sexual matters.

Harlow concluded from these observations that the attachment the infant expressed for its mother was not a learned or acquired motive, resulting from satisfaction of the hunger drive, as the behaviorists had maintained, but that "basic bodily contact was probably an unlearned, nativistic force that caused the child to love the mother" (Harlow, Gluck, and Suomi, 1972).

Article 5.1, by Harlow and Stephen J. Suomi, reviews some of Harlow's earlier studies and describes investigations designed to determine what makes monkey mothers attractive to their infants—appearance, contour, texture of covering, temperature, and motion. They conclude that all these variables are important in different ways and at different times during infancy. For example, infant monkeys prefer a heated wire surrogate mother to an unheated cloth surrogate during the first few weeks, but later spend more time clinging to the unheated cloth surrogate.

Harlow maintains that experiments of this type can tell us a great deal about the motivation of human infants. Research with inanimate mother surrogates, he says, may give us an idea of what qualities make a mother, human or monkey, an object of love to an infant (Harlow, Gluck, and Suomi, 1972).

5.1 Nature of love—simplified

Harry F. Harlow and
Stephen J. Suomi

The cloth surrogate and its wire surrogate sibling (see Figure 1) entered into scientific history as of 1958 (Harlow, 1958). The cloth surrogate was originally designed to test the relative importance of body contact in contrast to activities associated with the breast, and the results were clear beyond all expectation. Body contact was of overpowering importance by any measure taken, even contact time, as shown in Figure 2.

However, the cloth surrogate, beyond its power to measure the relative importance of a host of variables determining infant affection

Reprinted from the *American Psychologist*, 25 (1970): 161–168, with permission of the authors and the American Psychological Association. Copyright 1970 by the American Psychological Association.

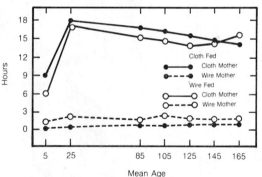

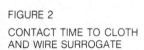

for the mother, exhibited another surprising trait, one of great independent usefulness. Even though the cloth mother was inanimate, it was able to impart to its infant such emotional security that the infant would, in the surrogate's presence, explore a strange situation and manipulate available physical objects (see Figure 3), or animate objects (see Figure 4). Manipulation of animate objects leads to play if these animate objects

FIGURE 3

INFANT MONKEY SECURITY IN
PRESENCE OF CLOTH
SURROGATE

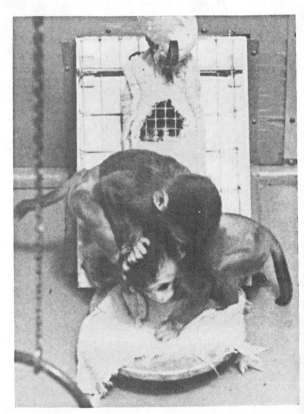

FIGURE 4

INFANT PLAY IN PRESENCE OF
SURROGATE

are age-mates, and play is the variable of primary importance in the development of normal social, sexual, and maternal functions, as described by Harlow and Harlow (1965). It is obvious that surrogate mothers, which are more docile and manipulative than real monkey mothers, have a wide range of experimental uses.

SIMPLIFIED SURROGATE

Although the original surrogates turned out to be incredibly efficient dummy mothers, they presented certain practical problems. The worst of the problems was that of cleanliness. Infant monkeys seldom soil their real mothers' bodies, though we do not know how this is achieved. However, infant monkeys soiled the bodies of the original cloth surrogates with such efficiency and enthusiasm as to present a health problem and, even worse, a financial problem resulting from laundering. Furthermore, we believed that the original cloth surrogate was too steeply angled and thereby relatively inaccessible for cuddly clinging by the neonatal monkey.

In the hope of alleviating practical problems inherent in the original cloth surrogate, we constructed a family of simplified surrogates. The simplified surrogate is mounted on a rod attached to a lead base 4 inches in diameter, angled upward at 25°, and projected through the surrogate's body for 4 inches, so that heads may be attached if desired. The body of the simplified surrogate is only 6 inches long, 2½ inches in diameter, and stands approximately 3 inches off the ground. Figure 5 shows an original cloth surrogate and simplified surrogate placed side by side.

As can be seen in Figure 6, infants readily cling to these simplified surrogates of smaller body and decreased angle of inclination. Infant monkeys do soil the simplified surrogate, but the art and act of soiling is very greatly reduced. Terry cloth slipcovers can be made easily and relatively cheaply, alleviating, if not eliminating, laundry problems. Thus, the simplified surrogate is a far more practical dummy mother than the original cloth surrogate.

SURROGATE VARIABLES

Lactation

Although the original surrogate papers (Harlow, 1958; Harlow & Zimmermann, 1959) were written as if activities associated with the breast,

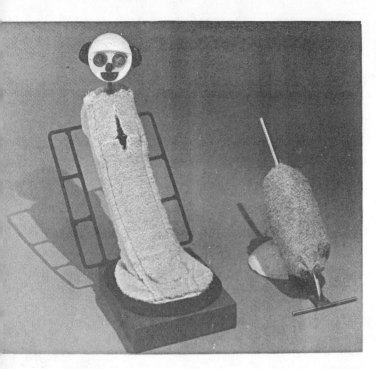

FIGURE 5

ORIGINAL SURROGATE
AND SIMPLIFIED
SURROGATE

FIGURE 6

INFANT CLINGING TO
SIMPLIFIED SURROGATE

particularly nursing, were of no importance, this is doubtlessly incorrect. There were no statistically significant differences in time spent by the babies on the lactating versus nonlactating cloth surrogates and on the lactating versus nonlactating wire surrogates, but the fact is that there were consistent preferences for both the cloth and the wire lactating surrogates and that these tendencies held for both the situations of time on surrogate and frequency of surrogate preference when the infant was exposed to a fear stimulus. Thus, if one can accept a statistically insignificant *level of confidence,* consistently obtained from four situations, one will properly conclude that nursing is a minor variable but one of more than measurable importance operating to bind the infant to the mother.

To demonstrate experimentally that activities associated with the breasts were variables of significant importance, we built two sets of differentially colored surrogates, tan and light blue; and using a 2×2 Latin square design, we arranged a situation such that the surrogate of one color lactated and the other did not. As can be seen in Figure 7, the infants showed a consistent preference for the lactating surrogate when contact comfort was held constant. The importance of the lactational variable probably decreases with time. But at least we had established the hard fact that hope springs eternal in the human breast and even longer in the breast, undressed.

FIGURE 7

INFANT PREFERENCE FOR
LACTATING CLOTH
SURROGATE

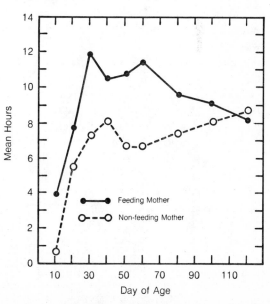

Facial variables

In the original surrogates we created an ornamental face for the cloth surrogate and a simple dog face for the wire surrogate. I was working with few available infants and against time to prepare a presidential address for the 1958 American Psychological Association Convention. On the basis of sheer intuition, I was convinced that the ornamental cloth-surrogate face would become a stronger fear stimulus than the dog face when fear of the unfamiliar matured in the monkeys from about 70 to 110 days (Harlow & Zimmermann, 1959; Sackett, 1966). But since we wanted each surrogate to have an identifiable face and had few infants, we made no effort to balance faces by resorting to a feebleminded 2×2 Latin square design.

Subsequently, we have run two brief unpublished experiments. We tested four rhesus infants unfamiliar with surrogate faces at approximately 100 days of age and found that the ornamental face was a much stronger fear stimulus than the dog face. Clearly, the early enormous preference for the cloth surrogate over the wire surrogate was not a function of the differential faces. Later, we raised two infants on cloth and two on wire surrogates, counterbalancing the ornamental and dog faces. Here, the kind of face was a nonexistent variable. To a baby all maternal faces are beautiful. A mother's face that will stop a clock will not stop an infant.

The first surrogate mother we constructed came a little late, or phrasing it another way, her baby came a little early. Possibly her baby was illegitimate. Certainly it was her first baby. In desperation we gave the mother a face that was nothing but a round wooden ball, which displayed no trace of shame. To the baby monkey this featureless face became beautiful, and she frequently caressed it with hands and legs, beginning around 30–40 days of age. By the time the baby had reached 90 days of age we had constructed an appropriate ornamental cloth-mother face, and we proudly mounted it on the surrogate's body. The baby took one look and screamed. She fled to the back of the cage and cringed in autistic-type posturing. After some days of terror the infant solved the medusa-mother problem in a most ingenious manner. She revolved the face 180° so that she always faced a bare round ball! Furthermore, we could rotate the maternal face dozens of times and within an hour or so the infant would turn it around 180°. Within a week the baby resolved her unfaceable problem once and for all. She lifted the maternal head from the body, rolled it into the corner, and abandoned it. No one can blame the baby. She had lived with and loved a faceless mother, but she could not love a two-faced mother.

These data imply that an infant visually responds to the earliest version of mother he encounters, that the mother he grows accustomed to is the mother he relies upon. Subsequent changes, especially changes introduced after maturation of the fear response, elicit this response with no holds barred. Comparisons of effects of babysitters on human infants might be made.

Body-surface variables

We have received many questions and complaints concerning the surrogate surfaces, wire and terry cloth, used in the original studies. This mountain of mail breaks down into two general categories: that wire is aversive, and that other substances would be equally effective if not better than terry cloth in eliciting a clinging response.

The answer to the first matter in question is provided by observation: Wire is not an aversive stimulus to neonatal monkeys, for they spend much time climbing on the sides of their hardware-cloth cages and exploring this substance orally and tactually. A few infants have required medical treatment from protractedly pressing their faces too hard and too long against the cage sides. Obviously, however, wire does not provide contact comfort.

In an attempt to quantify preference of various materials, an exploratory study was performed in which each of four infants was presented with a choice between surrogates covered with terry cloth versus rayon, vinyl, or rough-grade sandpaper. As shown in Figure 8, the infants demonstrated a clear preference for the cloth surrogates, and no significant preference difference between the other body surfaces. An extension

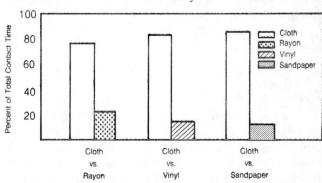

FIGURE 8
EFFECT OF
SURFACE ON
SURROGATE
CONTACT

of this study is in progress in which an attempt is being made to further quantify and rank order the preference for these materials by giving infants equal exposure time to all four materials.

Motion variables

In the original two papers, we pointed out that rocking motion, that is, proprioceptive stimulation, was a variable of more than statistical significance, particularly early in the infant's life, in binding the infant to the mother figure. We measured this by comparing the time the infants spent on two identical planes, one rocking and one stationary (see Figure 9) and two identical cloth surrogates, one rocking and one stationary (see Figure 10).

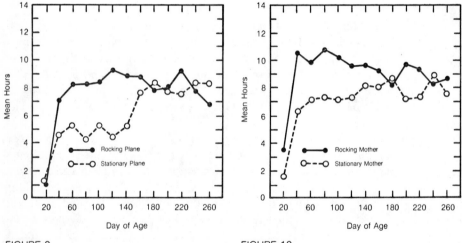

FIGURE 9

INFANT CONTACT TO STATIONARY AND
ROCKING PLANES

FIGURE 10

INFANT CONTACT TO STATIONARY AND
ROCKING SURROGATES

Temperature variables

To study another variable, temperature, we created some "hot mamma" surrogates. We did this by inserting heating coils in the maternal bodies that raised the external surrogate body surface about 10° F. In one experiment, we heated the surface of a wire surrogate and let four infant macaques choose between this heated mother and a room-temperature cloth mother. The data are presented in Figure 11. The neonatal monkeys clearly preferred the former. With increasing age this difference decreased, and at approximately 15 days the preference reversed. In a second experiment, we used two differentially colored cloth surrogates and heated one and not the other. The infants preferred the hot surrogate, but frequently contacted the room-temperature surrogate for considerable periods of time.

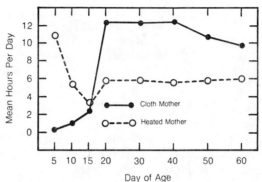

FIGURE 11

INFANT CONTACT TO HEATED-WIRE AND ROOM-TEMPERATURE CLOTH SURROGATES

More recently, a series of ingenious studies on the temperature variable has been conducted by Suomi, who created hot- and cold-running surrogates by adaptation of the simplified surrogate. These results are important not only for the information obtained concerning the temperature variable but also as an illustration of the successful experimental use of the simplified surrogate itself.

The surrogates used in these exploratory studies were modifications of the basic simplified surrogate, designed to get maximum personality out of the minimal mother. One of these surrogates was a "hot mamma," exuding warmth from a conventional heating pad wrapped around the surrogate frame and completely covered by a terry cloth sheath. The other surrogate was a cold female; beneath the terry cloth sheath was a hollow shell within which her life fluid—cold water—was continuously circulated. The two surrogates are illustrated in Figure 12, and to the untrained observer they look remarkably similar. But looks can be deceiving, especially with females, and we felt that in these similar-looking surrogates we had really simulated the two extremes of womanhood—one with a hot body and no head, and one with a cold shoulder and no

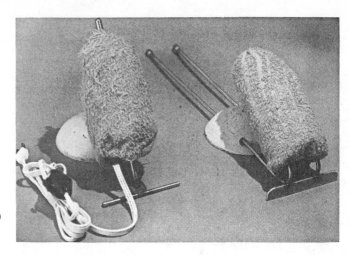

heart. Actually, this is an exaggeration, for the surface temperature of the hot surrogate was only 7° F. above room temperature, while the surface temperature of the cold surrogate was only 5° F. below room temperature.

In a preliminary study, we raised one female infant from Day 15 on the warm surrogate for a period of four weeks. Like all good babies she quickly and completely became attached to her source of warmth, and during this time she exhibited not only a steadily increasing amount of surrogate contact but also began to use the surrogate as a base for

FIGURE 13

INFANT CLINGING TO AND EXPLORING FROM WARM SIMPLIFIED SURROGATE exploration (see Figure 13). At the end of this four-week period, we decided that our subject had become spoiled enough and so we replaced the warm surrogate with the cold version for one week. The infant noticed the switch within two minutes, responding by huddling in a corner and vocalizing piteously. Throughout the week of bitter maternal cold, the amount of surrogate contact fell drastically; in general, the infant avoided the surrogate in her feeding, exploratory, and sleeping behaviors. Feeling somewhat guilty, we switched surrogates once more for a week and were rewarded for our efforts by an almost immediate return to previously high levels of surrogate contact. Apparently, with heart-warming heat, our infant was capable of forgiveness, even at this tender age. At this point, we switched the two surrogates daily for a total two weeks, but by this time the infant had accepted the inherent fickle nature of her mothers. On the days that her surrogate was warm, she clung tightly to its body, but on the days when the body was cold, she generally ignored it, thus providing an excellent example of naive behaviorism.

With a second infant we maintained this procedure but switched the surrogates, so that he spent four weeks with the cold surrogate, followed by one week with the warm, an additional week with the cold, and finally a two-week period in which the surrogates were switched daily. This infant became anything but attached to the cold surrogate during the initial four-week period, spending most of his time huddling in the corner of his cage and generally avoiding the surrogate in his exploratory behavior (see Figure 14). In succeeding weeks, even with the

FIGURE 14
TYPICAL INFANT REACTIONS TO COLD SIMPLIFIED SURROGATE

warm surrogate, he failed to approach the levels of contact exhibited by the other infant to the cold surrogate. Apparently, being raised with a cold mother had chilled him to mothers in general, even those beaming warmth and comfort.

Two months later both infants were exposed to a severe fear stimulus in the presence of a room-temperature simplified surrogate. The warm-mother infant responded to this stimulus by running to the surrogate and clinging for dear life. The cold-mother infant responded by running the other way and seeking security in a corner of the cage. We seriously doubt that this behavioral difference can be attributed to the sex difference of our subjects. Rather, this demonstration warmed our hopes and chilled our doubts that temperature may be a variable of importance. More specifically, it suggested that a simple linear model may not be adequate to describe the effects of temperature differences of surrogates on infant attachment. It is clear that warmth is a variable of major importance, particularly in the neonate, and we hazard the guess that elevated temperature is a variable of importance in the operation of all the affectional systems: maternal, mother-infant, possibly age-mate, heterosexual, and even paternal.

PROSPECTIVES

Recently we have simplified the surrogate mother further for studies in which its only function is that of providing early social support and security to infants. This supersimplified surrogate is merely a board 1½ inches in diameter and 10 inches long with a scooped-out, concave trough having a maximal depth of ¾ inch. As shown in Figure 15, the super-simplified surrogate has an angular deviation from the base of less than 15°, though this angle can be increased by the experimenter at will. The standard cover for this supremely simple surrogate mother is a size 11, cotton athletic sock, though covers of various qualities, rayon, vinyl (which we call the "linoleum lover"), and sandpaper, have been used for experimental purposes.

> Linoleum lover, with you I am through
> The course of smooth love never runs true.

This supersimplified mother is designed to attract and elicit clinging responses from the infant during the first 15 days of the infant's life.

We have designed, but not yet tested, a swinging mother that will

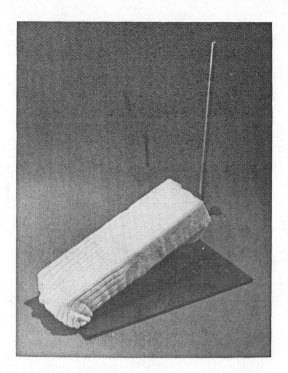

FIGURE 15

THE SUPERSIMPLIFIED
SURROGATE

dangle from a frame about 2 inches off the floor and have a convex, terry cloth or cotton body surface. Observations of real macaque neonates and mothers indicate that the infant, not the mother, is the primary attachment object even when the mother locomotes, and that this swinging mother may also elicit infantile clasp and impart infant security very early in life. There is nothing original in this day and age about a swinger becoming a mother, and the only new angle, if any, is a mother becoming a swinger.

Additional findings, such as the discovery that six-month social isolates will learn to cling to a heated simplified surrogate, and that the presence of a surrogate reduces clinging among infant-infant pairs, have substantiated use of the surrogate beyond experiments for its own sake. At present, the heated simplified surrogate is being utilized as a standard apparatus in studies as varied as reaction to fear, rehabilitation of social isolates, and development of play. To date, additional research utilizing the cold version of the simplified surrogate has been far more limited, possibly because unused water faucets are harder to obtain than empty electrical outlets. But this represents a methodological, not a theoretical problem, and doubtlessly solutions will soon be forthcoming.

It is obvious that the surrogate mother at this point is not merely a historical showpiece. Unlike the proverbial old soldier, it is far from fading away. Instead, as in the past, it continues to foster not only new infants but new ideas.

Families do much more than provide children with a source of love, as they constitute the group settings in which children have their first social experiences. The family is also a microcosm of the larger society to which it belongs. Family members occupy positions of varying amounts of status and prestige within the family and play the roles appropriate to these positions. The attitudes a child develops about himself and the world around him are a product not only of the values, beliefs, and norms of the larger society of which his family is a minute segment, but also of the feelings and expectations his parents and siblings have for him. The attitudes that prevail in families at different social-class levels and in different cultures have been studied extensively, and we shall discuss these studies further in Section 7; we are concerned here with the psycho-social effect of the attitudes characteristic of a given family on its child members. Studying this kind of influence is exceedingly complex, because of the uniqueness of each family and each family member. It is possible, however, to control some of the variation that results from this uniqueness by comparing the behavior of family members occupying one position with that of members in other positions. We can, for example, compare the opinions and attitudes of a sample of mothers with those of a sample of fathers, and thereby learn something about the personal characteristics of mothers in general and fathers in general. We can compare the attitudes of parents with those of their children, and we can study the behavior of children who occupy different positions in the family hierarchy.

Most of the research on the effect of children's positions in the family has been focused on the firstborn child. There are good historical reasons for this. The oldest child (usually the oldest *male* child) has traditionally held a higher status than his siblings. Not only does he usually have authority over them in the absence of the parents, but he may also have priority of rights and privileges and of inheriting family possessions. These traditional practices are not merely arbitrary; the firstborn occupies a unique position in a psychological sense, because his appearance makes his mother and father parents, instead of merely husband and wife, and gives them status with other parents. These points are brought out in the survey described by Paul C. Rosenblatt and Elizabeth L. Skoogberg in article 5.2.

5.2 Birth order in cross-cultural perspective

Paul C. Rosenblatt and
Elizabeth L. Skoogberg

This is a study of cross-cultural regularities in childhood events and adult roles of people of different birth orders. It is an attempt to put birth order effects into a cross-cultural perspective as Barry, Bacon, and Child (1957) have for sex roles. The study of birth order was based on the following conjectures.

In most societies, firstborns, as a result of birth priority, ordinarily care for, control, and discipline their other siblings. At the other end of the sibling array, last borns experience domination by elder siblings in play and when elder siblings have responsibility for their care. The likelihood of dominance by firstborns should be emphasized because it seems that children in the United States are deviant from children elsewhere in experiencing so little care from and care of other children (Minturn & Lambert, 1964, pp. 98, 107). It is true that firstborn children in the typical nonwestern society may, like later borns and last borns, experience care by other children, particularly by cousins and young aunts and uncles. However, they may still experience less care by other children, and it certainly is likely that they dominate in care relations with their own siblings. These child care arguments point to the possibility of sharp differences in adult role or personality related to birth order.

Reprinted from *Developmental Psychology*, 10 (1974): 48–54, with permission of the authors and the American Psychological Association. Copyright 1974 by the American Psychological Association.

But they are only part of the story. Because child care duties seem to fall more heavily on girls, these arguments are not sufficient to predict strong birth order differences in adulthood.

A second part of the story has to do with the importance of children in stabilizing parental marriage. It is not clear whether children stabilize marriage in the United States, though they may. By contrast, in many other societies a first child or a first son is clearly recognized as a marriage stabilizer. In these other societies, the parental marriage may not be more than a tentative relationship until a child is born, and the birth of a child may cement alliances between families. People may not even be recognized as adults until they are parents. Thus, a first child or a first son is an important person and may get treated as such. That treatment may help to produce certain dispositions in adulthood, both in the first child or first son and in the siblings who see him treated in that way.

A third part of the story has to do with the necessity to fill roles when someone dies or migrates. Americans may be less aware of this need because, in the United States, most people live to see their children grow to adulthood. In many other societies, parental death or migration frequently precedes the maturity of younger offspring. For these reasons, it is much more likely that an oldest son or older sons will be brought up with the contingency of parental loss in mind and with the notion that they may someday have to supervise the activities of the family, help in the rearing of younger siblings, and perform as adult sponsors for younger siblings.

Thus it was hypothesized that there are birth order differences in many societies, both in child rearing and in adult roles. Oldest children are expected to have more responsibility and authority over siblings and more often to stabilize parent marriage, augment parent status, and receive recognition for these special benefits they confer on their parents. Common forms of recognition may include elaborate birth ceremonies and the adoption of a parental teknonym based on the name of the first child. (Teknonymy is the naming of a parent after one of the parent's offspring.) At the adult level, oldest children, particularly sons, are more often expected to assume headship of a kin group, have authority over siblings, and receive respect from siblings. It is further hypothesized that kinship terms and modes of address frequently represent relative age of a child or adult within his group of full siblings.

METHOD

Sample

Murdock and White (1969) have delineated a universe of 186 representative, relatively independent, well-described cultures from around the world. Other reasonably well-described cultures in the culture areas of each of the 186 have been listed by Murdock (1967, 1968). Ethnographic materials from cultures in the 186 culture areas were examined with a goal of achieving a sample of approximately 40 unrelated cultures scattered throughout the world. This goal was achieved with the 39 societies that constitute the sample for the present study. Materials from 14 other societies were examined and found to be inadequate. Hence, the sample is opportunistic rather than a neat random sample from a defined universe. The 39 societies in the sample are listed in the Appendix to his article. [The Appendix has been omitted for reasons of brevity.]

Ratings

Ratings were made from photocopied ethnographic materials or, in a few cases, from hand-copied materials from the Human Relations Area File. A bibliography of materials used is available from the authors. As much as possible, the focus of each set of extracts was on a specific community in a specific time period. Ratings were made for ordinary people; special classes of people, such as royalty, were excluded from the ratings.

Four raters were used: Two independent raters worked on childhood materials and two other independent raters worked on adult materials. Materials for the two age periods were segregated so that raters of one period generally had no material from the other period. Separate ratings were made for firstborn sons, firstborn daughters, last-born sons, and last-born daughters. Ratings were not attempted for only children; only children, only from birth into adulthood, seem to receive poor coverage in the ethnographic literature. In each set of ratings, the experience of the specific kind of adult or child was compared with the experience of all siblings of that child's sex who were neither firstborn nor last born. For example, one of the childhood experience variables is "has authority over siblings." For each of the four combinations of sex and first versus last birth order positions, two raters evaluated whether the specific child had more, the same, or less authority over siblings than the average sibling of his sex not first- or last born. Reliability data for all but one of the measures made on a substantial number of cases or providing significant effects are presented in the tables.

The measure not included in the tables was whether naming, kinship terminology, or mode of address reflects relative age in some way. For that measure, ratings for both firstborn sons and firstborn daughters agreed in 26 of 26 cases both raters attempted to rate; ratings for last-born sons agreed in 24 of 25 cases both raters attempted to rate, and for last-born daughters in 23 of 23 cases both raters attempted to rate. Because more cases could be rated on naming, kinship terminology, or mode of address for firstborns than for last borns, analyses are reported only for firstborns. We assume that once birth order is represented somewhere in naming, in kinship terms, or in mode of address, it has an influence on all people regardless of birth order, making the significance of birth order salient on a daily basis.

Proportion of cases agreed on is used as an index of reliability because on many measures there is no variance; correlational indexes that require variance would belie the high level of rater agreement. Ratings for all measures listed in the tables and for kinship terminology, naming, and mode of address are tabulated in the Appendix section.

In combining ratings, all cases of rater disagreement were discarded. For some measures, combined ratings are available only for a very small fraction of the original 39 cases. For that reason, generalization is problematic. Although there is no evidence that the cases lost differ from the cases that were ratable on any given measure, evidence that they do not differ is weak. The possibility was examined that total number of ratings, an index of the prominence of birth order effects, might be related to type of kinship system, marital residence, presence of extended families, importance of agriculture, and community exogamy. For all societies in the sample except the Leyte, measures of these cultural attributes were available in the "Ethnographic Atlas," a compendium of ratings published in many issues of the journal titled *Ethnology*. It seemed possible to us that birth order effects might be stronger in societies with more power or land to control. But there was no significant relation of numbers of ratings to the aspects of culture for which Ethnographic Atlas ratings were examined. Despite these assurances that poorly ratable cases may not differ from richly ratable ones, the missing data reduce generalizability.

A number of variables could not be measured in adequate numbers of cases. In the Results section of this article, data were reported for all combinations of variable, sex, and birth order position for which there were at least eight combined ratings or for which there were significant effects. . . .

RESULTS AND DISCUSSION

In 24 of 26 societies for which there are combined ratings of the presence or absence of relative age in naming, kinship terms, or mode of address for firstborns, relative age is present. In the 24 societies where relative age makes a difference, a firstborn may be addressed in terms of birth rank, named in terms of birth rank, or hear himself referred to in terms of birth rank. Even if all 13 societies for which there are no ratings of presence of relative age in naming, address, or kin terms lack any representation of relative birth position, it seems that birth order is commonly a prominent part of identity for many people in the world. . . .

In Table 1 are data indicating that firstborn children or firstborn children of a given sex tend to increase parental status, to provide parents with a teknonym, and to make parent marriage stable or more stable. In many cases these effects are not reversible. If parenthood of a first child brings a person full adult status, the status cannot be lost. Teknonyms are not likely to be lost or altered as long as the offspring remains

TABLE 1
BIRTH ORDER AND EFFECT OF CHILD ON PARENT

Variable	Rater agreement	Yes[a]	No	p
Birth increases parent status				
Firstborn daughters	11/11	11	0	.001
Firstborn sons	13/13	13	0	.001
Parental teknonym for this child				
Firstborn daughters	5/5	5	0	.05
Firstborn sons	5/6	5	0	.05
Birth stabilizes parent marriage				
Firstborn daughters	13/13	13	0	.001
Firstborn sons	13/13	13	0	.001

a Includes both "yes" and "yes, provided the child is firstborn of all children in the marriage."

alive. Marriages that are tentative until a child is born are comparatively stable, at least as long as the child remains alive. Thus, these data may be taken to indicate that the birth of a first child or of a first child of a given sex has greater significance to parents than the birth of subsequent children, particularly children of the same sex as the firstborn. It seems plausible that the significance of a firstborn would lead to special treatment. Especially in societies in which parents use a teknonym for the firstborn, the significance of the firstborn is likely to be constantly in the awareness of parents and their offspring.

In Table 2 are included data about childhood experiences. Firstborns receive more elaborate ceremonies at birth and in the first weeks of life, are given more duties to perform (including care for other children, errand running, and household chores), have authority over siblings (in terms of telling them what to do and being able to punish them for wrongdoing), and receive more respect from siblings. Last borns tend to be more often spoiled or indulged but not significantly so. The trends in the data not reported in Table 2 because of lack of statistical significance and small numbers of cases suggest that in the areas of duties, authority, and respect, last borns are less like firstborns than are other

TABLE 2
BIRTH ORDER AND CHILDHOOD EXPERIENCES

Variable	Rater agreement	More	Same	Less	p
Elaboration of birth ceremonies					
Firstborn daughters	15/15	14	1	0	.001
Firstborn sons	16/16	15	1	0	.001
Given duties to perform					
Firstborn daughters	12/18	10	2	0	.05
Firstborn sons	12/17	8	4	0	
Has authority over siblings					
Firstborn daughters	9/9	9	0	0	.01
Firstborn sons	12/12	12	0	0	.001
Receives respect from siblings					
Firstborn daughters	7/8	7	0	0	.01
Firstborn sons	10/10	9	1	0	.05
Spoiled, indulged					
Last-born daughters	8/8	6	2	0	
Last-born sons	8/9	5	3	0	

later borns. That is, the weak trends are for last-born sons to have less authority over siblings, to receive less respect, and to have fewer duties than the average son who is not firstborn or last born.

The relationships between birth order and adult roles are given in Table 3. Firstborn sons are likely to have more authority over siblings (can tell them what to do or can punish them) than later-born sons, are likely to inherit or otherwise gain control of more family land, livestock, or other wealth, and are likely to be respected by siblings more than the average son not firstborn or last born. Last-born sons are likely to be respected less than the average son who is not firstborn or last born. Firstborn daughters, like firstborn sons, receive relatively more respect than their same-sex siblings. Firstborn adult sons are more likely than average adult sons to have power or influence over other people, and they are more likely to head a kin group (e.g., lineage) that includes some of their siblings.

Although the adult role data not tabulated in Table 3 represent small numbers of cases and nonsignificant effects, some people may find the tendencies in those data interesting. One tendency is for firstborn

TABLE 3
BIRTH ORDER AND ADULT ROLES

Variable	Rater agreement	More	Same	Less	p
Authority over siblings					
Firstborn sons	18/20	18	0	0	.001
Inherits or gains control					
Firstborn daughters	8/8	2	6	0	
Firstborn sons	18/19	13	5	0	.05
Last-born sons	9/12	3	5	1	
Respected by siblings					
Firstborn daughters	6/7	6	0	0	.05
Firstborn sons	16/16	16	0	0	.001
Last-born sons	7/8	0	0	7	.05
Power/influence over others					
Firstborn sons	21/22	21	0	0	.001
Heads a kin group					
Firstborn sons	7/10	7	0	0	.01
Has wealth					
Firstborn sons	10/16	6	4	0	

daughters to be like firstborn sons in every way except in heading a kin group. Another is for last-born sons to be average or below average in authority, power, heading a kin group, and wealth but to show some tendency to stay in the parental home, to be a protector of parents in parental old age, and to inherit or gain control of property more so than the average son not firstborn or last born. Firstborn sons also tend to be parental protectors.

It seems clear from the data obtained in this study that firstborns in many societies of the world increase parental status, stabilize parent marriage, and are more likely to grow up with authority over siblings, with respect from them, and with such special attention as comes from elaborate birth ceremonies, parental teknonym, and birth-order-relevant address, naming, or kinship terminology. Although the data allow no strong assertions about causality, it is not implausible that the childhood and adult events are related. Firstborns given special respect by siblings and having authority over them during childhood should surely be in a strong position to exercise authority and control over siblings in adulthood. The special attention given firstborns through ceremonies and teknonymy might well help to legitimate their assumption of authority, their control of property, and their control of a kinship group in adulthood.

A fascinating question is raised by the data of this study: What happens to firstborn daughters in adulthood? On our measures, they tend to differ from their female siblings only in receipt of respect from siblings. What other impact in adulthood might their special experiences in childhood have had? Presumably they have the same roles as other women, but perhaps they occupy them in special ways. One can speculate that they are either more likely than chance to be married to firstborn men, sharing their power and using the dispositions acquired in childhood in a behind-the-throne way, or that they are more likely to control husbands, especially if the husband is not firstborn. Alternatively, it is possible that the strength of the position of firstborn may only exist in relations with siblings. Siblings may have learned to defer to them, to be dominated by them, to treat them with respect, but other people perhaps have not. If that is so, it may be that a firstborn son or daughter is like other men or women once he or she is away from siblings.

Our society may have weaker birth order effects than most other societies. In many nonwestern societies, children care for other children, there are extended kinship groups, and there is a comparatively high likelihood of loss of family authorities while some children in a sibling group are short of adulthood. Also, in some nonwestern socieites, schooling away from home is absent, is available to only a fraction of all children, or is received for a shorter period of time than in western societies. Where schooling is less pervasive, siblings may not be as well insulated from siblings as they are here. For all of these reasons, birth order effects may be much stronger in many nonwestern societies. From that perspective, attempting to build a psychology of birth order effects using data only from Euro-American societies may be a mistake. Here, birth order effects are so subtle that Schooler (1972) has been able to make a case for such effects not even to be present. But it seems to us that there would be no question about the presence of such effects if data were gathered from any of a large number of nonwestern societies.

It is tempting to suggest that studies of birth order in the United States should examine interactions with ethnicity. For example, firstborn sons from homes heavily imbued with the traditions of Eastern European Jews may have been treated as very special by parents and have received more elaborate ceremony in infancy (Zborowski & Herzog, 1962, Part IV, chap. 3). However, it seems more reasonable to expect United States norms for child rearing and adult roles to smooth over most ethnic group differences, even in families that have migrated to the United States recently. It would be a rare ethnic group that would preserve teknonymy, marked status differences between adults who are parents and adults who are not, childhood birth order differences in duties, authority and respect, or adult birth order differences in inheritance or in authority over siblings. Nonetheless, this cross-cultural study of birth order suggests that studies of adolescent and adult birth order differences in the United States might profit from data on childhood experiences.

SUMMARY

In a worldwide sample of 39 societies, the birth of a first child of either sex is more likely than the birth of other children to increase parent status, stabilize parent marriage, and provide a parental teknonym. Firstborns are likely to receive more elaborate birth ceremonies and, in childhood, to have more authority over siblings and to receive more respect from siblings. In adulthood, firstborn daughters are likely to receive more respect from siblings than other daughters, and firstborn sons, in comparison to other sons, are likely to have more authority over siblings, more control of property, more power or influence over others, to be respected more by siblings, and to head a kin group.

The past decade has seen a dramatic increase in the number of research studies where birth order is included as a major variable. Birth order studies usually take one of two directions. One direction attempts to show that the discernible personality trends that appear during childhood and adulthood are related to the subjects' birth order. Although the results of these studies are somewhat contradictory, they do indicate that firstborns, even as adults, have a positive, or even a dependent, orientation toward authority figures and are generally more "socialized" in their behavior—more helpful, better liked, more responsible, more leader-like—than are individuals in other birth order positions. The other direction of birth order studies has involved searching for the reasons to explain why firstborns behave somewhat differently than later borns. This kind of research attempts to determine whether parents actually do treat firstborns differently from, for example, second borns. Studies of this type generally indicate that differences do exist. One such study, concerning the interaction between mothers and their four-year-old children, revealed that the mothers of the firstborns were more inclined to direct their children's behavior and to make overt gestures of love and emotional support than were mothers of later borns. The firstborns were more likely to display dependency behavior—for example, they more often ran to their mothers' side between testing sessions and more frequently asked them for help when working on assigned puzzles (Hilton, 1967).

The effects of birth order have also been demonstrated in research with monkeys. C. W. Stevens and G. Mitchell (1972) observed the behavior of individual first- and last-born rhesus monkeys, aged six to eleven months. Each monkey infant was placed in the company of another infant. In contrast to last-born monkeys, the firstborns were more inclined to vocalize, to be both more assertive and sociable, and to stay closer to the other infant. In other words, the firstborns were more socially active than the last borns, a difference suggesting that rhesus mothers treat their firstborns differently from their other infants, just as human parents do.

Although there is far from a one-to-one correspondence between the personality traits developed by firstborns in later years and the way they were treated during infancy and early childhood, a general survey of the evidence shows logical consistencies. The more highly socialized behavior patterns of firstborns seem to be the product of the greater attention they receive from infancy onward. Attention is both stimulating and rewarding. The more attention the child receives, the more he interacts with his parents; and conversely, the more he interacts with them, the more attention he receives.

A study by Joy D. Osofsky and Susan Oldfield, article 5.3 in this section, also contrasts the treatment that firstborn and last-born children receive from their parents. Their results show that parent-child interactions are complex, and that both birth order and the sex of the parents play significant roles. The fathers tended to be more attentive to their firstborn daughters than to their last borns, directing the firstborns' puzzle-solving activities and having more to say to them; the mothers, however, were inclined to speak more frequently to their last-born daughters. The fathers' behavior is consistent with what one would expect from other birth order research; the mothers' behavior is not. The study unfortunately did not include boys as subjects; it would have been interesting to see whether parents would treat boys in the two birth order positions differently from girls. In other words, would fathers be less helpful with firstborn boys, thus indicating they expected a higher degree of independence from them? And would mothers give more attention to firstborn boys than they do to firstborn girls? Such questions require further investigation.

Osofsky and Oldfield's report clearly demonstrates that children are not merely the passive recipients of parental attention. How a child behaves toward his parents has a great deal to do with how they treat him. The children in this study who asked for help with the puzzles got more attention than those who did not. An interesting difference was observed in how the fathers and mothers reacted to requests for help. The fathers tended to reinforce and encourage such requests, but the mothers did not. Perhaps the fact that the children were all girls had something to do with this, because fathers have traditionally been more inclined to foster their daughters' dependence than have mothers. Again, it would have been interesting to contrast parental patterns of dealing with boys' requests for help. If tradition is any guide, one would expect that the mothers would reinforce the boys' requests, but the fathers would not.

The Osofsky-Oldfield investigation presents a familiar model in dependency research. The child is given an easy or a difficult puzzle, and the experimenters observe both the extent to which he asks his parent for help, and the parental reaction to the child's requests and to his attempts to solve the puzzle. This experimental design has also been used successfully in studies devised to explore cross-cultural differences in parent-child interactions.

5.3 Children's effects on parental behavior: Mothers' and fathers' responses to dependent and independent child behaviors

Joy D. Osofsky and
Susan Oldfield

Most investigators of parent-child interaction have stressed the effects of parental behaviors on children. However, recent studies have indicated that such a unidirectional approach is limiting; children also influence the behavior and responses emitted by parents (Bell, 1968, 1971; Gewirtz, 1968; Moss, 1967; Osofsky, 1971; Yarrow, 1965). These investigations have provided evidence that infants and children are not simply passive, reactive organisms, but rather that they affect the kind, quantity, and quality of parental behavior that is emitted. A primary purpose of the present study was to further investigate the effects of children on parents, in order to gain a better understanding of the interactional relationship between parents and children.

Research investigating the socialization process and parent-child relationships has usually limited the study to a concern with mothers. The fathers' role in the family has rarely been defined as one directly concerned with the raising of children. When the father has been chosen as a subject for study, methods of gathering information have usually included indirect means, such as asking the mother how the father would react. There have been relatively few studies in which the father has been directly contacted for interviewing and questioning and even fewer in which the father-child relationship has been directly observed. Rosen

Reprinted from the *Proceedings of the 79th Annual Convention, American Psychological Association,* 6 (1971): 143–144, with permission of the authors and the American Psychological Association. Copyright 1971 by the American Psychological Association.

and D'Andrade (1959), Bee (1967), and Baumrind and Black (1967) have been among the few investigators who have directly studied fathers with their own children. A second purpose of the present study was to gain a greater understanding of the differential roles of mothers and fathers as parents, through the utilization of direct observations and interviews.

The early and important role of children's dependent and independent behaviors has been amply demonstrated in the literature (Beller, 1955; Hartup, 1963; Maccoby & Masters, 1970; Sears, Maccoby, & Levin, 1957). Many studies of dependency have elucidated and stressed parental antecedents in the development of dependent and independent child behaviors. In an investigation of the effects of children on parents, it would seem logical and appropriate to use the child's dependent and independent behaviors; therefore, such behaviors were included as a focus of the study.

METHOD

Subjects

The *S*s were 42 middle- and upper-middle-class parents and their daughters ranging in age from 4.5 yr. to 6.2 yr. (mean = 5.1 yr.). About one-half of the children were firstborn and one-half last born; one-half of the sample had been to nursery school and one-half had not. The names of the families were obtained from school lists of children who would be entering kindergarten the following year in the Ithaca, New York, school system.

Procedure

The *S*s were contacted first by letter and then by telephone and asked to come to Cornell University to participate in a study of parent-child relationships. The parents were offered a small sum of money to pay for expenses that might arise due to their participation in the project. Mothers and fathers were first observed separately, with their child, in structured and unstructured interaction situations. They were then interviewed separately concerning their child-rearing attitudes and behaviors, using a modified Sears et al. (1957) interview schedule. The *S*s were informed that they would be observed from behind a one-way mirror and that the entire session would be videotaped.

During the structured interaction situation, one of the tasks was designed to make the child act independent (assembling an easy puzzle) and the other to make the child act dependent (assembling a difficult puzzle). To further encourage the desired behaviors, the child was instructed to do the easy puzzle by herself and to obtain help from her parent with the difficult puzzle. The parent was asked to be with the child during the performance of these tasks. During the unstructured situation, the parent was requested to wait with the child while the other parent was being interviewed. The parent was told that any of the games and materials in the room could be used.

Using the videotapes, children's behavior was rated for the amount of independent and dependent behavior displayed. Independent child behaviors included the child working on her own, not asking for help, exhibiting independent behavior in general, and making a statement of confidence. Dependent child behaviors included asking for help, following directions, watching parent do the puzzle, and asking about the absent parent. Parents' behavior was evaluated for control, verbalization, physical interaction, positive reinforcement, and general encouragement of dependence and independence. Observational data was coded in 15-sec. intervals by two unbiased observers until reliability was established. Interrater reliabilities on a sample of the data ranged from .70 to .96 (mean = .80) for the parents' behaviors, and .66 to .91 (mean = .80) for the children's behavior. Following the establishment of reliability, one of the raters scored the remainder of the tapes. The interviews, conducted by two interviewers, stressed data concerning dependence and independence in children. After establishing reliability, which ranged from .65 to .97 (mean = .81), the remainder of the interviews were coded by one of the raters.

RESULTS

Analyses revealed that the structured laboratory tasks were effective in producing the desired dependent and independent child behaviors. Independent child behaviors occurred twice as frequently in the easy task as in the difficult task; dependent child behaviors occurred more than three times as frequently in the difficult task as in the easy task. The differences were highly significant. The amounts of dependent and independent child behaviors displayed did not relate to the sex of the participating parent.

As predicted, children's behaviors resulted in different parental responses. Parents (both mothers and fathers) interacted more, both verbally ($p<.001$) and physically ($p<.001$), when the children acted dependent. Parents were also more controlling when the children were dependent ($p<.001$). Two differences, based upon sex of parent, were noted. Fathers, but not mothers, positively reinforced the children more when they acted dependent than when they acted independent ($p<.02$). Although both parents were more controlling when the children acted dependent ($p<.001$), the mothers were even more controlling in their responses than were the fathers ($p<.05$).

In addition to the differential parental responses between mothers and fathers, which seem to have resulted from the children's behaviors, preliminary analyses of the observational data and interviews revealed differences in patterns of behavior related to other variables. There was a negative relationship between birth order of the child, with birth order rated from firstborn to last born, and fathers' controlling behaviors ($r=-.54$, $p<.01$) and amount of verbalization ($r=-.47$, $p<.01$). For mothers, there was a positive relationship between amount of verbalization and birth order ($r=.42$, $p<.05$). [*Editor's note:* In other words, fathers tended to control and to talk to firstborns rather than last borns, and mothers tended to speak more frequently to last borns.] For fathers, but not mothers, there was a positive relationship between the child's having nursery school experience and his reported strictness with the child ($r=.42$, $p<.05$), and a negative relationship between the amount of control he used when the child acted independent, during the behavioral observations, and his reported encouragement of independence during the interview ($r=-.53$, $p<.01$). More thorough analysis and reporting of the relationships between observational and interview data must await a longer paper.

DISCUSSION

The results of the present investigation would appear to demonstrate that, just as parents affect children's responses, children's behaviors affect parental responses in the parent-child relationship. Using structured observational situations, it was shown that children's behaviors could be adequately controlled to study the effects of dependent and independent child behaviors on parental responses. In addition, the feasibility of studying both the mothers' and the fathers' responses to differential child behaviors was demonstrated; the use of both parents would appear to be of potential importance for many types of investigations.

Children, in the controlled situations studied, did not act more dependent or independent with either parent. As predicted, the parents responded differently to the differentially evoked child behaviors. Both parents displayed more controlling behaviors and interacted more, physically and verbally, when the children acted dependent. This result is consistent with the position that stresses the importance of the children's, as well as the parents', role in the parent-child relationship. Children who are more dependent may encourage, or pull, controlling behaviors from the parents. If children continually ask parents for help and do not perform on their own, the parental response may be to accede to these demands. In determining the origins of child behaviors, it would appear important to study both the parents' and the children's responses.

The present study would also appear to demonstrate the importance of including the father, as well as the mother, in studies of parent-child relations. As noted, there were some important similarities both in the mothers' and fathers' responses to their daughters; however, there were also differences related to the sex of the parent. Fathers tended to reinforce their daughters' dependent behaviors more than did mothers, but were less controlling than were mothers when the child acted dependent. Birth order, nursery school experience, and reported encouragement of independence all differentially related to observed and reported parental responses, on the basis of parental sex. It would appear that mothers and fathers demonstrate different patterns of behaviors in response to their children, and their children's behaviors. These differences may relate to parents' differential involvement or expectations for their children. Daughters may pull different behaviors from fathers than they do from mothers. Whatever the explanation, without studying both mothers and fathers directly, it is not possible to gain an understanding of the similarities and differences in parental behavior and the parent-child relationship. Conclusive explanations of the effects of children on parents must await still further studies in a variety of areas.

Dependency is not the only personality variable to attract the attention of researchers interested in the effect of parents on their children's behavior. The effectiveness of any society depends on the willingness of its members to behave in prosocial, rather than in antisocial or asocial ways. Evidence from a large number of studies makes it fairly clear that antisocial trends in adult behavior can be attributed to parental punitivity and irresponsibility, but we have less data about the antecedents of prosocial behavior. A beginning has been made, however, in recent studies, which suggest not only that children need models who behave in prosocial ways, but that how the models act toward the children is also important. The study by Harris (4.4) in the preceding section demonstrated that children are more likely to share their winnings if their model shares, and especially if she shares with them. We also cited a study by Yarrow et al. (1973), which indicated that children are more likely to engage in helpful behavior if they observe a model who is helpful and who has reinforced them. Still other research shows that merely telling children how to behave when they encounter those in need of assistance has little effect (Staub, 1971). Apparently deeds, not words, are what count.

The first adult social models children encounter are, of course, their parents. It is quite likely that children subsequently react to other adults who are potential models much as they have learned to react to their parents. The effect of parents on children's generosity is the focus of the study by Anthony B. Olejnik and John P. McKinney that appears as article 5.4 in this section. The subjects were preschool children, and their generosity was measured by the number of M&M candies they were willing to donate to "poor children who didn't have any candy of their own."

In their search for an independent variable that might influence the amount of generosity displayed by the children, Olejnik and McKinney did not take the obvious course of asking the parents whether their children should share with others. Such questions would probably have elicited replies indicating approval, as nearly everyone is in favor of children's sharing. To have asked probing and leading questions about parental generosity—such as "How much did you give to the Community Chest last year?"—would, of course, have evoked resistance, resentment, and an unwillingness to participate in the research. Therefore, instead of attempting to find a subtle, if risky, measure of parental generosity, Olejnik and McKinney hypothesized that the more generous children would have parents whose attitudes toward child rearing were more *prescriptive* than *proscriptive*. The parents of the more generous children, in other words, would probably emphasize the prescriptive "thou shalt," rather than the proscriptive "thou shalt not," and would be more concerned with encouraging good behavior than with preventing bad behavior. The more generous children would probably also subscribe to prescriptive rather than proscriptive values. The results of the study are consistent with these expectations. Of particular interest is the finding that parental tendencies to reward or to punish, in and of themselves, had no relationship to the generosity of the children in the study. In other words, the *values expressed* by the parents and taken over by the children appeared to be the significant factor, rather than the extent to which the parents stressed rewards or punishments. In the larger sense, prescriptive values tend to go with openness, warmth, and trust, and proscriptive values tend to go with defensiveness and mistrust.

5.4 Parental value orientation and generosity in children

Anthony B. Olejnik and
John P. McKinney

A number of investigators (e. g., Hill, 1960; Hoffman, 1970) have observed that, until recently, research on moral values was confined largely to a study of the negative aspects of morality, namely wrongdoing and associated guilt. Hoffman (1963) has suggested that the reason research had focused on prohibitions is because "most research on the parental antecedents of moral development has been inspired by psychoanalytic theory, which stresses the importance of repression in the internalization of moral standards [p. 573]."

Recent research, however, (Baldwin & Baldwin, 1970; Bryan & Walbek, 1970 a,b; Elliot & Vasta, 1970; Harris, 1970; Midlarsky & Bryan, 1967; Rosenhan & White, 1967; Rutherford & Mussen, 1968; Staub & Sherk, 1970) has revived the interest in studying generosity, kindness, cooperation, and sharing behaviors in children. Two recent reviews (Bryan & London, 1970; Krebs, 1970) have summarized the recent research in this area.

Reprinted with permission of the authors. A condensed version of this report appeared in *Developmental Psychology*, 8 (1973): 311.

One area of interest has been the child-rearing antecedents of altruism. Aronfreed (1968) and Rosenhan (1969) argued that the acquisition of altruistic responses requires a history of reinforcement and the development of a self-reward mechanism. The research on parent-child relations and altruism (Becker, 1964; Hoffman, 1963; Mussen, Rutherford, Harris, & Keasey, 1970; Peck & Havighurst, 1960; Rosenhan & White, 1967; Rutherford & Mussen, 1968) has demonstrated that altruistic children tend to have parents who are warm, nurturant and non-punitive, or parents who are so perceived by their children.

While several of these studies have emphasized the non-punitive aspect of the child-rearing practices of parents of altruistic children, the present authors examined one aspect of the nature of the rewards and punishments which such parents administer; namely, whether their rewards and punishments are more prescriptive or proscriptive in their value orientation. This orientation, which refers to the "thou shalt" *vs* "thou shalt not" aspect of behavior, has been found to be a reliable dimension of the value statements of college students (McKinney, 1971).

According to both psychoanalytic theory and learning theory, children develop values as they are rewarded for doing what is right and punished for doing what is wrong. A recent modification of this two-fold process has suggested another dimension (McKinney, 1971) as instrumental in the development of moral behavior. According to this four-fold model, the child learns a prescriptive value orientation when he is rewarded for doing what is good and punished for not doing good (sins of omission); and he learns a proscriptive value orientation when he is punished for doing bad and rewarded for not doing bad. The difference in the two value orientations is the result of emphasis having been placed either on doing good (prescriptive) or doing bad (proscriptive) in both rewards and punishments. Earlier research (McKinney, 1971) has indicated that individual values do develop on a prescriptive-proscriptive dimension and that college students with a prescriptive value orientation perceived their parents as having been more rewarding and less punitive, while the proscriptively oriented subjects perceived the opposite.

Since it has been shown that parental warmth and nurturance are related to generosity (Rutherford & Mussen, 1968) and that subjects having a prescriptive value orientation perceive their parents as more rewarding, it was hypothesized that generosity would be related to a prescriptive value orientation in the family. The empirical evidence suggests the following hypotheses: (A) The value orientation can be measured and will be different for individuals holding prescriptive (ought to) values and those holding proscriptive (ought not to) values; (B) Parents who are more prescriptive and less proscriptive will have children who are more generous than parents with the opposite value orientation; (C) Parents who are more rewarding and less punitive will have children who are more generous than parents with the opposite discipline emphasis; (D) Children with a prescriptive value orientation will be more generous than those with a proscriptive orientation.

METHOD

Subjects

The parents (both mothers and fathers) of 34 boys and 44 girls between the ages of 4-0 and 4-11 years enrolled in nursery schools and day care centers in a university community in the midwest agreed to be subjects and allowed their children to participate in the experiment. While previous research on prescriptive and proscriptive value orientations was based primarily on college students, 4-year-old children were chosen for this study because it was assumed that this age was most appropriate to measure parental influence on the acquisition of moral behavior.

Procedure

There were two phases in the study. In the first phase, the children were observed for 20 minutes individually in a structured situation designed to determine the child's value orientation (either prescriptive or proscriptive) and the child's generosity to fictitious needy children. While the child was at either a day care center or a nursery school, the teacher introduced the experimenter to the child. Each subject was asked if he or she would like to play a game with the experimenter in another room. In the experimental room, the experimenter spent a few minutes developing rapport with each subject before the interview. Each male subject was then asked to answer two questions: "What makes a bad boy?" and "What makes a good boy?" Alternative questions such as, "When or why is a boy called a good boy?" were asked to make the questions clear and to obtain responses. Female subjects were asked these same questions about girls. These questions were asked in a random order.

After the brief interview each subject was then presented with a situational task of altruism, an adaptation of procedures used by Rutherford and Mussen (1968) and Midlarsky and Bryan (1967). Each child was asked if he liked M&M's and if he would like some. All children responded positively to both questions. Each subject was then given a bag of 18 M&M candies which were poured out on a table. The experimenter then gave the subject an opportunity to give away some of his candy to "poor children" who didn't have any candy of their own. Two pictures of "poor children" (one boy and one girl) and a donation can were placed in front of the child on the table. Subjects were assured that they were not required to give up their candy and that the amount of their donation, if any, was their decision. Each subject was told to put the candies he wanted to give in the donation can which was already partly filled, and the ones he wanted to keep for himself back into the plastic bag. In order to leave the donor free with his own choice, the experimenter left the room for a few minutes. The amount of each subject's donation was determined after subject was dismissed. All of the subjects' M&Ms were a different color than those in the can. The generosity score was simply the number of candies given away. Each child was told that he could pick up his bag of M&Ms from the teacher at the end of the day. Regardless of the amount of candy donated, all the subjects received a bag of 18 M&Ms to take home.

Value orientation measures

The value orientation of the child was determined by scoring the responses to the two questions. Children were allowed to make as many responses as possible to the questions. The responses were labeled prescriptive when they included either doing good or avoiding good behaviors, and proscriptive when they included either doing bad or avoiding bad behaviors. Responses which could not be classified as either prescriptive or proscriptive were not scored. The number of prescriptive and proscriptive responses were added separately, and the difference in the number of each type of response was taken as the child's value orientation score.

In the second phase of the experiment, the questionnaire which measured the value orientation of the parents was sent home with each child. The questionnaire consisted of a list of 24 behaviors a child might do or avoid (see Table 1). These behaviors were taken from a larger group of items suggested for this purpose by a group of parents attending an evening course in child psychology. The mothers and fathers in the present study were asked how much they would either reward or punish

TABLE 1
PARENTAL VALUE ORIENTATION ITEMS

1. not listening to parents when spoken to	13. playing nicely with friends
2. behaving well when out shopping	14. helping mother around the house
3. fighting with friends	15. purposely breaking toys
4. not bothering mother when she is busy	16. not getting new clothes dirty
5. not sharing his toys	17. playing with harmful objects
6. telling lies	18. not doing well in school
7. not running into the street	19. not coming to the dinner table when called
8. leaving toys scattered around the house	20. tracking dirt into the house
9. cleaning up his room	21. doing well at a new task
10. not being a poor loser in games	22. sharing his toys with friends
11. not behaving when visiting relatives	23. not keeping room clean
12. not cheating in school	24. not taking toys away from friends

each specific behavior. The behaviors included the four types suggested by the four-fold model of McKinney (1971). There were six examples of each of the following types of behavior: doing bad (items 3, 6, 8, 15, 17, 20), avoiding bad (items 4, 7, 10, 12, 16, 24), doing good (items 2, 9, 13, 14, 21, 22) and neglecting good (items 1, 5, 11, 18, 19, 23). These were listed in a random order and the parents were asked to circle one number from 1 to 5 (very little to very much) as to how much they would reward or punish their child for each of the listed behaviors. The value orientation and the discipline emphasis of the parents was determined by adding the scores for the six prescriptive reward items and the six prescriptive punishment items as well as the scores for the six proscriptive reward and the six proscriptive punishment items. Standard scores were computed for each subject for each of the four types of items. These scores were computed so that the prescriptive items could be separated from the proscriptive items in analyzing the relationship between parents' discipline emphasis (reward-punishment) and childrens' generosity. Conversely, the reward items could be separated from the punishment items in analyzing the relationship between parents' value orientation (prescriptive-proscriptive) and children's generosity. This was done to control for any extreme response set bias and a potential confounding of the two dimensions of discipline emphasis and value orientation, since earlier research (McKinney, 1971) had shown that most rewards tend to be stated prescriptively and most punishments tend to be stated proscriptively.

RESULTS

There were no significant sex differences . . . in the number of candies given away by the children. The mean number of candies given by boys was 4.29 M&Ms and by girls was 3.84 M&Ms. Among these, 21 boys and 23 girls gave from 1 to 18 M&Ms while 13 boys and 21 girls gave none away.

The reliability of the questionnaire was obtained by using the split-half technique corrected with the *Spearman-Brown formula*. Reliabilities were obtained for each of the four types of items: prescriptive-reward ($r = .75$); prescriptive-punishment ($r = .78$); proscriptive-reward ($r = .74$); and proscriptive-punishment ($r = .72$).

The results of t-tests showed that for both mothers' data and fathers' data, prescription scores were significantly higher for reward items than for punishment items while proscriptive scores were significantly higher for punishment items than for reward items. In other words, rewards were significantly more prescriptive than punishments, and punishments were significantly more proscriptive.

Because the reward and punishment items were significantly different in terms of their value orientation (prescription-proscription), it was necessary to analyze the two dimensions separately as independent variables affecting generosity. Children were classified either as givers (donated at least one M&M candy) or non-givers (did not donate any candies), and the value orientation of the parents was given as either prescriptive or proscriptive, while their discipline emphasis was given as either rewarding or punitive. The parents' value orientation was determined by comparing the standard scores for each subject, on the prescriptive reward items to those on the proscriptive reward items, as well as comparing the standard scores on the prescriptive punishment items to those on the proscriptive punishment items. The higher standard score in each comparison was used as an indicator of value orientation. Conversely, the discipline emphasis was determined by comparing prescriptive reward to prescriptive punishment standard scores, as well as comparing proscriptive reward to proscriptive punishment standard scores. Since standard scores were used to determine both value orientation and discipline emphasis, it must be pointed out that the prescriptive individuals were relatively more prescriptive than proscriptive; and that the rewarding individuals were relatively more rewarding than punitive. The reason for dichotomizing the donation data was simply that approximately half the children gave no candy, leaving a very skewed distribution. The questionnaire data were dichotomized because the use of a *Likert-type scale* is subject to an extreme response set bias when the intensity of the responses are scored.

When the value orientations of the parents of the givers and non-givers were analyzed for the reward items all comparisons were significant (see Table 2): mothers of girls ($\ldots p = .0055$); mothers of boys ($p = .0050$); fathers of girls ($p = .0318$); and fathers of boys ($p = .0162$). Parents whose value orientation was prescriptive had children who tended to be givers, while parents whose value orientation was proscriptive had children who tended not to give.

TABLE 2
NUMBER OF GIVERS OR NON-GIVERS WHOSE PARENTS HAD PRESCRIPTIVE OR PROSCRIPTIVE VALUE ORIENTATION ON REWARD ITEMS

| | *Reward items* | | | |
| | *Prescriptive* | | *Proscriptive* | |
	Givers	*Non-givers*	*Givers*	*Non-givers*
mothers–girls	14	4	9	17
mothers–boys	17	4	4	9
fathers–girls	14	6	9	15
fathers–boys	14	3	7	10

When the value orientation of the parents of givers and non-givers was analyzed for the punishment items, the same general findings emerged. The results were significant (see Table 3) for the following: mothers of girls ($p = .0011$); mothers of boys ($p = .0454$); and fathers of boys ($p = .0339$). Only in the case of the fathers of girls were the

TABLE 3
NUMBER OF GIVERS OR NON-GIVERS WHOSE PARENTS HAD PRESCRIPTIVE OR PROSCRIPTIVE VALUE ORIENTATION ON PUNISHMENT ITEMS

| | *Punishment items* | | | |
| | *Prescriptive* | | *Proscriptive* | |
	Givers	*Non-givers*	*Givers*	*Non-givers*
mothers–girls	18	6	5	15
mothers–boys	14	4	7	9
fathers–girls	12	7	11	14
fathers–boys	11	2	10	11

results not significant. Parents whose value orientation was prescriptive again had children who tended to be givers, and again parents whose value orientation was proscriptive had children who tended not to give. The relationship between the value orientation of the parents and the child's generosity was therefore consistent for both reward items and punishment items.

Turning to the parents' discipline (reward-punishment) emphasis, it was found that there were no significant differences when the value orientation was controlled. In other words, when the parents' discipline emphasis was analyzed separately for the prescriptive items and proscriptive items, there were no significant findings (see Tables 4 and 5). Therefore, whether the children were givers or non-givers was not related to the discipline emphasis of the parents, but rather to the value orientation within the sort of discipline to which they subscribe.

Finally the relation between the children's generosity and their own value orientation was analyzed. Only 35 of the 78 children gave answers to the two questions which were scorable for their value orientation.

TABLE 4
NUMBER OF GIVERS OR NON-GIVERS WHOSE PARENTS EMPHASIZED REWARDS OR PUNISHMENTS ON PRESCRIPTIVE ITEMS

| | Prescriptive items | | | |
| | Reward | | Punishment | |
	Givers	Non-givers	Givers	Non-givers
mothers–girls	11	9	12	12
mothers–boys	12	7	9	6
fathers–girls	12	7	11	14
fathers–boys	13	5	8	8

TABLE 5
NUMBER OF GIVERS OR NON-GIVERS WHOSE PARENTS EMPHASIZED REWARDS OR PUNISHMENTS ON PROSCRIPTIVE ITEMS

| | Proscriptive items | | | |
| | Reward | | Punishment | |
	Givers	Non-givers	Givers	Non-givers
mothers–girls	13	10	10	11
mothers–boys	10	4	11	9
fathers–girls	14	8	9	13
fathers–boys	12	4	9	9

Those children who gave more prescriptive answers to the questions about what makes a good and bad boy or girl, were categorized as prescriptive, while those who gave more proscriptive responses to those questions were categorized as proscriptive. Among the children with a prescriptive value orientation there were 16 givers and 3 non-givers, while among those children with a proscriptive value orientation there were 2 givers and 14 non-givers. A chi-square analysis, indicated that there were significantly more givers in the prescriptive group and non-givers in the proscriptive group ($\chi^2 = 38.0$, $p < .001$).

DISCUSSION

The hypotheses of the present study appear substantially confirmed. The data revealed that: (A) There is a reliable difference in responses between individuals holding prescriptive values and those holding proscriptive values; (B) Children whose parents have a prescriptive value orientation are more generous than children whose parents have a proscriptive orientation; (C) Children with a prescriptive value orientation are more generous than children with a proscriptive orientation. When value orientation is controlled, however, no differences are found in the generosity of children whose parents emphasize rewards and the generosity of children whose parents emphasize punishments.

The finding that there are no significant sex differences in generosity supports earlier research on altruism with nursery school children (Fischer, 1963) and elementary school children of both sexes (Handlon & Gross, 1959; Harris, 1968; Ugurel-Simen, 1952).

The results of this study indicate very clearly that parents who stress the "thou shalt" or right doing aspect of moral behavior are more likely to have generous children than are those parents who stress the "thou shalt not," or wrongdoing aspect. This proved true for both the rewards and the punishments that parents say they would administer to their children, for both boys and girls and when either the mothers or the fathers were the respondents. Somewhat unexpected was the finding that when this value orientation is controlled, it appears to matter not at all whether a parent is rewarding or punitive. The important thing is how a parent rewards or punishes, that is, what value orientation he stresses.

What of those studies, then, which have shown the relationship between generosity and such variables as non-punitiveness, nurturance, etc.? It should be remembered that, in the present study, the effect of value orientation was held constant when the discipline emphasis was studied, and vice-versa. Ordinarily, of course, parents reward good behavior and punish bad behavior. Less often do they punish the omission of good behavior, and rarely, under normal circumstances, do they reward the avoidance of bad behavior. Thus, a rewarding discipline regime would ordinarily involve a prescriptive orientation and a punitive regime a proscriptive orientation. This interaction has been demonstrated in an earlier study (McKinney, 1971) with college students. Generally subjects linked a prescriptive orientation with positive reinforcement and a proscriptive orientation with negative reinforcement. The value of the present study, then, lies in the discovery of an association between the value orientation of parents and the generosity of their children. It appears that emphasis on prescriptive values by parents teaches children what they ought to do, while emphasis on proscriptive values merely indicates to children what not to do without specific instructions on how they ought to behave.

SUMMARY

Generosity, value orientation (prescriptive-proscriptive), and discipline emphasis (reward-punishment) were studied in 78 4-year-old children and their parents. Generosity was measured by the number of M&M candies the children donated to fictitious needy children. An interview technique was used to measure the value orientation of the children, while a questionnaire was administered to the parents to measure value orientation and discipline emphasis. The finding of no significant sex differences in generosity scores is consistent with earlier research. Significant differences were found between giving and non-giving children in terms of their value orientation and the value orientations of their parents. Parents with a prescriptive value orientation had children who were more generous than children whose parents had a proscriptive value orientation. When the parental value orientations were controlled, there were no significant differences in the generosity of children with rewarding parents and the generosity of children with punitive parents.

Although parents, the initial environmental influences on an individual's behavior, are certainly the prime targets for blame when "things go wrong" in later years, they seldom get the credit when their children turn out well. It is difficult to say how much influence parents have on the personality and behavior patterns that appear in their children after the preschool years. Probably the safest conclusion to make is that the family environment, which is largely parent-created and controlled, interacts with the child's inborn temperament to shape the fundamental ways in which he comes to view himself and the world. How these basic elements are elaborated depends largely on the environment that the individual encounters outside the home during the middle and later years of childhood. The main sources of influence in that environment are the child's peers, whose effects on his behavior we will examine in the next section.

REFERENCES

Cofer, C. N. and Appley, M. H. *Motivation: Theory and Research.* New York: Wiley, 1964.

Harlow, H. F. "The nature of love." *American Psychologist* 13 (1958): 673–685.

Harlow, H. F., Gluck, J. P., and Suomi, S. J. "Generalization of behavioral data between nonhuman and human animals." *American Psychologist* 27 (1972): 709–716.

Harlow, H. F. and Harlow, M. K. "Learning to love." *American Scientist* 54 (1966): 244–272.

Hilton, I. "Differences in the behavior of mothers towards first- and later-born children." *Journal of Personality and Social Psychology* 7 (1967): 282–290.

Staub, E. "The use of role playing and induction in children's learning of helping and sharing behavior." *Child Development* 42 (1971): 805–816.

Stevens, C. W. and Mitchell, G. "Birth order effects, sex differences, and sex preferences in the peer-directed behaviors of rhesus infants. *International Journal of Psychobiology* 2 (1972): 117–128.

Watson, J. B. and Morgan, J. J. B. "Emotional reactions and psychological experimentation." *American Journal of Psychology* 28 (1917): 163–174.

5.1

Harlow, H. F. The nature of love. *American Psychologist,* 1958, 13, 673–685.

Harlow, H. F., & Harlow, M. K. The affectional systems. In A. M. Schrier, H. F. Harlow, & F. Stollnitz (Eds.), *Behavior of nonhuman primates.* Vol. 2. New York: Academic Press, 1965.

Harlow, H. F., & Zimmermann, R. R. Affectional responses in the infant monkey, *Science,* 1959, **130,** 421–432.

Sackett, G. P. Monkeys reared in visual isolation with pictures as visual input: Evidence for an innate releasing mechanism. *Science,* 1966, **154,** 1468–1472.

5.2

Barry, H., III, Bacon, M. K., & Child, I. L. A cross-cultural survey of some sex differences in socialization. *Journal of Abnormal and Social Psychology,* 1959, **55,** 327–332.

Minturn, L., & Lambert, W. W. *Mothers of six cultures: Antecedents of child rearing.* New York: Wiley, 1964.

Murdock, G. P. Ethnographic atlas. *Ethnology*, 1967, **6**, 109-236.

Murdock, G. P. World sampling provinces. *Ethnology*, 1968, **7**, 305-326.

Murdock, G. P., & White, D. R. Standard cross-cultural sample. *Ethnology*, 1969, **8**, 329-369.

Naroll, R. What have we learned from cross-cultural surveys? *American Anthropologist*, 1970, **72**, 1227-1288.

Naroll, R., & D'Andrade, R. G. Two further solutions to Galton's problem. *American Anthropologist*, 1963, **65**, 1053-1067.

Schooler, C. Birth order effects: Not here, not now! *Psychological Bulletin*, 1972, **78**, 161-175.

Zborowski, M., & Herzog, E. *Life is with people: The culture of the Shtetl.* New York: Schocken, 1962.

5.3

Baumrind, D., & Black, A. Socialization practices associated with dimensions of competence in preschool boys and girls. *Child Development*, 1967, **38**, 291-327.

Bee, H. L. Parent-child interaction and distractibility in 9-year-old children. *Merrill-Palmer Quarterly*, 1967, **13**, 175-190.

Bell, R. Q. A reinterpretation of the direction of effects in studies of socialization. *Psychological Review*, 1968, **75**, 81-95.

Bell, R. Q. Stimulus control of parent as caretaker behavior by offspring. *Developmental Psychology*, 1971, **4**, 63-72.

Beller, E. K. Dependency and independence in young children. *Journal of Genetic Psychology*, 1955, **87**, 23-25.

Gewirtz, J. L. On designing the functional environment of the child to facilitate behavioral development. In L. L. Dittman (Ed.), *Early child care.* New York: Atherton Press, 1968.

Hartup, W. Dependence and independence. In H. Stevenson (Ed.), *Child psychology.* Chicago: University of Chicago Press, 1963.

Maccoby, E., & Masters, J. Attachment and dependency. In P. Mussen (Ed.), *Carmichael's manual of child psychology.* New York: Wiley, 1970.

Moss, H. Sex, age, and state as determinants of mother-infant interaction. *Merrill-Palmer Quarterly*, 1967, **13**, 19-36.

Osofsky, J. D. Children's influences on parental behavior: An attempt to define the relationship with the use of laboratory tasks. *Genetic Psychology Monographs*, 1971, **83**, 147-169.

Rosen, B., & D'Andrade, R. The psychosocial origins of achievement motivation. *Sociometry*, 1959, **22**, 185-218.

Sears, R. R., Maccoby, E., & Levin, H. *Patterns of child rearing.* New York: Harper & Row, 1957.

Yarrow, L. J. An approach to the study of reciprocal interactions in infancy: Infant-caretaker pairs in foster care and adoption. Paper presented at Biennial meeting of Society for Research in Child Development, Minneapolis, 1965.

Aronfreed, J. *Conduct and conscience: The socialization of internalized control over behavior.* New York: Academic Press, 1968.

Baldwin, C. P., & Baldwin, A. L. Children's judgments of kindness. *Child Development,* 1970, *41,* 29-47.

Becker, W. Consequences of different kinds of parental discipline. In Hoffman, M. and Hoffman, L. *Review of child development research,* Vol. I. New York: Russell Sage Foundation, 1964.

Bryan, J. H., & London, P. Altruistic behavior by children. *Psychological Bulletin,* 1970, *73,* 200-211.

Bryan, J. H., & Walbek, N. H. Preaching and practicing generosity: children's actions and reactions. *Child Development,* 1970, *41,* 329-353. (a)

Bryan, J. H., & Walbek, N. H. The impact of words and deeds concerning altruism upon children. *Child Development,* 1970, *41,* 747-757. (b)

Elliot, R., & Vasta, R. The modeling of sharing: effects associated with vicarious reinforcement, symbolization, age, and generalization. *Journal of Experimental Child Psychology,* 1970, *10,* 8-15.

Fischer, W. F. Sharing in preschool children as a function of amount and type of reinforcement. *Genetic Psychological Monographs,* 1963, *68,* 215-245.

Handlon, B. J., & Gross, P. The development of sharing behavior. *Journal of Abnormal and Social Psychology,* 1959, *59,* 425-428.

Harris, M. B. Reciprocity and generosity: some determinants of sharing in children. *Child Development,* 1970, *41,* 313-328.

Hill, W. F. Learning theory and the acquisition of values. *Psychological Review,* 1960, *67,* 317-331.

Hoffman, M. L. Parent discipline and the child's consideration for others. *Child Development,* 1963, *34,* 573-588.

Hoffman, M. L. Moral Development. In Mussen, P. H. (Ed.) *Carmichael's manual of child psychology,* Vol. II, New York: John Wiley & Sons, 1970.

Krebs, D. L. Altruism—an examination of the concept and a review of the literature. *Psychological Bulletin.* 1970, *73,* 258-302.

McKinney, J. P. The development of values—prescriptive or proscriptive? *Human Development,* 1971, *14,* 71-80.

Midlarsky, E., & Bryan, J. H. Training charity in children. *Journal of Personality and Social Psychology,* 1967, *5,* 408-415.

Mussen, P., Rutherford, E., Harris, S., & Keasey, C. B. Honesty and altruism among preadolescents. *Developmental Psychology,* 1970, *3,* 169-194.

Peck, R. F., & Havighurst, R. S. *The psychology of character development,* New York: Wiley, 1960.

Rosenhan, D., & White, G. M. Observation and rehearsal as determinants of pro-social behavior. *Journal of Personality and Social Psychology,* 1967, *5,* 424-431.

Rosenhan, D. Some origins of concern for others. In Mussen, P. *et. al., Trends and issues in developmental psychology,* New York: Holt, Rinehart, and Winston, 1969.

Rutherford, E., & Mussen, P. Generosity in nursery school boys. *Child Development,* 1968, *39,* 755-766.

Staub, E., & Sherk, L. Relationship between need approval and children's sharing behavior. *Child Development,* 1970, *41,* 243-252.

Ugurel-Simen, R. Moral behavior and moral judgment of children. *Journal of Abnormal and Social Psychology,* 1952, *44,* 463-474.

6.
CHILD-PEER
RELATIONSHIPS

Even before there was a science of psychology, people were generally aware that the behavior and attitudes of parents are reflected in the behavior and attitudes of their children. "Like father, like son," is only one of a dozen old saws that acknowledge this relationship. Although we are aware that an individual's associates are also likely to influence behavior, we usually place a great deal of emphasis on parental, rather than peer, influence when we speculate about the causes of other people's behavior. We ask, "How could he have turned out so badly? His father and mother are such fine, upstanding people." Less often do we say, "It's easy to see why he turned out as he did. That crowd he went around with in junior high was pretty wild and irresponsible." We forget that the peer group competes with parents as a source of influence from the middle years of childhood onward, and for many children, the peer group is an easy winner.

There are at least two reasons why we often overlook the importance of peer influence in child development. One reason is that we are inclined to see the problems of influencing the behavior of children in terms of what adults—parents and teachers—can or cannot do. When we try to get Johnny more interested in learning to read, or try to inculcate better citizenship habits in our third grade class, we tend to think of the problem in terms of what we as adults should do about it, as though we were the sole source of influence on children's behavior. It usually does not occur to us that the peer group may be more influential than we are and that any maneuver we may execute will fail if we do not take peer power into account. The other reason for our inclination to ignore peer influence is that we are unaware of the extent to which our own behavior is influenced by the groups of which we are members.

The classic studies on group influence show that: first, in making judgments, we are likely to consider what other members of the group are saying or doing before we make up our minds; second, we are often unaware that we are being influenced by the group; third, even when we are aware of the group's attempts to influence us against our better judgment, we are nevertheless inclined to yield, at least to some extent; and fourth, the attitudes we form in a group setting are likely to endure for some time, even after we are no longer associated with that group (M. Sherif, 1936; S. E. Asch, 1956; R. S. Crutchfield, 1955; and S. Milgram, 1961, 1964).

The important points for our present discussion are: first, the groups in which we share membership exert considerable influence over our behavior; second, we are unaware of how influential they are; and third, their influence has a lasting effect. The reasons why groups have this power over us are very complex, but basically they derive from the fact that we tend to find our group associations rewarding—we need them for survival, we derive our identity from them, and we find interaction with other members stimulating. Conversely, exclusion from and censure by groups is upsetting and disturbing. We learn these facts during our preschool years, within the context of our first group—the family—and we learn it again and again when we venture forth from home and become members of neighborhood play groups, classroom groups, clubs, cliques, work groups, and so on. Becoming integrated into the groups that make up the social system is an essential part of growing up.

By the time a child enters school, he has already had some experiences in which adults and peers have made mutually contradictory attempts to influence him. Eventually he works out ways of coping with such conflicts. Perhaps he yields to adults in some situations and to peers in others; perhaps he prefers adults to peers, or vice versa. The paper by Robert H. Blinn and Leonard I. Jacobson (article 6.1) that begins this section describes an experiment in which elementary school children solved problems and were reinforced for correct answers either by their peers—boys or girls their own age from other classrooms—or by men or women experimenters. The authors' results showed that the children were more responsive to reinforcement by their peers, but that this peer advantage held only when the peers were the same sex as the subjects.

In interpreting these results, we should keep in mind that the experimental task was not a classroom assignment, and the adults were neither their teachers nor their parents. Nevertheless, the results do confirm the common observation that school children tend to be very anxious about being accepted by peer groups of their own sex; it is therefore not surprising that the approval of a same-sex peer stranger would be more important to them than approval from a strange adult of either sex. During the elementary school years, peers of the opposite sex have a lower reinforcement value; if the experiment had been conducted with adolescents, the results might have been different.

Effectiveness of peers and adults as social reinforcement and information feedback agents in conceptual learning

Robert H. Blinn and
Leonard I. Jacobson

In recent years there has been an increasing interest in the peer group as a major source of influence in the child's social development. Studies have indicated that with increasing age children become more responsive to social reinforcement delivered by peers (Charlesworth & Hartup, 1967; Patterson & Anderson, 1964), and that the factors of sex and friendship status of the peer agent significantly influence the child's responsiveness

Reprinted from the *Proceedings of the 81st Annual Convention of the American Psychological* Association, 8 (1973): 73–74, with permission of the authors and the American Psychological Association. Copyright 1973 by the American Psychological Association.

to reinforcement (Hartup, 1964; Tiktin & Hartup, 1965). Generally, these studies have concluded that peers may act as effective social reinforcement agents in certain situations.

However, the application of these findings to educational or therapeutic situations has been limited by two problems of experimental design common to most of the investigations. The first problem is the choice of a simple performance measure as the dependent variable. The marble-in-the-hole game (Gewirtz & Baer, 1958) in all its variations has been the most popular, but it is not clear if the findings obtained on such a simplistic performance measure have relevance for more complex learning situations (Wodthe & Brown, 1967). A second problem that has limited the generalizability of findings has been the lack of a comparison between the effectiveness of peer and adult social reinforcement agents. Although one such comparison has been conducted, Ss were from the highly specialized populations of the institutionalized and noninstitutionalized retarded (Harter & Zigler, 1968). Thus, no basis for evaluation of peer agent effectiveness has been determined for a normal population.

The present study was designed to evaluate the relative efficacy of peers and adults as sources of social reinforcement and information feedback in a conceptual learning situation. In addition, the sex of both agent and S, and the age and IQ of S were investigated also.

METHOD

Subjects

The 64 Ss were 32 boys and 32 girls drawn at random from the available population of second- and sixth-grade students at a public laboratory school in Coral Gables, Florida.

Feedback agents

Two male and 2 female advanced graduate students in psychology served as adult feedback agents. Each adult provided feedback to 8 Ss, equally divided with respect to sex and age. The 16 peer agents were drawn from the same population as the Ss, but were from different classrooms than their Ss in order to control for familiarity effects. They were divided equally with respect to sex and age also.

Apparatus

Three experimental units were developed expressly for this investigation. The concept attainment unit consisted of a slide projector and a screen visible to S. Below the screen was a panel with four numbered choice levers. The concept task itself was a modified version of the Intermediate Form of the Category subtest of the Reitan Organic Battery (Reitan, 1955) that used shortened versions of four of the concept problems included in this test.

The peer agent unit was a panel with six individually controllable instruction windows. In addition to GO and STOP, the words GOOD, YES, FINE, and O.K. were visible in the windows which lit up when desired by E. A third main unit was used to control and monitor the other units when the peer agent was providing feedback. When an adult was the agent, he or she provided feedback directly from a prepared schedule and also controlled the slide projector.

Peer agent training

Each peer agent was brought to the testing room prior to his participation in the experiment and was given the following instructions:

> This is a kind of game to see if you can recognize words that are flashed on this screen. The words are: FINE, GOOD, O.K., YES, GO, and STOP. I'll go back here [another room] and flash them on. Call them out when you recognize them loud enough so I can hear you. Watch the screen carefully so that you don't miss a word. O.K., ready?

Each instruction light was then flashed on at least twice or until the child had mastered the task. He was then asked if he would help some other children play a different game by doing the same thing. No peer agents refused to participate or had difficulty following the directions.

Procedure

After the peer agents were trained, Ss were brought to the experimental room and told that they had been selected to play a game where the object was to match pictures and numbers. They were seated in front of the concept unit and given a demonstration of how the "game" worked. Three demonstration slides were then presented where the correct concept was the number of objects on the screen. The Ss were told whether they were right or wrong. All of the Ss were told to do their best but not to worry if they did not get them all right since they were not expected to. In the peer agent condition, E monitored Ss' responses on the main unit and lit up appropriate feedback lights for the peer agent. Peer agents also told S when to GO and STOP via the instruction lights.

RESULTS AND DISCUSSION

A total percentage of correct responses was computed for each S and these scores were used in subsequent analyses. The correlation between Otis Alpha IQ available from school records and the concept attainment score was computed for each grade level. For sixth-grade Ss ($n = 32$), the correlation approached significance ($r = .311$, $p < .08$), but for second graders ($n = 32$) the relationship was nonsignificant ($r = .164$).

The effects of type of agent, sex of agent, grade of S, sex of S, and IQ of S were analyzed with a *multivariate analysis of variance* computer program (Clyde, 1969). A significant main effect of grade of S was found . . . ($p < .001$). Sixth graders gave a mean percentage of 47.81 correct responses ($SD = 10.01$), and second graders gave a mean percentage of 36.56 correct responses ($SD = 6.42$). Thus, sixth graders responded correctly more often than second graders.

A significant three-way interaction for Type of Agent × Sex of Agent × Sex of S was found to be significant also . . . ($p < .03$). Fig. 1 shows that both boys and girls gave a higher percentage of correct responses when the feedback agent was a like-sex peer than when peers of the opposite sex provided information feedback. In contrast, boys gave more correct responses when given feedback by a female adult agent than by a male adult, but sex of the adult agent had no effect on girls' responses. The most notable contrast, however, occurred between the effectiveness of peer and adult agents for boys. Male peers were highly effective feedback agents for boys, but male adults were the least effective. Female adults, however, were more effective agents for boys than were female peers. No other significant effects were in evidence ($ps < .10$).

The results of this study demonstrate clearly that not only are peers effective agents of social reinforcement and information feedback in a complex learning situation, but that they may be more effective for some Ss than adults. Boys, in particular, showed a stronger responsiveness to members of their same-sex peer group than to other types of feedback agents, but girls showed also some preference for same-sex peers over other agents. The results indicated that the like-sex peer group was a

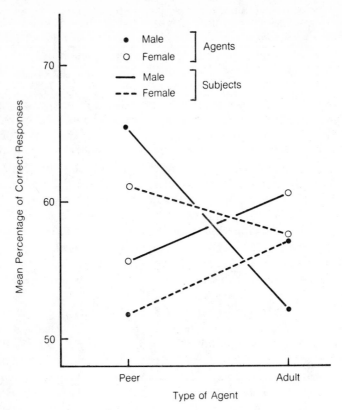

FIGURE 1

EFFECTS OF TYPE OF AGENT, SEX OF AGENT, AND SEX OF *S* ON CONCEPT ATTAINMENT

powerful source of influence for children between 8–12 years of age and that this factor could influence learning.

Since the present study dealt with a conceptual learning situation, the results may have significance for experimental teaching programs. The strong responsiveness of children to their peers suggests that effective teaching programs might do well to include peer teaching as an important element of the learning situation.

One of the rewards we receive from associating with others is reassurance. The early appearance of this learning is demonstrated in an experiment conducted by E. Paul Torrance, article 6.2 in this section.

Torrance's subjects were five-year-olds, who were asked to throw bean bags into a wastepaper basket target. The children participated in three task conditions—alone, in pairs, and alone before the class as part of a group competition. Torrance's dependent variable was not the success the children had in getting the bags into the target receptacle, but the distance they stood from the target. Markers were set at various distances from the target, and the children were free to make their throws from whatever distance they chose. The less confident and more anxious the children felt, the closer they stood to the target.

As might be expected, a large majority of the children chose the closest possible position when they performed alone before the class. Although it might appear that performing alone without an audience would cause the least anxiety, Torrance's results showed that the children were most relaxed when they worked in pairs. This effect can be explained in these terms: when we perform before a group, we are alone and exposed in a very significant way. Because we are not doing what the others are doing, we are not members of the group. They are watching, and we are performing. Furthermore, our worth as an individual is in question: failure or inability to perform up to standard carries with it the risk of ridicule, disapproval, or rejection. Our relationship to the group is in danger of compromise, as is our self-image. When we work with another individual, we become members of a group of two, where both members are in the same situation, and both are doing the same thing. The result is an equally shared, comfortable relationship.

We may wonder why performance alone, away from the classroom audience, was not freer from anxiety. Although Torrance does not comment on this particular circumstance, we may reasonably assume that he was present as an observer. Therefore, the child was not alone, but was performing for an audience of one adult.

6.2

Peer influences on preschool children's willingness to try difficult tasks

E. Paul Torrance

Some children apparently fail to learn because they are unwilling to try more and more difficult tasks. Others fail because they compulsively insist upon trying tasks too difficult for them to master. Thus, to guide a child's learning effectively a teacher must be able to influence his willingness to try tasks of appropriate difficulty.

In another source, the author (4, 5) has presented evidence to indicate that learners differing in tendencies to attempt the difficult need different kinds of feedback concerning their performance. Learners low in willingness to attempt the difficult appear to need evaluative feedback and external criteria. Those high in willingness to attempt the difficult seem to be hampered by this kind of feedback and need opportunities to test their own limits and push their limits forward. Thus, teachers should be aware of individual differences in willingness to attempt the difficult and to differentiate feedback experiences accordingly.

Almost all personality studies of productive, creative people show that such people enjoy a calculated risk in which success or failure depends upon their own ability (6). In fact, there seems to be a positive relationship between willingness to attempt difficult tasks and achievement. Studies of the lives of eminent people who have made important social contributions suggest that one of the essentials for high achievement is a strong tendency to attempt difficult tasks. Instead of just adapting or adjusting to their environment, they deliberately exposed themselves to possible failure and committed themselves to goals that required sustained expenditures of intellectual and physical energy and continued changes in behavior. Thus, it would appear that it is important to society that schools develop in children the ability to estimate their limits and a willingness to attempt difficult tasks.

Reprinted from *The Journal of Psychology* 72 (1969): 189–194, with permission of the author and The Journal Press. Copyright 1969 by The Journal Press.

The present study was conducted as a part of a sequence of activities to teach children to estimate more accurately their limits. It was designed specifically to determine the influence of three different peer conditions on willingness to attempt difficult tasks. The design of the study was suggested by the author's observations in working with United States Air Force personnel in advanced survival training that men were more likely to attempt difficult tasks and to test their limits in pairs than in individual or large group situations. The design of this study was also influenced by the finding of Miller, Bensen, Seidman, and Meeland (2) that men have a greater tolerance of electric shock in the presence of a partner than when alone.

It was hypothesized that the five-year-old children in the present study would be more willing to attempt the difficult when placed in pairs than when alone or before a large group (a class of 22 peers).

PROCEDURE

Subjects

The subjects were 44 five-year-olds enrolled in an experimental preprimary educational program following [a] creative-aesthetic approach (7, 8). The subjects were equally divided into two classes each taught by a master teacher assisted by a part-time teaching aide. The classes were integrated and roughly represented a stratified sample in a medium-sized Southern town. A deliberate attempt had been made to include some disadvantaged children in each class. While the majority of children in the two classes studied are white, almost all of the remaining children in the school are black.

The setting

Essentially the same behavioral settings were maintained in both classrooms. These behavioral settings were deliberately designed to encourage experimentation, manipulation, sociodramatic play, construction, and creative expression. The experimental materials (bean bags and waste baskets) used in this study had been available in both classrooms from the beginning of the school year but had been used almost entirely during free activity periods. The author was accustomed to working with each class for about one hour each week. Early in the school year during a free activity period, the author had encouraged some of the children to try to throw the bean bags into the basket from different distances.

No systematic work had been done either to teach the children to estimate their limits or to encourage them to try the task at distances difficult for them to succeed. Any such learning prior to the present study was incidental.

Experimental Material

The training and test task used in this study was adapted from Starkweather's (3) test of willingness to try difficult tasks. Starkweather's test apparatus consists of a target game in which a ball is rolled from varying distances to a target enclosed in a box. A marker consisting of a strip of cloth calibrated for distance is used in determining what is difficult for each child and in setting the easy and difficult task. Prior to the development of this instrument, Starkweather (3) had used a bean bag target game as a test of willingness to try difficult tasks but had abandoned it.

In the present study, the experimental equipment consisted of two sets of three 12-ounce bean bags each, a marker designating five levels of difficulty, and a waste basket. The equipment used in the study was quite similar to that which had been available in the classrooms from the beginning of the school year. However, no marker had been used prior to this time.

Orientation to the task

The target game was introduced as a part of the author's usual work with the children and was preceded by the reading and discussion of Mary McBurney Green's *Is It Hard? Is It Easy?* (1). As the book was read, the author and the children talked about whether it was easy for each of them to skip, tie shoelaces, climb trees, catch and throw a ball, take a bath, hold tickly worms, whistle, somersault, and pound nails so they go in straight. They were told that they could make the bean bag target game easy or difficult by standing close or far away from the target. In all three conditions, children were given opportunities to practice the task to "warm up" and to find out what was hard and easy for them.

Peer conditions

Under all three conditions, each subject was given a practice session, an explanation of the scoring system (5 points for hitting the target from E, 4 points for hitting it from D, 3 points for hitting it from C, etc.), and three trials to hit the target.

For Conditions A and B, children were called from the classroom in random pairs to play the target game in the wide hallway just outside the classroom. Two sets of targets and markers were set up in such a way that the players were back to back and could not see what the other was doing. Under Condition A, the children practiced and played the game in pairs; under Condition B, they practiced and played alone. Under Condition C, they performed before the entire class and each class competed with the other for the ownership of a large ball unlike any available to them. After each child had performed, he was allowed to add whatever points he scored to the class score being kept on the blackboard. (The two classes achieved identical scores.) This procedure netted 22 subjects each in Conditions A and B and 44 subjects in Condition C. The 44 children in Condition C were the same ones who were in Conditions A and B. The study was conducted after the children had been in the preprimary program for about five months.

RESULTS

A rough test of the hypothesis already stated can be obtained by comparing the proportion of easiest tasks chosen under each condition. These percentages were as follows: Condition A (Pairs), 13.7 percent; Condition B (Alone), 36.5 percent; Condition C (Class), 86.5 percent. In all cases, the differences in proportions are statistically significant at the one percent level of confidence. When working in pairs, children least frequently tried the target from the easiest position. When performing before the class, they were most conservative and most frequently tried the target from the easiest position.

A somewhat more precise test can be made by obtaining a distance score for trial, adding the distance score for the three trials by each child, and comparing the differences in means for the three conditions. The means and standard deviations, respectively, for the three conditions are as follows: Condition A (Pairs) 12.1, 3.3; Condition B (Alone), 6.7, 3.9; Condition C (Class), 3.8, 1.6. An analysis of variance yielded an F ratio of 64.64, significant at better than the .01 level. A t ratio of 4.61 was obtained for the difference in means for Conditions A and B and one of 1.91 was obtained for the difference between Conditions

B and C, the former being significant at better than the .01 level and the latter being significant at about the .05 level.

DISCUSSION

These results suggest that young children tend to be most willing to try difficult tasks when working in pairs and least willing to do so when performing before the entire class. In individual situations, they seem to be freer to adjust the difficulty of the task to their skill level than under the "pair" and "class" conditions.

One might question the extent to which one can generalize from the limited number of subjects included in this study. One might also wonder if the Creative-Aesthetic orientation of the program might not have influenced the results. Under the Creative-Aesthetic approach, there is constant emphasis on attempting difficult tasks and much effort is expended in developing a psychologically safe environment. Thus, it would be expected that children under the Creative-Aesthetic approach would feel freer than under other conditions to make errors or fail in the presence of the group. In both classes, however, the children were extremely reluctant to try the difficult before the class. Confidence in the results is strengthened by the fact that they were quite consistent within treatments and the differences between treatments were quite strong.

From these results, it would be expected that having children work on school tasks in pairs would influence them to try difficult tasks, while requiring them to perform before the entire class would discourage them from doing so. In the latter condition, none of the children in either class tried to hit the target from the five-point line and only two of them attempted to hit it from the four- or three-point line. When working in pairs, only three of the 22 children tried to hit the target from the easiest position; most of them held doggedly to the four- and five-point lines.

SUMMARY

In order to learn and to grow, children have to be willing to attempt difficult tasks. To facilitate learning and growth, teachers should be able to create the social or peer conditions conducive to attempting tasks of appropriate difficulty.

It was hypothesized that five-year-old children in an experimental preprimary school program would be more willing to attempt difficult tasks when placed in pairs than when alone or before their entire class.

The task used in this study was a target game in which the children attempted to throw bean bags into a basket from distances that made the task either easy or difficult, depending upon the choice of the child. In Condition A, the children played the game in pairs; in Condition B, alone; and in Condition C, before the entire class. There were 22 children each in Conditions A and B and 44 in Condition C.

The results clearly supported the hypothesis and further suggested that children are least willing to attempt the difficult when performing before the entire class.

Several experiments clearly show that the mere presence of others has an arousing effect on individuals (R. B. Zajonc, 1966). If a task is a familiar one or is monotonous, the presence of others may actually facilitate performance. In such instances, the arousal that comes from an audience or a partner may actually be helpful. If the task is unfamiliar, however, the presence of others is likely to be distracting or anxiety-provoking to some degree. Examples of this relationship between social arousal and performance are common in everyday life. We may learn a card trick and then fail miserably when we try it on our friends. A professional magician, however, actually performs better before an audience than without one. An inspector on an assembly line in a cannery may become careless or bored watching an endless row of cans come down the line, but he will suddenly become more efficient when he realizes he is being watched. During a political campaign, easy but dull tasks, such as sealing and stamping envelopes, go more rapidly when they are done in a group setting, but a committee that attempts to work as a group at the complex and demanding task of writing campaign speeches may find the work frustrating and extremely difficult.

If the arousal generated in an individual by his participation in a group reaches a sufficiently high level, it can have a "deindividuating" effect (P. G. Zimbardo, 1969). In an extreme case, a person who becomes a member of an excited mob no longer behaves as an individual, but as a mob member, and as such, will act in ways that may be quite different from his usual style of behavior. He has become deindividuated in the sense that he no longer exercises control over himself as an individual but has delegated this control to the mob group. Zimbardo describes other ways whereby deindividuation can take place—through taking drugs or alcohol, for example—but most instances of deindividuation occur when conformity to group norms, expectations, and demands takes precedence over individual responsibilities. Adults who are emotionally and socially mature generally resist the temptation to deindividuate, especially in situations where it is important for them to act in a responsible and moral way. Children, however, tend to be less sure of themselves. They have had fewer experiences making decisions in difficult situations and are much more accessible and vulnerable to influence from others. They are more impulsive and excitable than adults, and they succumb more readily to the extremes of panic, hilarity, and anger. It is therefore relatively easy for them to lose self-control, to surrender to the group mood, and to behave irresponsibly.

The experiment by Diener, Westford, Diener, and Beaman described in article 6.3 represents an ingenious manipulation of deindividuation effects. If a psychological theory has any validity, it ought to work in real-life settings, as well as in the laboratory, and the investigators in this study expended considerable effort to arrange an experimental situation that was both naturalistic and scientifically controlled. This experiment is especially interesting because it was set in private homes whose residents were solicited by Halloween trick-or-treaters.

The natural impulse of any young trick-or-treater, when offered candy, is to reach out and grab a handful. The researchers introduced an element of restraint by telling the children that they could have only one candy. They hypothesized that a child acting alone, without exposure to any deindividuating influences, would probably realize that this request is reasonable, and would therefore take only one candy. The more the child felt deindividuated, however, the more likely he would be to take more than one candy—to "steal," if we use the term employed by the investigators.

The experimenters introduced deindividuation influences into their experimental design in the form of vigorous physical exercise, scary noises, and the presence of partners. Under the exercise condition, the children played a fast game of "Simon says," which required them to jump up and down and to spin around. The excitement engendered by this form of arousal led each child to steal almost four times as many candies as he did under the nonstimulating control condition. The scary noises evidently produced even more excitement, for each child stole seven times as many candies under the noise influence as he did in the control condition. These two manipulations clearly demonstrate that physical and sensual arousal are enough to cause some deindividuation. However, the effect obtained when the children approached the candy bowl in pairs, rather than alone, is of particular interest. The presence of another child produced a much higher degree of deindividuation, and the average stealing rate was four times greater than it had been for children who approached the candy bowl alone, with or without stimulation.

The deindividuation effect is well known to people who deal with children. A child who is usually obedient, sensible, and civilized often behaves in an almost unrecognizable way when he is in a group composed of his peers. An ordinarily quiet, subdued child may race down the hall at school if he is with a group of energetic and high-spirited peers. A child who is attentive and who listens when others are speaking, may interrupt in an inconsiderate manner if he is in an excited, overstimulated group. Even the delinquent who enters a school at night and vandalizes classrooms is seldom alone.

Group influence can, of course, promote prosocial as well as antisocial or asocial behavior. When an atmosphere of attentiveness to work prevails in a classroom, an occasional child may refuse to work, but most of the students are likely to be picked up by the task-oriented norm and suppress whatever impulses they may have to engage in nonrelevant behavior. Indeed, an important part of classroom management consists of manipulating the group atmosphere so that prosocial and task-oriented norms become the prevailing patterns.

Deindividuating effects of group
presence and arousal on stealing by
Halloween trick-or-treaters

Edward Diener,
Karen L. Westford,
Carol Diener, and
Arthur L. Beaman

Deindividuation is one theoretical approach which has attempted to describe the situational factors which contribute to the disinhibition of antisocial behavior. Zimbardo (1969) has posited a number of "input" variables which can "release" behavior that is usually inhibited. External "deindividuating variables" are group presence and anonymity, with internal factors such as arousal and diffusion of responsibility also contributing to the deindividuated state. Most of the research derived from deindividuation has manipulated the variable of anonymity, with few studies focusing on group presence and the contributing rate of arousal on the expression of antisocial behavior.

In Zimbardo's laboratory investigations (1969), group presence and anonymity were manipulated in two separate experiments. He found that in the Group experiment, anonymous *S*s administered about twice the duration of shocks to the confederate as did individuated *S*s, while in the Alone experiment, anonymity produced changes in the opposite direction. However, because the two conditions were run in separate experiments, no valid comparison between Alone vs. Group aggression could be made. Paloutzian (1972) found *S*s in the Group condition to be more aggressive. The *S*s were seated in booths alone during the experiment and the group presence manipulation consisted of leading *S*s to believe that other individuals in booths were also administering distracting noise to another "subject." Fraser, Kelem, Diener, and Beaman (in press) investigated the effects of anonymity, group presence, and diffusion of responsibility on stealing by children on a Halloween expedition. The highest rate of stealing was in the Diffusion-

Reprinted from the *Proceedings of the 81st Annual Convention of the American Psychological Association*, 8 (1973): 219–220, with permission of the authors and the American Psychological Association. Copyright 1973 by the American Psychological Association.

Anonymous-Group condition where 80% stole, followed in rank order by the Anonymous-Group (57%), Anonymous-Alone (21%). Individuated-Group (21%), and Individuated-Alone (7%) conditions.

There were, however, several problems in these studies with the manipulation of group presence. For example, it can be argued that Paloutzian (1972) did not use groups at all since each person was in an individual booth and no verbal or nonverbal communication between *S*s was possible. Fraser et al. (in press) used a correlational rather than experimental approach to groups—the children came to experimental homes either alone or in self-made groups of various sizes. This raises several important questions about their results. Do children in a group exhibit more antisocial behavior just because they are in a group, because older children tend to come in groups more often than younger children, or because individuals more likely to transgress tend to come in groups?

The present study attempts to clarify the questionable past findings on the group presence factor and also to examine the contributing effect of the arousal variable. The study deals directly with questions raised by the Paloutzian and Fraser et al. studies by experimentally manipulating the composition of real groups. Two types of arousal inducement (physical exercise and scary "ghost" sounds) were used to study the effects of arousal on antisocial behavior. Arousal was manipulated in these two quite different ways in order to add generality to the findings and to be sure that the effects were due to general arousal rather than to some other by-product of the manipulations.

The hypotheses were: (*a*) There would be more stealing by groups than by individuals; (*b*) arousal produced by exercise would lead to an increase in stealing; and (*c*) noise would produce arousal, but because this arousal might be interpreted as fear, it might decrease or increase the tendency to steal.

METHOD

A 2×3 factorial design was used in which individuals or groups were either unaroused (controls), aroused through exercise, or aroused by a tape recording of scary ghost sounds.

Subjects

The *S*s were 841 children who trick-or-treated at 20 selected homes in Seattle, Wash., on Halloween evening, 1972, between 6 and 9 p.m.

Setting

Each participating home had set up in a room not visible from the front door a large bowl of bite-sized candies wrapped in colored tissue paper on a low table. Just behind the candy bowl was a decorated screen (with peep holes) that completely concealed a rater.

Procedure

At all homes the children were greeted by an adult female who amicably commented on the child's Halloween costume but let the child remain anonymous in all conditions. Because of the group presence manipulation, only those children arriving in groups of 3-6 were included as *S*s. Alternate groups of these sizes were sent to the candy bowl either in their group (Group condition) or individually (Alone condition). The children were told that they could take *one* candy only. While the children were at the candy bowl, the unobtrusive *O* recorded the number of children and the number of candies taken by each child.

In the control homes, arousal was not induced and only the manipulation of the Group or Alone condition took place. In the homes inducing arousal through scary ghost sounds, all procedures were the same except that a tape recording of frightening sounds was played in the candy room. Arousal through exercise was accomplished by leading the children in a game of "Simon Says," where the children clapped their hands, stomped their feet, jumped up and down, and spun around in an increasing tempo. For the groups, the exercise was done with all the children together; for the Alone condition, it was done with each child separately. The number of candies taken in excess of one was the dependent measure of antisocial behavior.

RESULTS

Manipulation check. To check the manipulation of arousal, a pilot study was run with eight children ranging from 6 to 9 yr. A base-line measure of arousal was taken and the children were then exposed either to a game of "Simon Says" or the tape-recorded sounds (order of presentation was counterbalanced) and asked to rate their arousal by saying which of seven arousal adjectives (none to all seven) described how they now felt. After a rest period, a second base-line measure was taken and the remaining arousal manipulation was induced and rated on the scale. The results showed that children were substantially aroused by both the exercise and scary noises used in the experiment. A *t* test for repeated measures revealed that arousal through exercise was significantly higher than base rate . . . ($p < .001$) and that arousal through tape-recorded ghost sounds was also higher than base rate . . . ($p < .005$).

Of the 841 children visiting experimental homes on Halloween, 487 came in groups of the appropriate size (3–6) and were included in the manipulated conditions of the experiment. There were six homes in the Control condition, five in the Noise condition, and nine in the Exercise condition. Any time a child took more than one candy, it was considered an antisocial act, and the number of candies in excess of one was recorded as the major dependent variable. Table 1 shows the mean number of candies stolen in each condition. The stealing data were analyzed in a 2×3 ANOVA [analysis of variance]. Group, arousal, and the Group × Arousal interaction all showed highly significant effects on stealing ($p < .001$).

TABLE 1
MEAN NUMBER OF CANDIES STOLEN PER CHILD

Arousal condition	Condition		M
	Individual	Group	
Control	.06 ($n = 93$)	.51 ($n = 89$)	.28
Noise	.42 ($n = 34$)	.49 ($n = 88$)	.48
Exercise	.23 ($n = 86$)	1.38 ($n = 97$)	.84
M	.19	.81	.54

[A comparative analysis of] the three arousal conditions showed that exercise induced significantly more stealing than did the noise ($p < .05$) or the control conditions ($p < .01$). The scary ghost sounds elicited a higher transgression rate than the control condition ($p < .05$).

A chi-square analysis for the number of stealers vs. nonstealers in the Group and Alone conditions showed that the two conditions were significantly different ($\chi^2 = 33.09$, . . . ($p < .001$), and a similar analysis for the arousal conditions also revealed them to be significantly different ($\chi^2 = 6.51$, . . . ($p < .05$).

DISCUSSION

The children in the Group condition were significantly more antisocial as shown by their greater incidence of stealing. This finding supports the findings of Fraser et al. (in press) and also Zimbardo's (1969) contention that arousal and group presence may act as deindividuating input variables, causing increases in antisocial behavior. Although alternative explanations can be offered for the effects of the exercise arousal manipulation, strength is added to the arousal argument by the fact that the scary noise produced a similar stealing effect. Also, both manipulations were shown to produce self-reports of arousal in the pretest.

Group presence and arousal interacted to produce relatively more stealing when both were present. The Fraser et al. study likewise found significant interactions between the deindividuation variables. Such findings indicate that the impact of the deindividuation variables is not simply additive and that when the factors act in concert, they are potent disinhibiting forces. Such results also indicate that a developing theory of deindividuation cannot consider the variables in isolation but must specify the interactions which seem to occur.

The present study strongly supports Zimbardo's contention that arousal and group presence can lead to antisocial behavior. The deindividuation variables manipulated in this study released antisocial behavior in children who were probably already motivated to steal because of the nature of the occasion. Several further studies are suggested by this research. One would be to study the group dynamics to see why group presence operates as it does. Is the effect mediated by modeling, diffused responsibility, or increased anonymity? Another possibility would be to investigate the prosocial effects arousal may have if the *S* initially had prosocial tendencies. It would also be important to discover how group presence and arousal interact with other deindividuation factors such as anonymity and diffusion of responsibility.

Article 6.4 by Lyle J. Buchanan, Jr., and Henry Clay Lindgren consists of an experiment in which involvement in a group activity was the independent variable and performance on a creativity task was the dependent variable. The task was one often used in creativity studies—that of asking subjects to think of as many unusual uses as possible for a simple object. The investigators found that children who wrote lists of unusual uses after they had participated in a class discussion devoted to making up a similar list, tended to make more creative and more numerous responses than those made by a control group who had previously made lists alone and had not participated in a group task.

The greater creativity of the experimental group can be explained both in terms of the children's having been aroused by participation in a group task and as a result of social learning or imitation. It is also possible that group participation set up a norm whose effect persisted when the children later worked alone. All of these explanations are consistent with our previously-examined studies demonstrating the effect of social interaction on individual behavior.

Brainstorming in large groups as a facilitator of children's creative responses

Lyle J. Buchanan, Jr., and
Henry Clay Lindgren

A number of experimenters have noted that brainstorming in small groups has a facilitative effect on creativity in subsequent individual brainstorming (1, 2, 3, 4). Lindgren and Lindgren (4), for example, found that university students who first brainstormed alone in writing cartoon captions, then brainstormed in small groups assigned the same type of task, and finally brainstormed alone, produced a larger number of responses and more creative responses in the third phase of the experiment than they had in the initial phase. Inasmuch as a control group that had not engaged in group brainstorming showed no such improvement, the enhancement of creativeness in the experimental group's third phase was attributed to the experimental treatment they had experienced in the second phase.

The present study was undertaken to determine whether (*a*) a similar facilitation of creativity through group brainstorming could be achieved with elementary school children, and (*b*) group brainstorming in formal

Reprinted from the *Journal of Psychology*, 83 (1973): 117–122, with permission of the authors and The Journal Press. Copyright 1973 by The Journal Press.

classroom settings would be effective in stimulating creativity in subsequent individual sessions.

METHOD

Subjects participating in the study were 122 fourth graders of both sexes attending three private schools having largely middle-class enrollments. At each school, subjects were randomly assigned to experimental or control treatments and seated in different classrooms. The two treatments were run simultaneously, with one experimenter randomly taking the experimental group, and the other, the control group. Tasks were six items utilizing the technique of Unusual Uses from Torrance's Test of Imagination, Form D (5), and were presented in randomized order in the two phases of the experiment.

Subjects in the experimental group were seated in formal, straight rows, all facing the experimenter, in traditional classroom style. Subjects were asked to brainstorm by thinking of as many unusual, interesting, and clever uses for the stimulus object (shoe box, paper clip, or whatever), to say them aloud so that everyone could hear them, and to write down their own responses, as well as others'.

This first phase of the experiment was concluded at the end of 10 minutes, whereupon subjects were given another item as a stimulus object and told to record on a second sheet of paper as many unusual, interesting, and clever uses for the second stimulus object as they could. During this individual brainstorming phase, which lasted five minutes, subjects did not speak.

Control groups sat in similar classrooms and brainstormed individually and silently for the same periods of time for both phases of the experiment (10 minutes for phase one and five minutes for phase two).

Creativity was measured in terms of the number of responses each subject produced during the second phase (individual brainstorming), and the level of creativity expressed in whatever responses he did produce. Level-of-creativity scores were obtained by summing the ratings assigned by three judges who operated independently. Judges were instructed to rate each set of responses in terms of their overall creativity—that is, the extent to which the responses could be characterized as original, clever, and interesting, as well as appropriate to the stimulus item in question. Response sheets completed by experimental and control subjects were first coded in a way that could not be recognized by the judges and then mixed together. Then they were sorted into batches of 16 or 17 sheets each and were kept separate for each school. The sheets in each batch were then rated on a seven-point scale in such a way that judgments were forced into an approximation of a crude normal curve. One response sheet in each batch was assigned the rating of "7" (most creative), and one sheet the rating of "1" (least creative). Two sheets were each given a rating of "6," and two were given a rating of "2," and so on. After a judge had completed the entire lot of 122 response sheets and recorded his scores, the response sheets of each school were reshuffled and randomly sorted into batches of 16 for the next judge. Interjudge correlations among the three judges were .83, .82, and .88, which compare favorably with those obtained by Lindgren and Lindgren (3, 4), who used the same method in assessing the level of creativity of cartoon captions.

RESULTS

Stepwise multiple regression analyses revealed that there was no significant relationship between subjects' sex, age, and grade-placement scores on the SRA Achievement Test, Form D (grades 2-4), on the one hand, and number of responses, or level-of-creativity score, on the other.

Stepwise multiple regression analyses did show, however, that the experimental groups in Schools 2 and 3 made significantly more responses ($p < .01$) and demonstrated a higher level-of-creativity ($p < .01$) than did the control groups. There were no significant differences between the experimental and control groups at School 1. Table 1 gives the means

TABLE 1
NUMBER OF RESPONSES FOR PHASE ONE AND PHASE TWO OF EXPERIMENT

| | Experimental groups | | | | Control groups | | | | |
| | Phase 1— group brainstorming | | Phase 2— individual brainstorming | | Phase 1— individual brainstorming | | | Phase 2— individual brainstorming | |
Samples	N	Number[a]	M	SD	N	M	SD	M	SD
School 1	27	11	5.8	2.8	24	5.2	3.1	5.3	3.3
School 2	16	30	17.8	5.8	22	4.4	3.5	4.5	3.8
School 3	19	35	20.8	5.9	14	9.1	5.4	10.1	5.7

a Total group responses.

TABLE 2
MEANS AND STANDARD DEVIATIONS OF PHASE TWO
OF LEVEL-OF-CREATIVITY SCORES

Samples	Experimental groups			Control groups		
	N	M	SD	N	M	SD
School 1	27	12.2	2.9	24	11.7	3.3
School 2	16	15.1	2.5	22	9.3	3.1
School 3	19	13.5	3.7	14	9.8	3.3

and standard deviations for the number of responses, and Table 2, for the level-of-creativity scores.

DISCUSSION

Results for two out of the three schools indicate that group brainstorming apparently has a subsequent facilitative effect on creativity for elementary children, just as it had for adults in previous studies, and formal, traditional classrooms apparently do not inhibit the effect.

The anomalous results from School 1 may have been due to unanticipated interference on the part of a teacher who insisted on remaining in the classroom during the experimental treatment in order to "help." He supplemented the experimenter's directions by ordering the children to cooperate, and later told the experimenter that he had done so because the school made no use of group discussion techniques, and the children, as a consequence, had had no experience with the method. Whatever the cause, the children in that school did not have a genuine group brainstorming experience. Table 1 shows that during the first phase of the experimental treatment in School 1, they produced only 11 responses, or an average of .41 per child, in contrast with averages of 1.88 for School 2 and 1.85 for School 3.

Another contributing factor to the poor performance of School 1 experimental subjects may have been the size of the group, which was half again larger than the corresponding groups in the other two schools. In other words, it may be that the size of the group is a limiting factor to the facilitating effects of group brainstorming on subsequent creativity.

If group brainstorming facilitates creativity in subsequent problem-solving sessions in the normal classroom situation, as the results from at least two of the schools suggest, further research should be directed to determining which aspect of the group brainstorming experience produces the facilitation effect. One possibility would appear to be *general arousal*—the result of participating in an active discussion. Competitiveness may also be a side-effect here. Enhanced performance may also be the result of the task becoming more salient. Such an explanation would depend on the operation of *group norms:* an individual who is not particularly interested in the kind of task set by the experimenter finds, as he observes other group members participating eagerly, that the task is more interesting than he had thought earlier. Still another explanation is *imitation*—the tendency of slower individuals to use more able group members as models. Members who participate in group brainstorming also find *reinforcement* in group approval, and even less active group members may find their subsequent performance enhanced as a vicarious gain from having observed the reinforced performance of others.

Each of these explanations appears to have merit, and their relative contribution to subsequent response enhancement can be determined only by a series of carefully controlled experiments.

SUMMARY

Six groups of fourth graders ($N = 122$) from three private schools seated in formal classroom settings were given an unusual-uses problem, and for a 10-minute period they either brainstormed as a total group or brainstormed individually. In the second phase of the experiment, all groups brainstormed individually for five minutes. In two schools (four groups), those who had engaged in group brainstorming in the first phase made significantly more responses and demonstrated a higher level of creativity than those who had brainstormed individually in both phases. Differences for the third school were not significant. Results for these two schools with their traditional classrooms are consistent with the results of experiments with adults showing that brainstorming in small, informal groups tends to facilitate creativity in subsequent problem-solving sessions. Additional research is needed to determine the extent to which such factors as general arousal, normative effect, imitation, or reinforcement contribute to the enhancement of creative responses in group brainstorming situations.

The values that prevail in a child's culture have a powerful effect on the way he behaves both in and out of groups. Bronfenbrenner's survey (1970) of Russian and American children's attitudes produced some interesting data on value differences in the two countries and on how the two groups of children respond to their peer groups. Bronfenbrenner asked the children what they would do in thirty different situations, each involving a moral conflict—for example, what would they do if they and their friends found the questions and answers for a quiz their teacher had planned for the following day? His results showed that American children had far fewer inhibitions about engaging in misbehavior than the Russian children did. The children were also asked how they would reply to the thirty questions if the other children in their school were told about their answers. Under the latter condition, the American children expressed a *greater* willingness to misbehave, but the Russian children reported less willingness.

Bronfenbrenner's research makes two points: first, that American children are less inhibited with respect to antisocial behavior than Russian children are; and second, that the norms of children's peer groups in America encourage misbehavior, but those of Russian children's groups discourage it. Because the attitudes prevailing in children's peer groups are likely to reflect the values of the society to which they belong, the differences Bronfenbrenner found between the two groups of children suggest that rebelliousness and resistance to authority are probably valued more highly by Americans of all ages than by the Russians. This interpretation seems to make sense. Even though American parents and teachers often complain about children's disobedience, they really do not especially value obedience as a personal trait. Like other American adults, they are inclined to prefer traits such as independence, spontaneity, and individuality. Data from cross-cultural surveys are consistent with this observation. When the members of a group of American university students were asked to rate themselves on fifteen personality traits, they placed achievement, dominance, and the need for autonomy and change at or near the top of the list, and deference, abasement, and the need for order—traits associated with obedience—near the bottom. Japanese students, incidentally, put deference and the need for order at the top of their list, and dominance and the need for autonomy and change near the bottom (M. Abate and F. K. Berrien, 1967). Probably Japanese children would have replied to Bronfenbrenner's questionnaire much as the Russian children did.

There is an accumulating body of evidence that American children are more competitive than children of other cultures. One study that demonstrates this characteristic consists of a series of experiments conducted by Spencer Kagan and Millard C. Madsen, article 6.5 in this section. The authors were interested in exploring the implications of earlier research (Kagan and Madsen, 1971), which found samples of Mexican children to be more cooperative and less competitive than American children. Although the results of the earlier study were interesting, they raised a question—were the Mexican children really more cooperative than the Americans because they placed a high value on helping others, or were they merely interested in avoiding competition?

Kagan and Madsen designed a series of experiments to answer this question. The first experiment in the series eliminated competition as a consideration. Pairs of children, matched by sex and ethnic group, were shown a box that contained either prizes for both of them or a prize for one of them. The box could be opened only by their working together, and the dependent variable was the amount of time they spent in doing so. There were no cultural differences in performance, but American boys proved to be more cooperative and helpful than Mexican boys, and American girls were less cooperative and helpful than Mexican girls. The results of the earlier study by Kagan and Madsen suggested that American children were less cooperative because they were unable or unwilling to be. This experiment indicated that such an interpretation was invalid, because when the children were not forced to choose between cooperation and competition, as they were in the earlier experiment, the Americans proved to be on the average just as able and as willing to cooperate as the Mexicans.

In the second experiment the children were again paired; one member of each pair was told that he could play the game in such a way that he could win the toy which had been given to the other child, and that the other child would do nothing to prevent the loss. In another version, the first child could play so that the other child would lose, but the experimenter would then take the toy. In the first version, Mexican children were almost as eager as the American children to win the other child's toy; in the second version, the Mexican children were more inclined to let the other child keep his toy, but the American children preferred to see him lose it. In other words, the Mexican children were almost as willing to compete as the American children, but only if they gained personally thereby; the American children were competitive even when the only reward was that of seeing another child lose a toy.

The third experiment was similar to the second, except that the second child could take an active part in the game and make moves to defend his position. The American children who started games without a toy generally played aggressively and attempted to take the other child's toy; their opponents countered just as aggressively to defend their possessions. The Mexican children without toys tended to play a more ambivalent game, and the toy owners responded just as ambivalently. The minority of the Mexican children who played an aggressive game met little resistance. In other words, the American children readily challenged and accepted challenges in their eagerness to compete for a prize, but the Mexican children were more inclined to avoid challenges.

In the fourth experiment, the pairs of children played a series of games. The winners received tokens that could be cashed in for prizes at the end of the series. A child could make his moves so that he blocked the other child and prevented him from winning, but as long as he was blocking, he could not win either. The game was considered a draw and no tokens were awarded if neither child won by the end of twenty-four moves. The American children again played the most aggressive game and did the most blocking. As a result, the American children won no prizes twenty-two times, but prizes were awarded every time the Mexican children played. One Mexican child won all eight of the toys, however, because he played aggressively and the other child did not block him; another Mexican child won seven out of eight toys. Such inequality did not occur among the American children, whose winnings tended to balance out.

Kagan and Madsen summarized their findings by observing that while the American children engaged in conflict to the point of irrationality, as they tended to compete even when it was in their best interest to be helpful or cooperative, the Mexican children were inclined to go to the other extreme and to avoid conflict, even when it was in their best interest to resist.

Experimental analyses of cooperation and competition of Anglo-American and Mexican children

Spencer Kagan and
Millard C. Madsen

The results of four experiments comparing the behavior of children from two settings are reported in this article. The children are residents of Los Angeles, California, and Nuevo San Vicente, Baja California, Mexico. Children from these two cultures have been shown to differ profoundly in the degree to which they cooperate or compete at a choice point. Two experiments (Kagan & Madsen, 1971; Madsen & Shapira, 1970), each using a different technique to force a choice between cooperation and competition, have demonstrated that Mexican children are much more cooperative and less competitive than their Los Angeles counterparts.

In view of these clear results, it was decided to inquire further into the psychological basis of the differences in cooperative-competitive behavior of children in the two cultural groups. Previous experimental situations forced children to choose between cooperation and competition. Experiment I was designed to assess the motivation and ability of children to cooperate in a problem situation with no obvious conflict of interest cues. In the absence of substantial differences between cultural groups in Experiment I, Experiments II, III, and IV were designed to successively increase the possibility of interpersonal conflict. In Experiment II, the investigations assess the degree to which children in the two cultural groups are competitive and rivalrous in a situation without direct social interaction and the necessity of mutual assistance. In Experiment III, rivalrous behavior in the presence of direct social interaction was examined. In Experiment IV, the tendencies of children to engage in and avoid direct interpersonal conflict was measured.

Reprinted from *Developmental Psychology* 6 (1972): 49–59, with permission of the authors and the American Psychological Association. Copyright 1972 by the American Psychological Association.

EXPERIMENT I: COOPERATION AND HELPFULNESS

In previous research children have been forced to choose between cooperation and competition. In these forced choice situations rural Mexican children are more cooperative than Anglo-American city children. The apparent cooperativeness of the Mexicans, however, may have little to do with their motivation or ability to cooperate. The Mexicans may be more cooperative than Anglo-American city children only in situations which force a choice between cooperation and competition, because of strong motivation to avoid competition (Kagan & Madsen, 1971; Madsen, 1967). Also, in the forced-choice situations, cooperative tendencies of the Anglo-American children may be masked by a strong tendency to compete. The question, therefore, remains as to whether the Mexican children are more cooperative than Anglo-American city children in situations which have no cues for competition.

In order to put to empirical test the hypothesis of a cultural difference in ability and motivation to cooperate independent of motivation to compete, an experimental task was created that had no cues for competition or the avoidance of competition; the task could be completed only by cooperation. The task was presented under two conditions, one to assess the ability of children to cooperate when motivated to do so, and the other to measure children's spontaneous motivation to help a partner. To test for developmental and sex trends, pairs of boys and girls of two ages were selected.

METHOD

Subjects

Subjects for all four experiments were drawn from the same areas in which previous research had shown cultural differences in cooperation-competition situations. The Mexican children were residents of Nuevo San Vicente (population 800), 88 kilometers south of Ensenada, Mexico. The children lived within a few miles of the town. The economy of the area is largely agricultural with a few small businesses in the town proper. The Anglo-American children were drawn from one elementary school and several day care centers located in lower income districts in and around Los Angeles, California. Eighty children in each culture, 40 of ages 7–9 years and 40 of ages 10–11 years, equally divided by sex, served as subjects.

Apparatus and procedure

Children in both experimental conditions were presented with a cooperation box ($68 \times 18 \times 23$ centimeters). The cooperation box has a hinged
lid which is secured in the closed position by four spring latches which
are spaced so that the simultaneous use of four hands (cooperation of
two children) is necessary to open the box (Figure 1b).

To minimize the possibility that groups differed in their familiarity
with the mechanical latches of the cooperation box, all children were
first presented for 1 minute with a smaller (18 centimeters square)
two-latch training box (Figure 1a). The experimenter placed the training
box in front of the child, put a toy in the box, closed the lid, and informed
the child that he could have the toy if he could open the box. Only
15 of the 160 children, 7 in Mexico and 8 in the United States, all
of the younger age groups except 1, could not open the box within
1 minute. These children were given instruction.

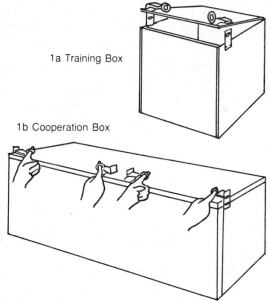

1a Training Box

1b Cooperation Box

FIGURE 1
THE (A) TRAINING BOX AND (B) COOPERATION BOX

Following pretraining, half of the children in each culture, age, and
sex subgroup participated in the cooperation condition and the other

half in the help condition. In both conditions the experimenter placed the cooperation box on a table in front of pairs of like-sexed children for five trials, informing them they could do anything they wished to open the box. In the cooperation condition, the experimenter placed two identical toys in the box and indicated that if the box was opened each child could have a toy. In the help condition, the experimenter placed only one toy in the box and indicated which of the two children would receive the toy if the box was opened.

RESULTS AND DISCUSSION

The mean time required by each subgroup to open the cooperation box is indicated in Table 1. The differences among means were analyzed by a $2 \times 2 \times 2 \times 2 \times 5$ (Culture $\times$ Condition $\times$ Sex $\times$ Age $\times$ Trial) analysis of variance. . . .

TABLE 1
MEAN SECONDS TO SOLUTION IN COOPERATION AND HELP CONDITIONS AS A FUNCTION OF CULTURE, AGE, AND SEX

Age & sex groups	Cooperation condition		Help condition	
	Anglo-American	Mexican	Anglo-American	Mexican
7-9 boys	2.8	8.9	8.0	13.6
7-9 girls	5.5	1.8	9.9	6.4
10-11 boys	2.8	3.7	5.0	11.8
10-11 girls	5.8	1.5	4.5	3.2

Note: Trials were collapsed.

The results indicated no significant effects due to culture, sex, or age, but significant effects due to condition ($p < .05$) and trials ($p < .001$). In all subgroups children were faster in the cooperation than in the help condition (Table 1). The trial effect indicated that children required more time to open the box on Trial 1 than on successive trials. The mean time on Trial 1, 16.6 seconds, differed significantly from the mean time on each successive trial ($p < .001$). Mean times on the remaining four trials ranged from 4.9 to 3.1 seconds and did not differ significantly from each other. The age difference approached, but did not reach, the .05 level of significance.

The only two-way interaction that reached significance was Culture × Sex ($p < .05$). As is evident from Table 1, the mean time was lower for Mexican girls than boys under both conditions at both ages. In the United States, in contrast, boys were faster than girls in three of the four subgroups. This interaction was due to scores on the first trial. On Trial 1, Anglo-American boys were faster than girls ($p < .05$) and Mexican girls were faster than boys ($p < .01$). No significant sex differences were found on subsequent trials. This Culture × Sex × Trial interaction is significant at the .05 level.

In view of these results, previous findings that rural Mexican children are more cooperative than Anglo-American city children at cooperation-competition choice points appear due to a cultural difference in tendency to compete rather than a difference in motivation or ability to cooperate. The results of the cooperation condition fail to support the hypothesis that the Mexican children are better able to cooperate than are Anglo city children. The results of the help condition fail to support the hypothesis that the Mexican and Anglo-American children differ in their motivation to help a peer. Typically, following instructions in the help condition, children would either begin working together or after only slight hesitation would ask, "Can I help him?" or "Can he help me?" When the instruction "You can both do anything you want" was repeated, almost all children worked together vigorously to open the box.

EXPERIMENT II: RIVALRY AND COMPETITION

The competitiveness of Anglo-American children at cooperation-competition choice points appears even more formidable in light of their ready cooperativeness in Experiment I. The results of the cooperation box experiment are consistent with the cooperation-competition experiments if one assumes that when both cooperative and competitive behavior is possible, the intense competitiveness of Anglo-American children masks their motivation and ability to cooperate.

The competitiveness of Anglo-American children may be due not only to a strong individual rather than mutual goal orientation, but also to a motivation to worst one's partner. The hypothesis of a strong motivation in Anglo-American children to lower the outcomes of their peers is consistent with the finding that Anglo-American children are strongly oriented toward relative rather than absolute gain (McClintock & Nuttin, 1969).

Mexican children may appear noncompetitive in cooperation-competition situations either because of a simple absence of competitive motivation or because of a reluctance to express competitive or rivalrous behavior. Competitive interaction is considered taboo in at least one Mexican rural population (Romney & Romney, 1963).

In an attempt to separate absence of competitive and rivalrous motivation from inhibition of such motivation in active interpersonal interaction, in the present experiment children were presented with a situation relatively free of social interaction. To distinguish competition from rivalry, competition was operationally defined in the present experiment as taking a toy from another for oneself and rivalry as taking the toy away to prevent one's pair mate from keeping it.

METHOD

Subjects

In both Mexico and the United States 32 like-sex pairs, ages 7–9, were randomly assigned to competition and rivalry conditions so that each condition contained 8 pairs of boys and 8 pairs of girls from each culture.

Apparatus

The circle matrix board (Kagan & Madsen, 1971) was used in this experiment. The circle matrix board is a 38-centimeter-square playing surface on which are drawn 7 rows of 2.5-centimeter-diameter circles with seven circles to a row (Figure 2). The circles are connected by 2.5-centimeter lines along which children can move a marker from one circle to another.

Competition condition

Children were seated on opposite sides of the circle matrix board. The marker was placed in the center circle (D4). One child was handed an inexpensive ball-point pen and was told, "this is a present for you; you may keep the pen and do anything you like with it." After the child had time to admire his present, he was asked to put it down by the center circle of the row nearest him (G4).

The second child was then informed that he could move the marker from the center circle along the lines wherever he wanted, one circle

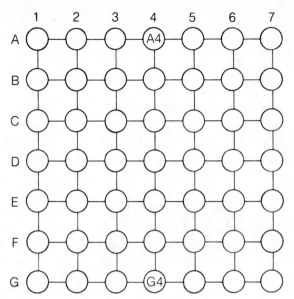

FIGURE 2

CIRCLE MATRIX BOARD

at a time for up to six moves. If the marker entered the circle nearest the pen (G4), he would take the first child's pen away and keep it for himself; if the marker entered the opposite circle (A4), the first child kept his present.

When the second child indicated he understood the goal contingencies, he moved the marker until it reached either the "take" or "let keep" circle, or until six moves were made. If no goal was reached by six moves, the first child was allowed to keep his pen. After the first trial, the procedure was repeated three times with different toys (magnifying glass, magnet, and ring).

Rivalry condition

The rivalry condition was identical to the competition condition except the second child had no opportunity to keep the first child's present. Instead, the second child was told that if the marker reached the take circle, the first child's toy would be taken from him and neither of the children would keep it. When the marker reached this circle, the experimenter simply placed the first child's present out of sight.

RESULTS

In both the rivalry and competition conditions, trials ended when the marker reached the take or let keep circle or when the six allotted moves were exhausted. The percentage of each type of response, for subjects in each culture and condition, is presented in Table 2. Because frequency of outcomes was not significantly affected by trials, trials were collapsed in all analyses so that each subject received a score representing the sum of his performance over trials. The Mann-Whitney U test was used for all analyses unless otherwise stated. No significant sex differences were found.

TABLE 2
EXPERIMENT II TRIAL OUTCOMES: PERCENTAGE OF TAKE, LET KEEP, AND AVOIDANCE IN EACH CONDITION BY CULTURE

Culture	Competition condition			Rivalry condition		
	Take	Avoid	Let keep	Take	Avoid	Let keep
Anglo-American	92	3	5	78	8	14
Mexican	77	9	14	36	22	42

Note: Trials were collapsed.

Take. Children in the competition condition took the toy from the other child more often than children in the rivalry condition ($p < .001$). Anglo-American children took more often than the Mexican children ($p < .001$). This cultural difference was significant ($p < .01$) in the rivalry condition, but a trend in the same direction did not reach significance in the competition condition (see Table 2).

The cultural difference in rivalry is mirrored also in the number of children always or never taking. Seven of the 16 Mexican children and only 2 Anglo-American children never took a toy in the rivalry condition ($p < .06$, Fisher test). Six Anglo-American children but only 1 Mexican child took on all four trials of the rivalry condition ($p < .05$, Fisher test).

Let keep. Children in the rivalry condition let the other child keep the toy more often than those in the competition condition ($p < .001$). Mexican children let their pair mate keep the toy more often than Anglo-American children ($p < .01$). This cultural difference was somewhat greater in the rivalry ($p < .02$) than in the competition ($p < .05$) condition.

In the competition condition, 7 Mexican and 3 Anglo-American children ever moved to let the other child keep his toy. In the rivalry condition, 13 Mexican and only 5 Anglo-American children ever moved to let the other child keep the toy. This difference was significant ($p < .02$, chi-square).

Avoidance. If children reached neither goal in the six allotted moves, the trial was labeled avoidance. Avoidance was the least common of the three outcomes. More avoidance behavior occurred in the rivalry than in the competition condition ($p < .05$). Considering both conditions together, more than twice as many Mexican (12) as Anglo-American (5) children avoided on at least one trial. This difference is a significant trend ($p < .10$, chi-square). The trend toward a cultural difference is indicated by the percentage of avoidance trials in each condition. The cultural difference in frequency of avoidance outcomes is marginally significant only in the rivalry condition ($p < .10$).

DISCUSSION

In this situation, which involves no active interpersonal interaction, both Mexican and Anglo-American children are quite willing to take a toy away from a peer to keep for themselves. If one accepts the generality of this finding, it means that previous cultural differences in cooperation-competition situations may not be due to simple absence of competitive motivation in Mexican children. It appears more likely that Mexican noncompetitiveness is due to avoidance of conflict in situations involving direct interpersonal interaction.

The results indicate a strong cultural difference in willingness to express rivalry. On 78% of the rivalry condition trials, Anglo-American children took the other child's toy away for apparently no other reason than to prevent the other child from having it. This rather striking willingness to worst another is expressed about half as often in the Mexican as in the Anglo-American children.

In the rivalry condition, Mexican children most often moved to let the other child keep his toy. That 22% of the Mexican trials ended in avoidance, however, suggests that Mexican children often had an impulse toward rivalry to which they did not give full expression. The relative absence of avoidance in the Anglo-American pairs suggests that they experienced little conflict in moving to separate another child from his toy.

EXPERIMENT III: SOCIAL INTERACTION IN A RIVALRY SITUATION

The results of Experiment II, when examined together with previous research, suggest that Mexican children are competitively motivated, but that they avoid competition which involves direct social interaction. In the third experiment, a rivalry situation was created so that children actively responded to the moves of their peers. It was thus possible to observe the tendency of Mexican children to avoid direct competitive interaction.

The behavior of the Anglo-American children in Experiment II is consistent with the results of cooperation-competition situations and raises the question of how far Anglo-American children will go to reduce the outcomes of a peer. While the present experiment did not examine outcomes worse than losing a toy, it did allow quantification of the extent children would compete in attempting to prevent another child from keeping his toy.

By comparison of the first moves of children in the present experiment with those in the rivalry condition of Experiment II, it is possible to examine the way in which a responding peer, and the potential for subsequent competitive social interaction, modify initial expression of rivalrous intent.

METHOD

Subjects and apparatus

In both Mexico and the United States, eight pairs of boys and eight pairs of girls 7-9 years of age participated. The children were seated, as in Experiment II, on opposite sides of the circle matrix board.

Procedure

The goal contingencies and the method of presentation were the same as for the rivalry condition of Experiment II. The only differences between the two situations were that in the present experiment children were informed they would take turns moving the marker, and that trials were terminated after a total of 20 moves if no goal were reached. Each pair received four trials. The child without the toy always moved first.

RESULTS

The data were analyzed in three ways. First, analysis was made of the direction of the first move on each trial, and these results were compared with the first moves of the rivalry condition in Experiment II. Second, the responses to initial "take" moves were examined. Third, as in Experiment II, analysis was made of the frequency of take, let keep, and avoidance outcomes. Unless otherwise stated, all analyses were made by the Mann-Whitney U test.

First moves. Children began each trial with a move in one of three directions: forward, to deny their peer his toy; backward, to let the peer keep the toy; or sideways, in the direction of neither goal, avoiding the decision (see Table 3).

TABLE 3
EXPERIMENT III INITIAL MOVES: PERCENTAGE OF TAKE, LET KEEP, AND AVOIDANCE IN EACH CULTURE

Culture	Take	Avoidance	Let keep
Anglo-American	81	16	3
Mexican	48	38	14

Note: Trials were collapsed.

Anglo-American children significantly more often than Mexicans began trials with a move to separate the other child from his toy ($p < .05$). The number of pairs beginning all four trials with take moves also reflects the cultural difference in initial intention. More Anglo-American (10) than Mexican (3) pairs always began with take moves ($p < .05$, chi-square).

The tendency for Mexicans more often to begin trials with a sideways move reached only trend proportions ($p < .10$). The tendency for Mexicans to begin their trials more often by moving to let the other child keep his toy was not statistically significant. Comparison of initial moves of the present experiment with those of the rivalry condition of Experiment II reveals no significant differences in frequency of any type of initial move for either cultural group.

Response to initial take moves. Fifteen Anglo-American and 12 Mexican children had an opportunity to respond to at least one initial take move. The 15 Anglo-American children were forced to respond to initial take moves on an average of 3.3 times; the 12 Mexican children were presented with an average of 2.6 initial take moves.

Children could make three types of responses to an initial take move: (*a*) conflict, moving the marker back into the circle from which the other child had just moved, away from the take goal; (*b*) sideways, moving the marker sideways to the other child's advance; and (*c*) submission, moving the marker in the direction of the other child's initial take move, toward the take goal. The percentage of moves in each direction for responding children of each culture is presented in Table 4.

TABLE 4
EXPERIMENT III RESPONSES TO INITIAL TAKE MOVES: PERCENTAGE OF CONFLICT, SIDEWAYS, AND SUBMISSION IN ANGLO-AMERICAN AND MEXICAN CHILDREN

Culture	Conflict	Sideways	Submission
Anglo-American	72	28	0
Mexican	14	65	21

Note: Trials were collapsed.

Nine of the 12 Mexican children never responded to an initial take move with a conflict move; only 1 of the 15 Anglo-American children was similarly restrained. This difference is significant ($p < .005$, Fisher test). Such an extreme difference cannot be explained by the fact that Anglo-American children had more opportunities to respond to initial take moves.

Most Mexican children preferred to move sideways rather than make a conflict or submission move. Eight of the 12 Mexican children moved sideways on 75% or more of their responses. Such a high frequency of sideways responses was observed in only 2 of the 15 Anglo-American children. This difference is significant ($p < .01$, Fisher test).

In both cultures the least common of all responses to initial take moves was submission. No Anglo-American child ever submitted. Four of the 12 Mexican children responded at least once with submission; 2 did so at every opportunity. The cultural difference in number of pairs ever resorting to submission is significant ($p < .05$, Fisher test).

Trial outcomes. The most frequent trial outcome for both Anglo-American and Mexican children was to reach neither the take nor the let keep goal circles. Anglo-American children significantly more often than Mexicans reached no goal ($p < .02$; see Table 5).

TABLE 5
EXPERIMENT III TRIAL OUTCOMES: PERCENTAGE OF TAKE, LET KEEP, AND NO GOAL OUTCOMES IN EACH CULTURE

Culture	Take	Let keep	No goal
Anglo-American	11	9	80
Mexican	22	36	42

Note: Trials were collapsed.

The intensity of the cultural difference in reaching goals is reflected in the number of pairs always and never reaching a goal. Eight Anglo-American and only three Mexican pairs never reached a goal. Six Mexican and only one Anglo-American pair reached a goal on every trial ($p < .05$, Fisher test).

Mexican children reached the let keep goal on a greater percentage of trials than did the Anglo-American children but that difference is not statistically significant. The difference in number of Mexican (six) and Anglo-American (one) pairs moving to the let keep circle more than once, however, is significant ($p < .05$, Fisher test).

There was no significant cultural difference in frequency of reaching the take circle which was the rarest trial outcome.

DISCUSSION

The initial response to a rivalrous move and the subsequent interactions differ dramatically between the Mexican and Anglo-American children. In response to another child's initial move to take away a toy, Anglo-American children most often made direct conflict moves. Although the Anglo-American children also sometimes moved sideways, they never submitted to the rivalrous intent. The Anglo-American refusal to submit to rivalry is analogous to their refusal to be exploited in a Maximizing Difference Game (McClintock & Nuttin, 1969). Mexican children, in contrast, almost always moved sideways or submitted; they almost never made conflict moves. The avoidant behavior of Mexican children in this experiment is similar to their behavior in cooperation-competition situations (Kagan & Madsen, 1971).

The initial responses set the pattern for the remaining moves in both cultural groups. Anglo-American children competed quite actively, with one child attempting to reduce the other's outcomes, and the second child attempting to defend himself. As a group, the Anglo-American children made 581 conflict moves, or an average of approximately 9 such moves per trial. The Mexican children totaled only 96 conflict moves, or approximately 1.5 per trial.

The presence of active interpersonal interactions in the present experiment reversed the tendency observed in Experiment II for Anglo-American children to reach goals more often. Although Anglo-American children more often than Mexicans made initial moves toward the take goal, the peer willingness to persist in interpersonal conflict prevented rivalrous children from reaching the take goals. Ironically, as a group the Mexicans significantly less often expressed initial rivalrous intentions but nonsignificantly more often reached the take goal. As a group more Mexicans reached the take goal because the few consistently rivalrous Mexicans met little opposition; their partners avoided conflict and allowed their toys to be taken away.

That the first moves of both cultural groups did not differ significantly from those of Experiment II indicates that the mere presence of a responding other and the potential for subsequent competitive social interaction does not significantly modify the initial expression of rivalrous intent.

EXPERIMENT IV: AVOIDANCE OF CONFLICT

The tendency observed in Experiment III for rural Mexican children to avoid interpersonal conflict has also been noted in anthropological (Romney & Romney, 1963) and experimental (Kagan & Madsen, 1971; Madsen, 1967) studies. The fourth experiment represents a more direct attempt to quantify the tendency of children to avoid interpersonal conflict.

To measure avoidance of conflict, children were set off in a direction that would necessarily result in conflict. Children in conflict had the alternatives of avoiding the conflict by moving aside or prolonging the conflict by refusing to move. The experimental situation was structured so that if both children remained in conflict for all of the allotted moves on any trial, neither child would obtain the toy for which he was striving. If a child always responded to conflict by stepping aside, however, he also would never obtain any toys. Thus, in terms of the children's own goals, strategies of uncompromising conflict or compulsive avoidance of conflict were irrational. The experiment therefore allows conclusions about the type and rationality of responses to conflict by children of each culture.

METHOD

Subjects and apparatus

In both Mexico and the United States, subjects of the experiment were eight boy and eight girl pairs of 7–9 years. The children were seated, as in Experiments II and III, on opposite sides of the circle matrix board.

Procedure

Subjects were informed that they would each command their own marker. The marker could be moved along the connecting lines to another circle, but it could not enter a circle occupied by the other child's marker. The subjects took turns moving the markers and on each turn a subject chose to move his marker or not, stating "move" or "stay." All children practiced taking both move and stay turns at least three times before the experimental trials.

When the children understood how they could command their markers, they were shown eight plastic chips and a large assortment of toys (ball-point pens, puzzles, whistles, etc.) and they were told that later each plastic chip could be traded for one toy. It was explained that on each trial a plastic chip would go to the first child whose marker reached the circle initially occupied by the other child's marker. If neither marker reached its goal by a total of 24 turns for the pair, however, neither child would receive a plastic chip for the trial. Children alternated moving first for eight trials.

Because children began by moving their markers toward each other in the direction of their goals, after the first child had completed three turns and the second child had completed two, each marker stood between the other marker and its goal with no circles between them. The second child was then forced either to block the first child's approach by staying or to move aside out of conflict. If the second child chose to block, the first in turn was forced to choose between blocking and moving. Thus the number of stay or blocking moves made by a pair when their markers each stood between the other marker and its goal with no circles between them is a measure of the willingness of the pair to remain in conflict. Because the pair was limited to 24 turns and because it took 5 turns for the markers to meet, children could block 0–19 times per trial.

RESULTS

Data from this experiment were analyzed in three ways: amount of blocking, number of toys lost by blocking, and distribution of toys received.

Blocking. All 16 Anglo-American pairs displayed at least some blocking. In contrast, only 5 of the 16 Mexican pairs ever blocked. This cultural difference in number of pairs ever blocking is significant ($p < .001$, chi-square). The cultural difference in intensity of blocking is equally significant. No Mexican pair averaged more than two blocking moves per trial; 10 Anglo-American pairs averaged over that number ($p < .001$, chi-square). In total, the Anglo-American pairs averaged 4.5 blocking moves per trial; Mexicans averaged .35 per trial. This difference is significant ($p < .001$, Mann-Whitney U test).

The Anglo-American children appeared increasingly willing to block as trials progressed. Fourteen of the 16 Anglo-American pairs showed more blocking on the second four than on the first four trials. This split-half difference is significant ($p < .005$, binomial test). Of the 5 Mexican pairs displaying blocking, 3 blocked more times on the second four trials. No significant sex differences were observed.

Toys lost. Twelve of the 16 Anglo-American pairs blocked each other sufficiently so that on at least one trial neither child received a toy. Seven Anglo-American pairs lost more than 1 toy. No pair lost more than 3 of the 8 possible toys. As a group, Anglo-American children lost 22 toys. No Mexican pair lost a toy by blocking. The cultural difference in number of pairs never losing a toy by blocking is significant ($p < .001$, chi-square).

Distribution of toys. Eleven Mexican and only 2 Anglo-American pairs divided the toys with four for each pair member. This difference is significant ($p < .01$, chi-square). Considering those pairs failing to distribute the toys four each, 12 of the 14 Anglo-American and only 1 of the 4 Mexican pairs distributed the received toys within one toy of equality (i.e., so that to make the distribution as equal as possible the child with fewer toys need take only one toy from the child with more toys). This difference is significant ($p < .01$, Fisher test). The two most unequal of all distributions occurred among the Mexican children: In one pair, one child received all eight toys and in another pair, one child obtained seven of the eight toys.

DISCUSSION

In this experiment Anglo-American pairs tended to remain in conflict even when to do so prevented them from getting as many toys as possible. The number of trials in which neither child obtained a toy may be seen as a measure of the pair's inability to avoid conflict when to do so is in their interest. Given this measure, Anglo-American children are significantly more irrational than Mexican children.

The Mexican children, however, tend to move aside even in the cases when to do so is irrational in terms of their individual interest. In those few cases where one Mexican child blocked in an attempt to receive more than half the toys, the other child seldom resisted, either by blocking or by verbal statements. In such cases the most extremely unequal distributions of toys resulted. Assuming that both children want as many toys as possible, failure of one child to block another from taking more than half the available rewards is irrational in terms of self-interest. Thus, considering those pairs in which some blocking occurs, the extent the received toys are distributed less equally than possible is a measure of irrational avoidance of conflict. Given this measure, Mexican children are irrationally avoidant. The blocked Mexican child appeared to move aside automatically. In two Mexican pairs, both children moved aside even though it was necessary for only one to do so. This tendency for compulsive avoidance of conflict in the Mexican children is consistent with the results of Experiment III and previous experiments (Kagen & Madsen, 1971; Madsen, 1967).

Among the Anglo-American children, every time one child attempted to obtain more than half the toys by blocking, the other child blocked in return. The willingness of Anglo-American children to block had a leveling effect which prevented the extremely unequal distribution of toys sometimes observed in the Mexican pairs. Sometimes, as noted, blocking led Anglo-American children to lose toys, but other times blocking was part of a heated interaction which allowed a just resolution of conflict. For example, when two Anglo-American girls had both stayed for some turns, the girl with fewer toys shouted at the other, "You pig!

You try to grab everything." The girl with more toys thereupon moved aside.

Spontaneous verbal comments and informal discussion with the children after the experiment revealed an interesting difference in the way children of each culture conceptualized the experimental situation. When Anglo-American children were asked why they moved aside in the conflict situation, they most often phrased their responses in terms of self-interest (e.g., "so I can get a chip next time"). The Mexican children never responded in terms of self-interest. When asked why they moved aside in the conflict situation, Mexican children most often responded, "to let him pass."

GENERAL DISCUSSION

Previous research has shown the irrational competitiveness of Anglo-American children in contrast with the rational cooperativeness of the Mexicans. The present four studies present a more balanced picture, demonstrating that the children of both cultures are, each in a different way, systematically irrational.

The irrational competitiveness of the Anglo-American children, while not as intense as at cooperation-competition choice points, is seen in Experiment IV. Taken as a pair, the Anglo-American children behave irrationally: They remain in conflict to an extent which denies them toys for which they are striving. The extreme rivalry of the Anglo-American children in Experiments II and III aims at decreasing their pair mate's outcomes without increasing their own. That almost all Anglo-American children find it reinforcing to lower the outcomes of their peers, throws into question the quality of peer interaction in the Anglo-American culture.

The Mexican children appear irrational in the opposite direction. In Experiment III, a significant proportion of Mexican children made no attempt to defend their toy against the advances of a rivalrous peer. The Mexican child's submission to the peer's attempts to lower his outcomes is irrational in terms of self-interest. Those Mexican children in Experiment IV who allowed their peers to take all or almost all the toys demonstrated compulsive rather than rational avoidance of conflict.

The present experiments demonstrate that Mexican children avoid and Anglo-American children remain in conflict to an irrational extent. That each culture is producing children who are systematically irrational in opposite directions suggests the possibility of cultural therapy. In the present experiments, no attempt has been made to determine the institutions and child-rearing practices responsible for the observed cultural differences. If causal relations can be established, the possibility exists of making systematic changes which would provide children of both cultures alternatives to irrational behavior.

SUMMARY

Four experiments were conducted to analyze cooperative and competitive behavior of Anglo-American city and Mexican rural children. Results of Experiment I failed to support the hypothesis of a cultural difference in motivation and ability to cooperate. In Experiment II, both Anglo-American and Mexican children appeared strongly motivated to take a toy away from a peer when they could keep it for themselves. Anglo-American children, however, were more motivated than Mexicans to lower another child's outcomes when they could obtain no gain themselves. In Experiment III, Anglo-American more than Mexican children responded with conflict to a peer's rivalrous intents in an interpersonal interaction situation; Mexican children were more submissive. In Experiment IV, Mexican children were more avoidant of conflict than Anglo-American children. The irrational reaction to conflict of both Anglo-American and Mexican children is discussed.

The research so far does not tell us why conflict is more attractive to American than to Mexican children, although there are several possible explanations. Perhaps American children have a greater need for excitement and stimulation. Such an interpretation would explain their greater willingness to challenge authority and to engage in antisocial behavior such as Bronfenbrenner observed. This interpretation would also be consistent with many observations of children in different cultures; children in Europe, Asia, and Latin America, for example, often sit quietly for long periods of time, but American children seem generally unable to do so. Your author, having spent a great many hours in airports throughout the world, has observed that the children who are walking or running about, calling to one another and to their parents, investigating and playing with displays and machines, are almost always American children, while children of other nationalities usually sit placidly or apathetically next to their parents. This difference between American and other children may of course be genetically determined, but a more reasonable explanation seems to be that the child-rearing practices of American parents are different from those of parents in other countries. These differences have attracted the attention of European observers, such as Alexis de Tocqueville and Charles Dickens, since the mid-nineteenth century.

Bronfenbrenner's research also suggests that American parents, by exercising less supervision over their children's behavior, have permitted children to create a childhood society with its own set of norms, which in some instances has more influence than parental values (Blinn and Jacobson, 6.1). Although this arrangement may make it easier for children to challenge parents and teachers, it does not make the individual child any more free, because he seems to substitute the authority of the peer group for that of significant adults.

Although conclusions such as these are consistent with research and everyday observation, they need to be substantiated by additional cross-cultural studies like those of Bronfenbrenner and of Kagan and Madsen. Nevertheless the cross-cultural research that has been done provides enough data to make us uneasy about conclusions concerning the social psychology of children and their peer groups, especially when such conclusions are based on research limited to North Americans.

REFERENCES

Abate, M. and Berrien, F. K. "Validation of stereotypes: Japanese versus American students." *Journal of Personality and Social Psychology* 7 (1967): 435–438.

Asch, S. E. "Studies of independence and conformity. A minority of one against a unanimous majority." *Psychological Monographs* 70 No. 9 (Whole No. 416), 1956.

Bronfenbrenner, U. "Reaction to social pressure from adults versus peers among Soviet day school and boarding school pupils in the perspective of an American sample." *Journal of Personality and Social Psychology* 15 (1970): 179–189.

Crutchfield, R. S. "Conformity and character." *American Psychologist* 10 (1955): 191–198.

Kagan, S. and Madsen, M. C. "Cooperation and competition of Mexican, Mexican-American and Anglo-American children of two ages under four instructional sets." *Developmental Psychology* 5 (1971): 32–39.

Milgram, S. "Nationality and conformity." *Scientific American* 205 No. 6 (1961): 45–52.

Milgram, S. "Group pressure and action against a person." *Journal of Abnormal and Social Psychology* 69 (1964): 137–143.

Sherif, M. *The Psychology of Social Norms.* New York: Harper, 1936.

Zajonc, R. B. *Social Psychology: An Experimental Approach.* Belmont, Calif.: Wadsworth, 1966.

Zimbardo, P. G. "The human choice: individuation, reason, and order, versus deindividuation, impulse, and chaos." In *Nebraska Symposium on Motivation, 1969,* edited by W. J. Arnold and D. Levine, Lincon: University of Nebraska Press, 1970.

6.1

Charlesworth, R., & Hartup, W. W. Positive social reinforcement in the nursery school peer group. *Child Development,* 1967, **38,** 993-1002.

Clyde, D. J. *Multivariate analysis of variance on large computers.* Miami, Fla.: Clyde Computing Service, 1969.

Gewirtz, J. L., & Baer, D. M. The effect of brief social deprivation on behaviors for a social reinforcer. *Journal of Abnormal and Social Psychology,* 1958, **56,** 49-56.

Harter, S., & Zigler, E. Effectiveness of adult and peer reinforcement on the performance of institutionalized and noninstitutionalized retardates. *Journal of Abnormal Psychology,* 1968, **73,** 144-149.

Hartup, W. W. Friendship status and effectiveness of peers as reinforcing agents. *Journal of Experimental Child Psychology,* 1964, **1,** 154-162.

Patterson, G. R., & Anderson, D. Peers as social reinforcers. *Child Development,* 1964, **35,** 951-960.

Reitan, R. M. An investigation of the validity of Halstead's measures of biological intelligence. *A.M.A. Archives of Neurology and Psychiatry,* 1955, **73,** 28-35.

Tiktin, S., & Hartup, W. W. Sociometric status and reinforcing effectiveness of children's peers. *Journal of Experimental Child Psychology,* 1965, **2,** 306-315.

Wodthe, K. H., & Brown, B. R. Social learning and imitation. *Review of Educational Research,* 1967, **37,** 514-538.

6.2

1. Green, M. M. Is It Hard? Is It Easy? New York: Young Scott Books, 1960.

2. Miller, I., Bensen, S. B., Seidman, D., & Meeland, T. Influence of a partner on tolerance for a self-administered electric shock. Paper presented at annual meeting of Western Psychological Association, Berkeley, California, March 29, 1956.

3. Starkweather, E. K. Preschool children's willingness to try difficult tasks. Final Report on Cooperative Research Project No. 5-0333, Oklahoma State University, Stillwater, Oklahoma, 1966.

4. Torrance, E. P. Different ways of learning for different kinds of children. In E. P. Torrance & R. D. Strom (Eds.), *Mental Health and Achievement.* New York: Wiley, 1965. Pp. 253-262.

5. _____. Does evaluative feedback facilitate creative thinking? Newsletter, Division 2 of the American Psychological Association, Spring-Summer, 1966.

6. _____. Comparative studies of stress-seeking in the imaginative stories of preadolescents in twelve different subcultures. In S. Z. Klausner (Ed.), *Why Man Takes Chances.* Garden City, N.Y.: Doubleday, 1968. Pp. 195-233.

7. Torrance, E. P., & Fortson, L. R. Creativity among young children and the creative-aesthetic approach. *Educ.,* 1968, **89,** 27-30.

8. Torrance, E. P., Fortson, L. R., & Diener, C. Creative-aesthetic way of developing intellectual skills among five-year-olds. *J. Res. & Devel. In Educ.*, 1968, **1** (3), 58–69.

6.3

Edwards, A. *Experimental design in psychological research.* New York: Holt, Rinehart & Winston, 1968.

Fraser, S., Kelem, R., Diener, E., & Beaman, A. The Halloween caper: The effects of deindividuation variables on stealing. *Journal of Personality and Social Psychology*, in press.

Paloutzian, R. *Some components of deindividuation and their effects.* (Doctoral dissertation, Claremont College) Ann Arbor, Mich.: University Microfilms, 1972, No. 30-578.

Zimbardo, P. The human choice: Individuation, reason, and order versus deindividuation, impulse and chaos. In D. Levine (Ed.), *Nebraska symposium on motivation.* Vol. 17. Lincoln: University of Nebraska Press, 1969.

6.4

1. Dunnette, M. D., Campbell, J., & Jaastad, K. The effect of group participation on brainstorming effectiveness for two industrial samples. *J. Appl. Psychol.*, 1963, **47**, 30–37.

2. Lindgren, H. C. Brainstorming and the facilitation of creativity expressed in drawing. *Psychol. Rep.*, 1967, 24, 350.

3. Lindgren, H. C., & Lindgren, F. Brainstorming and orneriness as facilitators of creativity. *Psychol. Rep.*, 1965, **16**, 577–583.

4. Lindgren, H. C., & Lindgren, F. Creativity, brainstorming, and orneriness: A cross-cultural study. *J. Soc. Psychol.*, 1965, **67**, 23–30.

5. Torrance, E. P. Rewarding Creative Behavior. Englewood Cliffs, N.J.: Prentice Hall, 1965.

6.5

Kagan, S., & Madsen, M. C. Cooperation and competition of Mexican, Mexican-American, and Anglo-American children of two ages under four instructional sets. *Developmental Psychology*, 1971, **5**, 32–39.

Madsen, M. Cooperative and competitive motivation of children in three Mexican sub-cultures. *Psychological Reports*, 1967, **20**, 1307–1320.

Madsen, M. C., & Shapira, A. Cooperative and competitive behavior of urban Afro-American, Anglo-American, Mexican-American, and Mexican village children. *Developmental Psychology*, 1970, **3**, 16–20.

McClintock, C. G., & Nuttin, J. M. Development of competitive game behavior in children across two cultures. *Journal of Experimental Social Psychology*, 1969, **5**, 203–218.

Romney, K., & Romney, R. The Mixtecans of Juxlahuaca, Mexico. In B. Whiting (Ed.), *Six cultures.* New York: Wiley, 1963.

7.

CULTURAL INFLUENCES

The social forces that influence children's personalities and behavior come from many sources. By the time a child enters school, he has been exposed to the values and beliefs expressed by his parents, siblings, and peers; by adults outside his immediate family; and by the mass media. Although each spokesman may give a special flavor to the expression of his unique views about the world and how people ought to behave, he is at the same time an unwitting representative of the cultural group to which he belongs.

If we were to examine a cross section of the society of any country, we would find a mosaic-like pattern of cultural groups. Each cultural group contains individual members who think of themselves and are thought of by others as behaving and thinking more or less differently than members of others groups do. The bases of these differences in group identity may be geographical, religious, educational, economic, or ethnic, or some combination of these. To the outsider, the differences between cultural groups in a given country may seem either trivial or considerable. Usually these differences are reflected in variations in how the world is viewed, as well as in speech. In Italy, for example, people from the Piedmont area in the north are seldom able to understand the dialect spoken five hundred miles to the south in Sicily, and their attitudes and values are likely to be as different from the Sicilians' as is their Piemontese dialect. This cross-cultural difference does not mean that no variations in values and language usage exist within the Piedmont area. In this province, as well as in every other area of the world, behavior and attitude patterns differ between social-class levels, because individuals who have more education use somewhat different language forms and express different life views than do those individuals with less education. Every Piedmontese, therefore, has at least two cultural identities, one regional and one social-class. The more complex a society, the greater the possibilities for multiple identities. In the United States, for example, an individual might be a first-generation Latin-American, Jewish, middle-class, and a resident of New York City. Each of these identities may uniquely influence his pattern of values and his linguistic behavior.

Differences between cultural groups in the United States are usually not so marked as they are in Italy. When individuals from the Pacific Northwest and the South Central states encounter each another, they are usually aware of differences in language styles and perhaps even of values and ways of looking at the world, but these differences are not nearly so great as the differences between the dialects and values characteristic of the northern and southern provinces in Italy. Class differences are also less sharply defined in the United States than they are in Italy and in other European countries. In the United States, the great amount of movement up, down, and across class lines has made some of the traditional differences less distinct. However, class differences do exist in the United States, and the contrasting life styles, values, and child-rearing practices characteristic of the different class levels are readily identifiable. In further contrast to Italy, the United States has a large number of ethnic groups—Puerto Ricans, Mexicans, blacks, American Indians, Asians, and so forth— each with its distinctive life style.

The question of whether social-class differences in values and life style are greater than ethnic differences is a matter of debate among behavioral scientists. Social-class and ethnic variables in cross-cultural research are difficult to control because they are so easily confounded. Most evidence indicates that social-class differences in the United States, especially those attributable to educational level, influence attitudes and behavior somewhat more than ethnic differences do. For example, behavioral differences between middle-class Puerto Ricans, blacks, Orientals, and Anglos tend to be slight. When psychological differences between different ethnic groups are found, most of the variance is attributable to the distribution of social classes within the groups. This point is often overlooked, and studies that compare attitudes and behavior patterns of white and black children, or Oriental and Latin-American children, without controlling for social class, are difficult to interpret. In most urban communities, the white population includes all social classes, the majority of which are middle-class. Black populations may include some middle-class members, but the majority are likely to be working-class, a sizable proportion of whom live at the poverty level. Oriental populations are likely to have a higher proportion of middle-class members than are any of the four groups, but the proportion of middle-class members among Mexican-Americans is usually small. It is only when samples are equated along a social-class variable such as education, that conclusions can be drawn regarding cultural differences between the groups.

The point that social-class differences in the United States are likely to be more significant than ethnic ones is demonstrated in the study by Anna Leifer that appears as article 7.1 in this section. In her study of cognitive development, she not only controlled for social class by drawing her subjects from preschools enrolling only disadvantaged children, but she used the Lowenfeld Mosaic test, a relatively "culture-free" measure. As might be expected, the children were considerably below the norm for their age—about one-and-one-half years. Her finding that there is essentially no difference between black children and white children is of special interest. Of the black children, 35 percent were able to make an identifiable pattern or design, as compared to 24 percent of the white children. The difference between these two percentages was not statistically significant for the 43 black and 46 white children who were the subjects in her study, however.

Mosaics of disadvantaged Negro and white preschoolers compared

Anna Leifer

While comparative studies of Negro and white intelligence in school-age children abound in the literature (8), relatively little work has been done comparing these two groups on projective tests. One study examined teen-age Negro and white Rorschach responses (4); another contrasted Rorschach and Lowenfeld Mosaic Test findings for both groups on the elementary school level (1); a third study reported differences in Mosaic responses of Negro and white primary-school students (2).

Despite the current interest in disadvantaged preschoolers, virtually no research has appeared that examines projective responses of Negro and white four-year-olds from economically deprived backgrounds. Moreover, no one has used the Lowenfeld Mosaic Test, a test ostensibly free of cultural parameters (3, 10), to assess the developmental level of these two groups.

Previous studies comparing Negro and white school-age children on projectives are generally in agreement with research indicating that Negro children have lower tested intelligence than that of supposedly matched white children (5). That is, Negro youngsters are reported to perform less adequately on projective tests than do their white counter-parts. However, careful analysis of the data on which these findings are based suggests that samples used for comparisons and described as "roughly" or "more or less" equivalent differ in important variables.

Ames and August (2), who reported Mosaic responses of Negro primary-school children to be considerably "less mature" than those of same age white children, described their white subjects as "more or less" approximating Negro subjects on *IQ* and socioeconomic status. Yet, Negro subjects, reflecting community patterns, attended all-Negro schools and had *IQ*s that averaged 15 points lower than the white group that it allegedly matched. Apparently the white group that was closest on relevant variables to the Negro group was characterized as "equivalent."

When Negro and white elementary-school students were examined with the Rorschach and the Lowenfeld Mosaic Test (1), Negro responses were described as "poorer," Lowenfeld patterns more "immature" than those of the white comparison group. However, parents of Negro subjects were classified as "slightly skilled," while parents of white subjects were of "clerical, skilled, or retail business" socioeconomic status.

Thus, in earlier studies, race is confusedly confounded with socio-economic and cognitive variables which cloud the data. Since affective behavior is multiply determined, unless all relevant variables are carefully matched, except race, no valid assessment of the comparative developmental status of Negro children is possible.

Present study compares the Lowenfeld Mosaic responses of Negro and white disadvantaged four-year-olds who live in the same neighborhood, attend the same school, all of whom, white as well as black, occupy the lowest socio-economic level in the community.

METHOD

Subjects were 43 Negro and 46 white children enrolled in a suburban Long Island, New York, prekindergarten for disadvantaged children. There were 21 Negro girls, 22 Negro boys, 20 white girls, and 26 white boys, ranging in age from 45 to 57 months. These children were eligible for this program, funded and sponsored by the New York State Department of Education, on the basis of priority of need, so they represented the poorest environmental circumstances in the community. Each child admitted to the program was felt to be educationally at a disadvantage and, therefore, handicapped in making an adequate kindergarten adjustment.

The Lowenfeld Mosaic Test was individually administered by the writer in the course of the school year as part of each child's psychological evaluation.

With the use of Ames and Ilg's classification scheme (3), each child's Mosaic product was evaluated according to the type of structure. Since Mosaic patterns have been shown to undergo an orderly progression with age from less (Nonrepresentational without pattern) to more mature constructions (Nonrepresentational with pattern and Representational), it was possible to assess the developmental level of Negro and white groups across sexes.

The Ames and Ilg (3) normative study further permitted comparisons between the Mosaic performance of present subjects with that of middle-class four-year-olds.

RESULTS

Table 1 shows the distribution of responses for Negro and white disadvantaged four-year-olds divided by sex. It is readily apparent that the greatest proportion of these children make a Nonrepresentational without-pattern type of structure, the most immature category of response. In fact, 71% of present subjects gave this type of construction compared with 28% of middle-class four-year-olds, 56% of middle-class three-year-olds, and 98% of middle-class two-year-olds (3). Thus poor children are considerably retarded in their psychological development which more

TABLE 1
MOSAIC RESPONSES OF ECONOMICALLY DEPRIVED NEGRO AND WHITE
FOUR-YEAR-OLD GIRLS AND BOYS

	Girls		Boys	
Type of structure	Negro (N=21)	White (N=20)	Negro (N=22)	White (N=26)
A. Nonrepresentational without pattern				
Drop or pile	1	0	2	3
Scatter	7	7	9	8
Prefundamental	3	3	3	1
Slab	1	5	0	3
Overall pattern	2	1	0	4
Lining up pieces	0	0	0	0
All A	14*	16*	14*	19*
B. Nonrepresentational with pattern				
Fundamental	0	0	1	1
Central design	2	1	1	1
Design along rim	2	0	0	1
All B	4	1	2	3
C. Representational				
Object	3	2	6	3
Scene	0	1	0	1
All C	3	3	6	4

*No significant differences found between proportions of Nonrepresentational without-pattern designs.

closely approximates the development of the middle-class two-and-one-half to three-year-old.

The most important thing, however, that Table 1 shows is that behavior in response to the Mosaic is approximately the *same* for both Negro and white children. *Both black and white children* in this sample are maturing at a much slower rate than middle-class children do. This is seen in Table 1 where proportion of Nonrepresentational without-pattern responses (starred items) made by Negro and white subjects failed to show significant differences when subjected to the chi-square statistical test.

Nor were there any appreciable differences between the relative numbers of Nonrepresentational without-pattern responses made by girls and those made by boys in Negro and white groups.

Quality of responses in the four groups of subjects was also comparable.

DISCUSSION

This research indicates that socioeconomic deprivation tends to retard psychological development in early childhood by approximately one-and-one-half-years. It further suggests that no developmental differences emerge between Negro and white preschoolers who grow up in similar marginal economic conditions. Environmental circumstances appear to be more closely articulated with developmental processes than is skin color. In other words, the effects of poverty on the maturation processes of young children seem to cut across race and ethnic origin.

Because the poorest children in any racially mixed community are generally Negro, it is usually extremely difficult to find a sample of white children comparable on all relevant variables except race. Thus basic assumptions about class and race differences in psychological development continue to rest on comparisons based on *nonequivalent* groups. Observations made thus far between Negro and white children, with respect to maturity status, can hardly be accepted as sufficient evidence that the Negro child is genetically less endowed or that cultural conditions other than those related to socioeconomic status serve to impede maturation.

Earlier studies have shown the Lowenfeld Mosaic Test to be useful in predicting school readiness (6) and in indicating individual's readiness to begin formal instruction in reading and spelling (9). The slow rate of development of economically disadvantaged children ill-equips them for the acquisition of skills in the beginning grades in school.

In considering the relative contribution of genetic and environmental influences in molding intellectual competence, Jensen (7) has postulated that genetic variables that inhere in the gene pools accessible to Negro children serve to strongly limit cognitive mastery. *IQ,* he states, is largely predetermined by fixed factors which prescribe a range of genetically based educability.

The study serves as one piece of evidence which calls into question the hypothesis that genetic factors are mainly responsible for the lower scholastic performance of Negro children. Present research suggests that when variables associated with marginal economic conditions interact in early development with the biogenetics of differing racial groups, the consequences for successful academic performance are equally unfavorable to both groups. Environmental forces indigenous to economic deprivation acting reciprocally with the genotypic potential of *white* children seem to similarly limit the potential of that group for school achievement. In short, poverty tends to shape similar ecological niches for developing children of different races.

SUMMARY

Comparison of Mosaic response of 43 disadvantaged Negro preschoolers with 46 equally disadvantaged white preschoolers shows products of both groups to be approximately one-and-one-half years below their chronological ages. This slower rate of psychological development leaves both Negro and white economically deprived children ill-equipped for formal school instruction.

Interaction of poor environmental conditions with the genotypic potential of children of both races appears to have the same unfavorable consequences for their academic success.

Criticism is directed at comparative statements about race differences in psychological development based on studies wherein race and socioeconomic status are confounded.

Other research reports included in this book have also presented data on differences between children that may be culturally relevant. Falbo (3.3) found that middle-class Hawaiian preschoolers were more likely to explain successful completion of a puzzle in terms of the child's having "tried hard," but children from welfare homes were more likely to explain success in terms of the ease of the task or of luck. Falbo found her results consistent with those of cross-cultural studies of achievement motivation. Children from poverty homes are more likely to be apathetic and to fear failure when confronted with unfamiliar tasks than are children from working-class and middle-class homes. This kind of response can, of course, result from the greater number of discouraging experiences that children from very poor families are likely to have; but the important point is that differences in attitude distinguishing the children of one class from those of other classes do exist, whatever the causes of those differences might be.

The second article (7.2) in this section is a study by Ruth Formanek and Pierre Woog of children's attitudes toward authority figures. Previous researchers had noted differences between middle-class and lower-class children with respect to their attitudes toward the police. Formanek and Woog hypothesized that these views might be part of a larger attitude toward authority and asked their subjects to express their feelings not only about policemen, but about teachers, principals, and parents as well. Their results indicate that lower-class preschool children are more apprehensive about authority figures than are middle-class children. This fear-level difference did not appear among the older children in this study, nor did it appear between the ethnic groups—black, white, and Puerto Rican. In general, the younger children were more inclined to see authority figures—especially the school principal—as threatening.

Attitudes of preschool and elementary school children to authority figures

Ruth Formanek and
Pierre Woog

Studies on attitudes to authority belong to the larger class of studies on political socialization. This is defined as the learning of political attitudes and behaviors acceptable to the present political system. The goal of political socialization is to train children to become well-functioning adult members of political society.

A major focus of attention of writers on political socialization has been the child's relationship to authority figures. Authority figures represent the child's first encounter with the political system and probably determine later orientations and behavior.

We have explored attitudes toward parents, teachers and the police in contrast to many such studies which have dealt only with attitudes toward political authority, but frequently have included the police. Our brief summary of the literature is classified according to authority figures.

Police. Derbyshire (1968) found that children of lower-class, culturally excluded minorities, living in the inner city, exhibit significantly more antipathy toward police than youngsters living in an upper middle class area. He attributes the difference to varying degrees of social distance between the community and the police. A public relations program, instituted by the Los Angeles Police Department, had as its aim the reduction of antipathy toward the police among lower-class third-grade children. The drawings of the police by lower-class children were compared to the drawings of middle-class children and higher levels of antipathy toward police on the part of lower-class children were found. Children of the Watts area were tested before and after exposure to the public relations program and showed significantly less antipathy

Reprinted, with minor editing, from Report No. ED 046 606, Educational Resources Information Center (ERIC), U. S. Office of Education, March, 1970, with permission of the authors. A draft of this paper was presented at the 1971 convention of the American Educational Research Association and published in the *Child Study Journal* 1 (1970–1971): 100.

toward the police after the presentation. Whether or not the new levels of antipathy remained stable over time was not investigated.

Greenberg (1970) studied the orientations to authority of middle-class and lower-class black and white children in grades three to nine. Similarities were found among younger children in that they tended to idealize authority figures. Above the third grade, a sharp divergence in the orientations of black and white children was found, consisting primarily in a decline of positive feelings toward the police among black students. Social class did not prove to be a powerful variable with one exception: black lower-class children showed a precipitous decline in positive feelings to the police. The author states that young black children idealize authority more than do white children, and lower-class children do so more than middle-class children. He hypothesizes that both black and lower-class children feel more vulnerable than do other children and tend to more readily idealize authority. Blacks are more fearful than whites, and lower-class children are more fearful than middle-class children. Differential levels of idealization may be traced to differential feelings of anxiety or vulnerability. Maturing black children appear to perceive the police with growing disaffection, their early attachment quickly eroding through personal experience with the police as well as through absorption of community attitudes.

While we did not question children on their attitudes towards the President, a number of such studies has recently appeared. A cross-cultural study by Greenstein (1973), *The Benevolent Leader: Children's Images of Political Leaders in Three Democracies*, includes up-to-date references to this literature.

Parents. Dubin and Dubin (1965) have summarized data from 56 studies dealing with children's social perceptions, and have organized their generalizations around children's perception of parental and non-parental authority figures. They state that ". . . from a methodological standpoint, the empirical literature appears inadequate to support broad generalizations by virtue of scatter in theoretical interest and limited research technologies employed . . ." Despite these limitations, certain of their conclusions are relevant to the hypotheses of the present study: in a wide age range, mother is preferred over father, to whom more power is ascribed, especially by boys; in relation to age and sex, perceptions (a) become more realistic with increasing age, with parents losing much of the power previously ascribed to them, and (b) perceptions are differentiated by sex, with girls more favorably oriented towards parents than boys. Cultural influences lead to quantitative differences in the perception of parental behaviors. No evidence was found to support the belief that there are qualitative differences as well. As regards social class, Hess and Torney (1962), who investigated the perception of authority structure within the families of 1861 children between the ages of 7 through 15, found no difference in children's perception by social class.

Schvaneveldt (1970) interviewed 86 nursery-school children in regard to their perceptions of what constitutes "goodness" or "badness" in mothers and fathers. Results indicated that boys and girls can readily verbalize their perceptions at this age. Parents are perceived as good by both sexes most of the time.

Schmidt (1970) studied the attitudes of children toward mother, father and teacher by means of rating scales. Younger children (ten-year-olds) judged persons in authority more positive than did older children (fourteen-year-olds), girls were more positive in their judgments than boys. In general, parents were judged more positively than were teachers. Since this study was done in West Germany, its findings may not have applicability in this country.

Teachers. Gregersen and Travers (1968) explored attitudes of elementary school children toward their teachers by means of drawings children made of their classes. Results are consistent with the hypothesis that boys are more rejecting of their teachers than are girls, and that boys show no increase in rejection of their teacher as age increases, but that girls show an increasing rejection. The degree to which girls show a negative attitude towards their teachers depends to some extent on the characteristics of the teacher.

Estvan and Estvan (1968) found a decline in enthusiasm for school shown by sixth graders as compared to first graders and interpret it as a result of increasing resistance to authority. Powers (in Gregersen and Travers, 1968) found girls were more accepting of the teacher as an authority figure than were boys, and that brighter students tended to be more accepting than less bright students.

METHOD

Purpose

The purpose of this study was to examine children's perceptions of authority figures as a function of the variables of sex, age, ethnic group and socio-economic status (SES). The authority figures included police-man, principal, teacher, father and mother. The hypotheses to be tested were arranged by two samples: pre-school children and elementary school children.

Pre-school sample

1. Boys will perceive authority figures as more threatening than will girls.

2. Lower SES children will perceive authority figures as more threatening than will middle SES children.

Elementary school sample

1. Boys will perceive authority figures as more threatening than will girls.

2. Lower SES children will perceive authority figures as more threatening than will middle SES children.

3. Black children will perceive authority figures as more threatening than will white or Puerto Rican children.

4. Older children (grades five and six) will perceive authority figures as more threatening than will younger children (grades one and two).

Procedures

Pre-school sample. Four questions from the Caldwell Pre-School Inventory (1967) were administered to a sample of 90 pre-school children.

1. What does a policeman do?
2. What does a teacher do?
3. What does a mother do?
4. What does a father do?

All responses were recorded verbatim. For purposes of reliability, or inter-judge agreement, five judges independently categorized the responses as: "threatening," "protective" or "neither." The response was left in the sample only when agreement as to its appropriate category was reached by four out of five judges. The procedure resulted in the following inter-judge agreement for each authority figure:

policeman	70%
teacher	77%
father	86%
mother	65%

Upon further analysis it was found that the percentage agreement was highly varied between "threatening" and "protective" responses. In all cases the agreement of threat responses was over 90%. As a result, the categories of "neither" and "protective" were collapsed to "non-threatening," which changed the percentage of agreement to over 90%.

Elementary school sample. The Caldwell Inventory was designed for pre-school children and did not include the authority figure of the principal. As a result, new statements had to be designed for the elementary school sample. The wording of the elementary school questions was deliberately open-ended to stimulate the student to enumerate more than one function of the authority figure.

1. Tell all the things you think of when I say policeman.
2. Tell all the things you think of when I say principal.
3. Tell all the things you think of when I say teacher.
4. Tell all the things you think of when I say father.
5. Tell all the things you think of when I say mother.
6. If you meet a friend and want to know how he feels about his parents, what questions would you ask him?

Statement 6 was constructed in order to gather more data of a descriptive nature. The six statements were pre-tested using 83 elementary school children who were not included in the study. From their responses, criteria to fit the categories of "threatening" and "protective" were established. When these criteria were used in the actual study, more than 95% of the responses could be so categorized.

Sampling

Pre-school sample. The population for the pre-school sample was drawn from an OEO day care center, a Headstart class in a public school, and a private nursery school. The children in the OEO and Headstart groups were low SES and the children in the private nursery school, middle SES. Of the total of 90 children, 49 were of low SES and 41 were of middle SES. Of the 49 low SES children, 30 were boys and 19 girls. Among the 41 middle SES children, 22 were boys and 19 were girls.

Elementary school sample. The elementary school sample consisted of 526 children from two Nassau County, New York, public school districts.

1st grade	96
2nd grade	60
3rd grade	62
4th grade	67
5th grade	122
6th grade	119

164 were low SES, 362 were middle SES, 193 were black, 40 were Puerto Rican and 303 were white. 240 were boys and 286 were girls.

RESULTS

All analyses were based upon the percent of responses among the total group that were characterized as threatening or protective. Chi Square was used in all cases with an alpha level of .05.

Pre-School

1. Boys vs. girls: significant differences for teacher and overall, i.e., boys perceive the teacher and authority figures in general as more threatening than girls do.

2. Lower SES vs. middle SES: significant differences found for teacher, policeman, father and overall, i.e., teacher, policeman, father, and authority figures in general are perceived as more threatening by children in the lower SES.

Elementary School Sample

1. Boys vs. girls—no significant differences found.

2. Lower SES vs. middle SES—no significant differences found.

3. Black children vs. Puerto Rican and white children—no significant differences found. When threat scores for black, white and Puerto Rican children were compared, it was found that authority figures outside the home received lower threat scores for Puerto Rican children in all cases with the exception of the teacher. Authority figures inside the home received higher threat scores for Puerto Rican children in all cases when compared to white and black children. However, these findings were not found to be significant.

4. Older children vs. younger children—significant differences were found for principal and overall. That is, authority figures in general and especially the principal are perceived as more threatening by the older children.

DISCUSSION

What developmental changes does the perception of authority undergo in the course of childhood? Does parental power become a prototype for later perceptions of non-parental authority? What is the influence of social class?

According to psychoanalytic theory, the perception of parental power undergoes considerable change in the course of development, beginning with "infantile omnipotence." This term refers to the infant's egocentric state, where the world centers on his own gratifications. He is totally dependent on the care of others who cater to his needs and whose ministrations lend him a sense of magical power. A gradual shifting of power, or lessening of infantile omnipotence reaches its zenith at the conclusion of the oedipal stage when the parent is viewed as the residue of all power and one's very existence appears feasible only through an "identification with the aggressor," i.e. "To accept his values, become like him, and repress the hostility one feels toward him" (Baldwin, 1967). Such a projection of total power unto the parent is almost as unrealistic as the infantile omnipotence of the earlier stage. It is, however, only another landmark in the acquisition of the more realistic perception of the power of the parents, who during the following years are then perceived as declining in power. Parental power during these years and presumably beyond these years, is perceived as somewhat more protective, less threatening and, on the whole, more realistic.

One might hypothesize a parallel development for the perception of power outside the home (e.g., police, teacher and principal power) with one omission of course: the stage of infantile omnipotence which occurs so early in life that no notice is taken of authority figures outside of the home. The perceptions of authority might begin with the attribution of an ever-increasing threatening power onto authority figures outside the home, similar to the power of the parental prototype which lasts through the end of the oedipal crisis. Beginning with the latency period, the threat of authority wanes and perception of non-parental power becomes more protective, less threatening and more realistic.

Our findings may be explained in the light of such theory. The pre-latency sample (pre-school) showed considerably more overall threat of authority than did the latency (elementary school) sample.

The finding that greater threat was associated with lower-class membership is however not explained by psychoanalytic theory.

Do class differences in the perception of authority figures by preschoolers reflect parental attitudes? Many investigators have concluded that the parent is the agent of transmission of cultural norms and attitudes, i.e. the primary agent of socialization. The lower-class black family has been labeled as the "crucible of identity" (Rainwater, 1966).

Furstenberg (1967) has made an attempt to obtain independent data from 475 pairs of parents and children in the same family in order to measure the extent to which children share their parents' attitudes and values. The most striking finding was that very little agreement was found to exist between parents and children on most attitudes.

Other recent research also found low rates of agreement between parents and children. For example, Niemi (1973) investigated two civil liberties issues, one whether a legally elected Communist should be permitted to hold office, and another, on allowing speeches on antireligious subjects. Parent-child correlations were .13 and .05 respectively. Dennis' (1969) study of the democratic orientations of younger children yielded a median of 27 parent-child correlations of only .13.

Our findings appear contradictory when viewed from a developmental position. If the preschool sample showed a class difference in the perception of threat of authority and the elementary school sample did not, can one assume that the lack of difference continues through high school into adult life? If one were to assume this development and hypothesize that no difference existed between adults of different classes, then one must ask the following question: what influences were active upon the preschool sample in direction of a threatening perception of authority? In the absence of influences other than those of the family, the preschool sample must get its perception of authority from the family. One might hypothesize that the present parent generation might have been shown to differ significantly as regards their perception of authority when analyzed for SES. This would mean that the school at this time with this generation has had the effect of neutralizing differences between social classes.

SUMMARY

Ninety preschool and 526 elementary school children were questioned on their attitudes toward authority figures. At the preschool level only, sex and SES were found to be significantly associated with attitude to authority: boys perceived the teacher as more threatening than did girls; lower SES preschoolers perceived father, teacher and policeman as more threatening than did middle SES preschoolers. In the elementary school sample, no significant differences were found for either sex, SES or ethnic group. Older children (grades 5 and 6) perceived the principal as significantly more threatening than did younger ones (grades 1 and 2).

Another variable that has attracted much attention from investigators interested in cross-cultural and socioeconomic differences is the willingness of children to delay gratification. W. Mischel (1958) conducted one of the first studies of this type when he asked Negro and East Indian children in Trinidad to perform a small service for him and offered them a choice of rewards—either a small (one-cent) candy bar immediately, or a large (ten-cent) candy bar a week later. The Negro children were twice as likely to prefer the immediate reward, but the East Indian children were twice as likely to prefer the delayed reward. The difference at first appeared to be an entirely cultural one, but further investigation showed that 30 percent of the Negro children and only 5 percent of the East Indian children came from homes where the father was absent. In every instance the children from fatherless homes chose the immediate reinforcement in preference to the delayed one. Negro children whose fathers lived with them were about evenly divided as to preferences for immediate and delayed rewards. The difference, instead of being a cultural one, was in fact related to the home situation and could therefore be more precisely characterized as socioeconomic, rather than ethnic. In a later study (1961) using Trinidad Negro children as subjects, but without controlling for socioeconomic status or father absence, Mischel found that the children who expressed preference for the delayed reward tended to score higher on measures of the need for achievement than did the children who preferred immediate rewards. The willingness to delay gratification therefore seems to be related to the ego-strength traits of internality of locus of control and motor response inhibition we discussed in Section 3.

The possibility that delay of gratification might have some meaning apart from socioeconomic considerations was explored by Victor M. Dmitruk, whose research report appears as article 7.3 in this section. Dmitruk's study is a partial replication of an earlier one by Strickland (1972). In Strickland's study, a black or white experimenter asked black or white sixth-grade students to complete a locus-of-control measure and then offered them a choice of one 45 RPM record as an immediate reward, or three records if they would wait three weeks for the experimenter's return. About 80 percent of the white students chose the delayed reward, irrespective of the experimenter's color. Only 33 percent of the black students chose the delayed reward when it was offered by the white experimenter, but 56 percent chose the delayed reward when it was offered by the black experimenter. Locus-of-control scores for the black students who delayed gratification and those who did not showed no difference, but the white students who delayed gratification showed more internality of control than those who were unwilling to wait. The black students in general showed less internality than the white students did.

Although Strickland's study provided some interesting insights into the way sixth graders from two ethnic groups react to the race of an experimenter, she did not control for socioeconomic status. We are therefore not sure whether the differences she reported are attributable to the social-class backgrounds of the children or to their ethnic status. In his partial replication of Strickland's study, Dmitruk attempted to equate his black and his white samples for socioeconomic status. He also thought that the rewards Strickland offered her subjects might not have been equally attractive to both black and white students. Dmitruk controlled for this possibility by permitting his subjects to choose their reward from displays of more desirable rewards whose delivery was to be delayed three weeks, or, if they preferred an immediate reward, they could select it from a display of less desirable items.

Dmitruk found no difference between black and white students in their willingness to delay rewards: 80 percent of the white subjects chose the delayed reward, as in Strickland's study, but 85 percent of Dmitruk's black subjects also chose to delay reinforcement. Of further interest is the finding that the race of the experimenter made no significant difference in the choice behavior of the black male students. Although there was a statistically significant experimenter

281

effect on the choices made by the black female students, the magnitude was not great: two subjects (5 percent) chose the immediate reward when the choice situation was presented to them by the black experimenter, and six subjects (about 21 percent) chose it when the experimenter was white.

Dmitruk attributed the difference in the findings of the two studies to the kinds of rewards offered to the students, but there are other possibilities he does not mention. One explanation may be that his subjects came from upper-lower to lower-middle class homes, whereas Strickland's black subjects were all from a poverty area. This difference in the sampling of the two studies suggests that delay of gratification may be a social-class phenomenon, as Mischel found much earlier in Trinidad, and as others have also noted. Delay of gratification, as tested in such studies, is partly impulse control and partly willingness to trust a strange adult. Perhaps what Strickland's research tells us is that poor children are more impulsive than children from higher-status homes, but they are more inclined to think about the choice and behave less impulsively if the experimenter who presents the options is of their own race, and therefore somewhat more familiar and reassuring. This interpretation would, of course, have to be tested by further research.

Delay of gratification as a function of incentive preference and race of experimenter

Victor M. Dmitruk

The ability to delay gratification is frequently used as a general index of personality development in children, and is assumed to be correlated with various behavioral measures of "morality," or "conscience," such as resistance to temptation (Hoffman, 1970). Although differences of opinion exist, a good deal of evidence supports the view that the decisions made by children in such experimental settings are largely determined

Reprinted with permission of the author. A summary of this report appeared as a one-page article in *Developmental Psychology*, 10 (1974): 302.

by factors in the immediate environment (Dmitruk, 1971, 1973a; Liebert & Ora, 1968; Medinnus, 1966; Thelen & Fryrear, 1971a, 1971b; Rosenkoetter, 1973). Dmitruk (1971, 1973a), for example, found (a) a very reliable, direct relationship between children's preferences for incentive items and probability of transgression in a temptation situation, and (b) evidence suggesting that certain "intangible" motives (e.g., competition with peers) influence the moral judgements of children in temptation situations, while others (e.g., experimenter "warmth") do not. Other authors have reported that probability of transgression is influenced by the sex-appropriateness of the temptation task (Keasey, 1973; Medinnus, 1966), nurturance and nurturance withdrawal (Burton, Allinsmith, & Maccoby, 1966; Saadatmand, Jensen, & Price, 1971), and by observation of deviant models (Rosenkoetter, 1973).

It seems that temptation behavior and the tendency to delay gratification should be subject to the same or to similar influences if they are, in fact, correlated measures of personality development (Hoffman, 1970). Several lines of evidence suggest that this may be the case. Bandura and Kupers (1964), for example, found that the standards for self-reward established by adult models have an effect upon the self-rewarding behavior of children. Children exposed to models setting high standards of performance for self-reward exhibited a tendency to limit their own self-rewards to exceptional performance. This type of self-imposed deprivation was not observed in children exposed to models setting low standards, or in those that did not observe a model. Other workers have shown that both live and symbolic models exert an influence upon the delay behavior of children (Bandura & Mischel, 1965), and that tolerance for delay can be increased through verbal persuasion (Staub, 1972).

The author of the present study was concerned with the extent to which decisions to accept immediate reward or to delay gratification are influenced by children's preferences for incentive objects. As indicated above, Dmitruk (1971) found that probability of transgression in temptation situations is directly related to incentive preference. It therefore seems reasonable to assume that children would be more willing to accept a delay in gratification to obtain a "preferred" incentive than they would to obtain an object that was not particularly appealing. The case for such an effect is even stronger when the results of a study of incentive preferences in children are considered. Dmitruk (1973b) attempted to test the validity of two techniques commonly used in selecting incentives for research with children. The first involves the use of a single incentive, selected somewhat arbitrarily and offered to all children (e.g., Grinder, 1962; Mischel & Metzner, 1962; Strickland, 1972). The second approach includes incentives "preselected" for their attractiveness to children on the basis of adult estimates of children's preferences for various objects (e.g., Saadatmand, Jensen, & Price, 1971). On the basis of his findings, Dmitruk suggested that both of these practices might better be abandoned in favor of other means of selecting incentives. Boys and girls (4–11 years old) were asked to indicate which of eight penny toys they liked the most and which they liked least, and all of the age- and sex-groups studied differed in their preferences for the items. In addition, although a group of adults asked to estimate the preferences of the children clearly believed age and sex differences in preference to exist among children, they were unable to estimate just what the preferences were for any of the groups.

These findings make it difficult to interpret the results of studies employing such techniques for the selection of incentives. Strickland (1972), for example, used 45 RPM records as incentives in a racial comparison of ability to delay gratification as a function of race of experimenter. Her results indicated, among other things, that black children were more likely to accept immediate rewards than the white children, irrespective of the race of the experimenter. The decision confronting the children was one of choosing between obtaining one 45 RPM record "immediately," or three such records "in three weeks." It is possible that the records were not equally appealing to the black and the white children, which could account for the differences observed in delay of gratification. If the records were not particularly appealing to the blacks, it probably would not make much difference if they had one record or three. This difficulty in interpretation was magnified in the Strickland study because the socioeconomic status (SES) of the black and the white groups differed.

The present investigation was essentially a replication of Strickland's experiment. However, an attempt was made to equate the black and the white groups for SES, and the children were given a choice of accepting a "preferred" incentive following a period of delay, or a less expensive, "nonpreferred" incentive on the day the experiment was conducted. It was hypothesized that giving the children the option of waiting for a truly appealing incentive object would significantly reduce, or eliminate the racial differences in ability to delay gratification reported by Strickland (1972) and others (Zytkoskee, Watson, & Strickland, 1971).

METHOD

Subjects

The subjects were 133 black (63 boys and 70 girls, 7–12 years old) and 85 white (38 boys and 47 girls, 7–12 years old) children enrolled in two public elementary schools in the Muskegon Heights, Michigan, school district. Both of the schools were integrated, but one was predominantly white (80%), and the other predominantly black (85%). Although no steps were taken to guarantee the homogeneity of the black and the white subjects with respect to SES, the two schools were separated physically by a distance of less than one mile, and school officials indicated that the SES of the parents of the children in the two racial groups was very similar.[1]

Apparatus

The materials employed consisted simply of 14 incentive objects arranged on two small tables. One of the tables held an assortment of 10 "expensive" incentives ($.25-.35), and the other, four "inexpensive" objects ($.05-.08). The expensive incentive items were (a) rubber ball, (b) yo-yo, (c) ID bracelet, (d) necklace, (e) squirt gun, (f) pencil with world globe at the top, (g) ball and jacks, (h) jumprope, (i) compass, and (j) number puzzle. The inexpensive incentives were (a) small plastic whistle, (b) beauty set, (c) plastic "pill" puzzle, and (d) magic slate. All of the incentive objects were purchased from a local novelty concern.

Procedure

The subjects were run individually by either a black or a white female experimenter, 26 and 23 years of age, respectively. Each child was led to a small room in the school and shown the table containing the expensive incentive objects. The subject was then asked to indicate which of the expensive incentives he liked "the very best of all" to determine his preferred incentive object. After this choice was made the subject was shown the assortment of inexpensive items and asked if he liked any of the inexpensive incentives better than the expensive object previously selected. If not, he was asked if he would rather wait three weeks

---

1 Three administrators within the school district in which the research was conducted independently rated the SES of area families as "upper-lower to lower-middle" when confronted with the classification developed by Warner and Lunt (1941). Among those asked to rate the families were the principals of each school.

to obtain the preferred incentive (in short supply), or receive his choice of the inexpensive items (in plentiful supply) at the end of the school day. The children selecting the immediate reward were given the object they chose at the end of the day, and those delaying gratification were given their preferred incentive three weeks later.

RESULTS

The preferred incentive choices of the black and the white subjects (Table 1) were contrasted by means of a [χ^2] analysis, and some indication of a racial difference in preference for the incentive objects was found ($\chi^2 = 17.058, \ldots p < .05$). Insufficient cell frequencies precluded the possibility of analyzing the incentive preference data by race and sex. Although the difference obtained was only marginally reliable, the data are suggestive as the sexual composition of the two racial groups was quite similar (53% female in the black group, and 55% female in the white group).

TABLE 1
FREQUENCY OF PREFERRED INCENTIVE CHOICES BY BLACK AND WHITE, MALE AND FEMALE SUBJECTS

| Incentive | Black | | White | |
	Male	Female	Male	Female
Rubber ball	2	0	5	2
Yo-yo	0	1	0	3
ID Bracelet	7	1	5	6
Necklace	9	37	4	16
Squirt gun	27	0	11	0
Pencil	13	17	8	9
Ball & jacks	1	6	1	4
Jumprope	0	4	0	4
Compass	2	0	3	1
Number puzzle	2	4	1	2

The delay data (Table 2) were then subjected to contingency analysis and no statistically significant overall differences between the black and

TABLE 2
NUMBERS OF SUBJECTS CHOOSING IMMEDIATE VERSUS DELAYED REWARDS: A
COMPARISON WITH STRICKLAND (1972)

Race of Experimenter	Subjects	Immediate choice		Delayed choice		z	p
		Strickland	Present	Strickland	Present		
Black	Black males	23	6	30	28	2.570	.01
	Black females	15	2	15	40	4.426	.0001
	White males	10	3	33	13	.381	ns
	White females	6	1	30	21	1.457	ns
White	Black males	26	4	10	25	4.795	.0001
	Black females	30	6	18	22	3.596	.0004
	White males	7	5	19	17	.344	ns
	White females	3	5	21	20	−.721	ns

the white boys and girls with respect to tendency to delay gratification were found ($\chi^2 = 8.291, \ldots p < .30$).

Comparison of the groups run by the white experimenter with those run by the black experimenter (Table 2) by means of a test for the significance of the difference between sample proportions *(two-tailed)* yielded only one statistically reliable result. The black females were significantly more likely to opt for an immediate reward when confronted by the white experimenter than when confronted by the black experimenter . . . ($p < .05$).

Finally, using the same analysis, the proportion of children delaying gratification in the various groups was compared with the findings reported by Strickland (Table 2). The white groups in this study did not differ from those in Strickland's study with respect to ability to delay gratification, but all of the black groups in this study were significantly more likely to delay gratification than Strickland's subjects.

DISCUSSION

The results obtained in the present study are clearly at odds with those reported by Strickland (1972) as far as racial differences in ability to delay gratification are concerned. None of the comparisons of the black and the white groups in this study yielded a statistically significant result, and all of the black groups were significantly more likely to delay gratification than were Strickland's black subjects.

This suggests that Strickland's findings may, in part, have been a function of differential appeal of the incentive used rather than an indication of any real differences between black children and white children in ability to delay gratification. The finding of a racial difference in incentive appeal supports this conclusion, even though the actual incentive object used by Strickland was not one of the choices confronting the subjects in the present study.

In sum, these findings seem to lend greater generality to the conclusion drawn by Dmitruk (1973b) in his study of the incentive preferences of children. The suggestion made was that differential incentive appeal may be a confounding factor in studies using capriciously selected incentives and comparing children differing with respect to age and/or sex. However, Dmitruk used only white subjects and it seems that such confounding is possible in racial comparisons as well. Thus, it appears that investigators should exercise greater care in the selection of incentives for research with children.

This conclusion is redundant in a sense because similar statements have been made both implicitly, and quite explicitly, in the past (e.g., Bijou & Sturges, 1959; Hartshorne & May, 1928-30). Such redundancy seems warranted, however, in light of current methodology in the study of child behavior and development. Hartshorne and May, for example, conducted extensive analyses of temptation behavior in children and concluded that (a) all children cheat, but differ with respect to the risk they will take, or effort they will expend, to do so, and (b) the critical determinants of risk taken and effort expended are to be found in the immediate situation in which the moral decision is to be made. Dmitruk (1971) has shown that incentive appeal is one "situational variable" influencing the amount of risk a child will take to cheat, and, as illustrated by the present study, the nature of the incentive objects employed also influences decisions to delay gratification. Bijou and Sturges (1959) made a more direct plea for careful selection of incentives following a review of the literature dealing with the use of tangible incentives in operant conditioning of children, suggesting that incentives be selected in light of the sex, age, and socioeconomic status of the subjects.

One additional point worthy of mention is the finding that the black girls in this study were less likely to delay gratification when the alternatives were offered by the white experimenter than when they were confronted by the black experimenter, a finding in agreement with one reported by Strickland (1972). Strickland suggested that this might be indicative of distrust of whites by black children, a seemingly plausible explanation although little direct evidence of such distrust exists. A study by Stabler, Johnson, and Jordan (1971) offers indirect support for Strickland's hypothesis, however. These investigators transmitted both positive and negative statements from two speakers, one black and one white. The transmissions were of equal intensity and were broadcast simultaneously through both speakers. Both black and white children were asked to guess the origin of the statements, and it was found that black children perceived significantly more negative statements emanating from the white speaker. This finding can, perhaps, be taken as evidence that black children distrust whites. Because delay of gratification is related to perceived probability that a delayed choice will be forthcoming (Hoffman, 1970), children should be less likely to delay gratification when the alternatives are presented by a distrusted adult.

Strickland (1972) also found that black males were less likely to delay gratification in the presence of a white experimenter, but this finding was not replicated in the present study. Several explanations can be offered for this discrepancy, but no conclusive statements can be made. One obvious possibility is that the difference is simply a function of the sex of the experimenters. Strickland's experimenters were male, while those in the present study were female. A second possibility is that the salience of the experimenter had a differential effect on black males and females. Strickland's experimenters stood in front of a classroom, exhibited the incentive, and asked the children to note their choice of an immediate or delayed reward on a sheet of paper. The subjects in this study were run individually and were in close physical proximity to the experimenters, who were trained to be "warm."[2] Perhaps this close contact served to overcome distrust of the white experimenter by the black males, but not in the case of the black females.[3]

Finally, the possibility exists that distrust of whites is greater in black females than it is in black males. Stabler, Johnson, and Jordan (1971) also found that black females perceived significantly more negative statements originating from the white speaker than did the black males.

---

2 "Warmth" was defined on the basis of results reported by Stevenson and Allen (1967).
3 Gewirtz and Baer (1958), for example, found a cross-sexed pattern in the preferences of children for adults when the adults were perceived as nurturant. Boys preferred and solicited social approval from adult females, and girls sought the approval of adult males. This pattern of preference changed when the adult was non-nurturant, with boys preferring males, and girls preferring females. Perhaps black males would be more likely to accept immediate rewards when confronted by non-nurturant adult females?

This reasoning is highly speculative, of course, and more work is needed before a definitive statement can be made with respect to the influence of experimenter race upon decisions to delay gratification.

SUMMARY

The ability of black and of white children to delay gratification was investigated as a function of incentive preference and race of experimenter. No reliable differences were found between the black and the white groups when the children were given the option of waiting for a "preferred" incentive selected from an assortment of 10 incentive objects. The black and the white groups did differ in their preferences for the incentives, however, suggesting that differential incentive appeal may be a confounding factor in delay of gratification studies using a single incentive object. Race of experimenter influenced only the behavior of the black females, who were significantly more likely to accept an immediate reward when confronted by a white experimenter.

The influence of social-class culture on children's behavior is exerted largely through the behavior of parents. In Section 3 we saw that working-class toddlers find verbal labels less useful than middle-class toddlers do in solving simple problems (Golden, Bridger, and Montare, 2.4); this behavioral difference is apparently related to the tendency of middle-class mothers to engage in more verbal interaction with their infants than working-class mothers do (Tulkin and Kagan, 1972). One of the effects of these differential rates of verbalization is reported in article 7.4 in this section, an observational study by Steven R. Tulkin which was conducted as part of the larger investigation by Tulkin and Kagan (1972) previously referred to. Tulkin's recent study clearly demonstrates that social-class differences begin to appear in children's behavior before they are a year old. Earlier researchers had concluded that social-class-related differences are not manifested in the behavior of children much before they reached the toddler stage, but Tulkin, who designed a well-controlled experiment and made use of sophisticated recording techniques, was able to capture response differences that had eluded earlier observers.

In Tulkin's study, working-class and middle-class infants heard a series of brief recordings of the voices of either their mother or another woman. He found that when a middle-class infant heard the recording of its mother's voice, it usually became very quiet. When the recorded passage ended, the infant was likely to vocalize and look at its mother, who was present during the experiment. When the infant heard the stranger's voice, it tended to look at the experimenter. The infant of a working-class mother, however, was more likely to become quiet on hearing the stranger's voice, and then to vocalize. When the infant heard the recording of its mother's voice, it tended to look at the experimenter, and when it heard the stranger's voice, it was more inclined to look at its mother. In general, the middle-class infant was likely to respond more appropriately in the experimental situation than was the working-class infant. Tulkin attributes these differences to the fact that the middle-class mothers talked to their babies more and responded more frequently to their vocalizations.

There were no differences between the two groups of mothers in the amount of attention and care they gave their infants; it was *how* they interacted with them, rather than *how much* they interacted, that seemed to make the difference in their infants' responses. Middle-class mothers evidently were more at ease than working-class mothers in talking to their babies. Tulkin and Kagan (1972) report that some of the working-class mothers thought it was ridiculous to try to talk to infants, because they believed that babies do not have feelings like adults and have no ability to communicate to others. These mothers evidently felt that there was no point in talking to children before the children had learned to talk. One working-class mother who deviated from the norm and talked a great deal to her infant daughter lamented that her friends were critical of her "talking to the kid like she was three years old." The point seems to be that the typical middle-class mother is not only more inclined to verbalize to her infant, but also to treat it as though it "had a personality."

Infants' reactions to mother's voice and stranger's voice: Social class differences in the first year of life

Steven R. Tulkin

Psychologists have paid insufficient attention to language development during the first year of life (Friedlander, 1968, 1970) primarily because of difficulties in assessing pre-verbal behavior. However, new procedures have recently been developed, and several researchers (Friedlander, 1968; Kagan, in press; Turnure, 1971) have begun to examine some of the dimensions of early language-related behaviors. The present study utilized these procedures to investigate social class differences in infants' responses to tape-recorded passages containing mother's voice and stranger's voice.

Studies of social class differences in infant development have been limited by the narrow range of infant behaviors which have been assessed. Thus the statement by Golden, Birns, Bridger, and Moss (1971) that "when such factors as birth complications and poor nutrition and health are ruled out, social class differences in intellectual performance have not been demonstrated until the third year of life (p. 43)" may simply reflect the insensitivity of our assessment procedures. The decision to examine class differences in language-related behaviors in the present study seems from reports that middle-class mothers have been found to engage in more "distinctive" or "meaningful" verbal interchanges with their children than working-class mothers (Hess & Shipman, 1965; Levine, Fishman, & Kagan, 1967; Tulkin & Kagan, 1972), and that class differences in infants' vocalization rates have also been reported (Irwin, 1948).

The importance of early pre-verbal behavior has been emphasized by several recent studies which have reported high correlations between infant vocalization and later intelligence. Moore (1967) found that the "speech quotient" of six-month-old girls was significantly correlated with vocabulary at three years of age ($p < .01$), and the speech quotient

Reprinted with permission of the author. A summary of this report appeared as a one-page article in *Developmental Psychology*, 8 (1973): 137.

of 18-month-old girls was correlated with vocabulary scores of eight-year-old girls (the oldest Moore tested). Similarly, Bayley (1968) reported a correlation of .80 between girls' vocalization scores during the first year of life and Wechsler-Bellevue Verbal IQ at 26 years of age.

METHOD

Subjects were 46 first-born white girls, ten months of age, who were part of a larger investigation (Tulkin, 1970). Twenty-seven infants came from middle-class families (defined by occupation and education of parents) and 19 from working-class families. Premature infants and infants with abnormal medical histories were excluded.

Subjects were seated in a high chair in front of a three-sided stimulus board. Their mothers sat behind them on their right, and a coder sat behind them on their left. A second coder stood behind the stimulus board and observed the subject through tinted plastic windows. Stimuli were presented through a speaker situated in front of the infant, and slightly to her right. Stimulus passages consisted of twenty-second tape-recorded passages containing a standard "fairy tale" read by the subject's own mother and by a stranger. Every subject heard the voice of a different stranger from her own social class group. Mother's voice and stranger's voice were presented alternately (four times each) for 20 seconds, separated by a 10-second interstimulus interval. There was a break between the first four stimuli (Series One) and the remaining four stimuli (Series Two) during which other procedures—not examined in the present report—were administered. Coders recorded amount of vocalization, looking at the mother, and looking at the coder. Reliabilities based on 20 pre-test infants (not included in the study) were .98, .97, and .91 for these three variables. Two additional measures were taken: Heartrate deceleration and physical activity. Heartrate was recorded by a Grass polygraph equipped with a Lexington Instruments Cardio-Tachometer. The magnitude of the deceleration was computed by taking the mean of the three lowest beats during the five seconds before the onset of the stimulus and subtracting from that value the mean of the three lowest beats during the first five seconds of the stimulus period. If there was no difference in the values, or the "stimulus" value was greater than the pre-stimulus value, the deceleration score was coded zero.

Activity was measured by a stabilimeter which was also connected to the polygraph. The instrument was sensitive only to movements of the top half of the infant's body. By emitting a high frequency sound wave and measuring the amount of time taken by the wave to bounce off the subject and return to a receiver on the stabilimeter, the instrument determined the distance between receiver and the child. Since every movement of the child involved a change of distance, movement was reflected in the stabilimeter output. Reduction of the stabilimeter data consisted of counting the number of seconds during each period in which the polygraph pen moved an arbitrary distance (equal to the child's moving a distance of approximately one foot). The stabilimeter data was divided into two variables: 1) *Differences* in activity were defined by comparing movement during two particular stimuli (e.g., mother's voice and stranger's voice) to determine if the infants were less active during one of the stimuli; and 2) *Quieting* was defined by comparing activity in the five-second period prior to a stimulus with activity during the first five seconds of the same stimulus to determine if the infants' decreased activity (i.e. attended) to a particular stimulus.

Data analysis consisted of comparing the degree of differential responding to the two stimuli in the two social class groups.

RESULTS

Comparisons of the infants' responses to mother's and stranger's voices (Table 1) suggest that middle-class infants showed greater differential response patterns, primarily in Series One.

Middle-class infants quieted more to the passages containing mother's voice than to the passages containing stranger's voice, while the working-class infants did not respond differentially (the second order comparison yielded a significant difference, $p = .058$). Middle-class infants also vocalized more following the passages containing mother's voice than following the passages containing stranger's voice (second order comparison yielded significance level of .090). These two differences were not found in Series Two, possibly because the infants became restless and cranky, and thus their physical activity and vocalizations were less likely to be related to the stimuli.

The most dramatic differences, however, involved the infants' looking behaviors. Middle-class infants showed greater differential looking patterns (looking more at mother after hearing mother's voice and more at the coder following the stranger's voice) than did the working-class subjects. In Series Two, the only significant difference involved looking

TABLE 1
DIFFERENTIAL RESPONSES TO MOTHER'S AND STRANGER'S VOICES

| Variable | Working class | | Middle class | | p^a |
	Mean	S.D.	Mean	S.D.	
Series One					
Vocalization during stimuli	.25	1.66	.02	.38	n.s.
Vocalization following stimuli	−.18	.67	.06	.35	.090
Look at mother during stimuli	−.59	7.04	−1.24	4.75	n.s.
Look at mother following stimuli	−.27	.79	.35	1.43	.055
Look at stranger during stimuli	−.02	4.21	.55	3.34	n.s.
Look at stranger following stimuli	.78	1.37	−.46	2.31	.03
Heartrate deceleration	.88	2.28	.13	2.32	n.s.
Activity	.38	3.17	−.31	2.89	n.s.
Quieting	−1.18	2.45	.55	3.08	.053
Series Two					
Vocalization during stimuli	.28	1.52	.21	1.21	n.s.
Vocalization following stimuli	−.09	.89	−.15	.85	n.s.
Look at mother during stimuli	.54	5.76	1.15	8.64	n.s.
Look at mother following stimuli	−.37	.93	−.16	1.03	n.s.
Look at stranger during stimuli	.80	1.64	−1.29	3.44	.05
Look at stranger following stimuli	.52	2.00	−.57	2.89	n.s.
Heartrate deceleration	−.15	2.43	.35	2.23	n.s.
Activity	−1.25	3.05	−1.15	4.12	n.s.
Quieting	.27	3.03	.00	3.14	n.s.

a Independent *t* tests; two-tailed

Note: Each variable represents the magnitude of response to the mother's voice passages minus the magnitude of response to the stranger's voice passages. Thus a positive number indicates a greater response to the mother's voice passage, while a negative number indicates a greater response to the stranger's voice. Units for all values except for heartrate deceleration are number of seconds.

behavior. Here, the middle-class infants differentially gazed at mother and stranger *during* the passages.

DISCUSSION

The present findings are consistent with other investigations of infants' reactions to language stimuli. Turnure (1971) found greater motor quieting to mother's voice passages with age, and concluded that infants were increasingly attentive to the stimuli. The present data also point to the importance of motor quieting as an index of attention to auditory stimuli.

The importance of the infants' looking responses has also been emphasized by other investigators. Kagan (in press) presented meaningful and nonmeaningful speech passages to a group of eight-month-old infants, and found that "upper-middle-class" infants looked longer at the speaker baffle than infants from other social class groups following the high meaning-high inflection stimulus. Both Kagan's subjects and the present subjects seemed to be searching for the source of the speech. Since there was no stranger visible to the infants in Kagan's experiment, their looking at the speaker baffle paralleled the middle-class infant's looking at the "correct person" in the present study.

Further evidence for the importance of looking for the source of auditory stimuli comes from the finding that infants tested in experimental procedures in which they could not search for their mothers upon hearing her voice have begun to cry (Laroche and Tcheng, 1963; Turnure, 1971). Turnure hypothesized that the distress developed because "the infants' usual responses to his mother were contingent . . . on more of her attributes being perceived than just her voice." More research is necessary to understand this phenomenon more completely, but one cannot resist noting the similarity between these findings and Hebb's (1946) classic study of the nature of fear, which demonstrated that a familiar stimulus which is missing some of its critical elements is likely to elicit fear.

The major importance of the present findings is that they demonstrate that with more refined assessment procedures, social class differences—or, more correctly, the effects of experience—can be examined in the first year of life. The greater differential responding to mother's and stranger's voices by the middle-class infants is likely related to the fact that these infants have experienced more verbal stimulation from their mothers at home—quantitatively in the form of more frequent maternal vocalization, and qualitatively in the form of distinct face-to-face verbalization and reciprocal vocalizations (Tulkin & Kagan, 1971).[1]

---

1 Correlations between the previously reported home observations and the laboratory variables reported in the present paper are only suggestive, however. None of the home observation variables was correlated with the differential looking behaviors, but some of the maternal verbal behaviors at home were correlated with differential vocalizations following mother's and stranger's voices. Distinct face-to-face vocalization at home and differential vocalization following the first presentation of mother's and stranger's voices, for example, yielded correlations of .464 ($p < .05$) for middle-class subjects and .444 ($p < .05$) for working-class subjects.

These data, as well as reports from other laboratories, emphasize the importance of exploring language-related behaviors in the first year of life, and attempting to understand the relationships between these behaviors and infants' experiences.

The final paper in this section, a survey conducted by Tien-Ing Chyou Niem and Roberta R. Collard (article 7.5) deals with differences that characterize child-parent relationships in American and Chinese cultures.

In the studies we have discussed or presented so far, American children have been shown to be more willing than children from other cultures to engage in antisocial behavior and to defy adult authority (Bronfenbrenner, 1970), and to behave in ways that are relatively more aggressive and competitive (Kagan and Madsen, 6.4). The general public is well aware of these differences. Mass media commentators often characterize American children as more disobedient, disruptive, ill-mannered, and inconsiderate than children from other countries. The usual explanation offered is that American parents, in contrast to other parents, are too easy-going and permissive, and are generally unwilling to punish misbehavior. Niem and Collard's study of American and Chinese preschool children and their parents suggests that this interpretation is largely incorrect. They did find, as have other investigators, that American children are more disobedient and more physically aggressive than other children. They did *not* find that American parents are less punitive than other parents, but just the opposite. Only 12 percent of the Chinese children in the study were spanked during the thirty-day observation period, in contrast to 65 percent of the American children. Although the Chinese parents made more attempts to control the behavior of their children than the American parents did, the methods they used differed from those of the American parents. The Chinese parents were more likely to use love-oriented methods (persuasion, reasoning, appeals to conscience, withdrawal of acceptance, and so forth), but the American parents more often employed non-love-oriented methods (physical punishment, shouting, scolding, loss of privileges, threats of punishment, and so forth). In general, the Chinese parents seemed more interested than the American parents were in helping their children achieve impulse control.

Although the number of subjects in the study was small, the

observed differences were consistent with data from related studies and with social learning theory. The fact that the American children were more physically aggressive seems related to the physically aggressive ways in which their parents behaved toward them. The fact that American fathers and family relatives were less involved in controlling the misbehavior of the children than were the Chinese family groups also tells us something about cultural values. In America, discipline is usually a matter between mother and child, and fathers become involved only if the matter is serious. Relatives and persons outside the family generally take a hands-off position even when they disapprove of a child's behavior, because the attempts of others to discipline or even admonish a child are resented by its parents. In traditional cultures like the Chinese, children's misbehavior is a matter of general concern, and it is quite appropriate for an outsider to chide a destructive or aggressive child, especially if his parents are not around.

Parental discipline of aggressive behaviors in four-year-old Chinese and American children

Tien-Ing Chyou Niem and
Roberta R. Collard

Previous studies comparing Chinese and Chinese-American children and adolescents to Caucasian-American ones have all indicated that children 5 yr. of age and older living in Chinese culture are less aggressive than are children the same age in American culture (Hsu, Watrous, & Lord, 1960–61; Scofield & Sun, 1960; Sollenberger, 1968). In the present study, the aggressive behaviors of groups of 4-yr.-old Chinese (Taiwanese) children and American children were compared to see if differences in kind and amount of aggression would also be found at an earlier stage of socialization. The methods of discipline used to control the children's aggressive behaviors were compared in the two groups in terms of whether they were love oriented or non-love oriented, because children reared by love-oriented methods have been found to show a lower level of aggression, higher conscience development, more dependence on parents, and consequently a better identification with them than do children reared by non-love-oriented methods (Bandura & Walters, 1959; Sears, Maccoby, & Levin, 1957; Whiting, 1959).

The lower amount of physical aggression and delinquent behavior shown by Chinese children and adolescents has been explained as resulting from the greater stability of Chinese families compared to American families (Hsu et al., 1960–61) and from the use of less permissive discipline for aggression by the former and more permissive discipline in other areas of child rearing (Scofield & Sun, 1960; Sollenberger, 1968). Before 1949, most Chinese were raised in extended families where they received support from and were disciplined by many persons, whereas for at least two generations, most Americans have been raised in nuclear families where they are disciplined mainly by their parents. In the extended family, children are supervised more closely, and they are more a part of the adult world. In America, children spend much of their time with their peers and thus learn to handle their conflicts in more primitive ways (Bronfenbrenner, 1970). In an extended family, where many people live in the same household, the expression of aggression in children cannot be tolerated easily, because of the difficulties it would cause among the adult members of the family (Whiting, 1959).

Although Chinese and Chinese-American parents have been reported to be less permissive of the direct expression of hostile aggression in their children, they have not been reported to use a high degree of physical punishment (Sollenberger, 1968). High use of physical punishment has been found to be associated with a high level of physical aggression in children, possibly because it involves hostile aggressive acts on the part of the parent, who is a model for the child's behavior (Bandura & Walters, 1959; Sears, Whiting, Nowlis, & Sears, 1953).

According to Whiting (1959), parents who use love-oriented techniques of child rearing are accepting, affectionate and nurturant, tend to reward desired behavior by love and punish undesired behavior by withdrawal of love, have firm, consistent standards of behavior, and use reasoning often. Non-love-oriented techniques include physical punishment, restriction of privilege, taking away possessions, and using tangible rewards.

The purpose of the present study was to determine whether there were differences in kinds and amount of aggressive behaviors between groups of Chinese and American 4-yr.-old children and differences in the amounts of love-oriented vs. non-love-oriented discipline used by the parents to control their children's aggressive behaviors. Four-year-old children were chosen because, in American culture, it is between the ages of 3 and 5 yr. that the expression of aggression tends to shift from more diffuse and direct expression to more use of verbal aggression and other less direct methods (Jersild & Markey, 1935).

In line with results of previous studies, it was predicted that the Chinese children in the present study would show less physical aggression than would the American children; although it was possible that because these Ss were at an early stage of socialization, such differences might not be found. It was also predicted that the Chinese parents would use more love-oriented techniques in dealing with aggression, because the use of such discipline has been found to lead to less aggressive behavior in older children, and older Chinese children show a low level of aggression.

METHOD

Subjects

The Ss were 17 Chinese children living in Taipei, Taiwan, and 17 American children living in two university towns in Massachusetts. Each group consisted of 7 girls and 10 boys between the ages of 4 yr. 2 mo. and 4 yr. 6 mo. All Ss were from middle-class families; they were cared for predominantly by their mothers, and all attended preschools in the morning or afternoon.

Procedure

Mothers were asked to record each incident of their children's aggressive behavior every day for 30 days on a form adapted from Goodenough (1931). The form included questions concerning the situation in which the aggressive behavior occurred, persons handling the behavior, discipline method(s) used, and the child's reaction afterwards.

Aggressive behaviors were classified into physical aggression, verbal aggression, diffuse discharge, and "mother's categories," which included primarily disobedience and going out of boundaries. Discipline methods were classified into non-love-oriented techniques, love-oriented techniques, and other methods. Non-love-oriented methods consisted of physical punishment or control, material reward, scolding or shouting at, deprivation of privilege, and threat of punishment. Love-oriented methods consisted of withdrawal or threat of withdrawal of love, reasoning, coaxing, soothing, meeting the child's needs, and promise of future gratification. Other methods included ignoring, forbidding, commanding, distracting, disciplining the other child in the conflict, etc.

Interrater agreement was 99.0% for kinds of aggressive behavior, 81.1% for a specific category of discipline, and 98.2% for whether the discipline was love oriented or non-love oriented. In order to control for inaccuracies of reporting, the z test *(one tailed)* of percentage difference (Mendenhall, 1969) was used to analyze the differences between the two groups. A result was considered significant if its occurrence by chance was equal to or less than 5%.

RESULTS

Kinds and amount of aggressive behaviors

The Chinese mothers reported more aggressive incidents of their children over the 30 days than did the American mothers (408-304); however, if the total number of aggressive responses within the incidents are counted, there is little difference between the two groups. The Chinese reported 559 aggressive responses and the Americans, 519. The Chinese children were subjected to more parental controls of their aggressive behaviors than were the American children (597-416). The American children were more disobedient (75-56) and went out of bounds more often (11-0).

The Chinese children were reported to show less physical aggression (125-162 responses) and more verbal aggression (329-238) than did the American children, and these differences were statistically significant. The American children used physical attack more often than the Chinese children (132-86), but the Chinese children showed more diffused discharge of aggression (41-25).

Parental discipline methods

Although both the Chinese and American parents reported using more love-oriented than non-love-oriented methods in handling their children's aggressive behaviors, the Chinese parents reported a significantly higher use of love-oriented methods (421 times) than did the Americans (187 times) and a lower use of non-love-oriented techniques (55-117 times, respectively).

There was a significant difference between the groups in use of methods not classified into love-oriented or non-love-oriented discpline. The American mothers used a higher percentage of ignoring (including letting the children settle their own differences) and more commanding, while the Chinese mothers more often disciplined the other child in the conflict. Under love-oriented methods, the Chinese parents used less withdrawal of love (isolation), more reasoning and meeting the child's needs, and more appeals to conscience or empathy.

The Chinese parents reported using physical punishment 15 times, while the American parents reported 33 instances. Only 2 of the Chinese children were spanked (a total of 6 times), while 11 of the American children were spanked a total of 23 times over the same period.

The Chinese children were disciplined more by relatives and persons other than parents (59 times) than were the American children (19 times), which may indicate that the extended family was more common in the Chinese sample than in the American one. The Chinese boys were disciplined by their fathers (46 out of 243 incidents) almost twice as often as the American boys were (24 out of 182 incidents), indicating that the Chinese fathers were probably more often involved in the discipline of their sons.

DISCUSSION

The finding that the Chinese parents used more reasoning and less physical punishment and the Chinese children showed more verbal and less physical aggression than did their American counterparts may be evidence of the children's identification with their parents' behavior. The American children, whose parents used spanking as punishment, showed more physical attack. Because the Chinese children were confined to a smaller space with more persons to watch them, they were probably supervised more closely and their aggressive behaviors more often controlled. The American children (who were usually free to play in the neighborhood) probably received more intermittent reinforcement of their aggressive behaviors, which would make them more likely to persist.

Perhaps the greatest difference in methods of controlling aggression between the two groups of parents lies in the subtle ways the Chinese parents helped their children learn impulse control. They more often tried to help their children to understand and resolve the conflict situation leading to aggression by asking for motives, explaining the conflict situation to them, pointing out the consequences of their aggressive behavior, and suggesting other ways of solving the conflict. These mothers also helped their children to control their aggression by meeting their needs or by reducing frustration. They did this by helping the children to do or get what they wanted, by helping them succeed at a task, by promise of future gratification (which was later carried through), by partial gratification, and by substitute gratification. Except for "substitute gratification," the Chinese parents used these discipline methods two or three times as often as the American parents did.

The findings that the American children showed more disobedience, more physical aggression, more running away, and also received less discipline from their fathers may be related to the greater tendency of American children to show delinquency later on.

A cross-cultural study whose findings are somewhat similar to those of Niem and Collard was conducted by Margaret and David Steward (1973), who observed Anglo-American, Chinese-American, and Mexican-American mothers who had been asked to teach their three-year-old sons some simple games. The investigators noted that Chinese-American mothers were more matter-of-fact and were concerned primarily with the child's performance. This approach is consistent with the American stress on achievement and independence training. Mexican-American mothers tended to be more critical and negative than the other mothers. According to the investigators, the Chinese-American mothers obviously enjoyed teaching their children, but the Mexican-American mothers found the role uncomfortable, saying that they were mothers and not teachers—teaching is something that the schools do. Anglo-American mothers perceived teaching as one of the several roles appropriate for mothers, although they were unsure about what they should be teaching their children.

Ethnic identity and social class are the two major variables that influence child-rearing patterns and, consequently, children's behavior. As we noted at the beginning of this section, it is often difficult to keep the two variables separate in doing cross-cultural research, especially when socioeconomic status is distributed differently in the social classes being compared. Steward and Steward, in the study just cited, were careful to control for both social class and ethnic identity; but because so many investigators have failed to take these necessary precautions, it is difficult to place the results of many otherwise interesting cross-cultural studies in any kind of meaningful frame of reference.

REFERENCES

Mischel, W. "Preference for delayed reinforcement: An experimental study of a cultural observation." *Journal of Abnormal and Social Psychology* 56 (1958): 57-61.

Mischel, W. "Delay of gratification, need for achievement, and acquiescence in another culture." *Journal of Abnormal and Social Psychology* 62 (1961): 543-552.

Steward, M. and Steward, D. "The observation of Anglo-, Mexican-, and Chinese-American mothers teaching their young sons." *Child Development* 44 (1973): 329-337.

Strickland, B. R. "Delay of gratification as a function of the race of the experimenter." *Journal of Personality and Social Psychology* 22 (1972): 108-112.

7.1

1. Ames, L. B. Academic promise in Negro pupils. *J. Learn. Disabil.*, 1968, **1**, 16-23.

2. Ames, L. B., & August, J. Comparison of mosaic response of Negro and white primary-school children. *J. Genet. Psychol.*, 1966, **109**, 123-129.

3. Ames, L. B., & Ilg, F. L. Mosaic Patterns of American Children. New York: Harper, 1962.

4. Downing, G., Edgar, R. W., Harris, A. J., Kornberg, L., & Storm, H. F. The Preparation of Teachers for Schools in Culturally Deprived Neighborhoods (The Bridge Project). Flushing, N.Y.: Queens Coll., 1965.

5. Dreger, R. M., & Miller, K. S. Comparative psychological studies of Negroes and whites in the U. S. *Psychol. Bull.*, 1960, **57**, 361-402.

6. Ilg, F. L., & Ames, L. B. School Readiness. New York: Harper, 1964.

7. Jensen, A. R. How much can we boost *IQ* and scholastic achievement? *Harvard Educ. Rev.*, 1969, **39**, 1-123.

8. Kennedy, W. A., Van de Reit, V., & White, J. C. A normative sample of intelligence and achievement of Negro elementary school children in the southeastern United States. *Monog. Soc. Res. in Child Devel.*, 1963, **28**(6), 1-112.

9. Leifer, A. Relation of mosaic patterns to spelling and reading in low achievers. *Educ. & Psychol. Meas.*, 1970 **30**(2) 463-467.

10. Lowenfeld, M. The Lowenfeld Mosaic Test. London: Newman Neame, 1954.

7.2

Baldwin, A. L. *Theories of Child Development.* New York, Wiley, 1967.

Caldwell, Bettye. *The Caldwell Pre-school Inventory.* Syracuse University, 1967.

Dennis, Jack. Political Learning in Childhood and Adolescence: A Study of Fifth, Eighth and Eleventh Graders in Milwaukee, Wis. Madison: Center for Cognitive Learning, Technical Report No. 98, 1969.

Derbyshire, Robert L. Children's Perceptions of the Police: A Comparative Study of Attitudes and Attitude Change. *Journal of Criminal Law, Criminology and Police Science*, Vol. 59: 183, 1968.

Dubin, Robert and Dubin, Elizabeth R. Children's Social Perceptions: A Review of the Research. *Child Development*, Vol. 36: 809, 1965.

Easton, David and Dennis, Jack. The Child's Image of Government. *Annals of the American Academy of Political and Social Science*, Vol. 361: 40, 1965.

Estvan, F. J. and Estvan, E. W. *The Child's World: His Social Perception*. New York, Putnam, 1959.

Furstenberg, F. F. Jr. Transmission of Attitudes in the Family. Ph.D. Thesis, Columbia University, 1967.

Greenberg, S. Edward. Orientation of Black and White Children to Political Authority Figures. *Social Science Quarterly*, Vol. 51: 561, 1970.

Greenstein, Fred I. The Benevolent Leader Revisited: Children's Images of Political Leaders in Three Democracies. *American Political Science Review*. (In press)

Gregerson, Gayle F. and Travers, R. A Study of the Child's Concept of the Teacher. *The Journal of Educational Research*, Vol. 61: 324, 1968.

Hess, Robert D. and Torney, Judity V. Religion, Age and Sex in Children's Perception of Family Authority. *Child Development*, Vol. 36: 809, 1965.

Niemi, Richard G. Political Socialization. In *Handbook of Political Psychology*, J. Knutson, editor. San Francisco, Jossey-Bass, 1973.

Rainwater, as quoted by Proshansky, H. and Newton, P., in *Social Class, Race and Psychological Development*, M. Deutsch et al., editors. New York, Holt, 1968.

Schmidt, R. Lothar. Einstellungen gegenüber Autoritätspersonen und selektives Gedächtnis bei Kindern, *Dissertation* Abstracts International, Vol. 3, No. 5-B, 1970.

Schvaneveldt, Jay D., and Fryer, M., and Ostler, R. Concepts of 'Badness' and 'Goodness' of Parents as Perceived by Nursery School Children. *Family Coordinator*, Vol. 19: 98, 1970.

Sears, David O. Political Socialization, Part II: Partisan Predispositions and the Life Cycle. To be published in *Handbook of Political Science, Vol. II*. Edited by Fred I. Greenstein and Nelson W. Polsky. Reading, Mass., Addison-Wesley, 1974.

7.3

Bandura, A., & Kupers, C. J. Transmission of patterns of self-reinforcement through modeling. *Journal of Abnormal and Social Psychology*, 1964, *69*, 1-9.

Bandura, A., & Mischel, W. Modification of self-imposed delay of reward through exposure to live and symbolic models. *Journal of Personality and Social Psychology*, 1965, *2*, 698-705.

Bijou, S., & Sturges, P. T. Positive reinforcers for experimental studies with children. *Child Development*, 1959, *30*, 151-170.

Burton, R. V., Allinsmith, W., & Maccoby, E. E. Resistance to temptation in relation to sex of child, sex of experimenter, and withdrawal of attention. *Journal of Personality and Social Psychology*, 1966, *3*, 253-258.

Dmitruk, V. M. Incentive preference and resistance to temptation. *Child Development*, 1971, *42*, 625-628.

Dmitruk, V. M. Intangible motivation and resistance to temptation. *Journal of Genetic Psychology*, 1973a, in press.

Dmitruk, V. M. A test of the validity of two methods of selecting incentives for research with children. *Developmental Psychology*, 1973b, in press.

Gewirtz, J. L., & Baer, D. M. The effect of brief social deprivation on behaviors for a social reinforcer. *Journal of Abnormal and Social Psychology*, 1958, 56, 49–56.

Grinder, R. E. Parental childrearing practices, conscience, and resistance to temptation in sixth-grade children. *Child Development*, 1962, 33, 803–820.

Hartshorne, H., & May, M. S. *Studies in the nature of character:* Vol. I, *Studies in deceit;* Vol. II, *Studies in self-control;* Vol. III, *Studies in the organization of character.* New York: MacMillan, 1928–30.

Hoffman, M. L. Moral development. In P. Mussen (Ed.), *Carmichael's manual of child psychology, Vol. 2.* New York: John Wiley & Sons, 1970.

Keasey, G. B. Sex differences in yielding to temptation: A function of the situation. *Journal of Genetic Psychology*, 1973, in press.

Liebert, R. M., & Ora, J. P. Children's adoption of self-reward patterns: Incentive level and method of transmission. *Child Development*, 1968, 39, 537–544.

Medinnus, G. R. Age and sex differences in conscience development. *Journal of Genetic Psychology*, 1966, 109, 117–118.

Mischel, W., & Metzner, R. Preference for delayed reward as a function of age, intelligence, and length of delay interval. *Journal of Abnormal and Social Psychology*, 1962, 64, 425–431.

Rosenkoetter, L. I. Resistance to temptation: Inhibitory and disinhibitory effects of models. *Developmental Psychology*, 1973, 8, 80–84.

Saadatmand, B., Jensen, L., & Price, A. Nurturance, nurturance withdrawal, and resistance to temptation. *Developmental Psychology*, 1970, 2, 450–456.

Stabler, J. R., Johnson, E. E., & Jordan, S. E. The measurement of children's self-concepts as related to racial membership. *Child Development*, 1971, 42, 2094–2097.

Staub, E. Effects of persuasion and modeling on delay of gratification. *Developmental Psychology*, 1972, 6, 166–177.

Stevenson, H., & Allen, S. Variables associated with adults' effectiveness as reinforcing agents. *Journal of Personality*, 1967, 35, 246–264.

Strickland, B. R. Delay of gratification as a function of race of experimenter. *Journal of Personality and Social Psychology*, 1972, 22, 108–112.

Thelen, M. H., & Fryrear, J. L. Imitation of self-reward standards by black and white female delinquents. *Psychological Reports*, 1971a, 29, 667–671.

Thelen, M. H., & Fryrear, J. L. Effects of observer and model race on the imitation of standards of self-reward. *Developmental Psychology*, 1971b, 5, 133–135.

Warner, W. L., & Lunt, P. S. *The social life of a modern community.* New Haven, Conn.: Yale University Press, 1941.

7.4

Bayley, N. Behavioral correlates of mental growth: Birth to thirty-six years. *American Psychologist*, 1968, 23, 1–17.

Friedlander, B. Z. The effect of speaker identity, voice inflection, vocabulary and message redundancy on infants' selection of vocal reinforcement. *Journal of Experimental Child Psychology,* 1968, *6,* 443–459.

Friedlander, B. Z. Receptive language development in infancy: Issues and problems. *Merrill-Palmer Quarterly,* 1970, *16,* 7–51.

Golden, M., Birns, B., Bridger, W., and Moss, A. Social class differentiation in cognitive development among black preschool children. *Child Development,* 1971, *42,* 37–45.

Hebb, D. O. On the nature of fear. *Psychological Review,* 1946, *53,* 259–276.

Hess, R. D., and Shipman, V. C. Early experience and the socialization of cognitive modes in children. *Child Development,* 1965, *36,* 869–886.

Irwin, O. C. Infant speech: The effect of family occupational status and of age on use of sound types. *Journal of Speech and Hearing Disorders,* 1948, *13,* 224–226.

Kagan, J. Change and continuity in the first two years: An inquiry into early cognitive development. New York: Wiley, in press.

Laroche, J. L., and Tcheng, F. *Le Sourire du Nourrisson: La Voix comme Facteur Declenchant.* Louvain: Publications Universitarires, 1963.

Levine, J., Fishman, G., and Kagan, J. Sex of child and social class as determinants of maternal behavior. Paper presented at the meeting of the Society for Research in Child Development, New York, March, 1967.

Moore, T. Language and intelligence: A longitudinal study of the first eight years. *Human Development,* 1967, *10,* 88–106.

Tulkin, S. R. Mother-infant interaction in the first year of life: An inquiry into the influences of social class. Unpublished doctoral dissertation. Harvard University, 1970.

Tulkin, S. R., and Kagan, J. Mother-infant interaction in the first year of life. Child Development, 1972, *43,* 31–41.

Turnure, C. Response to voice of mother and stranger by babies in the first year. *Developmental Psychology,* 1971, 4, 182–190.

7.5

Bandura, A., & Walters, R. H. *Adolescent aggression.* New York: Ronald Press, 1959.

Bronfenbrenner, U. *Two worlds of childhood.* New York: Russell Sage Foundation, 1970.

Goodenough, F. L. *Anger in young children.* Minneapolis: University of Minnesota Press, 1931.

Hsu, F. L. K., Watrous, B., & Lord, E. Culture pattern and adolescent behavior. *International Journal of Social Psychiatry,* 1960-61,7, 33–53.

Jersild, A. T., & Markey, F. V. Conflicts between preschool children. *Child Development Monographs,* 1935, No. 21.

Mendenhall, W. *Introduction to probability and statistics.* Belmont, Calif.: Wadsworth Publishing, 1969.

Scofield, R. W., & Sun, C. W. A comparative study of the different effect upon personality of Chinese and American child-rearing practices. *Journal of Social Psychology,* 1960, **52,** 221–224.

Sears, R. R., Maccoby, E. E., & Levin, H. *Patterns of child rearing.* Evanston, Ill.: Row, Peterson, 1957.

Sears, R. R., Whiting, J. W. M., Nowlis, V., & Sears, P. S. Some child-rearing antecedents of aggression and dependency in young children. *Genetic Psychology Monographs,* 1953, **47,** 135–234.

Sollenberger, R. T. Chinese-American child-rearing practices and juvenile delinquency. *Journal of Social Psychology,* 1968, **74,** 12–23.

Whiting, J. W. M. Cultural and sociological influences on development. In. *Maryland Child Growth and Development Institute,* 1959.

8.
Manipulating children's environments

In the discussion that introduced Section 1, we noted that American psychologists, regardless of how much they may be interested in basic research, are usually sensitive to the practical or applied aspects of their findings. This, we observed, is probably the effect of the pragmatic, problem-centered orientation of the American culture. We also noted that educators and government officials are especially interested in having psychologists supply them with data for use in policy-making decisions that directly or indirectly affect the welfare of children.

In recent years, much of this problem-oriented research has been in the form of studies concerned in one way or another with increasing children's competence, in its most general sense. Several investigations and experimental programs have focused on children with more than average difficulty at school. Problems such as these are matters of concern because of the general tendency to equate school failure with some deficiency in the child, or with an inability on the part of the child to cope adequately with the problems of adulthood. Both of these interpretations are matters of controversy. Some behavioral scientists claim that school success has little, if anything, to do with success as an adult, and that school failure is probably due more to deficiencies in the school than to deficiencies in the child. Although there are compelling arguments to support both points of view, most psychologists who work with children believe that in general, children who encounter difficulties in the classroom also have problems at home, problems in getting along with other children, or problems with their health, and that a child who has one of these problems, frequently has the others as well. Therefore, even if we grant that the child's ability to adjust to school is not the most crucial adaptation he must make, we must admit that it is often an index of his overall adjustment to life.

We should also take note of another element in our picture of a child's psycho-social development. In school a child's behavior is subject to systematic observation, and his performance as a junior member of society is compared to that of his peers. Whether comparisons such as these should be made at all is again a matter of controversy. Some professionals believe that comparisons are always psychologically damaging; others maintain that comparison making is a natural and fundamental part of all kinds of social interaction, and that while most people unconsciously judge others and are themselves judged in everyday life, the school personnel who make appraisals are aware and objective about what they are doing. The research-oriented psychologist tends to favor making comparisons, for without comparisons of some kind, there can be neither science nor research.

There are many reasons why a child might have difficulties, but because children who get a poor start in life may logically have problems later, one of the best places to look for causes is in birth records. There is little disagreement over this assumption. Investigators agree that infants whose birth weight is markedly below normal—that is, "premature" infants—are more likely to have problems later on. Low-birth-weight children are born to mothers at all social levels, but there is a higher percentage of such births àmong mothers who live in poverty and who are malnourished.

D. V. Caputo and W. Mandell (1970) reviewed the research literature on this topic and concluded that low birth weight was frequently associated with significant neurological and physiological impairment in infancy and in later years. These children are more likely than the average child to score low on intelligence tests and to constitute a higher percentage of those children classified as mentally retarded or institutionalized for various disabilities. Those who reach high school are more likely to drop out. There is also a greater likelihood that low-birth-weight children will be hyperkinetic (overactive, disruptive, and tense) both in and out of school.

What can be done to help low-birth-weight infants? Extra stimulation seems beneficial. S. Scarr-Salapatek and M. L. Williams (1973) conducted a controlled experiment in which low-birth-weight infants born to young, unmarried mothers were divided into experimental and control groups. Attendants in the nursery to which the experimental group was assigned were instructed to pick up the infants frequently, to play with them and talk to them, and to hold them in a rocking chair while feeding them. Brightly colored mobiles were suspended over the infants' cribs to provide extra visual stimulation. Low-birth-weight neonates in the control group received the kind of treatment the hospital normally gave such infants. By the end of four weeks, the infants in the experimental group had gained more weight than those in the control group, and when rated on a scale of neurological and developmental status, showed greater advancement. When the mothers of the infants in the experimental group took them home, they were each given a mobile and brightly colored posters to hang near the babies' cribs. A social worker who made weekly visits to the mothers' homes also brought additional toys from time to time.

At the end of a year both groups of infants were observed and tested on intelligence and developmental scales. Results showed that the infants who had received the experimental treatment scored close to normal, but those in the control group were significantly retarded for their age. Children in the experimental group whose mothers lived alone with them and who played with them and stimulated them a great deal made the most progress.

The investigators made some observations that were especially interesting. Hospital staffs ordinarily treat premature infants as extra-uterine fetuses and consider them to be relatively unresponsive to their environment, but the premature infants in the experimental group of this study surprised both investigators and previously skeptical nurses by looking at the mobiles and gazing at the faces of the attendants who fed them. The social workers who visited the mothers, all of whom lived at the poverty level, found the mothers to be interested in doing the best for their babies but uninformed about matters such as proper diet and the importance of giving their infants stimulation through talking to them, playing with them, and handling them frequently.

The study by Scarr-Salapatek and Williams is one of several investigations during the last decade indicating that infants have a "need for stimulation" and that, within reasonable limits, more stimulation is better than less. Y. Brackbill (1973) found, for example, that stimuli in the form of continuous noise, bright light, swaddling clothes, and relatively high room temperature caused one-month-old infants to spend twice as much time sleeping, and reduced the time they spent in crying by 78 percent.

The experiment by Ottinger, Blatchley, and Denenberg, the first article (8.1) in this section, shows that normal newborn infants who receive extra stimulation are likely to be more attentive to their surroundings than are other newborns. Because cognitive development involves a process of becoming familiar with the environment and learning to cope with it, becoming aware and observant of the environment is an essential first step. The infant who receives extra stimulation evidently gets an early developmental start, but the child who is understimulated is handicapped.

Stimulation of human neonates and visual attentiveness

Donald R. Ottinger,
Mary E. Blatchley, and
Victor H. Denenberg

During recent years there has been a rapid growth in theory and research regarding the role of experience preceding and affecting the beginning of cognitive development. The work of Piaget and Hebb are noteworthy; Hunt (1961) has emphasized that infantile experience plays a role in cognitive, as well as emotional, development; and Denenberg (1966) has argued that variation in stimulus input is necessary for optimal adjustment and performance.

Reprinted from the *Proceedings of the 76th Annual Convention of the American Psychological Association* 3 (1968): 355–356, with permission of the authors and the Association. Copyright 1968 by the American Psychological Association.

8. Manipulating children's environments

Institutionalized infants were given increased stimulation in the form of rocking by White and Castle (1964) starting at 6 days of age for 30 days. Although the eyes of the experimental Ss were covered during rocking, at 6 weeks of age the experimental Ss exhibited more visual attention than a nonrocked control group.

Casler (1965), again using institutionalized babies, gave an experimental group extra tactile stimulation for 10 weeks and found the experimental group exceeded a control group on Gesell scores on adaptive, language, and personal-social scales.

The purpose of the present study was to determine if supplementary stimulation experiences would alter visual attentiveness if applied during the neonatal period.

METHOD

Subjects

The Ss were 28 full-term neonates, equally divided into experimental and control groups. Both males and females were used. Permission to use S was obtained from both the mother and the responsible physician.

Test apparatus

A modification of the Fantz (1958) technique for measuring visual fixation was used. A display board constructed of plywood, painted blue, 32 inches above the floor and tipped forward at an angle of 75° to the floor, held the visual targets. Two targets were presented simultaneously on the board, and an observation hole was placed midway between the targets.

These targets, painted black on white posterboard, were used and were presented in all combinations in random order and balanced for side of presentation. The targets were 1, 3, or 5 black dots within the black outline of a circle. S was held by an assistant and placed midway between the targets, oriented to the center, and 19 cm. from the display board. E remained behind the display board and presented the stimuli without awareness as to identity of targets and observed the reflection of targets on the pupils of Ss eyes. E presented each set of targets for 30 seconds and operated electrical timers recording the time eyes were open and time eyes were open and on target. Lighting was provided by lamps on either side of S below his field of vision. Approximately 25 to 28 foot-candles were reflected from the targets and field.

Procedure

All *S*s were pretested on the morning of the day following delivery, at least 12 hours after the event, and in a quiet room. *S*s were again tested for visual attentiveness on the morning of the fourth postpartum day.

Supplementary experiences

As soon as the pretesting was completed, *S*s in the experimental group were subjected to several types of stimulation:

1. *S*s were held at the shoulder of *E* approximately 19 cm. from a rotating multicolored wheel for a period of 5 min.

2. *S*s were held on *E*'s lap and their backs gently rubbed for 10 min.

3. Again while being held to the shoulder of *E*, *S* was exposed for 5 min. to a flat circle on which a schematic face was painted. This rotated continually (30 rpm) around a brightly painted semisphere, thus passing in and out of *S*'s field of vision.

4. Five min. of rocking and "mother talk" were given.

5. At the completion of the above routine, an electrical crib rocker was placed on the crib for 15 min. This provided a gentle shaking of the crib and baby.

This 25-min. procedure, exclusive of the crib rocker, was carried out twice a day, morning and late afternoon, for 3 days. The crib rocker was employed for 15 min., 6 times a day, at approximately 4-hr. intervals.

Totaling all forms of stimulation, there were 140 min. of supplementary experience for each of 3 days given to the experimental *S*s. In addition, a plastic mobile was placed at the head of the crib, a pinwheel at the side, and abstract designs were used as crib liners.

Except for the pretesting, the hospital routine for the control *S*s was not altered until posttesting. All babies were taken to their mothers 6 times a day for feeding. Each feeding period lasted approximately 1 hr. and if the baby finished before that time the mother had the option of holding the baby or replacing him in his crib. Flexibility of routine was provided by allowing any mother to hold her baby between feedings. Additional routine stimulation to the baby was provided by the hospital attendants who could pick up and comfort the babies if it seemed necessary. Each nursery was provided with continuous music if the attendant on duty desired to listen to it. Thus, hospital routine was left as undisturbed as possible and no baby was denied any attention or stimulation that existed in the usual routine.

RESULTS

The design thus consisted of experimental and control groups divided unequally into males and females, and pre- and post-test scores.

The data were analyzed by an unweighted means analysis of variance. Analyses were performed on the total time S's eyes were open and also on the proportion of this "eyes-open" total time that S's eyes were fixated on a target.

The analysis of variance on the total time the eyes were open during the testing periods produced a significant main effect for pre- and posttest at the .01 level. The eyes of both experimental and control groups were open more on the posttest on the fourth postpartum day than they had been during the pretest on day one. There were no other significant main effects of interactions on this variable.

Visual fixation time on target was expressed as a proportion of the total time that each S had his eyes on target for the time he had them open during a presentation. . . . The interaction of groups by pre- and post-test scores was significant at the .01 level. Experimental babies fixated on targets a higher proportion of time than did the control babies during the posttest. Thus, on the posttest all babies had their eyes open more than on the pretest, but the experimental babies spent a greater proportion of that time with their eyes fixated on the targets than did the controls. Group means are shown in Table 1, and the analysis of variance is shown in Table 2. (Omitted in the interests of brevity.)

TABLE 1
PROPORTION OF EYES-OPEN TIME SPENT ON TARGET ARC-SIN TRANSFORMATION

Group	N	Pretest	Posttest
Experimental male	6	1.5704	1.7555
Experimental female	8	1.6957	2.0437
Control male	7	1.7159	1.5841
Control female	7	1.7502	1.7339

DISCUSSION

The purpose of this experiment was to determine if supplementary stimulation experiences would increase visual attentiveness during the neonatal period. This phenomenon has been previously demonstrated in older infants and after longer periods of treatment than is employed in the present study, but this is the first time this has been demonstrated during the neonatal period.

The finding that both control and experimental groups had their eyes open significantly more during the testing on Day 4 than on Day 1 is interpreted as a maturational change or at least an interaction between maturation and the level of stimulation available from the hospital routine. The effects on fixation time are apparently related to experiences provided by the experimental treatment. The present study does not contain any information on the permanence of this produced behavioral change. The demonstrated plasticity of visual behavior in the human neonate would appear to be important if subsequent experiences were to follow that built upon this behavioral modification. The increase in amount and variability of stimulus input for the experimental group acted upon the neonate to increase visual attentiveness. Such an increase in visual attentiveness would appear to be beneficial for the organism in enabling him to attend to more complex aspects of the visual world at an earlier age. This capacity to respond to experiences while yet in the neonatal period and increase the development of an act as basic as attention suggests that a systematic program of stimulation and experience can be initiated during the neonatal period with the goal of increasing cognitive development. The determination of appropriate developmental experiences remains to be determined, but the goal of increasing the rate of cognitive development clearly calls for the necessary research to determine this program.

Although the findings of studies of early stimulation present some surprises, they are generally consistent with the view held by most people that children do best when they are raised by adults who love them. However, these studies show that love in the form of emotional attachment is not enough, for love must be actively expressed in the form of looking at the child, handling him, playing with him, and talking to him. One of the most interesting of the studies on the need of children for loving attention and stimulation is an investigation conducted by Wayne Dennis, article 8.2 in this section. For the last two decades. Dennis has been observing children who were placed in a crèche (a foundling home) in Beirut. Lebanon. The five nuns in charge of the hundred or so children in the crèche did the best they could, but the ratio of one adult to twenty children meant that each child received a subnormal amount of attention, stimulation, and love. It is hardly surprising therefore that the children's average IQ was about 50, the lowest that has ever been reported for an otherwise normal group of children. Once the children were adopted, however, they began to develop at a normal rate. Those children who left the crèche during the first year of life made the best progress and achieved normal levels of intelligence, but those who were adopted later left the crèche with a handicap that was likely to prevent their reaching normal levels.

The mental growth of certain foundlings before and after adoption

Wayne Dennis

This report is concerned with the intellectual development of children who are severely retarded from environmental causes early in life and who are later adopted into normal families. The subjects consist of foundlings admitted within two weeks after birth by the Crèche of St. Vincent de Paul in Beirut, Lebanon. The post-adoption tests of these children were conducted in the spring of 1964 and 1965, and a full report of the results, as well as follow-up data, was published by me in 1973 under the title, *Children of the Crèche* (see complete reference at the end of this article).

MENTAL DEVELOPMENT IN THE CRECHE

We began to gather data on the mental development in the Crèche in 1955. However, thus far, only two reports have appeared, one by

A previously unpublished paper, delivered by the author at the American University of Beirut in 1965, and edited by him in 1974. It is reprinted here with permission of the author.

Dennis and Najarian (1957) and one by Dennis and Sayegh (1965). Both show that severe behavioral retardation occurs in the Crèche. While the Dennis and Najarian study showed that there was little retardation on certain tests among Crèche children attending nursery school between the ages of four to six years, more general tests of intellectual performance show decided retardation at these ages. The instruments recently used have been the Cattell Infant Scale and the Stanford-Binet (form L-M). Each scale, by supplying alternate items, permits some choice of test items on the part of the examiner. We have taken advantage of this prerogative to choose those items on which, on the basis of our experience, Crèche children are least handicapped. The Stanford-Binet was used with any child who was able to achieve a basal age of two years (the lowest Stanford-Binet level). If he could not achieve a basal age of two, we used the Cattell scale, which begins at two months. The testing was done by Mrs. Yvonne Sayegh, who is fluent in Arabic and French. Since French is the chief language used in the Crèche, instructions were usually given in that language, but, if the child did not understand, Arabic also was tried.

Unless they are adopted, foundlings remain in the Crèche to the age of five years and sometimes even to age seven. At some point between ages five and seven they are transferred to institutions for older children which are operated by the same religious order.

Since 1956 we have tested a total of 112 children in the Crèche who were between four months and six years of age. Those to be tested were chosen in terms of age groups; i.e., in one series of tests all children aged four months to twelve months were tested, in another all between one year and two years, at another all between two years and six years. In other words, there was no individual selection for testing. Testing was done only for research purposes, not as a basis for adoption. In only a few cases were scores made available to the institution.

The over-all mean I.Q. for children tested between the age of 4 months to six years was 53. There is no significant age trend in this age range. So far as we are aware, this is the lowest institutional mean which has been found. A slightly higher mean previously reported by Dennis and Najarian for the first year of life in the Crèche was due to the inclusion of three-month-olds in the mean, but the full effect of the Crèche is not apparent before the age of four months. Whether the higher scores of infants below four months of age are real or are due to test inadequacies has not been determined.

The question arises as to whether or not the choice of adoptive infants is based in part upon impressions of behavioral development, even though test scores were not provided to the prospective parents. Many infants who were adopted had never been tested. In each age group that was tested in a particular year, the scores of the children who were adopted and those who were not adopted at some arbitrary date after their testing were compared. In no group was there a significant difference between the two sub-groups.

This should not be surprising inasmuch as judgment of the infant I.Q. from observation requires a skilled estimate of behavioral level relative to age norms. The Crèche children are small, and undersized children are usually judged to be younger than they are. Thus they do not appear to be as retarded as they are. An additional factor operating against intellectual selection is that the adoptive parents in almost all cases are childless and may have had only vague notions of the relation between age and children's behavior.

There *are* selective factors in adoption from the Crèche but they are not behavioral. As revealed by conversations with the nuns and with adoptive parents, there appears to be a preference for blue or gray eyes and yellow or brown hair. There is also preference for a child who bears a real or fancied facial resemblance to one or both of the adoptive parents. Neither of these preferences is likely to have any relation to intelligence scores.

In brief, the mean behavioral quotient of foundlings while they are in the Crèche, both those who remain in the Crèche and those who are later adopted, is in the neighborhood of 50. There are, of course, individual differences, but the upper range of differences is limited. Of the 112 children tested while in the Crèche, only 16 tested over 70 and only one of these tested above 100. Thus there is very little overlapping between Crèche scores and the scores of family-reared children. This statement is not based merely on American norms. Considerable experience with the Cattell test and the Stanford-Binet in Lebanon show that Lebanese children approximate the American norms on each test.

While the foregoing data on mental development in the Crèche may seem shocking, we wish to say that the five nuns who are responsible for the welfare of the 100 or more children in the Crèche are devoted to correcting the retardation of Crèche children. The initiation of a program of adoption was the first step taken in this direction. The Crèche, at this time, is the only institution for children in Lebanon, indeed the only one in several Middle Eastern countries, which has such a program. Within the crèche itself, major reforms are underway. The wholehearted cooperation of the institution in our studies over a period of nearly ten years provides evidence of its desire to improve the condition of foundlings, an aim which cannot be achieved simply by abolishing the Crèche. But it is beyond the scope of this paper to attempt to present a full picture of the difficulties which are faced by those who seek to assist homeless children in the Mediterranean and Near Eastern areas.

MENTAL GROWTH AFTER ADOPTION

Following their adoption we have given mental tests, primarily Stanford-Binets, to 34 children. [This number was later increased to 86.] The tests were given in the early months of 1964 and 1965. While we were testing, the nun who is chiefly in charge of adoption at the Crèche could locate only 35 adoptive families in Lebanon and Syria. Of these, 34 cooperated with us. Because of geographic mobility in Lebanon, and because the Crèche has no social workers and no other staff to maintain follow-up contacts, many adopted children could not be located. It is possible that additional cases, adopted prior to 1965, can be contacted later. In any case, new adoptions are occurring, and these will be studied in later years. Aside from those adoptions in Lebanon and in Syria, Crèche children have also been adopted in the United States and in France. [Results obtained from American adoptees are reported in *Children of the Crèche*.] One mulatto child has been adopted in Africa. We have not as yet attempted to study these adoptees in foreign countries.

Despite the considerable amount of testing which we have done in the Crèche, we find that only 6 of the 34 subjects of this study were tested prior to adoption. Their mean pre-adoption score was 57 which is not significantly different from the mean of Crèche children as a whole. This finding, as well as the evidence reviewed previously, tends to show that our subjects, prior to adoption, progress mentally at a rate approximately 50% of that of the ordinary Lebanese family-reared child.

Our 34 cases were adopted at ages ranging from shortly after birth (2 cases) to six years (3 cases). They have been adopted for periods as short as 4 months and as long as 10 years. Their ages when tested following adoption vary from one year to 15 years. Since in all of these respects they are very heterogeneous, and it is therefore not possible to separate them into several groups homogenous in respect to age at adoption, the length of the post-adoption period, and age at testing.

In what kinds of homes have these children lived? Naturally homes vary, but no adoptive parent was illiterate, no adoptive father was employed as an unskilled laborer and very few fathers were in the skilled manual laborer class. Many fathers were business or professional men. Aside from two professional women, no adoptive mothers worked outside the home. While there were a few poor and humble homes, most of the homes were middle class. Of the cases in Beirut, most were located in Ashrafieh or Ras Beirut, which are considered to be good neighborhoods. Most of those adopted outside of Beirut were in progressive villages.

All adoptive parents were Roman Catholics, or Maronites, who constitute a very old Near Eastern branch of the Roman Catholic church. The Order of St. Vincent de Paul requires such placement.

Most of the adoptive parents preferred to have the child tested at home. We were therefore able to meet one or both parents and observe home conditions. Only a few parents preferred to bring the child to the Crèche for testing.

How does the mental development of the Crèche adoptee change following his adoption? From our data, our conclusion is that soon after his adoption his rate of mental development changes from 50 to 100.

Let us define our terms. The I.Q. of a child describes his average rate of mental development between and his birth and the date of his testing. To obtain the I.Q. the mental age is divided by the chronological age and is then cleared of decimals. The rate of development prior to adoption is shown by the conventional I.Q. To indicate the rate of development after adoption we must introduce a similar but different index. This is the rate of mental gain over a shorter period of time, in this case the period between the date of adoption and the date of post-adoptive testing. This is obtained by dividing the gain in mental age during this period, by the chronological length of the period. As is traditional with the I.Q., the rate of gain will be expressed in two or three digits with the decimal point omitted. A normal rate of gain for any period of childhood is, of course, 100; i.e., is in the usual case the increase in mental age is equal to the increase in chronological age. On this basis, the typical Crèche child prior to adoption shows an advance of 50.

Among our 34 adopted subjects, the mean rate of gain between the date of adoption and the date of testing is 106. In other words these children who prior to adoption were progressing slowly advanced at the normal rate in their varying periods of post-adoption life.

The rate of post-adoption gain, so far as our present data are concerned, is not related to the duration of the adoption. At present, we have data on only four cases who have been adopted for less than a year. Their mean rate of gain has been 104. Eleven cases have been adopted for periods ranging from four years five months to ten years four months. The mean rate of gain after adoption for these cases is 75. This is not significantly different from that of those recently adopted. No sub-group differs significantly from 100. Conceivably a much larger number of cases may change this finding, but it is not likely to change it appreciably.

Within the limitations of our present data, the age at adoption as well as the duration also has no bearing upon the subsequent rate of progress. Those adopted late (i.e., at 4, 5 and 6 years of age) progress as rapidly, but not more rapidly, than those adopted earlier.

While the figure 100 approximates the observed mean rate of post-adoption development, there are, of course, individual differences. The lowest individual rate of gain found following adoption is 72, the highest is 142. These figures indicate that there is little overlap between the rate of intellectual development among children when in the Crèche and their rate of gain subsequent to their adoption.

Since individual rates of gain are based upon a relatively small number of test items, and in some cases upon short adoption periods, the individual measures of rate of development are subject to a considerable error of measurement. For this reason, our stress is placed upon group means.

The obvious interpretation suggested by the findings just presented is that if the *typical* Crèche foundling progresses at half the normal rate prior to adoption, and at a normal rate thereafter, the mental age of an adopted Crèche child at any time, if he is *typical,* can be predicted by adding to a mental age which is equivalent to one half of his chronological age at adoption a subsequent mental age gain equivalent to the duration of his adoption. To obtain his I.Q. one divides this figure by his chronological age at post-adoptive testing.

Using this procedure we have predicted the I.Q. for each of our 34 cases. It should be noted that the predictions refer to the average child, we have at present no way of predicting individual differences. Nevertheless our predictions of I.Q. at post-adoptive testing based on the formula presented above vary, on the average, by 9 I.Q. points from the empirically determined I.Q.'s. The mean of the predicted I.Q.'s differs from the actual mean by less than one point. The correlation between predicted I.Q.'s and empirical I.Q.'s is .73. If we had a sufficient number of sub-groups, so that sub-groups, rather than individual scores, could be scored as a basis of prediction presumably the correlation would approach 1.00.

That there should be such a correlation is a theoretical interpretation, not a mathematical necessity. That is, the observed fact that the mean rate of gain between the dates of adoption and of testing is close to 100 can be accounted for in a variety of ways, such as that the real rate of gain is high immediately following adoption and then becomes slower, or is slow at first and then becomes faster, or that it is slow between January and July and fast between July and January, or vice versa. But none of these or other possible explanations of our findings seem likely to prove correct. The most direct test of our theory will consist of testing the adoptees at more than one point in time following adoption, and this we shall do in our later studies.

Perhaps it needs to be pointed out that a normal rate of gain subsequent to adoption does not bring about a quick improvement in I.Q. This is because the retardation which exists at the time of adoption, when expressed in terms of the I.Q., is only slowly reduced by the lengthening duration of post-institutional experience. For example, if a child is adopted at 8 months of age and at that time has a mental age of 4 months, he has an initial retardation of 4 months in respect to mental age. If he develops at the rate of 100, the deficit of 4 months will remain and on his first birthday his mental age will be 8 months, on his fifth birthday it will be 4 years 8 months, at age 10 it will be 9 years 8 months. His I.Q. will increase with age because the initial retardation of four months becomes an increasingly smaller fraction of his chronological age. According to our theory he can closely approach but not attain an I.Q. of 100.

For children who are adopted at later ages the consequences of this principle are more drastic. Let us take the case of a Crèche foundling who is adopted at 6 years of age. At this time, if he is a normal Crèche foundling, he will have a mental age of 3 years. Let us assume that, being typical, his rate of gain is 100 thereafter. Four years later at 10 years of age he will have added 4 years of mental age to his initial 3, attaining a mental age of 7. His I.Q. is now 70. This is a big gain over his earlier I.Q. of 50. It is still far from the norm of 100.

However, by age 13 the average Crèche child adopted at age 6 should have a mental age of 10 and thus an I.Q. of 77, a gain in I.Q. of 27 points. In fact the only three cases in our files which approximate these conditions do have at one post-adoption testing at a mean age of 13 years one month a mean I.Q. of 77. To be sure, such a fit between theory and fact seems too good to be true.

Taking our cases as a whole, the mean I.Q. on post-adoption testing is 81. This is a gain of approximately 30 points. That it is so high is due to the fact that several children were adopted at an early age and were tested after a long period of adoption. This mean gain is of little significance since it does not take into account age at adoption and age at post-adoptive testing. . . .

Let us for a moment drop our preoccupation with the Crèche in order to make the point that not all institutional environments result in intellectual retardation. We are acquainted with foundling homes in which the mean rate of intellectual development is 100. The figure of 50 for the Crèche is an empirical figure, not a theoretical one. But if it were, let us say, 60 or 80, the principles which we have stated and illustrated above would presumably be the same, although the values in the equation would be different.

Indeed, we can envisage a situation in which home environments are less stimulating than some institutional environments, in which case, of course, we would expect the rate of gain, and the I.Q., to decrease following adoption.

Why, in Lebanon, is the mean rate of gain after adoption almost exactly 100? It is, of course, the mean I.Q. in many modern countries. It would seem, therefore, that this is the rate of gain, whether from birth or from a later period, to be expected of children of ordinary heredity in ordinary modern homes. Whether unusual environments can produce a rate of gain higher than 100 on the part of average children remains to be determined.

As we have noted previously, the Lebanese families into which Crèche foundlings have been adopted vary widely. While our present data are not definitive, they suggest that Crèche children adopted by the best educated and most well-to-do parents do not have a higher rate of gain than those in less privileged homes. On the other hand, very few severely underprivileged homes are represented in our sample.

THEORETICAL CONSIDERATIONS

While our present data are limited, certain deductions from them seem to be clearly indicated. For one thing, Crèche foundlings cannot be considered to be biologically inferior to a serious extent, despite a mean institutional I.Q. of 50, since after adoption the rate of gain is 100 and their subsequent mean I.Q. increases considerably. Furthermore it is evident that an early period of life which depresses the I.Q. to a mean of 50, does not, even if it lasts to age 6, prevent a normal rate of intellectual gain in later years.

On the part of some theorists, the intellectual retardation of institutional children has been attributed to emotional factors. While we do not wish to minimize the general importance of the emotions, the finding that the course of post-institutional intellectual development can be fairly accurately predicted from the duration of institutionalization and the duration of adoption seems not to require a dynamic explanation.

Recently considerable attention has been given to the concept of "critical periods" in development. While evidence for critical periods may exist in other areas of behavior in other species, there appears to be no critical period for intellectual development in children, if we are correct in interpreting our data as showing that whatever the duration of intellectual stultification, a normal rate of mental development can be initiated at any subsequent time at least up to six years of age. [Additional data presented in *Children of the Crèche* suggest that a critical period for permanent effects of experiential deprivation occurs around the age of two years.]

Perhaps the most important theoretical suggestion which emerges from this study is that the age of the child, after the age of four months, is of little significance with respect to what can be gained from intellectual experience. That is to say one year of normal experience appears to produce only one year of increase in mental age whether the normal experience begins at four months or at six years. It is commonly held by many psychologists that for biological reasons the older the child the faster he learns. Our data suggest that if a child is biologically normal but is retarded by a paucity of intellectual experiences, a year of normal experience is required for one year of mental development, regardless of the age at which normal experience begins. In making this statement we are referring to the kind of mental differences which are measured by the Stanford-Binet, not to motor performances such as sitting or walking or stair climbing.

Many persons have observed that children who have been for several years in poor institutions appear to have a long-lasting intellectual retardation. Our data support this observation, but we think the data provide an explanation for the phenomenon. Although development may take place at a normal rate after children leave the Crèche, the initial retardation remains and cannot be erased by a normal rate of development. Mental development must proceed beyond its normal speed if an initial deficit is to be overcome, or it must continue for a longer period than it does in the case of ordinary children.

From the above considerations, two practical and humanitarian principles can be deduced. To begin with, we assume on the basis of our experience that it will continue to be necessary to place some children in institutions. We assume this to be true because we believe that certain circumstances such as the illness or death of the mother, earthquakes, typhoons, fires and war, and social attitudes toward illegitimacy will continue to require institutional care. If our interpretations are correct, children placed temporarily in institutions must have an intellectually normal environment or retardation in mental growth will occur. Mere nutrition and good health are not enough to insure mental growth. For this reason "good" institutions should be developed. There are institutions in existence which show that institutions need not produce mental retardation. Secondly if placement in a "bad" institution is unavoidable, placement should be for the shortest possible period, since the longer the period of institutionalization under stultifying conditions the greater the child's mental retardation when he leaves the institution and the more difficult the task of rehabilitation. These are not novel ideas, all that we have contributed are facts which support them.

While the preceding comments have been phrased in terms of institutions, they should be stated as applying to any environment which results in a rate of gain of less than 100. A deprivation of normal experiences, whether it occurs in a family or in an orphanage, appears to have consequences which cannot easily or quickly be corrected.

SUMMARY

In a particular foundling home it has been found that infants from the age of 4 months until they leave the institution have mean I.Q.s on the Cattell Infant Scale and the Stanford-Binet of approximately 50. Some of these children are adopted. In 1964 and 1965, 34 children from this institution who had been adopted were tested at ages varying from one to 15 years. The findings of the study are interpreted as indicating that after adoption the rate of mental development becomes normal; i.e., in each post-adoption year the average child gains one year in mental age. But since the mean rate of gain after adoption is only 100, an initial retardation in mental age remains. The I.Q. increases after adoption because the pre-adoption years become a relatively smaller part of the child's life period as his age increases. It has been shown that after adoption the adopted children as a whole reach a mean I.Q. of 81. This gain is based upon limited periods of adoption. Whether a mean I.Q. of 100 eventually will be reached by these children remains for future determination.

The bearing of these findings upon several theories of intellectual development have been considered. Their implication for institutional practices and for the care of underprivileged children have also been discussed.

What happens, however, if institutions provide extra amounts of stimulation and attention? Are they able to present a psychological environment that is an adequate substitute for family life? A study by B. Tizard and J. Rees (1974) answers some of these questions. These investigators studied four groups of British children, aged four-and-one-half years. One group lived in nurseries run by voluntary societies. These nurseries were especially well-staffed and provided many toys, books, and outings. The prevailing policy in the nurseries, however, was one of discouraging personal relationships with the children, apparently to avoid favoritism and jealousy. Each child was therefore provided with a great deal of stimulation but with no close and continuous relationship with a parent figure. The second group included children from the nurseries who had been taken back by their mothers between the ages of two and four. The third group contained children who had been adopted by families most of whom were middle- and upper-middle class. The fourth group, included solely for purposes of contrast, was composed of children who had never stayed at the nurseries, but who lived in London with their own families, all of which were small and of working-class status.

Intelligence tests administered to these four groups provided evidence supporting the concept that stimulation of some kind is important to satisfactory cognitive development in children, as the mean IQs of the groups turned out to be normal or better. The third group, which was adopted by largely middle-class families, had the highest mean IQ—115; the children who were restored to their natural mothers had the lowest—100. Of these natural mothers, half lived alone and were in poor circumstances; the other half were married to men who, in most cases, were not the fathers of the children who had been taken back from the institutions. In other words, the homes of the children in this group probably had more than the usual number of problems. The group of children who remained in the nurseries had a mean IQ of 105. Although they were read to more often than the children in any other group and owned the greatest number of toys, they tended to be socially unresponsive and highly distractible when intelligence tests were being administered to them. The working-class children who were living with their natural parents also tended to be socially unresponsive and distractible, but their mean IQ was 111.

One of the most important variables identified by these investigators was the frequency of the children's literary experiences. When the children in all four groups were combined and reclassified according to their IQs, 42 percent of those who had IQs of 110 and over had been read to at least three times a week and had been taken to a children's library at least once a month; the children with IQs under 110 were seldom read to and rarely or never visited libraries.

The findings of Tizard and Rees are consistent with those of other studies: if children are to attain a normal level of cognitive development, stimulation is essential, personal attention from interested and involved adults is important, and verbal interaction (through being talked to and read to) is especially facilitating. Discoveries like these formed the basis of the large-scale programs of intervention—attempts to improve children's psycho-social environment—that were initiated in the United States during the 1960s. Two examples of such programs are Project Head Start and "Sesame Street."

The Head Start Program was initiated by the U.S. Office of Education during the summer of 1965, as a result of legislation passed by Congress in the previous year. The general idea of the program was to provide preschool-age children from economically deprived homes with "enriched" learning experiences, which would presumably facilitate their cognitive and social development and prepare them to enter school better able to cope with classroom tasks. The program draws heavily upon research findings like those we have discussed in this book. Head Start groups are kept small, and the high ratio of adults to children gives each child an opportunity to receive a great deal of personal attention and stimulation.

One feature of the Head Start program is that the mother of each child is involved in activities designed to facilitate his development, especially along cognitive lines. The importance of this feature is demonstrated in an experiment conducted by R. Highberger and H. Brooks (1973), where the mothers of an experimental group of Head Start children read to them for at least fifteen minutes a day over a seventeen-week period. Children in the control group could take toys home from the center's toy library, but their mothers were asked not to work with them. At the end of the experiment, children who had received the experimental treatment tended to make higher scores on a nonverbal "culture-fair" test of mental ability than did members of the control group.

Program Head Start has been evaluated by a number of studies. The one that attracted the most attention was conducted by Ohio University and the Westinghouse Learning Corporation (1969). The investigators studied cognitive and affective (emotional and attitudinal) progress made in the first three grades of school by comparing a sample of children from more than one hundred Head Start centers throughout the country with other disadvantaged children who had not participated in the Head Start program. The body of data gathered was extensive and in some instances ambiguous and contradictory, but it did indicate that some of the full-year programs, especially those serving black children in certain inner-city areas and in the southeastern states, seemed to have facilitated the development of cognitive skills. There was no evidence that Head Start activities had any effect on affective development, nor was there any significant effect on children who attended only the summer programs. The investigators also noted that the parents voiced strong approval and support for Project Head Start.

During its first ten years, Program Head Start involved well over a million children and their parents. Although this number is impressive, it represents only a small percentage of the children who, for one reason or another, could have benefited from enriched preschool learning experiences. Shortages in trained personnel, housing, and funds have made it impossible to provide Head Start experiences for more children. There is also the additional problem faced by busy mothers, many of whom are employed outside the home, of getting children to and from Head Start centers. The television program "Sesame Street," which first appeared in 1969, seems to be at least a partial answer to these problems. "Sesame Street" is a series of programs produced by Children's Television Workshop specially designed to capture and hold the interest of preschool children and to get them involved in a cognitive exploration of their environment. These programs attempt, for example, to make children more aware of similarities and differences between objects, and of how symbols—like letters and numbers—are related to objects and ideas.

"Sesame Street" has the advantage of being available in the home. It is not necessary for a mother to go through the routine of enrolling her child in a center some distance away and of making arrangements for his transportation. It does have the disadvantage, however, of leaving the question of involvement up to the child. He may watch the program or not; if he does watch it, he can look at it passively, as he might some other kind of entertainment; and there are no supervised activities to follow up on whatever concepts are presented. A question can therefore be posed as to whether the programs are really worthwhile.

An answer to this question is made by Gerry Ann Bogatz and Samuel Ball, whose paper appears as article 8.3 in this section. Bogatz and Ball report the results of a survey of nearly a thousand children undertaken by the Educational Testing Service. These findings show that the more frequently children viewed the program, the more gains they made in using numbers, letters, and geometric forms, in problem-solving, and in understanding concepts such as size and location of objects.

"Sesame Street": An evaluation of its effects on preschoolers

Gerry Ann Bogatz and
Samuel Ball

"Mommy, let's talk about something." A two-year-old is squirming in her high-chair. Mommy looks up. "What do you want to talk about?" "I wanna talk about the letter J." Mommy does a double-take and beams at the unexpected exchange.

In a city playground, a three-year-old is playing catch with his mother and father. The father starts to walk to a bench when suddenly he hears his youngster scream, "Dad, you can't go now. You'll mess up the triangle."

In a rural town, a mother walks into her kitchen and finds her retarded five-year-old playing with three spoons and a knife and singing to himself. "One of these is not like the others, one of these things doesn't belong. . . ."

Throughout the country during the past year, a surge of stories about "budding geniuses" and new-found skills has been heard. Somehow, preschool children were behaving in ways previously attributed to kindergarten and first-graders. Even tales of 15-month-old babies suddenly saying 1-2-3-4-5 were heard. And those who were attuned to the world of toddlers suspected the source of this change. An educational television show, "Sesame Street," designed to help teach certain skills to preschoolers, particularly disadvantaged children, had captured the attention of millions of youngsters.

The show is a daily, hour-long medley of fast-paced animation, puppetry, film, and actors performing as expertly as any you will meet on the commercial networks. The show is amusing, lively, and entertaining. But is it achieving its educational objectives?

Anything as innovative as "Sesame Street" is bound to have its doubters, and slowly these voices also began to be heard. Was "Sesame

Reprinted from *American Education* 7(3) (April 1971): 11–15, a publication of the U. S. Office of Education, with permission of the authors. Original article entitled: "Some things you've wanted to know about 'Sesame Street.' "

Street" teaching the many disadvantaged minority group children for whom the show was primarily geared? Were these stories of budding geniuses mainly typical of white middle-class children? Or were they even typical of them? Even if "Sesame Street" was helping children memorize the ABC's and 1-2-3's, was the show capable of teaching more complex skills? Was "Sesame Street" creating a generation of passive robotlike creatures who were absorbing the fascinating material presented but who would later turn away from traditional education when they reached school?

Some of these questions have now been answered or are currently being studied in an evaluation of the show conducted by Educational Testing Service. And the results so far are not only encouraging but in some cases truly remarkable. They show that "Sesame Street" had a marked effect on the learning of three- through five-year-old children from widely diverse backgrounds—including a strong and positive effect on disadvantaged children.

The effect was seen in many goal areas including letters, numbers, forms, classification, and sorting skills. This evaluation was dependent upon the work of many hundreds of people and the cooperation of the parents of over a thousand children. It is one of the most extensive and intensive evaluations ever undertaken of any educational program.

November 10, 1969, was a memorable occasion for U.S. television. On that date "Sesame Street" began telecasting on some 130 noncommercial TV stations across the United States. Unlike most television shows for preschoolers, it was well publicized and well financed. It received a budget of $8 million over more than two years for research and development and actual broadcasts. Surprisingly, a conscious, well-financed attempt to educate as well as entertain on television had never occurred before. In fact, the traditional view, based on the contrast between the lively and popular style of commercial network's children's shows and the slow and labored style of most low budget, locally produced, educational programs for children, probably sees educational television and entertaining television as mutually exclusive.

The evaluation of "Sesame Street" was a job that began in the summer of 1968 and [continued] through 1971. The participation of Educational Testing Service in the "Sesame Street" venture dates back to a series of curriculum conferences set up by the show's producer, the Children's Television Workshop. The meetings were called to establish the specific behavioral goals of the show. What selected set of

8. Manipulating children's environments

instructional objectives could a television show reasonably be expected to teach millions of children in 130 hours? By the end of the summer 1968—more than a year before the show was to go on the air—a highly specific, behaviorally stated set of goals had been provisionally selected.

Children's Television Workshop decided that research could be divided into two parts—formative and summative. The formative research was conducted by an in-house research team. Its role was one of helping the producers develop the show as effectively as possible. Children's Television Workshop selected Educational Testing Service to become the summative, out-of-house research group to carry out an independent, objective, overall evaluation of "Sesame Street" in terms of the goals of the show.

ASSESSING THE GROWTH

Our first major task was to develop an entirely new battery of measuring instruments expressly reflecting the curriculum goals of the show. Previously existing tests were not suitable. One set of instruments we designed was given individually to 1,300 three- through five-year-old children to assess growth in the specific goal areas and in the areas where unanticipated learning might occur. For example, we were not only concerned with measuring whether children learned to label letters and numbers (two of the specific goals of "Sesame Street"), but also whether children would learn to recognize common words in their environment. [See Figure 1 for a sample item.]

Another set of measuring instruments that was developed was intended to assess the background variables whose presence might affect the amount of learning achieved by a child viewing "Sesame Street." Examples of such variables included the vocabulary level of the child, whether stories were read to him by his parents or siblings, and the mother's educational aspirations for the child.

A final group of measures dealt with assessing how many of the 130 hours were viewed by each child, what the child did while viewing (his motor, verbal, and visual behavior), and what was actually on the show. This group of measures was an important supplement to the other measuring instruments we developed. It enabled us to indicate not only which children learned what, but to link these learning phenomena to the amount of viewing, to the particular television techniques used in

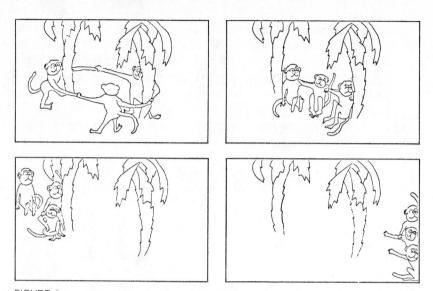

FIGURE 1

A PAGE FROM ETS TEST ASKS YOUNGSTERS TO POINT TO THE MONKEYS
BETWEEN THE TREES.

the program to achieve the goals, and to the way the children reacted
(tuned in, tuned out) to these techniques.

The test locations selected were Boston; Phoenix; Durham, N.C.
(inner-city black and white); suburban Philadelphia (middle class), and
northern California (rural).

EVALUATING THE MEDIUM

What seemed to be appreciated in all the communities we worked in
and what was crucial in the areas suspicious of outsiders was our decision
to assure that matters of local concern would be dealt with locally. In
each area we appointed a coordinator who was indigenous to the community in which we were working. Local cooperation was enhanced when
we emphasized that all testing would be performed by community residents who would be properly trained and adequately paid, that our
tests were specific to the goals of "Sesame Street," that we were not
trying to evaluate their children but rather that we were trying to evaluate
the show.

The research design was predicated on these major questions:

1. What, overall, is the impact of "Sesame Street"?
2. What are the moderating effects of age, sex, prior achievement level, and socioeconomic status on the impact of the program?
3. Do children at home watching "Sesame Street" benefit in comparison with children at home who do not watch it?
4. Do children in preschool classrooms benefit from watching the program as part of their school curriculum?
5. Do children from Spanish-speaking homes benefit from "Sesame Street"?
6. What are the effects of home background conditions on the impact of the show?

After extensive analyses of the massive amount of data obtained during the six months of the show, several generalizations can be accurately made: "Sesame Street" has shown that television can be an effective medium for teaching children important simple facts and skills and complex cognitive skills. The program benefited children from disadvantaged inner-city homes and from middle-class suburban and rural areas, both at home and in school. Children who watched the most, learned the most, with the amount of learning increasing in relation to the amount of time the children watched the show. Those skills that received the most time on the show were generally the skills that were best learned.

The vast amount of specific data supporting each of the above statements is contained in the full report: "The First Year of 'Sesame Street': An Evaluation." What the data show is the tremendous potential impact of this program and television as an educational medium.

"Sesame Street" is the first show ever to attempt to educate an entire population through national television in the guise of an extremely entertaining package, and that attempt has been remarkably successful in terms of the educational goals it has set for itself. Not only is the show being viewed by millions of youngsters—a milestone in itself for a show televised on educational television—it is also giving children of all backgrounds some basic skills they will need in their years in school.

The effect of the show can be demonstrated dramatically in three comparisons. The first is among the three age groups who watched the show—disadvantaged children of ages three, four, and five. The word disadvantaged can be, and is, defined in several different ways, but for our purposes economic status, educational opportunity, and attitudinal factors are all considered.

Pretests and post-tests were given to all the disadvantaged children [Figure 2]. The children were divided into four sections based on the amount they had viewed "Sesame Street." Children in Quarter 1 (Q1) viewed never or once a week; Q2 viewed two to three times a week; Q3 viewed four to five times a week; Q4 viewed more than five times a week. Before "Sesame Street" went on the air, older children almost invariably performed higher on the test than younger children. After "Sesame Street," however, three-year-olds who watched most (Q4) scored higher at post-test than three of the four-year-old groups and two of the five-year-old groups, although these three-year-olds had a pretest score lower than all five-year-olds and all but one of the four-year-old groups.

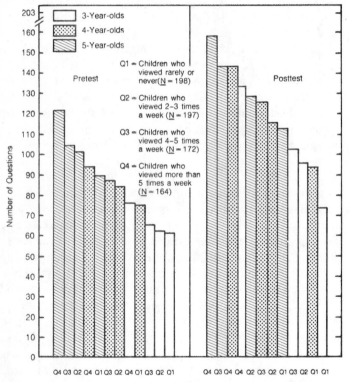

FIGURE 2

PRETEST AND POSTTEST SCORES OF 3, 4 AND 5-YEAR-OLD DISADVANTAGED CHILDREN

In other words, the placement of the children along the scale measuring the goals of "Sesame Street" was very dependent on age at pretest, while at post-test it was much more related to amount of viewing. These data also suggest that three- and four-year-olds are capable of learning many of the skills traditionally reserved for the five-year-old in school. And the data also support the general result of the evaluation: that children who watched the most (Q4 and Q3), learned the most.

A second comparison can be made between the middle-class four-year-old children in the study and the four-year-old disadvantaged children. Recent history of research has warned that such comparisons are often unwise to make primarily because so many things differentiate the two groups that a comparison is likely to be an invidious one, unfairly discriminating against the disadvantaged group. However, in this instance, the comparison allows us to discover the differing impact of the show on different children.

It was found that at pretest time every group of advantaged children scored higher than every group of disadvantaged children. However, at post-test, the gains of Q3 and Q4 disadvantaged children resulted in a realignment; no longer were scores directly related to social class, but rather social-class effects were clearly modified by amount of viewing. Disadvantaged children who watched "Sesame Street" often performed better on the measures of the show's goals than advantaged children who watched "Sesame Street" rarely or never [Figure 3].

A third comparison that we made we termed the "Age Cohorts Study." It involved two matched groups of children. Group 1 was 53 to 58 months of age at the time of pretesting. Group 2 was 53 to 58 months of age at the time of post-testing. In addition to being of the same chronological age at the point of comparison, the two groups were of comparable mental age and they lived in the same communities. There were, in short, no observable differences between the two groups in important matters of previous attainments, IQ, and home background. There were more than 100 disadvantaged children who were not attending school in each group.

The pretest scores of Group 1 (before the children could have watched "Sesame Street") were compared with the post-test scores of Group 2 after the Group 2 children had watched the program. The frequent viewers in Group 2—children in Q3 and Q4—scored about 40 points higher on the 203 common items than the comparable children in Group 1 who had never watched the show. Equally significant is

FIGURE 3

PRETEST AND POSTTEST SCORES OF DISADVANTAGED AND ADVANTAGED
4-YEAR-OLD CHILDREN

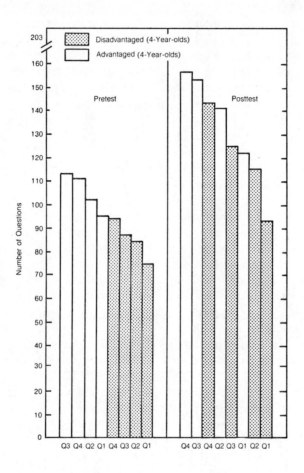

the fact that the infrequent viewers (Q1) in Group 2 differed by only
about 12 points from comparable children in Group 1 who had not
viewed "Sesame Street" at all. In short, holding maturational effect,
IQ, previous attainments, and home background constant, the frequent
viewers made large and important gains.

INTERPRETING THE RESULTS

In general, the skills that received the most time and attention on the show itself were, with rare exceptions, the skills that were best learned. This is a welcome finding but not one that appears as self-evident as it perhaps should.

The greatest percentage gains were in the areas of letters, numbers, forms, and classification, and in the first three areas, it was mainly naming and recognizing. Our analysis of the amount of time spent on each goal of the show indicated that the greatest amount of time was spent on letters and numbers—14 and 10 percent respectively—the two areas where gains were greatest. In addition, these goal areas were taught primarily through the use of animation and puppets, the two techniques that seem to be most appealing to these youngsters.

One result of the study dealing with Spanish-American children is particularly intriguing. There were only 43 Spanish-speaking children included in the study, and there was considerable variation among them in the extent to which they had been exposed to English before watching "Sesame Street." Owing to this variability and the small size of the sample, conclusions must be drawn with great caution.

The largest concentration of Spanish-speaking children was in Q1, leaving only 18 in the more frequent-viewing groups. These frequent-viewing children gained almost incredible amounts; in fact, the gains among Q3 Spanish-speaking children were as high as those for Q4 in the rest of the study. In the letters test, the Q4 Spanish-speaking children started lowest at pretest and scored highest at post-test. Other letters subtests and tests of numbers, scoring, relational terms, and classification showed the same phenomenon: a low start with subsequent very high gains for the children who viewed most.

These results suggest two things: first, Spanish-speaking children, even when encouraged to watch "Sesame Street," watched less than the other groups in the study. Special efforts may be needed to encourage these children and their parents to watch. Second, and more importantly, language did not appear to be a barrier to the learning of these children. When they watched, they consistently learned very large amounts.

The results of the research conducted during the first year of "Sesame Street" suggest many areas for future investigation during the second season. Among them are:

1. Will the gains made by the viewers of "Sesame Street" continue beyond the testing conducted after the first six months?
2. Will the gains, if maintained, help the children once they enter school?
3. Will the knowledge these children have absorbed, if maintained, influence the treatment they receive—both intellectual and emotional—in their homes and schools?
4. Do the tentative results obtained with the small groups of Spanish-speaking children hold for larger groups?

"Sesame Street" was never intended as a replacement for preschool experience. Its goals are largely limited to the cognitive areas, and assessment of the affective areas has not been done. Yet the possibility of the show continuing to benefit large segments of the population that never attend preschool is certainly suggested by the research conducted during the first year.

EXPANDING THE GOALS

The goals of "Sesame Street" now have been expanded to include such subjects as sight vocabulary, addition and subtraction, and multiple classification. Whether television is able to teach these more complex skills to very young children is of particular interest. As well, the evaluation in the second year will investigate in more detail such side effects as children's attitudes to school activities and the effects of parent-child interaction on the child's learning.

To those of us who have been studying the show since its creation, a good deal of what has been noted here seems rather remarkable. We remember the pre-"Sesame Street" days only two years ago when many educators were questioning if nationally televised educational television was capable of teaching even the most simple skills, such as reciting the alphabet.

"Sesame Street" has proven that television can be a very successful educational medium, and its potential has only just begun to be realized. Right now, through "Sesame Street" it's teaching our children some basic facts and important cognitive skills.

The fact that "Sesame Street" is a major success story does not mean that it is anything more than an initial step in solving the problems of socially deprived children. Although Bogatz and Ball's data show that children at all social-class levels benefited from watching the program—even Spanish-speaking children made gains—they also indicate that the middle-class children in their sample gained more than the disadvantaged children for whom the program was designed. A possible explanation for the greater gain made by the middle-class children might be that they are more favorably disposed to educational programs than are disadvantaged children, and therefore watch more programs of this type. Support for this explanation appears in a study by T. E. Jordan (1970), who surveyed a sample of three-year-olds and found that only about a fifth of the black children saw the program, in contrast to about half of the white children. Approximately the same proportion of watchers and nonwatchers was found when the sample was broken down along social-class lines. The research we discussed and presented in Section 7 suggests that the relevant variable here is socioeconomic status, rather than ethnicity. The success of "Sesame Street" therefore impels to solve a new problem—how can we get disadvantaged children to watch it more often?

REFERENCES

Brackbill, Y. "Continuous stimulation reduces arousal level: Stability of effect over time." *Child Development* 44 (1973): 43–46.

Caputo, D. V. and Mandell, W. "Consequences of low birth weight." *Developmental Psychology* 3 (1970): 363–383.

Highberger, R. and Brooks, H. "Vocabulary growth of Head Start children participating in a mothers' readings program." *Home Economics Research Journal* 1 (1973): 185–187.

Jordan, T. E. "Social characteristics of children watching "Sesame Street." Reprinted from Report No. ED 039 943 "Discriminating characteristics of families watching 'Sesame Street.' Early Developmental Adversity Program: Phase III, EDAP Technical Note 15.1." Educational Resources Information Center (ERIC), U. S. Office of Education, March 1970.

Ohio State University and Westinghouse Learning Corporation. *The impact of Head Start: An evaluation of the effects of Head Start on children's cognitive and affective development.* Springfield, Va.: Clearinghouse for Federal Scientific and Technical Information, 1969. Two vols. (Documents, PB-184328 and PB-184329).

Scarr-Salapatek, S. and Williams, M. L. "The effects of early stimulation on low-birth-weight infants." *Child Development* 44 (1973): 94–101.

Tizard, B. and Rees, J. "A comparison of the effects of adoption, restoration to the natural mother, and continued institutionalization on the cognitive development of four-year-old children." *Child Development* 45 (1974): 92–99.

8.1

Casler, L. The effects of extra tactile stimulation on a group of institutionalized infants. *Genetic Psychology Monographs*, 1965, 71, 137–175.

Denenberg, V. H. Animal studies on developmental determinants of behavioral adaptability. In O. J. Harvey (Ed.), *Determinants of behavioral adaptability.* New York: Springer Publishing, 1966.

Fantz, R. L. Pattern vision in young infants. *Psychological Record,* 1958, 8, 43–47.

Hunt, J. McV. *Intelligence and experience.* New York: Ronald Press, 1961.

White, B. L., & Castle, P. W. Visual exploratory behavior following postnatal handling of human infants. *Perceptual and Motor Skills,* 1964, 18, 497–502.

8.2

Dennis, W. *Children of the Crèche.* New York/Englewood Cliffs. N. J.: Appleton-Century-Crofts/Prentice-Hall, 1973.

Dennis, W., and Najarian, P. "Infant development under environmental handicap." *Psychological Monographs* 71 (1957): No. 7.

Sayegh, Y., and Dennis, W. "The effect of supplementary experiences upon the behavioral development of infants in institutions." *Child Development* 36 (1965): 81–90.

9.

Intelligence: Its meaning and its development

The field of psychology has generated controversies from the time of its inception, but none of its facets has been more controversial than intelligence and its measurement. There are today two major controversies in this area—one over whether intelligence tests should be used at all, and the other over the causes of variation in measured intelligence. The disagreement over what intelligence test scores or IQs mean constitutes a further controversy underlying the other two. These controversies result from differences of opinion among both psychologists and laymen, and involve issues concerning the procedures for scientific research, the applicability of psychological techniques and research findings to the solution of human problems, the self-esteem of individuals and ethnic groups, and the political aspects of funding educational programs and research projects.

Intelligence tests, as we know them today, were developed over seventy years ago by Alfred Binet and Theodore Simon for the purpose of identifying Parisian school children for placement in classes for slow learners. Lewis M. Terman adapted their scale for use with American children and introduced IQ measurement as a convenient indication of a child's intellectual advancement or retardation in comparison to the average for his age. The term IQ was readily assimilated into everyday language as a synonym for intelligence, even with reference to adults. Intelligence testing was given its greatest impetus by the development of paper-and-pencil measures, the Army Alpha and Beta tests, which were used by the U.S. Army in World War I as a basis for decisions regarding promotion and assignment to special training. The 1920s saw a proliferation of intelligence tests and their widespread use in government, in business and industry, and especially in schools.

There were two basic motives for the use of intelligence tests in the schools. Because of the underlying assumption that IQ test scores are a valid index of a child's learning ability, these tests were used as the basis for administrative decisions in placing children into slow, average, or fast learning groups. The motive was to make the schools more efficient through "homogeneous grouping," which would presumably make it possible for a teacher to organize her presentations especially for the learning ability level of the class assigned to her. The second motive for widespread intelligence testing came from a concerted attempt to individualize education and to make it less impersonal. Each child's test scores were recorded in his cumulative file; his teacher was urged to read it and to record her own anecdotal information about the child's behavior, in order to promote understanding of the "child as an individual."

Both of these uses of intelligence tests have been somewhat discredited over the years. In studies where relevant variables were adequately controlled, homogeneous grouping has been shown to be of no advantage to children's learning progress (Borg, 1964; Goldberg, Passow, and Justman, 1966). Indeed, there has been some evidence showing that the morale and self-esteem of children assigned to "slow" classes are likely to suffer (E. J. Ogletree, 1970). Many schools still group children by IQ, however, probably because teachers tend to prefer homogeneous to heterogeneous, or mixed, classes. The apparent reason for this preference is that teaching homogeneous groups is viewed as simpler and less demanding.

The practice of administering intelligence tests to all pupils and recording the results in their cumulative files has also been criticized in recent years on the grounds that such data influence the teachers' attitudes and expectations of their students. Some research evidence shows that teachers tend to focus more attention on children with higher IQs and to ignore those with lower ones (Rosenthal and Jacobson, 1968; Rosenthal, Underwood, and Martin, 1969). It is very difficult to maintain adequate experimental controls in such studies, and the results are less clear-cut than those of studies about the effects of homogeneous grouping; but they do tend to support the contention that teachers preform opinions of students' intelligence from both their IQ scores and the anecdotal history in the cumulative files.

The main impetus of the move against mass administration of intelligence tests has come from civil rights groups. They accuse school personnel of using IQ scores to label children from deprived minority groups as inferior, and to use these labels as rationalizations for withholding advantages, for denying these children admission to prestigious educational programs, and for exposing them to possible ridicule. As a result of these charges, a number of communities, including New York City, no longer administer intelligence tests to all children. The question has been raised within the psychological profession as well as among laymen, about whether the administration of intelligence tests—or of any standardized tests—is ever justified.

These criticisms notwithstanding, intelligence tests continue to be used by clinical and school psychologists to gather information about children who have been referred to them, and to make decisions about their treatment. Furthermore, a scanning of any journal devoted to child research will show that the intelligence test is still in widespread use by investigators in this field. Why, then, do psychologists persist in using a measuring technique that is so widely criticized? There are many answers to this question, one of which is that intelligence measures make it possible to compare findings from various studies and to examine the effects of environmental factors such as differences in child-rearing practices and teaching methods. In reviewing research literature related to experimental methods of teaching mathematics, for example, it is important to know whether the children who served as subjects in the various studies had high, low, or average IQs.

The most compelling reason for its continuing use, however, is that IQ has become the most acceptable standard measure of general competence. In a review of the attempts of behavioral scientists through the years to define the parameters of human competence, S. Anderson and S. Messick (1974) observed that IQ is now both the major yardstick of child development and the principal criterion of the effectiveness of intervention programs of the type we described in Section 8. They concluded that IQ has taken on this function not only because it has a long history of use and has been well tested, but because it is highly correlated with success in a wide variety of human endeavors and can therefore be said to incorporate a great many other variables, in whole or in part.

The IQ tests continue to be widely used as indirect measures not only of cognitive development, but of a variety of other competence-related variables. This point is brought out in the first paper (article 9.1) in this section, a correlational study by Lynn Dorman of various measures of competence. Dorman employed an ingenious and ingenuous method for measuring assertiveness in preschool children. Each child in her sample was shown a pyramid of six plastic glasses behind which an attractive toy had been placed in clear view. The child was told that he could have the toy as a reward if he would knock the glasses over. The child's assertiveness was then scored according to the number of seconds it took him to knock over the pyramid. The less time he took to recognize that the request was bona fide and should be acted upon, the lower his score, and the higher his rated assertiveness. Observers and teachers made separate ratings of each child's assertiveness, based on his behavior in a variety of situations; the teachers were asked to include in their ratings the children's ability to maintain interest in a task. In addition to these ratings, the Stanford-Binet Intelligence Test was administered to the children.

There were significant intercorrelations between all of these measures. The children who acted promptly in the pyramid test were likely to be the ones who were rated as highly assertive by observers and teachers and who also had higher IQs. These results tell us that whatever the qualifications of the Stanford-Binet as a test of cognitive ability—intelligence—it also is an indirect but fairly powerful measure of a child's willingness to deal directly with his environment and to face it in a venturesome and unhesitating fashion. Cognitive abilities are developed through interacting with the physical and social environment; if a child is overly cautious and shrinks back to avoid encounters with the environment, he will have less opportunity to make progress in cognition.

The highest correlation in Dorman's study was between the Stanford-Binet and the teacher's ratings. The fact that they are in such close agreement indicates that the Stanford-Binet scores and the teachers' ratings were measuring much the same thing. In other words, the Stanford-Binet and the teachers were both responsive to differences in the children's competence in dealing with their environment.

9.1 Assertive behavior and cognitive performance in preschool children

Lynn Dorman

There has been a great deal of recent interest in certain behaviors which have action on the environment as their common characteristic. These behaviors, such as asking questions, exploring the environment, manipulating the environment, and destroying the environment, may be subsumed under one category of behavior—assertion. As thus defined, assertion would include the usual concept of aggression.

Assertive behaviors have been studied under many labels: attention, curiosity, competence, leadership, and aggression. Assertion is an early or innate human behavior in its exploratory manipulative sense, as well as in its destructive sense. An infant actively scanning its environment choosing one stimulus over another, and the young child creating and recreating responses in the environment, such as in Piaget's notion of making interesting sights last (4), provide us with examples of early assertion. The autonomous three-year-old who wants to do everything "by myself," and the young child directing the activities of others are also examples of children behaving assertively—acting on their environments.

Destructive assertion, also present from birth, exists in at least two forms: instrumental and noninstrumental. Man can destroy his environment for legitimate, as well as for illegitimate, purposes. Instrumental destructive assertion is seen in the young child who tears open a box to get the contents inside; noninstrumental destructive assertion parallels our usual notion of aggression: that is, destruction with no apparent legitimate purpose.

Reprinted from the *Journal of Genetic Psychology* 123 (1973): 155–162, with permission of the author and The Journal Press. Copyright 1973 by The Journal Press.

Beller (1, 2) explored the relationship between instrumental and noninstrumental aggression in nursery school children. He devised a task which required the child to knock over a barrier to obtain a toy behind it or to knock over the barrier when there was no toy behind it. In general, he found that the two behaviors were negatively correlated; children responded either instrumentally or noninstrumentally, but not both, or not both equally. The relationship between instrumental and noninstrumental destructive assertion needs further study, especially as concerns the development of these behaviors and the relationship between these types of assertion and other characteristics in children. This study focused on instrumental destructive assertion as present in preschool children and as related to manipulative assertion and to cognitive performance.

Cognitive performance requires instrumental assertive interaction with the environment. In cognitive activities, the organism interacts with the environment in many assertive ways: the organism *perceives* the environment, *interprets* what it perceives, and then does something with the interpretation. If assertive behaviors are necessary for learning, as it seems they are, then we should find a relationship between instrumental assertion and general cognitive performance.

The two types of assertion studied were exploratory manipulative assertion and instrumental destructive assertion. Exploratory assertion was measured by teacher and observer ratings of children's behavior, and instrumental destructive assertion was measured by a task adapted from Beller (1, 2). Cognitive performance was measured by the Stanford-Binet Intelligence Test, Form L-M, since it taps a variety of cognitive abilities.

It is predicted (a) that all measures of assertion—the teacher ratings, the observer rating, and the measure of instrumental destructive assertion—are related to intelligence scores; (b) that all three measures of assertion are related to each other.

METHOD

Subjects

Subjects were 25 boys and 25 girls enrolled in the Brockton, Massachusetts, Head Start program. The mean age was 5 years 9 months and included 11 black and 39 white children. Ss had been in the program for 10 months before the present study began.

Procedure

All observers and testers were introduced to the teachers and the children before data collection began, so that the children were familiar with them. Testing was done individually. There were four Es, each of whom administered one task to all subjects, in order to reduce experimenter bias. All Es were white female graduate students.

a. Instrumental destructive assertion. E asked each child to come and play a new game with her in another room. The child was seated at a table and saw a four-sided container, open on top. E removed the side facing the child allowing him to see a small colorful top behind a pyramid of six clear plastic glasses. E said, "Do you see that toy in there? It is a top. You can have that top to keep by knocking over the tower of glasses in front of it." Immediately after the last word of the instructions, a stop watch was started and was not stopped until at least one glass was completely knocked over. If the child did not respond, the instructions were repeated at 30 seconds and at 60 seconds. Children's questions concerning how and when to knock over the tower were answered with "however you want" and "whenever you want." If, at the end of 120 seconds, a child had not knocked over the tower, E said, "Well, I guess you don't want to knock over the tower today. That's okay, you can have the top to keep anyway." E then gave the top to the child, telling him again that he could keep it. The child's reaction time from the last word of the instructions to the fall of at least one glass was his score for instrumental destructive assertion and is hereafter called the IDA score of 120 seconds, the time at which the task was terminated.

b. Observer rating of assertion. An observation schedule was designed to include those behaviors thought to be representative of assertive behaviors. There were eight items: asking the teacher for information, asking the teacher for directions, asking other children for information, asking other children for directions, directing other children, making suggestions, playing with manipulative toys, and exploring the environment.

The observation schedule had been pretested, and the two observers were trained until they were in high agreement with each other on the observations. Each of the observers watched individual children for almost 15 minutes per child. The observation procedure was to look for 20 seconds and record for 15 seconds. This resulted in 25 observation periods per child, and each child's score was the total number of assertive behaviors checked during the 25 periods.

c. Teacher rating of assertion. The teachers were asked to rate the children in their classes on a five-point scale consisting of the same items as the observation schedule, and, in addition, the child's ability to sustain interest in a task. The score was the total of all nine ratings.

d. Measure of cognitive performance. The measure of cognitive performance was the Stanford-Binet Intelligence Test, Form L-M, which was administered by three experienced testers. The children were brought individually to a room by *E* and were told that *E* was going to ask them some questions. All testing began with Opposite Analogies: items IV, 3; VI, 5; and VIII, 5. The starting level for the test was determined by the highest level at which the child was correct. Standard scoring procedures were used, as presented in the manual (6).

RESULTS

There were no significant sex or race differences on the Stanford-Binet, or on any of the three measures of assertion. The data from all children were combined for all later analyses. Table 1 gives the means, ranges, and standard deviations of all measures. . . .

TABLE 1
RANGES, MEANS, AND STANDARD DEVIATIONS FOR ALL MEASURES OF ASSERTION AND OF COGNITIVE PERFORMANCE

Measure	Range	Mean	Standard deviation
IDA	3–120	54.99	43.19
Teacher rating	12–45	28.60	7.69
Observer rating	0–25	7.52	5.85
Stanford-Binet[a]	42–133	91.98	18.12

a The Stanford-Binet data are based on only 49 children; one boy would not answer any questions. His IDA score, incidentally, was 120 seconds.

The three measures of assertion—the IDA task, the teacher rating, and the observer rating—were each significantly correlated with total intelligence scores. In addition, all three measures of assertion were significantly intercorrelated. The results of these correlations are presented in Table 2.

TABLE 2
INTERCORRELATIONS AMONG EXPERIMENTAL MEASURES

Measure	IQ	Teacher rating	Observer rating
IDA	−.36	−.26	−.29
	(p<.005)	(p<.05)	(p<.025)
IQ		.61	.23
		(p<.005)	(p=.05)
Teacher rating			.28
			(p<.025)

Observers were thus able to see in 15 minutes what teachers saw over several months, and both of these ratings were related to instrumental destructive assertion.

Eleven of the children (22%) never knocked over the glasses to get the top. These children squirmed in their chairs, bit their nails, stared off into space, or stared at E. Since they all said afterwards that they had wanted the top, it is assumed that they were motivated to knock over the glasses but the conflict engendered stopped them from asserting themselves as asked.

Since the major hypothesis, that assertion is related to cognitive performance, was supported, an item analysis of the Binet was done with the use of the IDA scores and the Binet items from year IV through year VIII. In order to have equal numbers at each age level, all subjects were given an assumed failure for all items above their ceiling level and an assumed pass for all items below their basal level. This is in line with the basic assumptions of the Stanford-Binet.

The point biserial correlations indicated that seven of the 36 items were significantly related to instrumental destructive assertion. Children who passed certain items were significantly more assertive than children who failed the items. The seven items, their point biserial correlations, and their significance values are presented in Table 3.

At year V, the basal age level for the average five-year-old, half of the six items are related to IDA scores.

DISCUSSION

Each of the measures of assertion was a reflection of the child's ability to come to grips with his environment, to learn about it, to master it, to respond to it. The child who could do all these things, as rated by

TABLE 3
STANFORD-BINET ITEMS SIGNIFICANTLY RELATED TO IDA

Year	Item description	Correlation	Significance
IV, 4	Pictorial identification	.287	.05
IV, 6	Comprehension II	.287	.05
V, 3	Definitions	.287	.05
V, 4	Copying a square	.287	.05
V, 5	Pictorial similarities and differences II	.341	.05
VI, 1	Vocabulary	.311	.05
VI, 4	Number concepts	.379	.01

the teacher and observer, and as indicated by the IDA task, was the child with the highest *IQ*. Intelligence tests often consist of items which measure knowledge of the environment, and assertive children who are more in touch (both literally and figuratively) with their environment will have more information about their environments. The data supported the major hypothesis that assertion and cognitive performance are related.

The second hypothesis, that all measures of assertion are related, was also supported by the data. The correlation between teacher rating and the observation indicates that assertive behavior is a relatively stable characteristic of the preschool child, a characteristic which he brings to many situations and which can be seen even in 15 minutes in the play yard.

The seven items significantly related to the IDA task were mostly items from years V and VI, indicating that perhaps assertion is most necessary for learning those cognitive tasks most age appropriate. The items seemed also to fall into two categories: (*a*) verbal, comprehension items, and (*b*) discrimination, number items. Learning about the environment in order to pick up general information requires some assertion. Vocabulary, definitions, comprehension, and identification (the verbal, comprehension items that were related) all require being "in tune" with the environment. To learn words and meanings, and to comprehend, one must be attending to the appropriate environmental stimulation or must ask questions to find out information. As determined by the measures, the nonassertive children did not ask for information and were generally passive in relation to the environment. This was seen also in their behavior on the IDA task. On this task 13 children asked for directions of the "how" and "when" variety, and all 13 eventually knocked over the glasses. None of the nonresponders asked any questions.

Why the nonresponders, the less assertive children, act as they do is not answered by this study. It may be that they were never reinforced for asking questions, and thus this behavior was extinguished. The child may have been punished for exploratory behavior, and punishment inhibits specific behaviors. It is also possible that the nonassertive child is attending to and learning about his environment, but the "something" he is learning is not the specific cognitive activity about which we are asking. That the problem is not solely attentional is indicated by the present study.

After the task was terminated, all nonresponders were questioned to determine their understanding of the problem and their possible motivation. All said that they wanted the top, that the glasses would not break, but that they did not know why they failed to respond.

It is possible that, although they understood what was said, they interpreted the cues differently or did not trust E or perhaps themselves. This might explain their failing discrimination items on the Binet. These items (copying a square, pictorial similarities and differences, and number concepts) require attention to the appropriate cues—not just to the given instructions. They also require physical assertion; the child must make a move, either to draw, point, or pick up blocks. Here also, distrust of self and others might partially explain their failure as might inappropriate attention.

Items requiring discrimination, comprehension, and verbal ability were the ones most related to instrumental destructive assertion and are typical of the kinds of tasks with which the child will be faced in future schooling. Verbal and discrimination skills are basic to the learning of reading and basic to most thought processes.

Obviously more research needs to be done concerning the determinants of assertion and the variables that foster or hinder its development. This question must be answered both developmentally and situationally. What is it within the home environment, or the early environment, that leads to the ability or the nonability to assert oneself at age five? What is it within the immediate situation that allows or does not allow for the expression of assertion? The answers to these questions bear many implications for child rearing and for teaching, important enough implications to warrant further study.

That nonassertive children are not adequately studied is indicated in the numbers of children dropped from research studies. For example, in social reinforcement studies using "marble dropping" (e.g., 5), children who did not drop marbles during the first minute of baseline measure or those who stopped dropping marbles before they were asked were eliminated from the study. Other authors purposely omitted "noncooperative" children and eliminate nonresponders (e.g., 3).

As the present results indicate, nonassertive children do not respond—even two minutes after being so asked. How many other studies drop nonassertive children from their samples? Perhaps such children cannot be tested as required by the experiment, but if they are a sizeable part of the general population, the results of studies which eliminate such children are restricted to a selected sample. In light of all our present knowledge, it would be interesting to compare nonresponders to children remaining in studies, since nonresponders often represent up to 20% of the originally tested population.

SUMMARY

Assertive behaviors, as measured by teachers, observers, and an experimental task, were related to each other and to Stanford-Binet intelligence scores. All measures of assertion were correlated with each other and with total *IQ*. Subsequent item analysis of the Binet showed that the more assertive children did better on certain items: comprehension, verbal, and discrimination. These results are discussed as are possible reasons for nonresponsiveness of 20% of the sample and the implications of this for future research.

Why do some children function at a higher level of competence than others? Why do children vary in the ratings they receive on the Stanford-Binet and other measures of cognitive development? Attempts to answer questions like these are another source of controversy. One group, represented by Arthur R. Jensen (1969), claims that by far the greater part of the variation between childrens' IQs is genetically determined (inherited); the other group, represented by J. McV. Hunt (1969), maintains that intelligence is highly responsive to environmental differences, especially during early childhood. These two points of view are often called "hereditarian" and "environmentalist." The controversy centers upon the causes of mean IQ differences between races, ethnic groups, and social classes. The hereditarians contend that these differences are primarily genetically determined, but the environmentalists claim that they result from intergroup variations in environment, which may be created by the groups themselves, or imposed upon them by society. The environmentalists maintain that these conditions are likely to have a significant effect on children during their most formative years and thus produce corresponding variations in IQ.

Psychologists have long believed that individual variation in IQ is partially determined by differences in inherited factors, or genes, and by differences in environment. The case for genetics is based on studies of the IQs of twins. These investigations show that a pair of identical twins, who come from the same fertilized ovum and therefore have identical genes, is much more likely to have similar IQs than is a pair of nonidentical (fraternal) twins, whose genetic similarity is no different from that of nontwin siblings. Identical twins raised apart also show greater IQ similarity than fraternal twins raised apart, but the greater the difference in the amounts of schooling they receive, the greater the difference in their IQs (Newman, Freeman, and Holzinger, 1937). These findings are compatible with the concept that although inherited traits may set limits for an individual's cognitive development, the extent to which he develops these abilities is determined by his environment. Most psychologists, however, do not believe that the data on genetics and IQ support the interpretation that mean IQ differences between ethnic groups and social classes are genetically determined. Not only is such an interpretation unsupported by the available data, but to set up properly controlled studies to prove or disprove this contention would be difficult, impractical, and unethical.

When the *Harvard Educational Review* published Jensen's paper (1969) saying that special programs like Head Start were bound to fail, because racial and social-class differences in IQ are genetically determined, a controversy involving not only psychologists but the lay public as well, was opened up. The second paper (article 9.2) in this section is an analysis by Sandra Scarr-Salapatek of Jensen's arguments and of statements made by R. Herrnstein (1971) and H. J. Eysenck (1971), two other hereditarians who support Jensen's contentions. Scarr-Salapatek's position is consistent with the concept of a "both-and" interaction between heredity and environment accepted by most psychologists, and she maintains that the data on which the three hereditarians base their conclusions could be used just as well to support an environmentalist interpretation. She also questions the wisdom of Jensen's raising an issue that is bound to aggravate in, tergroup tensions and that at the same time rests on shaky assumptions.

9.2

Unknowns in the IQ equation

Sandra Scarr-Salapatek

IQ scores have been repeatedly estimated to have a large heritable component in United States and Northern European white populations (*1*). Individual differences in IQ, many authors have concluded, arise far more from genetic than from environmental differences among people in these populations, at the present time, and under present environmental conditions. It has also been known for many years that white lower-class and black groups have lower IQ's, on the average, than white middle-class groups. Most behavioral scientists comfortably "explained" these group differences by appealing to obvious environmental differences between the groups in standards of living, educational opportunities, and the like. But recently an explosive controversy has developed over the heritability of between-group differences in IQ, the question at issue being: If individual differences within the white population as a whole can be attributed largely to heredity, is it not plausible that the average differences between social-class groups and between racial groups also reflect significant genetic differences? Can the former data be used to explain the latter?

Reprinted from *Science* 174 (1971): 1223–1228, with permission of the author and of the American Association for the Advancement of Science. Copyright 1971 by the American Association for the Advancement of Science.

Scarr-Salapatek's paper is a review of three publications:
(1) "Environment, heredity, and intelligence," a collection of articles comprising a statement by Arthur R. Jensen and rebuttals by leading psychologists. *Harvard Educational Review*, Spring 1969 (subsequently published by the *Review* as a special reprint).
(2) H. J. Eysenck, *The IQ Argument*. New York: Library Press, 1971.
(3) Richard Herrnstein, "I.Q." *Atlantic* 288 No. 3 (1971): 44–64.

To propose genetically based racial and social-class differences is anathema to most behavioral scientists, who fear any scientific confirmation of the pernicious racial and ethnic prejudices that abound in our society. But now that the issue has been openly raised, and has been projected into the public context of social and educational policies, a hard scientific look must be taken at what is known and at what inferences can be drawn from that knowledge.

The public controversy began when A. R. Jensen, in a long paper in the *Harvard Educational Review*, persuasively juxtaposed data on the heritability of IQ and the observed differences between groups. Jensen suggested that current large-scale educational attempts to raise the IQ's of lower-class children, white and black, were failing because of the high heritability of IQ. In a series of papers and rebuttals to criticism, in the same journal and elsewhere (2), Jensen put forth the hypothesis that social-class and racial differences in mean IQ were due largely to differences in the gene distributions of these populations. At least, he said, the genetic-differences hypothesis was no less likely, and probably more likely, than a simple environmental hypothesis to explain the mean difference of 15 IQ points between blacks and whites (3) and the even larger average IQ differences between professionals and manual laborers within the white population.

Jensen's articles have been directed primarily at an academic audience. Herrnstein's article in the *Atlantic* and Eysenck's book (first published in England) have brought the argument to the attention of the wider lay audience. Both Herrnstein and Eysenck agree with Jensen's genetic-differences hypothesis as it pertains to individual differences and to social-class groups, but Eysenck centers his attention on the genetic explanation of racial-group differences, which Herrnstein only touches on. Needless to say, many other scientists will take issue with them.

EYSENCK'S RACIAL THESIS

Eysenck has written a popular account of the race, social-class, and IQ controversy in a generally inflammatory book. The provocative title and the disturbing cover picture of a forlorn black boy are clearly designed to tempt the lay reader into a pseudo-battle between Truth and Ignorance. In this case Truth is genetic-environmental interactionism (4) and Ignorance is naive environmentalism. For the careful reader, the battle fades out inconclusively as Eysenck admits that scientific evidence to date does not permit a clear choice of the genetic-differences interpretation of black inferiority on intelligence tests. A quick reading of the book, however, is sure to leave the reader believing that scientific evidence today strongly supports the conclusion that U.S. blacks are genetically inferior to whites in IQ.

The basic theses of the book are as follows:

1) IQ is a highly heritable characteristic in the U.S. white population and probably equally heritable in the U.S. black population.

2) On the average, blacks score considerably lower than whites on IQ tests.

3) U.S. blacks are probably a non-random, lower-IQ, sample of native African populations.

4) The average IQ difference between blacks and whites probably represents important genetic differences between the races.

5) Drastic environmental changes will have to be made to improve the poor phenotypes that U.S. blacks now achieve.

The evidence and nonevidence that Eysenck cites to support his genetic hypothesis of racial differences make a curious assortment. Audrey Shuey's review (5) of hundreds of studies showing mean phenotypic differences between black and white IQ's leads Eysenck to conclude:

> All the evidence to date suggests the strong and indeed overwhelming importance of genetic factors in producing the great variety of intellectual differences which we observe in our culture, and much of the difference observed between certain racial groups. This evidence cannot be argued away by niggling and very minor criticisms of details which do not really throw doubts on the major points made in this book [p. 126].

To "explain" the genetic origins of these mean IQ differences he offers these suppositions:

> White slavers wanted dull beasts of burden, ready to work themselves to death in the plantations, and under those conditions intelligence would have been counter-selective. Thus there is every reason to expect that the particular sub-sample of the Negro race which is constituted of American Negroes is not an unselected sample of Negroes, but has been selected throughout history according to criteria which would put the highly intelligent at a disadvantage. The inevitable outcome of such selection would of course be a gene pool lacking some of the genes making for higher intelligence [p. 42].

Other ethnic minorities in the U.S. are also, in his view, genetically inferior, again because of the selective migration of lower IQ genotypes:

It is known [*sic*] that many other groups came to the U.S.A. due to pressures which made them very poor samples of the original populations. Italians, Spaniards, and Portuguese, as well as Greeks, are examples where the less able, less intelligent were forced through circumstances to emigrate, and where their American progeny showed significantly lower IQ's than would have been shown by a random sample of the original population [p. 43].

Although Eysenck is careful to say that these are not established facts (because no IQ tests were given to the immigrants or nonimmigrants in question?), the tone of his writing leaves no doubt about his judgment. There is something in this book to insult almost everyone except WASP's and Jews.

Despite his conviction that U.S. blacks are genetically inferior in IQ to whites, Eysenck is optimistic about the potential effects of radical environmental changes on the present array of Negro IQ phenotypes. He points to the very large IQ gains produced by intensive one-to-one tutoring of black urban children with low-IQ mothers, contrasting large environmental changes and large IQ gains in intensive programs of this sort with insignificant environmental improvements and small IQ changes obtained by Head Start and related programs. He correctly observes that, whatever the heritability of IQ (or, it should be added, of any characteristic), large phenotypic changes may be produced by creating appropriate, radically different environments never before encountered by those genotypes. On this basis, Eysenck calls for further research to determine the requisites of such environments.

Since Eysenck comes to this relatively benign position regarding potential improvement in IQ's, why, one may ask, is he at such pains to "prove" the genetic inferiority of blacks? Surprisingly, he expects that new environments, such as that provided by intensive educational tutoring, will not affect the black-white IQ differential, because black children and white will probably profit equally from such treatment. Since many middle-class white children already have learning environments similar to that provided by tutors for the urban black children, we must suppose that Eysenck expects great IQ gains from relatively small changes in white, middle-class environments.

This book is an uncritical popularization of Jensen's ideas without the nuances and qualifiers that make much of Jensen's writing credible or at least responsible. Both authors rely on Shuey's review (5), but Eysenck's way of doing it is to devote some 25 pages to quotes and paraphrases of her chapter summaries. For readers to whom the original Jensen article is accessible, Eysenck's book is a poor substitute; although he defends Jensen and Shuey, he does neither a service.

It is a maddeningly inconsistent book filled with contradictory caution and incaution; with hypotheses stated both as hypotheses and as conclusions; with both accurate and inaccurate statements on matters of fact. For example, Eysenck thinks evoked potentials* offer a better measure of "innate" intelligence than IQ tests. But on what basis? Recently F. B. Davis (6) has failed to find any relationship whatsoever between evoked potentials and either IQ scores or scholastic achievement, to which intelligence is supposed to be related. Another example is Eysenck's curious use of data to support a peculiar line of reasoning about the evolutionary inferiority of blacks: First, he reports that African and U.S. Negro babies have been shown to have precocious sensorimotor development by white norms (the difference, by several accounts, appears only in gross motor skills and even there is slight). Second, he notes that by three years of age U.S. white exceed U.S. black children in mean IQ scores. Finally he cites a (very slight) negative correlation, found in an early study, between sensorimotor intelligence in the first year of life and later IQ. From exaggerated statements of these various data, he concludes:

> These findings are important because of a very general view in biology according to which the more prolonged the infancy the greater in general are the cognitive or intellectual abilities of the species. This law appears to work even within a given species [p. 79].

Eysenck would apparently have us believe that Africans and their relatives in the U.S. are less highly evolved than Caucasians, whose longer infancy is related to later higher intelligence. I am aware of no evidence whatsoever to support a within-species relationship between longer infancy and higher adult capacities.

The book is carelessly put together, with no index; few references, and those not keyed to the text; and long, inadequately cited quotes that carry over several pages without clear beginnings and ends. Further-

---

*A measure of the electrical activity in the brain.

more, considering the gravity of Eysenck's theses, the book has an occasional jocularity of tone that is offensive. A careful book on the genetic hypothesis, written for a lay audience, would have merited publication. This one, however, has been publicly disowned as irresponsible by the entire editorial staff of its London publisher, New Society. But never mind, the American publisher has used that and other condemnations to balance the accolades and make its advertisement (7) of the book more titillating.

HERRNSTEIN'S SOCIAL THESIS

Thanks to Jensen's provocative article, many academic psychologists who thought IQ tests belonged in the closet with the Rorschach inkblots have now explored the psychometric literature and found it to be a trove of scientific treasure. One of these is Richard Herrnstein, who from a Skinnerian background has become an admirer of intelligence tests—a considerable leap from shaping the behavior of pigeons and rats. In contrast to Eysenck's book, Herrnstein's popular account in the *Atlantic* of IQ testing and its values is generally responsible, if overly enthusiastic in parts.

Herrnstein unabashedly espouses IQ testing as "psychology's most telling accomplishment to date," despite the current controversy over the fairness of testing poor and minority-group children with IQ items devised by middle-class whites. His historical review of IQ test development, including tests of general intelligence and multiple abilities, is interesting and accurate. His account of the validity and usefulness of the tests centers on the fairly accurate prediction that can be made from IQ scores to academic and occupational achievement and income level. He clarifies the pattern of relationship between IQ and these criterion variables: High IQ is a necessary but not sufficient condition for high achievement, while low IQ virtually assures failure at high academic and occupational levels. About the usefulness of the tests, he concludes:

> An IQ test can be given in an hour or two to a child, and from this infinitesimally small sample of his output, deeply important predictions follow—about schoolwork, occupation, income, satisfaction with life, and even life expectancy. The predictions are not perfect, for other factors always enter in, but no other single factor matters as much in as many spheres of life [p. 53].

One must assume that Herrnstein's enthusiasm for intelligence tests rests on population statistics, not on predictions for a particular child, because many children studied longitudinally have been shown to change IQ scores by 20 points or more from childhood to adulthood. It is likely that extremes of giftedness and retardation can be sorted out relatively early by IQ tests, but what about the 95 percent of the population in between? Their IQ scores may vary from dull to bright normal for many years. Important variations in IQ can occur up to late adolescence (8). On a population basis Herrnstein is correct; the best early predictors of later achievement are ability measures taken from age five on. Predictions are based on correlations, however, which are not sensitive to absolute changes in value, only to rank orders. This is an important point to be discussed later.

After reviewing the evidence for average IQ differences by social class and race, Herrnstein poses the nature-nurture problem of "which is primary" in determining phenotypic differences in IQ. For racial groups, he explains, the origins of mean IQ differences are indeterminate at the present time because we have no information from heritability studies in the black population or from other, unspecified lines of research which could favor primarily genetic or primarily environmental hypotheses. He is thoroughly convinced, however, that individual differences and social-class differences in IQ are highly heritable at the present time, and are destined, by environmental improvements, to become even more so:

> If we make the relevant environment much more uniform (by making it as good as we can for everyone), then an even larger proportion of the variation in IQ will be attributable to the genes. The average person would be smarter, but intelligence would run in families even more obviously and with less regression toward the mean than we see today [p. 58].

For Herrnstein, society is, and will be even more strongly, a meritocracy based largely on inherited differences in IQ. He presents a "syllogism" (p. 58) to make his message clear:

1. If differences in mental abilities are inherited, and
2. If success requires those abilities, and
3. If earnings and prestige depend on success,
4. Then social standing (which reflects earnings and prestige) will be based to some extent on inherited differences among people.

Five "corollaries" for the future predict that the heritability of IQ will rise; that social mobility will become more strongly related to inherited IQ differences; that most bright people will be gathered in the top of the social structure, with the IQ dregs at the bottom; that many at the bottom will not have the intelligence needed for new jobs; and that the meritocracy will be built not just on inherited intelligence but on all inherited traits affecting success, which will presumably become correlated characters. Thus from the successful realization of our most precious, egalitarian, political and social goals there will arise a much more rigidly stratified society, a "virtual caste system" based on inborn ability.

To ameliorate this effect, society may have to move toward the socialist dictum, "From each according to his abilities, to each according to his needs," but Herrnstein sees complete equality of earnings and prestige as impossible because high-grade intelligence is scarce and must be recruited into those critical jobs that require it, by the promise of high earnings and high prestige. Although garbage collecting is critical to the health of the society, almost anyone can do it; to waste high-IQ persons on such jobs is to misallocate scarce resources at society's peril.

Herrnstein points to an ironic contrast between the effects of caste and class systems. Castes, which established artificial hereditary limits on social mobility, guarantee the inequality of opportunity that preserves IQ heterogeneity at all levels of the system. Many bright people are arbitrarily kept down and many unintelligent people are artificially maintained at the top. When arbitrary bounds on mobility are removed, as in our class system, most of the bright rise to the top and most of the dull fall to the bottom of the social system, and IQ differences between top and bottom become increasingly hereditary. The greater the environmental equality, the greater the hereditary differences between levels in the social structure. The thesis of egalitarianism surely leads to its antithesis in a way that Karl Marx never anticipated.

Herrnstein proposes that our best strategy, in the face of increasing biological stratification, is publicly to recognize genetic human differences but to reallocate wealth to a considerable extent. The IQ have-nots need not be poor. Herrnstein does not delve into the psychological consequences of being publicly marked as genetically inferior.

Does the evidence support Herrnstein's view of hereditary social classes, now or in some future Utopia? Given his assumptions about the high heritability of IQ, the importance of IQ to social mobility, and the increasing environmental equality of rearing and opportunity, hereditary social classes are to some extent inevitable. But one can question the limits of genetic homogeneity in social-class groups and the evidence for his syllogism at present.

Is IQ as highly heritable throughout the social structure as Herrnstein assumes? Probably not. In a recent study of IQ heritability in various racial and social-class groups (9), I found much lower proportions of genetic variance that would account for aptitude differences among lower-class than among middle-class children, in both black and white groups. Social disadvantage in prenatal and postnatal development can substantially lower phenotypic IQ and reduce the genotype-phenotype correlation. Thus, average phenotypic IQ differences between the social classes may be considerably larger than the genotypic differences.

Are social classes largely based on hereditary IQ differences now? Probably not as much as Herrnstein believes. Since opportunities for social mobility act at the phenotypic level, there still may be considerable genetic diversity for IQ at the bottom of the social structure. In earlier days arbitrary social barriers maintained genetic variability throughout the social structure. At present, individuals with high phenotypic IQ's are often upwardly mobile; but inherited wealth acts to maintain genetic diversity at the top, and nongenetic biological and social barriers to phenotypic development act to maintain a considerable genetic diversity of intelligence in the lower classes.

As P. E. Vernon has pointed out (10), we are inclined to forget that the majority of gifted children in recent generations have come from working-class, not middle-class, families. A larger percentage of middle-class children are gifted, but the working and lower classes produce gifted children in larger numbers. How many more disadvantaged children would have been bright if they had had middle-class gestation and rearing conditions?

I am inclined to think that intergenerational class mobility will always be with us, for three reasons. First, since normal IQ is a polygenic characteristic, various recombinations of parental genotypes will always produce more variable genotypes in the offspring than in the parents of all social-class groups, especially the extremes. Even if both parents, instead of primarily the male, achieved social-class status based on their IQ's, recombinations of their genes would always produce a range of offspring, who would be upwardly or downwardly mobile relative to their families of origin.

Second, since, as Herrnstein acknowledges, factors other than IQ—motivational, personality, and undetermined—also contribute to success or the lack of it, high IQ's will always be found among lower-class adults, in combination with schizophrenia, alcoholism, drug addiction, psychopathy, and other limiting factors. When recombined in offspring, high IQ can readily segregate with facilitating motivational and personality characteristics, thereby leading to upward mobility for many offspring. Similarly, middle-class parents will always produce some offspring with debilitating personal characteristics which lead to downward mobility.

Third, for all children to develop phenotypes that represent their best genotypic outcome (in current environments) would require enormous changes in the present social system. To improve and equalize all rearing environments would involve such massive intervention as to make Herrnstein's view of the future more problematic than he seems to believe.

RACE AS CASTE

Races are castes between which there is very little mobility. Unlike the social-class system, where mobility based on IQ is sanctioned, the racial caste system, like the hereditary aristocracy of medieval Europe and the caste system of India, preserves within each group its full range of genetic diversity of intelligence. The Indian caste system was, according to Dobzhansky (11), a colossal genetic failure—or success, according to egalitarian values. After the abolition of castes at independence, Brahmins and untouchables were found to be equally educable despite—or because of—their many generations of segregated reproduction.

While we may tentatively conclude that there are some genetic IQ differences between social-class groups, we can make only wild speculations about racial groups. Average phenotypic IQ differences between races are not evidence for genetic differences (any more than they are evidence for environmental differences). Even if the heritabilities of IQ are extremely high in all races, there is still no warrant for equating within-group and between-group heritabilities (12). There are examples in agricultural experiments of within-group differences that are highly heritable but between-group differences that are entirely environmental. Draw two random samples of seeds from the same genetically heterogeneous population. Plant one sample in uniformly good conditions, the other in uniformly poor conditions. The average height difference between the populations of plants will be entirely environmental, although the individual differences in height within each sample will be entirely genetic. With known genotypes for seeds and known environments, genetic and environmental variances between groups can be studied. But racial groups are not random samples from the same population, nor are members reared in uniform conditions within each race. Racial groups are of unknown genetic equivalence for polygenic characteristics like IQ, and the differences in environments within and between the races may have as yet unquantified effects.

There is little to be gained from approaching the nature-nurture problem of race differences in IQ directly (*13*). Direct comparisons of estimated within-group heritabilities and the calculation of between-group heritabilities require assumptions that few investigators are willing to make, such as that all environmental differences are quantifiable, that differences in the environments of blacks and whites can be assumed to affect IQ in the same way in the two groups, and that differences in environments between groups can be "statistically controlled." A direct assault on race differences in IQ is vulnerable to many criticisms.

Indirect approaches may be less vulnerable. These include predictions of parent-child regression effects and admixture studies. Regression effects can be predicted to differ for blacks and whites if the two races indeed have genetically different population means. If the population mean for blacks is 15 IQ points lower than that of whites, then the offspring of high-IQ black parents should show greater regression (toward a lower population mean) than the offspring of whites of equally high IQ. Similarly, the offspring of low-IQ black parents should show less regression than those of white parents of equally low IQ. This hypothesis assumes that assortative mating for IQ is equal in the two races, which could be empirically determined but has not been studied as yet. Interpretable results from a parent-child regression study would also depend upon careful attention to intergenerational environmental changes, which could be greater in one race than the other.

Studies based on correlations between degree of white admixture and IQ scores *within* the black group would avoid many of the pitfalls of between-group comparisons. If serological genotypes can be used to identify persons with more and less white admixture, and if estimates of admixture based on blood groups are relatively independent of visible characteristics like skin color, then any positive correlation between degree of admixture and IQ would suggest genetic racial differences in IQ. Since blood groups have not been used directly as the basis of racial discrimination, positive findings would be relatively immune from environmentalist criticisms. The trick is to estimate individual admixture reliably. Several loci which have fairly different distributions of alleles in contemporary African and white populations have been proposed (*14*). No one has yet attempted a study of this sort.

h² [HERITABILITY] AND PHENOTYPE

Suppose that the heritabilities of IQ differences within all racial and social-class groups were .80, as Jensen estimates, and suppose that the children in all groups were reared under an equal range of conditions. Now, suppose that racial and social-class differences in mean IQ still remained. We would probably infer some degree of genetic difference between the groups. So what? The question now turns from a strictly scientific one to one of science and social policy.

As Eysenck, Jensen, and others have noted, eugenic and euthenic strategies are both possible interventions to reduce the number of low-IQ individuals in all populations. Eugenic policies could be advanced to encourage or require reproductive abstinence by people who fall below a certain level of intelligence. The Reeds (*15*) have determined that one-fifth of the mental retardation among whites of the next generation could be prevented if no mentally retarded persons of this generation reproduced. There is no question that a eugenic program applied at the phenotypic level of parents' IQ would substantially reduce the number of low-IQ children in the future white population. I am aware of no studies in the black population to support a similar program, but some proportion of future retardation could surely be eliminated. It would be extremely important, however, to sort out genetic and environmental sources of low IQ both in racial and in social-class groups before advancing a eugenic program. The request or demand that some persons refrain from any reproduction should be a last resort, based on sure knowledge that their retardation is caused primarily by genetic factors and is not easily remedied by environmental intervention. Studies of the IQ levels of adopted children with mentally retarded natural parents would be most instructive, since some of the retardation observed among children of retarded parents may stem from the rearing environments provided by the parents.

In a pioneering study of adopted children and their adoptive and natural parents, Skodak (*16*) reported greater *correlations* of children's IQ's with their natural than with their adoptive parents' IQ's. This statement has been often misunderstood to mean that the children's *levels* of intelligence more closely resembled their natural parents', which is completely false. Although the rank order of the children's IQ's resembled that of their mothers' IQ's, the children's IQ's were higher, being distributed, like those of the adoptive parents, around a mean above 100, whereas their natural mothers' IQ's averaged only 85. The children, in fact, averaged 21 IQ points higher than their natural mothers. If the (unstudied) natural fathers' IQ's averaged around the population mean of 100, the mean of the children's would be expected to be 94, or 12 points lower than the mean obtained. The unexpected boost in IQ was presumably due to the better social environments provided by the adoptive families. Does this mean that phenotypic IQ can be substantially changed?

Even under existing conditions of child rearing, phenotypes of children reared by low-IQ parents could be markedly changed by giving them the same rearing environment as the top IQ group provide for their children. According to DeFries (*17*), if children whose parents average 20 IQ points below the population mean were reared in environments such as usually are provided only by parents in the top .01 percent of the population, these same children would average 5 points *above* the population mean instead of 15 points below, as they do when reared by their own families.

Euthenic policies depend upon the demonstration that different rearing conditions can change phenotypic IQ sufficiently to enable most people in a social class or racial group to function in future society. I think there is great promise in this line of research and practice, although its efficacy will depend ultimately on the cost and feasibility of implementing radical intervention programs. Regardless of the present heritability of IQ in any population, phenotypes can be changed by the introduction of new and different environments. (One merit of Eysenck's book is the attention he gives to this point.) Furthermore, it is impossible to predict phenotypic outcomes under very different conditions. For example, in the Milwaukee Project (*18*), in which the subjects are ghetto children whose mothers' IQ's are less than 70, intervention began soon after the children were born. Over a four-year period Heber has intensively tutored the children for several hours every day and has produced an enormous IQ difference between the experimental group (mean IQ 127) and a control group (mean IQ 90). If the tutored children continue to advance in environments which are radically different from their homes with retarded mothers, we shall have some measure of the present phenotypic range of reaction (*19*) of children whose average IQ's might have been in the 80 to 90 range. These data support Crow's comment on h^2 in his contribution to the *Harvard Educational Review* discussion (p. 158):

> It does not directly tell us how much improvement in IQ to expect from a given change in the environment. In particular, it offers no guidance as to the consequences of a new kind of environmental influence. For example, conventional heritability measures for height show a value of nearly 1. Yet, because of unidentified environmental influences, the mean height in the United States and in Japan has risen by a spectacular amount. Another kind of illustration is provided by the discovery of a cure for a hereditary disease. In such cases, any information on prior heritability may become irrelevant. Furthermore, heritability predictions are less dependable at the tails of the distribution.

To illustrate the phenotypic changes that can be produced by radically different environments for children with clear genetic anomalies, Rynders (*20*) has provided daily intensive tutoring for Down's syndrome [i.e., so-called Mongoloid] infants. At the age of two, these children have average IQ's of 85 while control-group children, who are enrolled in a variety of other programs, average 68. Untreated children have even lower average IQ scores.

The efficacy of intervention programs for children whose expected IQ's are too low to permit full participation in society depends on their long-term effects on intelligence. Early childhood programs may be necessary but insufficient to produce functioning adults. There are critical research questions yet to be answered about euthenic programs, including what kinds, how much, how long, how soon, and toward what goals?

DOES h^2 MATTER?

There is growing disillusionment with the concept of heritability, as it is understood and misunderstood. Some who understand it very well would like to eliminate h^2 from human studies for at least two reasons. First, the usefulness of h^2 estimates in animal and plant genetics pertains to decisions about the efficacy of selective breeding to produce more desirable phenotypes. Selective breeding does not apply to the human case, at least so far. Second, if important phenotypic changes can be, produced by radically different environments, then, it is asked, who cares about the heritability of IQ? Morton (*21*) has expressed these sentiments well:

> Considerable popular interest attaches to such questions as "is one class or ethnic group innately superior to another on a particular test?" The reasons are entirely emotional, since such a difference, if established, would serve as no better guide to provision of educational or other facilities than an unpretentious assessment of phenotypic differences.

I disagree. The simple assessment of phenotypic performance does not suggest any particular intervention strategy. Heritability estimates can have merit as indicators of the effects to be expected from various types of intervention programs. If, for example, IQ tests, which predict well to achievements in the larger society, show low heritabilities in a population, then it is probable that simply providing better environments which now exist will improve average performance in that population. If h^2 is high but environments sampled in that population are largely unfavorable, then (again) simple environmental improvement will probably change the mean phenotypic level. If h^2 is high and the environments sampled are largely favorable, then novel environmental manipulations are probably required to change phenotypes, and eugenic programs may be advocated.

The most common misunderstanding of the concept "heritability" relates to the myth of fixed intelligence: if h^2 is high, this reasoning goes, then intelligence is genetically fixed and unchangeable at the phenotypic level. This misconception ignores the fact that h^2 is a population statistic, bound to a given set of environmental conditions at a given point in time. Neither intelligence nor h^2 estimates are fixed.

It is absurd to deny that the frequencies of genes for behavior may vary between populations. For individual differences within populations, and for social-class differences, a genetic hypothesis is almost a necessity to explain some of the variance in IQ, especially among adults in contemporary white populations living in average or better environments. But what Jensen, Shuey, and Eysenck (and others) propose is that genetic racial differences are necessary to account for the current phenotypic differences in mean IQ between populations. That may be so, but it would be extremely difficult, given current methodological limitations, to gather evidence that would dislodge an environmental hypothesis to account for the same data. And to assert, despite the absence of evidence, and in the present social climate, that a particular race is genetically disfavored in intelligence is to scream "FIRE! . . . I think" in a crowded theater. Given that so little is known, further scientific study seems far more justifiable than public speculations.

Some of the research that Scarr-Salapatek (1971) has done suggests that environmental limitations may be a major factor in the low IQs commonly found among slum children. In one of her investigations she studied IQs and school achievement among Philadelphia school children, black and white, twins and nontwins. She reasoned that if the hereditarian position were valid, the variance in IQs among the children at each social-class level should be approximately the same, because differences in environment would have little effect. She also reasoned that if, on the other hand, the environmentalist position were valid, the IQs of middle-class children would show much variance, but the IQs of children from the slums would vary within a much narrower range. The rationale for the latter hypothesis was that middle-class children would experience relatively fewer restraints to cognitive development and that their IQs would "seek their own level." The IQs of slum children, which under better circumstances should have been high, would instead be depressed by their unfavorable environment. What Scarr-Salapatek found was that IQ variance among slum children was less than that for middle-class children. These results, which held for black children as well as for white, supported an environmentalist position.

The next article (9.3) in this section is a longitudinal study by Emmy E. Werner. Her findings are relevant to the hereditarian-environmentalist controversy and are based on a large mass of data, meticulously gathered by a team of workers over a period of more than ten years. Of further interest is the population she and her coworkers studied—the children of the island of Kauai, Hawaii—which was more than 90 percent nonwhite.[1] Werner's findings suggest that heredity has some influence on children's IQs, for there were significant correlations between the IQs of the children and those of their

---

1. For a more complete account of the study, see E. E. Werner, J. M. Bierman, and F. E. French, *The Children of Kauai.* Honolulu: University of Hawaii Press, 1971.

parents. She found further evidence, however, to indicate that environmental factors may have had an even greater influence, because the highest correlations in her study were between the children's IQs and the amount of educational stimulation in their homes. Even higher correlations between educational stimulation and IQ were reported by Wolf (1964), who interviewed mothers of fifth-grade children living near Chicago. Wolf found especially strong relationships between children's IQs and the ratings of such environmental variables as parents' intellectual expectations for their children, opportunities available for enlarging vocabularies, the extent to which parents provided learning situations in the home, and the amount of help children received with problems and tasks involving learning. In both the Kauai and the Chicago studies, the parents' attitudes toward cognitive stimulation and development appeared to play a major role in the scores their children made on intelligence tests.

9.3 Sex differences in correlations between children's IQs and measures of parental ability and environmental ratings

Emmy E. Werner

Recently, Bayley and Schaefer (1964) presented an interesting hypothesis concerning sex differences in intellectual development. Reporting on longitudinal data from a sample of 26 boys and 27 girls from the Berkeley Growth Study, they noted that the correlations between children's IQs and the parents' estimated IQ was higher for girls. They also found a more lasting relationship between early maternal behavior and the child's later IQ for boys. They suggested that the intellectual performance for boys was more responsive to environmental events, while that of the girls had a larger component of genetic control.

In search for additional evidence for this hypothesis of a sex difference in response to environment, Bayley (1966) reviewed a series of

Reprinted from *Developmental Psychology* 1 (1969): 280–288, with permission of the author and the American Psychological Association. Copyright 1969 by the American Psychological Association.

eight studies that showed higher parent-daughter than parent-son correlations in mental abilities. (IQ, education) at ages 2 through 11.

Maccoby (1966) in her review of research on sex differences in intellectual functioning pointed out that this hypothesis remains to be checked against other bodies of data. Both Kagan and Moss (1959) and Honzik (1963) found in their longitudinal samples in Ohio and California that while the correlations between measures of parental ability (education, IQ) and child's IQ develop earlier in the girls, the correlations become significant for the boys by school entrance.

Data from the Fels longitudinal study and the Berkeley Guidance Study also showed significant relations between parental behavior and the intellectual development of girls (Crandall, Dewey, Katkovsky, & Preston 1964; Honzik, 1967). Maccoby concluded that existing data do not permit us either to support or reject the Bayley-Schaefer (1964) hypothesis unequivocally and that the issue must remain open for further evidence.

The purpose of the present study was to report correlations between son's and daughter's IQs and measures of parental ability and environmental ratings for 485 children who were participants in a longitudinal study on the island of Kauai, Hawaii. The findings of this study with a considerably larger sample than the Berkeley and Fels Growth studies, and representing children from all socioeconomic status (SES) and intelligence levels, may contribute additional evidence on sex differences in parent-child correlates of ability.

METHOD

The 485 children in this study group, 231 boys and 254 girls, were participants in the Kauai Pregnancy and Child Study (KPS), a longitudinal investigation of the outcome of all pregnancies on the island of Kauai, Hawaii in 1955. Major objectives of the 2- and 10-year follow-up phases of the study were to identify problems affecting children's physical, intellectual, social, and emotional development and relate them to degree of perinatal complications and quality of environment. Detailed descriptions of this study have appeared elsewhere (Werner, Bierman, French, Simonian, Connor, Smith, & Campbell, 1968; Werner, Simonian, Bierman, & French, 1967).

The economy of the island centers around large-scale growing and processing of sugar cane and pineapple. The skills required approach those of a large-scale industrial enterprise. Rates of pay are comparatively high in these two fields, but employment opportunities in other jobs are limited. Recently, tourism has begun to offer additional work outlets in a somewhat depressed economy.

Although three-fourths of the 30,000 inhabitants of the island were born in Hawaii, the population has a varied ethnic background. Of all the live births occurring in 1955, 33% were Japanese, 23% Hawaiian and part Hawaiian, 18% Filipino, 6% Portuguese, and 3% Anglo-Saxon Caucasian. The remaining 17% were principally mixtures of ethnic groups other than Hawaiian, mostly children of Japanese-Filipino marriages.

The Anglo-Saxon Caucasians are predominantly found in the "above average" SES groups, contributing a higher percentage of professional, proprietor, and managerial positions than any other ethnic group on the island. The Japanese represent the majority of the "average" SES (skilled and technical trades); they are the only other ethnic group that has a sizable number of professional, managerial, and business men. The Portuguese are concentrated in the "below average" group with some members in the skilled trades and among technically trained people. The part and full Hawaiians and the Filipinos make up the bulk of the semiskilled and unskilled workers on the plantations.

Measures of children's ability

During the first follow-up, in 1957/58, the Cattell Infant Intelligence Test (Cattell, 1940) was administered to the children at mean age 20 months by two well-qualified psychologists from the University of Hawaii. The mean IQ for boys on the Cattell is 97 and for the girls 100; the comparable SDs are 13 and 12.

During the second follow-up, in 1965/66, the SRA Primary Mental Ability Tests (PMA), Elementary Form (Thurstone & Thurstone, 1954) was administered and scored by trained examiners according to standard directions to groups of about 15 children, yielding a total PMA IQ and five factor scores. For children who scored below the mean on the PMA or who showed marked discrepancies on PMA subtests, an individual test, usually the Wechsler Intelligence Scale for Children (WISC), was administered by a clinical psychologist to check the results of the group test. The mean age of the children at the time of the testing was 10 years, 6 months, with a range from 9 to 11 years. The mean IQ for boys on the PMA is 102 and for the girls 104; the comparable SDs are 13 and 12.

Measures of parental ability

A search was made of the cumulative records in the Kauai public and parochial schools for parents who had attended schools on the island. Group intelligence test scores were obtained for one or both parents of the 485 children. For 233 children, both mothers' and fathers' IQ was available, for 199 children only the mother's IQ could be obtained, for 58 children only the father's IQ was recorded. The overwhelming majority of the parents had taken the California Test of Mental Maturity, which yields a verbal, a nonverbal, and a full IQ. A few parents had taken the Terman McNemar Test of Mental Ability or an individual Stanford-Binet test. The tests chosen for this study as measures of parental ability had been administered to the parents when they were between 10 and 15 years old, at an age close to that of their children in the last follow-up.

Environmental ratings

Environmental ratings are based on home interviews conducted by two public health nurses and a social worker, familiar with the community and trained in the use of a standardized interview form. The main purpose of the interview was to obtain information from the family, usually the mother, pertinent to the quality of the environment in which the child had grown up to age 10.

A clinical psychologist rated this information for all children on three dimensions: SES, educational stimulation, and emotional support. Ratings were made on a 5-point scale from very favorable (1) to very unfavorable (5).

The socioeconomic rating combined information on father's occupation, income level, steadiness of employment, and condition of housing. It was based primarily on father's occupation which was categorized into five groups: professional (1), semiprofessional, proprietor, and managerial (2), skilled trade and technical (3), semiskilled (4), day labor and unskilled (5).

The rating on educational stimulation took into account the opportunities provided by the home for enlarging children's vocabulary, the quality of language models available, the intellectual interests and activities of the family, the work habits emphasized in the home, the availability of learning supplies, books and periodicals, and the opportunity provided for the child to explore various aspects of the larger environment (library use, special lessons, recreational activities). It was based on items from an interview first used by Wolf (1964) in a study of the relationship between environmental process variables and the intelligence of fifth graders in the Midwest and was adapted for the Kauai setting. Reliabilities reported by Wolf for the environmental ratings ranged from .89 to .95.

The rating on emotional support was based on information given in the home interview on interpersonal relations between parents and child, opportunities for satisfactory identification, kind and amount of controls used, and the presence or absence of traumatic experiences. Items concerning methods of discipline, ways of expressing approval, and tension and conflict in the family were included among the interview questions. The items on which the ratings were based had been shown to be related to children's cognitive development (Freeberg & Payne, 1967). Only those items were included in which a percentage of agreement in the 90s had been reached in a pilot study of interrater reliability.

RESULTS AND DISCUSSION

Correlations between the IQs of sons and daughters at age 20 months and measures of parental ability, education, and SES are presented in Table 1.

TABLE 1
CORRELATIONS BETWEEN CHILDREN'S IQS AND MEASURES OF PARENTAL ABILITY AND SOCIOECONOMIC STATUS AT AGE 20 MONTHS

Variable	No. cases		Cattell IQ at age 20 mo.	
	Boys	Girls	Boys	Girls
Father's IQ				
Total	104	96	.13	.29**
Verbal	104	96	.19	.33**
Nonverbal	104	96	.14	.33**
Mother's IQ				
Total	152	165	.05	.19*
Verbal	152	165	.06	.03
Nonverbal	152	165	.09	.26**
Father's education	171	179	.15	.26**
Mother's education	179	191	.19*	.21**
Socioeconomic status	180	192	.23**	.09
Father's occupation	179	191	.21**	.14**

*$p < .05$.
**$p < .01$.

Correlations between the IQs of sons and daughters at age 10-11 years and measures of parental ability, education, and environmental ratings are presented in Table 2.

TABLE 2
CORRELATIONS BETWEEN CHILDREN'S IQS AND MEASURES OF PARENTAL ABILITY AND ENVIRONMENTAL RATINGS AT AGE 10

Variable	*No. cases*		Group intelligence test		Individual intelligence test	
			PMA IQ		"Best" IQ	
	Boys	Girls	Boys	Girls	Boys	Girls
Father's IQ						
Total	129	131	.21*	.32**	.24**	.31**
Verbal	129	131	.31**	.40**	.32**	.37**
Nonverbal	129	131	.13	.24**	.04	.22*
Mother's IQ						
Total	196	213	.30**	.28**	.30**	.30**
Verbal	196	213	.29**	.20**	.22**	.21**
Nonverbal	196	213	.32**	.38**	.29**	.36**
Father's education	219	238	.31**	.31**	.31**	.27**
Mother's education	225	250	.33**	.28**	.34**	.29**
Educational stimulation	231	254	.40**	.53**	.37**	.52**
Socioeconomic status	231	254	.24**	.34**	.23**	.32**
Emotional support	231	254	.23**	.28**	.21**	.28**

*$p < .05$.
**$p < .01$.

In 8 out of 10 correlations at age 20 months, the IQs of girls on the Cattell Infant Intelligence Scale showed higher relations with measures of parental ability and education than the IQs of boys at the same age.

At age 10, in 7 out of 11 sets of correlations, the IQs of daughters had a higher relation to measures of parental ability (IQ) and the environmental ratings (educational stimulation, SES, emotional support) than the IQs of sons. The pattern was the same for parent-child correlates of ability on both *group* and *individual* intelligence tests. The difference between the sexes in favor of the girls was significant ($p < .001$) for all three environmental ratings.

However, while at age 20 months the correlations between measures of parental ability (IQ, education) were significant *only* for the girls, parent-child correlates of mental ability were significant for *both* boys and girls at ages 10 and 11 years.

The findings of the present study are in agreement with Honzik (1963) at comparable ages. Honzik also reports earlier appearance of parent-child resemblance for the girls in the Guidance Study sample (a representative sample of children born in Berkeley) and notes a continuing increase in parent-son resemblance through middle childhood.

At both ages 20 months and 10 years, there was a slightly, but not significantly higher correlation between father-daughter IQs than between father-son IQs in the Kauai sample. For the total and the verbal part of the parental IQ test this correlation was also higher than the mother-daughter correlates of ability at ages 20 months and 10 years.

For the sons, mother's IQ (total and verbal) correlated slightly, but not significantly higher than father's IQ with their own IQ at age 10, and so did mother's education.

This finding, suggestive of a higher opposite-sex relationship, is similar to the one reported by Honzik (1963) for the Guidance Study and by Bing (1963) in a study of child-rearing practices in families of 60 fifth graders divided into high- and low-verbal ability groups on the PMA.

All three environmental ratings (educational stimulation, emotional support, and SES) correlated significantly with the IQs of *both* boys and girls at age 10.

Similarly, Honzik (1967) reports from the Guidance Study significant correlations between parental concern for educational achievement at 21 months and both sons' and daughters' IQs at age 10. In the same study affectional relationships between parents and child at 21 months were shown to have positive correlations with IQs of both sons and daughters at age 10.

In the Fels longitudinal study, parental stress on the importance of intellectual mastery at early school age (4-7) was also found to be positively correlated with both boys' and girls' IQs at age 9 (Kagan & Freeman, 1963).

Likewise, in a study of 118 English children, Kent and Davis (1957) reported a significant relationship between parental concern and ambition for their children and the IQs of their sons and daughters at age 8. Unconcerned parents, with few ambitions, indifferent to success or failure, giving little guidance and encouragement, had children with significantly lower Stanford-Binet and WISC IQs than those from normal homes. In a more recent longitudinal study in Great Britain, Moore (1968) followed children from 6 months to 8 years and found significant correlations between mental growth at age 8 and ratings of the educational stimulus quality and emotional climate of the home.

In the Kauai study higher correlations were found for *both* sexes between the children's IQs at age 10 and the educational stimulation in the home than between measures of parental ability and children's IQs. This finding is similar to the results of a study by Wolf (1964) of the relationship between environmental process variables and the intelligence of 60 fifth graders in a Midwestern community. He also reports higher correlations between ratings of intellectual stimulation in the home and children's IQs than those usually found between children's IQ and parental IQ, SES, or parents' education.

In the Kauai sample girls' IQs correlated higher than those of the boys with all environmental ratings at age 10, especially with the ratings of educational stimulation in the home. This finding is similar to that reported by Crandall et al. (1964) in a study of 40 early grade school children at the Fels Institute. Parents' attitudes and behaviors toward their children's intellectual achievement efforts were associated more frequently and more significantly with their daughters' performance on scholastic tests than with those of their sons. Crandall et al. hypothesized that the girls' achievement strivings were more related to the desire of approval from adults while the boys' achievement behaviors were more autonomously determined. Because of this, parents' attitudes and behaviors (such as satisfaction-dissatisfaction with the child's intellectual performance, parental instigation, and participation in intellectual activities with the children) might have less impact and be less predictive of the scholastic performance of boys this age than girls.

While most of the findings with the Kauai sample agree with those of the Berkeley Guidance Study and the Fels longitudinal study, the data in this report showed one relationship that has not been reported in other longitudinal samples. At 20 months and 10 years fathers' *verbal* IQs correlated slightly but not significantly higher with *both* sons' and daughters' IQs than the nonverbal and total IQ scores. In contrast, mothers' *nonverbal* IQ scores correlated slightly but not significantly higher with *both* sons' and daughters' IQ scores than the verbal and total IQ.

We do not know how much this finding is an artifact of this sample. A sizable number of parents and children on Kauai were born and reared in bilingual homes. Among foreign languages spoken at home by parents and other adults are Japanese, Spanish, Portuguese, and Filipino dialects. Many islanders speak a dialect, a modified pidgin English with primitive grammar and word structure. This pidgin includes many Hawaiian words and unusual uses of common English words and phrases. These language habits may also explain why the correlations between group tests of parental ability and children's IQs in the Kauai sample are generally somewhat lower than those found in populations on the United States mainland.

In conclusion, the findings with the Kauai sample do not support the Bayley-Schaefer hypothesis that the intellectual performance of boys is more responsive to environmental events while that of the girls has a larger component of genetic control. Were this the case one would expect higher same-sex correlations between mothers and daughters, and lower correlations between the environmental ratings and girls' IQs than were found in this study.

The findings of the present study agree with those of the Berkeley Guidance Study and the Fels longitudinal study, and point to sex differences in rate (size and timing) of intellectual maturation, favoring the girls, and to a greater responsiveness of the girls to achievement demands and educational stimulation in the home in middle childhood.

SUMMARY

Correlations between sons' and daughters' IQs at 20 months and 10 years and measures of parental ability and environmental ratings are reported for a time sample of 485 children, participants in a longitudinal study on the island of Kauai, Hawaii. The findings point to sex differences in rate of intellectual maturation favoring the girls and to a greater responsiveness of the girls to achievement demands and educational stimulation in the home in middle childhood. Ratings of educational stimulation in the home yielded higher correlations with IQs of both sons and daughters than measures of parental ability, scioeconomic status, and emotional support.

The evidence implies that a child has a better chance of attaining an above-average IQ if his parents believe in the importance of intellectual competence and are willing to devote considerable time, energy, and expense to stimulating and encouraging his cognitive development. It is very likely that the concerned parents are themselves interested in intellectual activities and thereby provide models that invite imitation. Such parents are more frequently found at middle-class levels of society, rather than at working-class or lower levels. A question therefore arises about whether parents who are not middle class and who have had little education can create the kind of environment that raises children's IQs.

Article 9.4, a report by Howard Garber and Rick Heber, describes an experimental program that seems to answer the preceding question. The program is the Milwaukee Project, an undertaking of the University of Wisconsin Research and Training Center. This project has attracted nationwide attention because of the unexpectedly high IQs registered by the children who participated in it. The results are all the more phenomenal in that all of the children tested came from impoverished homes, and all of their mothers had IQs of 75 or less. The children first became actively involved in the program between the ages of three months and six months, when teachers visited homes, established rapport with mothers, and began to work with the infants. Once a mother had developed confidence in the teacher, the child was taken each day to the program's center. The mothers for their part were encouraged to participate in a thirty-week program that stressed basic academic skills and featured on-the-job training in laundering, housekeeping, food service, and practical nursing. The program also included instruction in community-oriented social studies, home economics, interpersonal relations, and child care (Heber et al., 1972).

In their report, Heber and Garber describe in detail the intensive training in linguistic and other cognitive skills received by the experimental group of children at the center. There seems to be no question that these children developed in markedly different ways from children in control groups. For one thing, their IQ, which averaged about 120, was dramatically higher than the mean of 95 attained by a control group. For another, their relationships with their mothers, which are described in the section on mother-child relationships, were qualitatively different. The experimental child, for example, tended to interact with the mother on a more sophisticated plane and actually "taught" her something about problem solving.

The Milwaukee Project demonstrates that many children who are relegated to "slow sections" in schools actually can function at normal levels of competence, provided they are involved in intellectually and socially stimulating environments and their parents are given opportunities to learn vocational skills. What is even more significant, the results reported by Garber and Heber constitute a persuasive argument that IQ differences between ethnic and social-class groups result from environmental, rather than genetic, causes.

9.4 The Milwaukee Project: Early intervention as a technique to prevent mental retardation

Howard Garber and Rick Heber

The evidence that a certain population of disadvantaged children suffer depressing events through the early years is derived from the performance discrepancy typically exhibited between them and their counterparts, the "normal, middle-class, advantaged child." Virtually all the studies of such early "deprivation" have attempted to ameliorate the intellectual deficiency that seems to attend developmental disadvantagement by using some sort of enrichment or compensatory education procedure. The enrichment procedure is intended to intellectually rejuvenate children who have been deprived of the stimulation appropriate for intellectual development. Moreover, it seemed entirely reasonable to attempt to close the performance gap for these children by implementing a "catch-up" compensatory program just prior to the time the children enter school.

Reprinted with permission of the authors and the University of Connecticut from *National Leadership Institute—Teacher Education/Early Childhood*, University of Connecticut Technical Paper, March, 1973.

Unfortunately, most gains in performance proved tenuous, as the discrepancy between the children reappeared after a few years of schooling. It appears that most of these attempts to rehabilitate the developmental process for such children did not begin intervention early enough to mitigate whatever depressing events occur most powerfully in the early environment, particularly since nearly all began after most of the critical periods. The human organism is an extremely complex organism and therefore cannot be expected to respond normally when the appropriate stimulation necessary for growth is not available. There is, rather, a biologically related sequence of critical periods in early life at which times both optimum nutrition and stimulation must be available—i.e., if development is to be normal.

There are both strong and weak aspects to this notion of compensation which is known more generally by the rubric: *social deprivation hypothesis.* Its strong points are that it has provided intellectual and nutritional benefits to otherwise disadvantaged children; and probably its strongest point is that it has helped children to adjust emotionally and attitudinally to the requirements of formal schooling, particularly since a major problem with the education of the disadvantaged in elementary school has been one of motivation, discipline, and maintenance of classroom decorum. The weak point is the fallacious notion that compensatory education would be a panacea for children with severe developmental histories.

The Milwaukee Project is at once similar in concept to the early education studies, but it is also *quite* different. It is because of its outward similarity that the difference in concept and design between the Milwaukee Project and other "early education studies" could be overlooked and even confused. True, the project is an intervention project concerned with the education of very young children who are quite disadvantaged: but the Milwaukee Project is much more than that.

The Milwaukee Project, as it has come to be known, represents an attempt to prevent intellectual deficits in "high-risk" children by early intervention. The intervention technique employs an intensive educational program for the very young high-risk child, beginning before six months of age. The label "high-risk" is a statistically based term which reflects that certain children have a critically high probability of being mentally retarded by the time they have reached maturity. This probability level is determined by a number of factors which include low maternal IQ, low socio-economic status (SES), low IQ of siblings, large-sized families, etc. Evidence from extensive survey work showed that the offspring of mentally retarded, low SES mothers, although testing at retarded levels on IQ instruments at maturity, test at normal levels very early in life. *The Milwaukee Project undertook to prevent this decline from occurring by having a group of children participate in an intensive early education program, beginning before six months of age.*

It is just this point that may not be well understood. The Milwaukee Project was designed as a study to prevent mental retardation—cultural-familial mental retardation—by intervening very early in life. The study was not designed to raise IQ levels, but to permit continued normal intellectual development by mitigating environmentally depressing events. . . .

Approximately ten years ago, faced with problems associated with early detection of mental retardation, the University of Wisconsin Research and Training Center established the High-Risk Population Laboratory. The main purpose of this effort was to provide opportunity for prospective longitudinal investigation into the problems of mental retardation, in contradistinction to the almost exclusive reliance upon retrospective techniques. Further, the intent of the laboratory was to bring into accessibility for research purposes the sub-population of the mentally retarded labeled the cultural-familial retarded, which previously has been essentially unavailable to investigators. This group of retarded reside in the community and remain undetected for two reasons: (1) they have relatively mild intellectual deficits which are most difficult to detect in the very young; and (2) they are without major related physical problems. Ordinarily, neither of these characteristics alone would be sufficient to precipitate the attention of responsible agencies to these individuals.

The approach used by the High-Risk Population Laboratory in its search for a technique for early detection was to develop sufficient information to permit the diagnosis of cultural-familial retardation. In order to compile this information, a door-to-door survey was conducted in an area of the metropolitan community of Milwaukee which had previously been identified as having an extremely high prevalence of retardation. This area of the city has the lowest median educational level, the lowest median family income, the greatest population density per living unit, and the highest rate of dilapidated housing in the city. *Though the area comprises about 2 percent of the population of the city, it yielded approximately 33 percent of the total number of children identified in school as educable mentally retarded.* In our first survey, all families residing in this area who had a newborn infant and at least one other child of the age of six were selected for study. All members of the family, both children and adults, received an individual intellectual appraisal. In addition, extensive data were obtained on family history, including the social, educational and occupational history and status. This approach provided us with some key variables that appear to be sufficiently sensitive to the existence of cultural-familial retardation to be used as a signal for such.

The population survey data produced some striking data on the

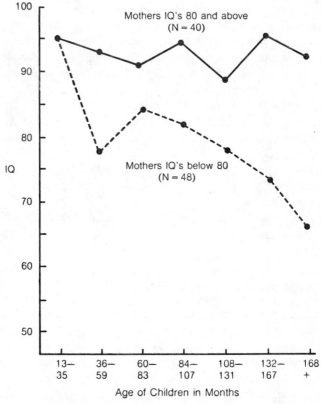

FIGURE 1

IQ CHANGE IN THE OFFSPRING OF DISADVANTAGED MOTHERS AS A FUNCTION OF MATERNAL IQ (HEBER, ET AL., 1968)

prevalence of retardation in depressed urban areas, on the distribution of retardation among families living in the high-risk area, and on trends in intelligence as a function of age of children and adults residing in the area. *For example, it was found that the high prevalence of mental retardation identified with Milwaukee's inner core population was strikingly concentrated among families where maternal intelligence was depressed, particularly where the family was large.* From our survey sample it was found that the prevalence of IQs of 75 and below was 22 percent, i.e. in these families where there was a newborn and at least one child of age six or greater. This selection procedure resulted in a sample of much larger than average families, and an increased prevalence of sub-75 IQs. However, it was found that 45.4 percent of the mothers who had IQs below 80 accounted for 78.2 percent of all children with IQs below 80. Moreover, it was found that depressed maternal intelligence was even a better predictor of depressed child intelligence for the older (above age six) than for the younger children. The most startling aspect of this data is that on infant intelligence tests, children of mothers above 80 IQ and below 80 IQ did about equally well. *After the infancy period, though, the children whose mothers had IQs greater than 80 appeared to maintain a fairly steady intellectual level, while the children whose mothers had IQs less than 80 exhibited a marked progressive decline in their intellectual level.* [See Figure 1] This trend toward a decline in measured intelligence for children in disadvantaged environments has wide acceptance as a general characteristic of a "slum" environment population, although this set of data indicates that this trend of declining intelligence as age increases is restricted to offspring of the "less bright" mothers.

SELECTION OF RESEARCH FAMILIES

As a consequence of the survey data, we have utilized maternal IQ as a basis for selection of a group of newborns, with confidence that a substantial percentage would be identified as mentally retarded. In other words, to identify the "high-risk" families within the "high-risk" residential area, the variable of maternal intelligence was utilized as a selection criterion since it proved to be the most efficient predictor of low school-age offspring intelligence.

The High-Risk Population Laboratory maintained a survey of births in the high-risk area. By first screening and then administering individual tests of intelligence, we identified those mothers of newborns who were mentally retarded, i.e. who had full-scale WAIS IQs less than 75. From this pool of candidates, accumulated over an eighteen-month period, we drew 40 mentally retarded mothers and randomly assigned them to either the Experimental or Control condition, after they had been invited to participate in a study of child development being conducted by the University of Wisconsin. All of the families selected were of Negro extraction.

The Experimental group, beginning within the first few months of life, was to undergo a comprehensive intervention in their social environment, the objective of which was to displace all of the presumed negative factors in the social environment of the infant being reared in the slum by a mother who is herself retarded. We are, thereby, testing the "social deprivation" hypothesis of etiology by seeing whether it is possible to prevent retardation from occurring in the offspring of these retarded mothers.

Should the Experimental children enter school and exhibit normal intellectual functioning we will know that it is possible, through our experimental program, to prevent mental retardation from occurring at the present high frequency of children raised in these circumstances. If the children are assigned to classes for the retarded at the rate of those without training, our program has not been successful.

The experimental intervention is comprised of two components: (1) the maternal rehabilitation program and (2) the infant stimulation program which are described below.

THE MATERNAL REHABILITATION PROGRAM

A two-phase program was initiated to better prepare the experimental mothers for employment opportunities and to improve their homemaking and child-rearing skills. Through improved employment potential, increased earnings, and self-confidence, it was hoped that positive changes in the home environment would occur. The rehabilitation program consisted of adult education classes to teach the mothers basic academic tools necessary for vocational adaptability, and finally, an occupational training program to teach specific vocational skills.

The job training program utilized two large, private nursing homes in Milwaukee. The choice of the nursing homes as a site for training was made because of the appropriate job skill areas represented in these facilities, the availability of professional staff with some understanding of rehabilitation problems, and the employment opportunities available in nursing homes and other chronic care facilities.

During the educational phase of the program, the basic academic skills of reading, writing and arithmetic were emphasized. In addition, their curriculum included community-oriented social studies, home economics, interpersonal relations, and child care.

While the occupational habilitation component of the maternal program appears to have been quite successful to date, major problems with respect to adequacy of homemaking skills and care and treatment of children remain to be resolved with a number of experimental families. With many of the mothers now successfully employed, the maternal program is shifting to an increased emphasis on training in general care of family and home, budgeting, nutrition, and food preparation.

THE INFANT STIMULATION PROGRAM

The program is, in its most basic sense, designed to facilitate intellectual development of very young children. The plan is concerned with (1) a physical location which promotes learning, (2) a staff to manage and arrange instruction for children, and (3) the educational program.

Physical plant

Over the years, the project has been located in several facilities. When all of the children were around six months of age, a large fourteen-room duplex served our needs very well because of the many "nooks and crannies" where teachers could work with children on a more intimate one-to-one basis. . . . The entire program is now housed in a leased school facility located adjacent to one of the inner-city's churches. This building, complete with six classrooms, a gymnasium, office space, and a lunch room is well suited to the needs of the program.

The staff

At the onset of the stimulation program we chose to employ a paraprofessional staff. The persons chosen were, in our judgment, language facile, affectionate people who had had some experience with infants or young children. The majority of these "teachers" resided in the same general neighborhood as the children, thus sharing a similar cultural milieu. The teachers ranged in age from approximately eighteen to forty-five with most of the teachers in their mid-twenties. Their educational experience ranged from eighth grade to one year of college. The teachers were both black and white.

The teacher of an infant had the major responsibility of establishing initial rapport with the infant's mother. This was done during a brief period, ranging from two to eight weeks, when the teacher worked with her child in the home until the mother expressed enough confidence in the teacher to allow the child to go to the center. . . .

Educational program

When the children first entered the project (by six months of age), they were each assigned a teacher. If the match proved satisfactory, the child remained with her as his primary teacher until he reached twelve months of age. At that time the child was gradually paired with other teachers and children. By the time he was fifteen to twenty months old, depending on the child, he was grouped with two other children and came into contact with three different teachers. This situation held for just his academic-learning environment. Actually each child was in contact with most of the other children and teachers.

The teacher who was assigned to an infant was responsible for his total care, including: feeding and bathing, cuddling and soothing, reporting and recording general health as well as organizing his learning environment and implementing the educational program. Within the context of the educational program, the teacher was expected to follow and expand upon a prescribed set of activities. Her job was to make these activities interesting, exciting and varied. She was also required to "objectively" evaluate and report the child's progress, pointing out areas of apparent difficulty.

The present groupings and teacher-pupil ratios vary with the age level of the child, but are flexible to allow for individual child needs. Under most circumstances, the infant remained with a teacher on a one-to-one basis up to twelve months, at which time another teacher and child were paired with him to encourage the expansion of relationships. Around fifteen months of age, a transition period began during which two children were assigned to one teacher. By age eighteen months we began to form the children into small groups so that by about 24 months all children of the same age level (about a five-month span) were grouped together with enough teachers to provide a one-to-three teacher-child ratio. During structured learning periods, the teacher-pupil ratio may be 1:2, 1:3, 1:4 depending on the age and the ability of the children. Within each age group, behavioral and educational evaluations were made by the teachers, teacher supervisor, and curriculum supervisors in bi-monthly conferences, at which time decisions on whether to regroup children, provide individual instruction or curriculum changes were made.

To facilitate learning and teacher effectiveness, a structured program was planned for each age group. The schedule remained constant to aid the child in developing realistic expectations and time orientation. For children under 24 months of age, the teacher varied the schedule in consideration of the child's moods and attention, while teachers of children older than 24 months followed the schedule somewhat more closely, gradually increasing the demands made on the child's attention span. The daily schedule for each child was as follows:

8:45	Arrival
9:00–9:30	Breakfast
9:30–10:00	First structured learning period
10:00–10:30	Second structured learning period
10:30–11:00	Self-directed activities in free play environment
11:00–11:30	Third structured learning period
11:30–12:00	Sesame Street
12:00–12:30	Lunch
12:30–1:45	Nap
1:45–2:00	Snack
2:00–2:30	Fourth structured learning period
2:30–3:00	Fifth structured learning period
3:00–3:30	Sixth structured learning period
3:30–4:00	Motor period
4:00	Departure

Though a child was never forced to remain in a learning area, the teacher was encouraged to make it exciting for him to do so. . . .

The intent of the education program was to provide an environment and a set of experiences which would allow children to develop to their potential intellectually as well as socially, emotionally, and physically. The specific focus of the educational program was to prevent from occurring those language, problem-solving, and achievement motivation deficits which are associated with mild mental retardation and severe disadvantagement.

The general educational program is best characterized as having a cognitive-language orientation implemented through a structured environment by prescriptive teaching techniques on a daily basis (seven hours per day, five days per week). This program and schedule was coupled with a high teacher-child ratio, affording an opportunity to present a variety of cognitive tasks, to evaluate their effectiveness, and to provide both direct and non-direct teaching within both small and large groups.

Although there are many theories which have implications for an educational program; e.g., Skinner, Piaget, Montessori, Bruner; none is complete while all are relevant. By necessity the theory which has guided the development of the curriculum for the Milwaukee Project's Educational Program is eclectic yet structured in its presentation. There were no suitable programs available as guides for intervention in the first few months of life. Consequently, the project staff has continually adapted existing methods and materials for the purposes of our program.

The educational program had two major emphases: (1) language and (2) cognition. We considered language not only as essential to social communication, but essential to the ability to manipulate symbols, the tool by which one stores and recovers information and a major influence on how one interprets his environment. It was our intent that tasks or experiences be presented to the child with considerable emphasis on verbal expressiveness in order to facilitate this development.

The cognitive development of the children was of primary concern because we did not want to simply identify and provide children with those facts which are the supposed elements for success in school. A child must have at his disposal the technique not only to incorporate, integrate, refine, and utilize this information, but (and most importantly) to be able to act spontaneously whenever the situation changes.

Thus while a handle for the term cognitive development is difficult to find, there were certain identifiable developmentally important cognitive skills, e.g. classification, association, generalization, integration, interpretation. We have focused on these and have attempted to facilitate their development by incorporating into the educational program specific tasks, which were begun as soon as the children entered the program.

Importantly, although language was emphasized as a tool for processing information as well as for communication, and cognitive development was emphasized for the development of thinking creatively as well as providing the child with a repertoire of responses, we recognized that the energy to make this system work is the desire to utilize these skills. Therefore, a third area of concern was motivation. We attempted to develop achievement motivation by both designing tasks and creating an atmosphere which would maximize interest, provide success experiences, provide supportive and corrective feedback from responsive adults, and to gradually increase the child's responsibility for task completion.

The educational program took place within a structured learning environment. By utilizing a structured learning approach, the emphasis was on educating the teacher to plan and present relevant and organized learning situations. The content of instructional units was presented in small logical steps. The children's progress was evaluated and corresponding program adjustments made as part of an ongoing process. Yet within this structured environment, we still emphasized flexibility as essential in order to meet the needs of the children and the teacher. Opportunities could be provided for both directed and non-directed instruction. There was greater opportunity for direct child-teacher intervention.

Thus the Milwaukee Project attempted to change the expected course of children who were at high-risk for mental retardation. The plan was to implement a comprehensive family intervention, beginning in the home.

The program for the retarded mothers was designed to modify those aspects of the environment which the mother herself creates or controls. Each day, her child was picked up at home and brought to the Infant Education Center for the entire day. These children are the Experimental group. The Control group is essentially the same kind of children whose mothers were in the original pool of high-risk families from which were drawn both the Experimental and Control group families. The children in the Control group are seen only for testing, which is done on a prescribed schedule for both groups of children.

ASSESSMENT OF DEVELOPMENT

In order to assess the effects of the kind of comprehensive intervention we have made with the natural environment of the infant reared by a retarded mother, we have undertaken an intensive schedule of measurements.*

---

*Because of the obvious limitations of this report, only a portion of the measurements are reported here.

Our schedule of measurement includes measures of physical maturation, standardized and experimental measures of developmental schedules of infant adaptive behavior, standardized tests of general intelligence, an array of experimental learning tasks, measures of motivation and social development, and a variety of measures of language development.

Both the Experimental and Control infants are on an identical measurement schedule. Infants are scheduled for assessment sessions every three weeks. The particular measures administered at a given session depend upon the predetermined schedule of measures for that age level. A particular test or task is administered to both Experimental and Control infants by the same person; the testers are not involved in any component of the infant stimulation or maternal program.

In the first 24 months of life, the measurement schedule was largely restricted to general developmental scales and emerging vocalization and language.

Gesell data

The Gesell Developmental Schedules were administered to Experimental and Control infants at the ages of six, ten, fourteen, eighteen, and 22 months. Through six, ten, and fourteen month testings, both groups appeared reasonably comparable on the four schedules: Motor, Adaptive, Language, and Personal-Social. These data can be seen in the graph [Figure 2] which is a composite of the four schedules plotted in terms of the mean scale developmental age norms for each age level tested. There is some divergence in performance at fourteen months, due mainly to the significant ($p < .05$) difference on the Motor and Adaptive schedules in favor of the Experimental group. The Control group at this time also performs above average. At eighteen months the Control group begins to fall three to four months below the Experimental group, although still performing at or close to Gesell norms. The Experimental group at eighteen months is significantly ($p < .001$) ahead of the Controls on all but the Personal-Social Gesell Schedule. At 22 months the Experimental group scores are from four and one-half to six months in advance of the Control group ($p < .001$) on all four schedules, while the Control group has fallen below the Gesell norms on the Adaptive and Language schedules.

In summary, the Gesell data is roughly comparable for both groups to fourteen months with performance on all scales slightly in advance of test norms. At 22 months, performance of the Experimental group

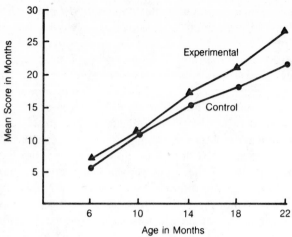

FIGURE 2

COMPOSITE OF FOUR GESELL SCORES

is clearly accelerated while the Control group performs at or slightly below norms for the four scales.

Learning

Beginning at 24 months, increased emphasis was given to experimental, direct measures of learning and performance, as well as to the standardized tests of general intelligence.

The learning tasks chosen were those that, on the one hand, would characterize the developmental learning process and on the other hand were tasks that could be repeated yearly. By repeating tasks we could keep pace with the increasing CA's of our Ss and yet maintain a continuity of task which would permit evaluation of developmental changes in performance. *Obviously, the exceedingly complex nature of cognitive growth required more than a single measure of intellectual development, such as is obtained from IQ tests. Thus, a more comprehensive picture of the growth of cognitive abilities was attempted by an array of experimental learning tasks (see, e.g., Stevenson, 1972).*

Most importantly, we were concerned with delineating some of the characteristics of early learning behavior that are either facilitating or interfering with learning. We wanted information on the response patterns or behavior style, and we wanted information about the role of attention in early learning. These tasks, therefore, not only provided

9. Intelligence: Its meaning and its development

a measure of the differential development of the learning process in the children, but increased our understanding of how certain performance variables relate to cognitive growth.

One experimental task has been concerned with development of the child's attention to color and form and the response strategy employed. It is a color-form matching task in which the child may respond consistently according to one of the dimensions: color or form. He cannot respond consistently if he does not attend to one dimension or the other, especially if he uses a response strategy such as position responding or alternation responding. In this case, responding to the dimension of either color or form is more developmentally advanced than ignoring the color-form dimension and responding, e.g., to position. This test has been administered four times. During the third year of life, none of the Controls demonstrated a dimensional response (i.e., in terms of color or form). By contrast, over half of the Experimental group (55 percent) showed unidimensional responding. In the fourth year of life and during the fifth and sixth years as well, this differential performance was maintained. There are two notable points: (1) three-fourths or more of the Experimental group showed unidimensional responding at each successive testing, while even at the fifth and sixth year testings the percentage of the Control group showing unidimensional responding was comparable only to the Experimental group's first test performance, nearly two years before; and (2) the Experimental group showed a significant shift to form, which is quite consistent with other research indicating advanced developmental performance. Quite interestingly, of those children in both groups who did not show dimensional preference, by far a greater percentage of the Controls, at each testing, showed response perseveration. In other words, little or no attempt was made, it seems, to attend to either color or form since most (over two-thirds) responses were made purely to position. As of the last testing (when children are between the ages of five and six) only twenty percent of the Experimentals showed such responding, as compared to nearly two-thirds of the Control group.

Additional evidence for perseverative responding and the development of strategies was gained from a probability learning task. In this task no response is always correct, but a strategy of responding can help to increase the child's percentage of payoff. In fact, although both groups were reinforced at about the same rate (i.e. payoff)—they were very different in their use of strategy. The Control group showed a greater tendency to perseverate, i.e., they continued to respond to either a stimulus or position irrespective of the consequence of their previous response. Further, whereas only one-third of the Experimental group showed a tendency to perseverate, 80 percent of the Controls perseverated. By the second testing, nearly two years later, nearly three-fourths of the Control children continued to perseverate as compared to only one-fourth of the Experimental group. This tendency to perseverate suggests that the children are insensitive to the reinforcement contingencies—i.e., they do not seem to appreciate the feedback to be gained from their response and therefore perseverate their response to position.

Thus, we feel that in spite of the apparent simpleness of these tasks, they demonstrate the association of early intellectual development with an ability to impose order on the environment—an ability which is basic and essential to intellectual development. This difficulty in the performance of various learning tasks may be similar to the input phenomena found in studies of short-term memory (Calfee, 1969). In that kind of an experimental paradigm, and perhaps in ours as well, there appears to be a critical lack in the ability to organize stimulation for input where there is sub-average intellectual functioning.

A deficiency in this critical ability becomes quite apparent in the performance of various problem-solving and concept formation tasks. For example, we have studied the performance of the children in an oddity discrimination task. The child is presented with a horizontal array of three stimuli, each of which has four component dimensions: color, form, size, and number. In order for the child to be able to select the odd stimulus on each trial, he must first separate the dimensions into relevant, irrelevant, and quiet. This is an extremely complex conceptual task for very young children.

This task has been presented three successive times, and the data show superior performance by the Experimental children. We have analyzed the data further by a breakdown of the concept categories. These results show a superior performance on all dimensions and particularly on the form dimension for the Experimental children, which is consistent with their performance on our most recent replication of the matching study. Obviously this preference can facilitate performance, but it is just this point that underscores our earlier remark regarding the development of attentional processes. Though it may be that dimensional preferences lead in some situations to response biases, it can also index the developmental process of selective organization of the stimulus environment, especially for very young children. The earlier that such behavior occurs, the greater the facilitation of learning performance on just such kinds of tasks. In our case, the data point obviously to a developmentally related facilitation of performance as a function of the degree to which the early dimensional preferences have been established.

Language development

A child's acquisition of language occurs in a surprisingly short period of time. Although grammatical speech rarely begins before eighteen months of age, the basic process appears complete by the age of three and one-half. Furthermore, at this age level, it is probably language facility which most clearly differentiates the cultural-familial retardate from his non-retarded peers. It is for this reason that we have given so much emphasis to both the development of the children's language abilities and the measurement of this aspect of behavior. Our concern is both with the quantitative and qualitative differences in the developing language structures of these two groups.

The development of language depends on a number of organic and environmental factors. The main variable in the social environment critical to language development in the child is the primary responsible adult: usually the mother. Brown and Bellugi (1964) suggest three processes operating in the learning of language. The first process is one of imitation with reduction by the child of the adult utterances in the environment. The young child seems to reduce adult utterances to a form which is much like that of a telegram; i.e., it utilizes the high content, low-function words of the adult utterance. Thus, where an adult might say something like, "I see the big chair," the child might say, "See chair." This telegraphic language can communicate a situation known to the adult and the child.

The second process appears to involve the imitation of the child's utterances by the adult. What might happen is, when a child says something, the adult repeats the utterance and expands it slightly. The resulting utterance is a perfectly formed model sentence in the adult language which apparently has, as its purpose, the effect of saying to the child, "This is the way you could have said what you just said." Thus, where a child might say something like, "There doggie," the adult might say, "Yes, there is a doggie." This type of imitation occurs in about 30 percent of the utterances.

The third process is one of induction of the latent structure: this requires that the child learn the rule of language, which he appears to do in some covert manner. The basic learning of the language system is usually complete by the time the child enters school. It is obvious, therefore, that if the responsible adult in a child's environment is language deficient and somewhat nonresponsive, there can be serious retardation in a child's language development.

The first statistically significant difference in language development appeared at eighteen months on the Language scale of the Gesell Developmental Schedule. At this testing age the Experimental children were two months above the norm and three months ahead of the Controls. By 22 months the Experimental children were over four months ahead of the norm and six months ahead of the Controls. This trend of differential language development has continued, and perhaps in even a more dramatic way. In fact, some of the most striking differences in the performance of the Experimental and Control children are reflected in the research measures of language performance.

Research in developmental psycholinguistics usually divides language into three areas: imitation, comprehension, and production. We are using both tests developed in our laboratory and such standardized instruments as the Illinois Test of Psycholinguistic Abilities (ITPA), in order to assess language development. Imitation, the child's ability to repeat certain grammatical structures presented to him as models, is tested through a sentence repetition test; comprehension, the understanding of grammatical structures, is assessed through a grammatical comprehension test; while production, spontaneous language facility, is measured through gross feature tabulation of free speech samples. Together, the results of these measures have provided us with a comprehensive picture of the children's language development for five years.

Samples of conversation between each child and our language tester (a black, middle-aged woman) have been analyzed since the child's eighteen-month birthday. The free speech sampling technique is quite useful with such young children since the situation is relaxed, unstructured, and the child is quite comfortable in conversation. Structured test situations, on the other hand, particularly at these very early ages, tend to restrict the behavior of the child and thereby reduce the validity of the speech sample somewhat.

The analysis of this language sample indicated that the Experimental children between the ages of one and one-half and three say a lot more in conversation. Using this measurement technique, we find that it is not until three years of age that the Control group produces the same amount of utterances as the Experimental children. However, since the measure provides a rather gross picture of language as language becomes more complex, it actually masks the considerable linguistic differences that exist between the children. These differences show up in the group's performance on the more sophisticated language measures.

Still, we feel that this considerable early difference in language behavior is basic to the more sophisticated language skills yet to come. We are not quite sure why, but the repetition and verbal expressiveness characteristic of the Experimental group between one and one-half and three seems fundamental to the continued differential development of language skills by the E group over the C group. The amount of utterances at the eighteen-month level for the Experimental group is not achieved by the Control group until nearly a year later.

The mean number of unique words, lexical growth in free production, was also measured. Vocabulary range is always greater on the part of the Experimental group. This is so even when the Control group produces more utterances than the Experimental group; the Experimental group still produces more unique words.

At the age of three we began to test imitation by means of a sentence repetition test. It is an easily administered instrument: you ask the child to repeat what the tester says. The children's replies are analyzed for omissions, substitutions, and additions. The omissions are significantly greater for the Control group at every age level from 36 months on while there is a significant decrease in omissions by the Experimental group every six months. Also, the Experimental group has made significantly fewer substitutions and additions to the repetitions. The Experimental group by the age of four has significantly more exact repetitions than the Control group, whose performance is comparable to the Experimental group's performance at three. This same performance differential continues through age five.

Also at age three we tested grammatical comprehension with a modified version of a test developed by Dr. Ursula Bellugi-Klima (Fraser, 1963). It is a game in which the child manipulates objects in order to demonstrate his ability to comprehend various grammatical constructions, such as the active and passive voice. In this test you might have, for example, two toy animals and you ask the child to show "the pig chases the cow" and then you ask the child to show you "the pig is chased by the cow." The child is expected to act out these situations, which requires just comprehension, not production. The game is played with the child across sixteen syntactic areas: e.g., active-passive voice, embed-ded sentences, singular-plural, possessive nouns, and prepositions. The results show that the Experimental group's performance is significantly superior at all age levels tested (three, four, and five). Their grammatical comprehension is at least one year (and more) in advance of the Control group.

Our standardized language instrument has been the ITPA, which has been administered to all children over four and one-half. The results have, basically, supported the differential performance of the Experi-mental and Control groups on our other measures. The mean psycholin-guistic age of the Experimental group is 63 months (measured at 54 months) as compared to a mean of 45 months for the Control group, a difference in favor of the Experimental group by over a year and one-half.

In describing the language behavior of the Experimental children one would find them volubly expressive, verbally fluent, and according to the ITPA linguistically sophisticated. They speak their own dialect and they are proud of their own speech and yet their performance is developmentally advanced on sophisticated tests of the English language.

MOTHER-CHILD RELATIONSHIP

Each mother . . . creates an environment for her child which is quite different from that created by other mothers, even though all live in the same environment. Indeed, it is the very nature of the environment created by the mother which influences social, emotional, and cognitive development. The investigation of this relationship has been studied in detail by Hess and Shipman (e.g. 1968). They found that the mother's linguistic and regulatory behavior induces and shapes the information-processing strategies and style in her child and can act to either facilitate or limit intellectual growth.

Mildly retarded mothers tend to regulate behavior by using imperatives and restricted communication—a behavior control system which can [limit] intellectual growth in her child. Furthermore, the nature of this interaction is such that it induces a passive-compliant attitude by weakening the child's self-confidence and dampening motivation. We are quite con-cerned, therefore, in determining the nature of the mother-child rela-tionship, especially after having intervened in this critical process.

In the mother-child interaction most sophisticated behavior—such as the initiation of problem-solving behavior by verbal clues and verbal prods, or the organization of tasks with respect to goals in problem-solving situations, etc.—is done by the mother. However, where the mother is of low IQ, the interaction is more physical, less organized, and less direction is given to the child. Indeed, while this was the case in the Control group mother-child dyads, it was quite different in the Experimental dyads.

We used a specially prepared mobile laboratory for all experimental sessions. The testing room was equipped with videotape and sound recording equipment, so that the entire session with each family was recorded for later analysis. The mother and child are brought to the laboratory and seated at a table. Part of this research involved explaining to the mother the tasks she and the child were to perform. First, she was to tell the child a story based on a picture, which afforded us the opportunity to measure the mother's language facility. Second, the mother was told to teach the child a block sorting task and how to copy three designs on a toy Etch-A-Sketch. The behavior between the mother and child was rated on a scale with rating categories divided into various kinds of physical and verbal behaviors, with additional categories to indicate whether the behavior was active or passive.

We found that the Experimental dyads transmitted more information than the Control dyads, and this was a function of the quality of the Experimental child's verbal behavior. The Experimental children supplied more information verbally and initiated more verbal communication than found in the Control dyads. The children in the Experimental dyad took responsibility for guiding the flow of information— providing most of the verbal information and direction. The mothers of both dyads showed little differences in their teaching ability during the testing session. However, in the Experimental dyads, the children structured the interaction session either by their questioning or by teaching the mother. As a result, a developmentally more sophisticated interaction pattern has developed between the Experimental children and their mothers, which contributed to faster and more successful problem completion.

It is apparent from this description of a portion of the data of the mother-child interaction, that the intervention effort has effectively changed the expected pattern of development for the Experimental dyads. Moreover, the result of what might be termed a reciprocal feedback system, initiated by the child, has been to create a more sophisticated and satisfying interaction pattern in the Experimental dyad. In fact, there is some evidence that the Experimental mothers may be undergoing some changes in attitude and self-confidence. The Experimental mothers appear to be adopting more of an "internal locus of control"—an attitude that 'things happen' because of their decisions and actions and not purely by chance or fate. Thus, the intensive stimulation program, undergone by the Experimental children, has benefited both the Experimental child and the Experimental mother by broadening their verbal and expressive behavioral repertoire.

MEASURED INTELLIGENCE TO 66 MONTHS

The standardized tests of intelligence included the Cattell, Stanford-Binet, and Wechsler Preschool-Primary Scale of Intelligence (WPPSI). The Cattell test, extending into the Binet, was scheduled at three month intervals beginning at CA 24 months and at six month intervals from CA 48 months on. The graph illustrates the course of intellectual development for the two groups from twelve months until 66 months of age. The data presented use scores derived from the Gesell schedules from 12 to 21 months, and Cattell and Binet scores from 24 to 66 months. The mean IQ at the upper age level of 66 months is based on approximately half of the group, because at this time not all of the subjects have reached this age.

The mean IQ for the Experimental group based on the means at each age interval from 24 to 66 months is 123.4. For the Control group, mean IQ for all testings is 94.8. At the latest age point the Experimentals are just above their mean, at 125 (s.d. = 8.5) while the Controls have slipped below their overall mean to 91 (s.d. = 9.1). The discrepancy between Experimental and Control group performance at each three month test interval varies from a minimum of 23 IQ points at 24 months to over 30 IQ points at 66 months.

These data summarize the present differential development between the Experimental and Control groups. The dotted line on the graph [Figure 3] represents the mean IQ's of offspring of mothers with IQ's below 75, taken from our original population survey. This is referred to in our study as the Contrast group. It depicts the pattern of development expected for our actual Control group. You will recall that our hypothesis was in terms of preventing the relative decline in development of the Experimental group which we see in the Contrast group and

FIGURE 3

MEAN IQ PERFORMANCE WITH INCREASING AGE FOR THE EXPERIMENTAL AND
CONTROL GROUPS IN COMPARISON TO THE HIGH RISK SURVEY CONTRAST GROUP

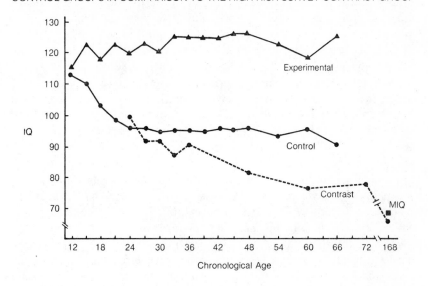

Chronological Age

which we can begin to see in the Control group. In sharp contrast is
the Experimental group's performance, to date, on the standardized tests
of measured intelligence, indicating a remarkable acceleration of intellectual development on the part of these children exposed to the infant
stimulation program. Further, their performance is quite homogeneous
as contrasted with that of the Control group where less than one-fourth
of the Ss test at or above the norms with the remainder trending toward
sub-average performance.

It is important to point out that there is reason for caution in the
interpretation of such data, particularly when one considers the numerous
pitfalls and hazards of infant measurement. The Experimental children
have had training, albeit fortuitously, on items included in the curriculum
which are sampled by the tests, while the repeated measurements have
made both groups test-wise. It is well to point out, however, that curriculum materials and tests used are standard fare for early education programs everywhere. All in all, it does seem that the Experimental group
has benefited from the intensive training program, a program to which
no comparable group of infants has ever been exposed, to the best of

our knowledge. We have tried very hard to answer whether it has been simply a matter of training and practicing specific skills. In fact, extraordinary precaution has been taken to separate the development of the curriculum and the assessment program. Two separate staffs have been employed. It is obvious to most researchers that, to some extent, infant intelligence tests must contain material which approximates material used in preschool curricula, primarily because of the limited variety of material for this age. To circumvent this problem somewhat, we have employed other measures of performance, which minimized the stock item, and thereby afforded additional insight into the differential development of these children. As could be seen in the measures of learning and language development, the differential performance discrepancy is consistent with the IQ measures, indicating advanced intellectual development of the Experimental group. What is more, there is considerable difference in the pattern or style of behavior between the groups—particularly the tendency to stereotypy of response exhibited by the Control group, which certainly is antagonistic to successful learning performance.

Thus, infant testing difficulties notwithstanding, the present standardized test data, when considered along with performance on learning tasks and language tests, indicate an unquestionably superior present level of cognitive development on the part of the Experimental group. Also, the first "wave" of our children are now in public schools. *None* have been assigned to classes for the retarded and we are collecting data on school performance generally.

CONCLUSION

We are particularly concerned with the social-emotional development of our children, which was encouraged through the interpersonal relationship developed between the teachers and the children and their families. We felt that this was fundamental to developing intellectual strength in children. Intellectual strength we defined as the ability to meet new experiences with not only considerable creativeness and ingenuity, but with self-confidence and the kind of motivation that is based on the natural curiosity to learn. The child who feels himself to be intellectually strong enters new learning situations with eagerness, unafraid of failure, and filled with curiosity and excitement with each new adventure in knowledge gathering. Unfortunately, this natural desire to pursue and discover and learn about our world, that is within each of us, can be dampened or shut down by negative learning experiences. In all too many cases a child's failure to learn is due to the restricted learning environment created for him in early life. As a result, children who have such developmental histories develop a behavior system which is antagonistic to the learning they must do for successful school performance.

Learning need not be forced if there is excitement. Experiences must not be restricted, opportunities for learning must be varied, solutions must have alternatives, and discovery must be shared in. The environment for preschool age children must be at once so rich, so varied, so intriguing, and so organized that a child has before him considerable opportunity to learn and make use of his own natural tendencies to discover.

It appears, however, that the mitigation of the environmental influences for which cultural-familial retardation is a consequent can be accomplished, though not by any single source. Most importantly, though, help must be given to that large population of mothers who are unaware of the critical nature of early childhood and also unaware of their own needs during pregnancy. *In large part, it is these mothers who consequently contribute to the growing number of children so poor in development that they are at high risk for mental retardation.* Therefore, existing early stimulation programs notwithstanding, there is considerable need for a comprehensive, nation-wide program for the prevention of mental retardation. The implementation of this program with any consideration for success will require an active community service program for which there probably is no previous model, but there is now available information of the kind we have just presented to you. Indeed, if our country is to seriously challenge the problem of cultural-familial retardation, we must do so at its doorstep and that will require a strategy for prevention, with increased emphasis on early detection and early intervention.

Although we have given intelligence a section all to itself, we do not intend to imply that the pursuit and measurement of the IQ tells us as much about children's behavior as does the study of, for example, their cognitive and affective development. IQ is not the most important variable in child psychology, although the nonpsychologist often gets the impression that it is, but it does serve as a useful index. Measures of intelligence can provide us with an estimate of a child's cognitive status at a given moment, but they cannot, in themselves, tell us why children vary. Investigations into the probable causes of this variance have yielded considerable information about the effect of different kinds of environment on children's development, data which are consistent with other investigations. Study after study shows that children are likely to thrive if they are stimulated, talked to, and loved, and it comes as no surprise to find a correlation between such inputs and IQ. Whether IQ measurements should be used by educators, personnel workers, and other nonpsychologists is a question that has political overtones and that may affect the morale, self-esteem, and interpersonal relations of individuals and groups. This is an important question, and one to which answers must be found; but because of the breadth and intensity of this controversy, its solution is beyond the scope of this book.

REFERENCES

Anderson, S. and Messick, S. "Social competency in young children." *Developmental Psychology* 10 (1974): 282-293.

Borg, W. R. *An Evaluation of Ability Grouping.* Cooperative Research Project, No. 577. Logan: Utah State University, 1964.

Eysenck, H. J. *The IQ Argument.* New York: Library Press, 1971.

Goldberg, M. L., Passow, A. H., and Justman, J. *The Effects of Ability Grouping.* New York: Teachers College Press, 1966.

Heber, R., Garber, H., Harrington, S., Hoffman, C., and Falender, C. *Rehabilitation of Families At Risk for Mental Retardation.* Progress Report of the Rehabilitation Research and Training Center in Mental Retardation, University of Wisconsin, Madison, Wisc., December, 1972.

Herrnstein, R. "I. Q." *Atlantic* 228 No. 3 (1971): 44-64.

Hunt, J. McV. "Has compensatory education failed? Has it been attempted?" *Harvard Educational Review* 39 (1969): 130-152.

Jensen, A. R. "How much can we boost IQ and scholastic achievement?" *Harvard Educational Review* 39 (1969): 1-123.

Newman, H. H., Freeman, F. N., and Holzinger, K. J. *Twins: A Study of Heredity and Environment.* Chicago: University of Chicago Press, 1937.

Ogletree, E. J. "Ability grouping: Its effect on attitudes." *Journal of Social Psychology* 82 (1970): 137-138.

Rosenthal, R., Baratz, S. S., and Hall, C. M. "Teacher behavior, teacher expectations, and gains in pupils' rated creativity." *Journal of Genetic Psychology* 124 (1974): 115-121.

Rosenthal, R. and Jacobson, L. *Pygmalion in the Classroom.* New York: Holt, Rinehart, and Wilson, 1968.

Rosenthal, T., Underwood, B., and Martin, M. "Assessing classroom inventive practices." *Journal of Educational Psychology* 60 (1969): 370-376.

Scarr-Salapatek, S. "Race, social class, and IQ." *Science* 174 (1971): 1285-1295.

9. Intelligence: Its meaning and its development

Wolf. R. M. "The identification and measurement of environmental process variables related to intelligence." Unpublished doctoral dissertation. University of Chicago. 1964.

9.1

1. Beller. E. K.. and Haeberle. A. W. Dependency and the frustration-aggression hypothesis I. Paper presented at the 30th annual meeting of the Eastern Psychological Association. Atlantic City. New Jersey. 1959.

2. _____. Dependency and the frustration-aggression hypothesis II. Paper presented at the 32nd annual meeting of the Eastern Psychological Association. Philadelphia. 1961.

3. Lovaas. O. I. Interaction between verbal and nonverbal behavior. *Child Devel.* 32 (1961): 329–336.

4. Piaget. J. The Origins of Intelligence in Children. New York: Norton. 1963.

5. Stevenson. H. W. Social reinforcement with children as a function of *CA*. sex of *E*. and sex of *S. J. Abn. & Soc. Psychol.* 63 (1961): 147–154.

6. Terman. L.. and Merrill. M. Stanford-Binet Intelligence Scale. Boston: Houghton Mifflin. 1961.

9.2

1. For a review of studies. see L. Erlenmeyer-Kimling and L. F. Jarvik. *Science* 142. 1477 (1963). Heritability is the ratio of genetic variance to total phenotypic variance. For human studies. heritability is used in its broad sense of total genetic variance/total phenotypic variance.

2. The *Harvard Educational Review* compilation includes Jensen's paper. "How much can we boost IQ and scholastic achievement?." comments on it by J. S. Kagan. J. McV. Hunt. J. F. Crow. C. Bereiter. D. Elkind. L. J. Cronbach. and W. F. Brazziel. and a rejoinder by Jensen. See also A. R. Jensen. in J. Hellmuth. *Disadvantaged Child*. vol. 3 (Special Child Publ.. Seattle. Wash.. 1970).

3. P. L. Nichols. thesis. University of Minnesota (1970). Nichols reports that in two large samples of black and white children. seven-year WISC IQ scores showed the same means and distributions for the two racial groups. once social-class variables were equated. These results are unlike those of several other studies. which found that matching socio-economic status did not create equal means in the two racial groups [A. Shuey (5); A. B. Wilson. *Racial Isolation in the Public Schools*, vol. 2 (Government Printing Office. Washington. D.C.. 1967)]. In Nichols's samples. prenatal and postnatal medical care was equally available to blacks and whites. which may have contributed to the relatively high IQ scores of the blacks in these samples.

4. By interaction. Eysenck means simply $P = G + E$, or "heredity and environment acting together to produce the observed phenotype" (p. 111). He does not mean what most geneticists and behavior geneticists mean by interaction; that is. the *differential* phenotypic effects produced by various combinations of genotypes and environments. as in the interaction term of analysis-of-variance statistics. Few thinking people are not interactionists in Eysenck's sense of the term. because that's the only way to get the organism and the environment into the same equation to account for variance in any phenotypic trait. How much of the phenotypic variance is accounted for by each of the terms in the equation is the real issue.

5. A. Shuey. *The Testing of Negro Intelligence* (Social Science Press. New York. 1966). pp. 499–519.

6. F. B. Davis, *The Measurement of Mental Capacity through Evoked-Potential Recordings* (Educational Records Bureau, Greenwich, Conn., 1971). "As it turned out, no evidence was found that the latency periods obtained . . . displayed serviceable utility for predicting school performance or level of mental ability among pupils in preschool through grade 8" (p. x).

7. *New York Times*, 8 Oct. 1971, p. 41.

8. J. Kagan and H. A. Moss, *Birth to Maturity* (Wiley, New York, 1962).

9. S. Scarr-Salapatek, *Science*, in press.

10. P. E. Vernon, *Intelligence and Cultural Environment* (Methuen, London, 1969).

11. T. Dobzhansky, *Mankind Evolving* (Yale Univ. Press, New Haven, 1962), pp. 234-238.

12. J. Thoday, *J. Biosocial Science* 1, suppl. 3, 4 (1969).

13. L. L. Cavalli-Sforza and W. F. Bodmer, *The Genetics of Human Populations* (Freeman, San Francisco, 1971), pp. 753-804. They propose that the study of racial differences is useless and not scientifically supportable at the present time.

14. E. W. and S. H. Reed, *Science* 165, 762 (1969); *Am. J. Hum. Genet.* 21, 1 (1969); C. MacLean and P. L. Workman, paper at a meeting of the American Society of Human Genetics (1970, Indianapolis).

15. E. W. Reed and S. C. Reed, *Mental Retardation: A Family Study* (Saunders, Philadelphia, 1965); *Social Biol.* 18, suppl., 42 (1971).

16. M. Skodak and H. M. Skeels, *J. Genet. Psychol.* 75, 85 (1949).

17. J. C. DeFries, paper for the C.O.B.R.E. Research Workshop on Genetic Endowment and Environment in the Determination of Behavior (3-8 Oct. 1971, Rye, N.Y.).

18. R. Heber, *Rehabilitation of Families at Risk for Mental Retardation* (Regional Rehabilitation Center, Univ. of Wisconsin, 1969). S. P. Strickland, *Am. Ed.* 7, 3 (1971).

19. I. I. Gottesman, in *Social Class, Race, and Psychological Development,* M. Deutsch, I. Katz, and A. R. Jensen, Eds. (Holt, Rinehart, and Winston, New York, 1968), pp. 11-51.

20. J. Rynders, personal communication, November 1971.

21. N. E. Morton, paper for the C.O.B.R.E. Research Workshop on Genetic Endowment and Environment in the Determination of Behavior (3-8 Oct. 1971, Rye, N.Y.).

9.3

Bayley, N. Developmental problems of the mentally retarded child. In I. Philips (Ed.), *Prevention and treatment of mental retardation,* Basic Books, 1966.

Bayley, N., and Schaefer, E. S. Correlations of maternal and child behaviors with the development of mental abilities: Data from the Berkeley Growth Study. *Monographs of the Society for Research in Child Development,* 1964, 29 (6), 1-80.

Bing, E. Effect of child-rearing practices on the development of differential cognitive abilities. *Child Development,* 1963, 34, 631-648.

Cattell, P. *The measurement of intelligence of infants.* New York: Psychological Corporation, 1940.

Crandall, V. J., Dewey, R., Katkovsky, W., and Preston, A. Parents' attitudes and behaviors and grade school children's academic achievements. *Journal of Genetic Psychology,* 1964, 104, 53-66.

Freeberg, N., and Payne, D. Parental influence on cognitive development in early childhood: A review. *Child Development,* 1967, 38, 66–87.

Honzik, M. P. A sex difference in the age of onset of the parent-child resemblance in intelligence, *Journal of Educational Psychology,* 1963, 54, 231–237.

Honzik, M. P. Environmental correlates of mental growth: Prediction from the family setting at 21 months. *Child Development,* 1967, 38, 337–364.

Kagan, J., and Freeman, M. Relation of childhood intelligence, maternal behaviors and social class to behavior during adolescence. *Child Development,* 1963, 34, 899–911.

Kagan, J., and Moss, H. A. Parental correlates of child's IQ and height: A cross-validation of the Berkeley Growth Study results. *Child Development,* 1959, 30, 325–332.

Kent, N., and Davis, D. R. Discipline in the home and intellectual development. *British Journal of Medical Psychology,* 1957, 30, 27–34.

Maccoby, E. E. (Ed.) *The development of sex differences.* Stanford University Press, 1966.

Moore, T. Language and intelligence: A longitudinal study of the first eight years. Part II: Environmental correlates of mental growth. *Human Development,* 1968, 11, 1–24.

Thurstone, L. L., and Thurstone, T. G. *SRA Primary Mental Abilities (Elementary Form) Examiner's Manual.* (Rev. ed.) Chicago: Science Research Associates, 1954.

Werner, E., Bierman, J. M., French, F., Simonian, K., Connor, A., Smith, R., and Campbell, M. Reproductive and environmental casualties: A report on the ten year follow-up of the Kauai Pregnancy Study. *Pediatrics,* 1968, 42, 112–127.

Werner, E., Simonian, K., Bierman, J. M., and French, F. Cumulative effect of perinatal complications and deprived environment on physical, intellectual and social development of pre-school children. *Pediatrics,* 1967, 39, 490–505.

Wolf, R. M. The identification and measurement of environment process variables related to intelligence. Unpublished doctoral dissertation, University of Chicago, 1964.

9.4

Brown, R. and Bellugi, U. Three processes in the child's acquisition of syntax. *Harvard Educational Review,* 1964, 34, 133–151.

Calfee, Robert C. *Short-Term Retention in Normal and Retarded Children as a Function on Memory Load and List Structure.* University of Wisconsin Center for Cognitive Learning, Technical Report No. 75, 1969.

Fraser, C., Bellugi, U., and Brown, R. Control of grammar in imitation, comprehension and production. *Journal of Verbal Learning and Verbal Behavior,* 1963, 2, 121–135.

Heber, R., Dever, R., and Conry, J. The influence of environmental and genetic variables on intellectual development. In H. J. Prehm, L. A. Hamerlynck, and J. E. Crosson (Eds.) *Behavioral Research in Mental Retardation,* Research and Training Center, Monograph 1, University of Oregon, 1968, 1–22.

Hess, R. D. and Shipman, V. C. Maternal influences upon early learning. In R. D. Hess and R. M. Bear (Eds.) *Early Education.* Chicago: Aldine, 1968, 91–103.

Stevenson, Harold W. The taxonomy of tasks. In F. J. Monks, W. W. Hartup, and Jan de Wit (Eds.) *Determinants of Behavioral Development.* New York: Academic Press, 1972, 75–88.

Epilogue

When I have finished a book, I customarily ask myself why I undertook to write it. The question is not easily answered, because an author's motives, like the themes underlying all complex forms of human behavior, are exceedingly complicated, and it is sometimes difficult to determine which of several possible aims are the principal ones.

Nevertheless, as I recall the feelings and reactions I had while searching the literature for the ideas and articles this book comprises, it seems to me that my primary motive was to make children seem more *interesting*. Although we often say that children should be more tractable, cooperative, civilized, or self-controlled, the idea that they should be more interesting is virtually never uttered. If we assume that children are interesting enough already, why do we tend to treat them in such off-hand, irritable, and unthinking ways? We behave like this for many complex and even unconscious reasons, but one major factor is undoubtedly our preoccupation with other concerns and interests. The demands children make on our time and attention are frequently annoying and unwanted, and we become impatient with behavior that does not meet our expectations and requirements. Anyone who studies children or works with them professionally is clearly aware that the average adult's tolerance and acceptance of children is often superficial and short-lived, an attitude in sharp contrast with the general precept that children are a source of unending interest and enjoyment.

One of the reasons for our often shallow and transitory interest in children is that our capacities for understanding them are rather limited. Although common sense and our own childhood memories can help to give us a basis for coping with children's behavior, we very quickly "come to the end of the line" when we have to deal with an unexpected problem or new development. Our limited knowledge makes it easy for us to misinterpret or to ignore significant responses and patterns of behavior, and so, with a sigh of exasperation or resignation, we turn to matters that interest us more.

A textbook in child psychology cannot, of course, remedy this regrettable situation, but it can serve as a stimulus to move its readers beyond the limits of everyday understanding and experience where children are concerned. It can present its readers with ways of looking at children's behavior that transcend conventional modes of thinking and reacting. In our opening paper, for example, Patricia Marks Greenfield's observations of her infant daughter's attempt to cope linguistically with the world of reality extend far beyond the reactions of a fond parent. Although her observations are occasionally somewhat technical, they still convey the sense of excitement that psychologists feel when they are in the process of unravelling some interesting detail of human behavior. The other researchers whose work I have presented in this book, also depart from everyday, commonplace concepts in how they look at children's behavior.

Psychological research in child development can make children more interesting to us because it helps us understand them better. We acquire some of this understanding from what psychologists tell us about children's behavior, but most of what we gain comes from looking at children in new ways—through psychologists' eyes, so to speak. We will never be able to understand all we observe, of course; but reading the research is certain to give us a different perspective on children and their behavior, and we should then begin to notice significant details that we might otherwise overlook. We may even gain helpful insights into our own behavior.

Will our newfound understanding enable us to deal with children more effectively? Perhaps so, but this should not be our major goal. If we focus on improving our understanding, and if understanding children makes them more interesting to us, we are bound to respond to them in a different way, and we should become more effective as a result. We may even discover that children are, after all, a source of unending interest and enjoyment.

Contributors

Gerald R. Adams received his master's degree in psychology at the University of Nebraska in Omaha, and is now at the College of Human Development, Pennsylvania State University. The co-author of his contribution, Norman H. Hamm, also served as his thesis adviser and co-researcher.

Samuel H. Ball is a native of Australia and received his doctorate at the University of Iowa. He taught at the Newcastle Teachers College in New South Wales and is currently a research psychologist at the Educational Testing Service, Princeton, New Jersey. He is also on the faculty of Teachers College, Columbia University.

William Ball was formerly a co-researcher with Edward Tronick at the Center for Cognitive Studies, Harvard University.

Jarvis Barnes has worked with Stephen Nowicki, Jr., as a research associate in the Psychology Department of Emory University, Atlanta, Georgia.

Arthur L. Beaman is in the Psychology Department of the University of Montana at Missoula.

413

Mary E. Blatchley has been associated with Donald R. Ottinger and Victor H. Denenberg as a research worker in the Psychology Department, Purdue University.

Robert H. Blinn has worked with Leonard I. Jacobson as a psychological researcher at the University of Miami in Florida.

Gerry Ann Bogatz is Assistant Program Director of Elementary and Secondary School Programs at the Educational Testing Service, Princeton, New Jersey.

Beverly W. Brekke is a member of the faculty of the Department of Special Education, University of North Dakota at Grand Forks.

Wagner Harold Bridger received his M.D. from New York University and is presently professor of psychiatry at the Albert Einstein College of Medicine in New York City. He has done extensive research in developmental, experimental, and cognitive psychology, as well as in physiology, psychopharmacology, and ethology.

Lyle J. Buchanan, Jr., received his master's degree in psychology at San Francisco State University. Henry Clay Lindgren, his co-author, was his thesis adviser and co-researcher.

Roberta Randall Collard is on the faculty of the University of Massachusetts at Amherst. She received her degree from the University of Chicago and has done research in birth order, creativity, and emotional adjustment in young children.

Arthur F. Constantini is a member of the faculty of the Department of Child Psychology and Family Relations of the University of Connecticut at Storrs. He received his training from Kent State University in Ohio.

Victor Hugo Denenberg is a professor of biobehavioral science at the University of Connecticut in Storrs. He received his degree at Purdue University and has done extensive research in comparative, physiological, and experimental psychology.

Wayne Dennis is an emeritus professor of psychology of Queens College. He is well known for his studies with Hopi, Iranian, Sudanese, and Lebanese children, and is currently involved in a research program at the American University of Beirut.

Carol Diener and Edward F. Diener have worked as researchers in the field of social psychology at the University of Washington.

Victor M. Dmitruk received his degree from the University of Michigan and is a member of the psychology faculty at Grand Valley State College, Allendale, Michigan.

Lynn Dorman is a former kindergarten teacher who received her degree from Boston University. Her contribution to this book is based on her doctoral dissertation.

Toni Falbo has done work in psycholinguistics and cross-cultural psychology as a researcher with the Psychology Department of the University of California at Los Angeles.

Ruth Formanek received her degree from the University of Vienna. She is a member of the staff of the Jewish Community Services of Long Island and of the education faculty at Hofstra University, Hempstead, Long Island.

Seymour J. Friedland received his degree from Clark University and is on the faculty of Tufts University. He also serves as psychological consultant to the city school system of Lowell, Massachusetts.

Howard Lawrence Garber is a research associate in the Department of Behavioral Disabilities at the University of Wisconsin at Madison. His chief responsibility is that of coordinating research and assessment of the Family Rehabilitation, also known as the Milwaukee Project. In addition, he serves as a consultant to inner-city elementary schools that are developing curricular materials designed to facilitate cognitive development. He holds his doctorate from the University of Wisconsin.

Mark Golden has done research in the social psychology of children. He received his degree from the University of California at Los Angeles, and is on the faculty of the Albert Einstein College of Medicine.

Patricia Marks Greenfield worked with Jerome S. Bruner at the Center for Cognitive Growth at Harvard University, where she received her doctorate.

She has been on the faculties of Syracuse University, Stanford University, and the University of California at Santa Cruz and at Los Angeles.

Norman H. Hamm has done considerable research in the social psychology of children. He is on the psychology staff of the University of Nebraska at Omaha.

Harry F. Harlow has had a distinguished career as an experimental psychologist, working with primates on such diverse topics as problem solving, maternal deprivation, brain lesions, and sexual behavior. He served a term as the president of the American Psychological Association and is research professor at the University of Wisconsin.

Steven D. Harlow is a member of the faculty of the College of Education, Kansas State University at Manhattan.

Mary B. Harris received her degree from Stanford University and is on the staff of the Educational Foundations Department of New Mexico State University at Las Cruces.

Richard Franz Heber is Director of the Waisman Center on Mental Retardation and Human Development of the University of Wisconsin at Madison. A Canadian by birth, he has been educated at the University of Arkansas and Michigan State University, as well as at George Peabody College, where he received his doctorate. He has written extensively in the field of mental retardation.

Edmund H. Henderson is the director of the McGuffey Reading Center of the University of Virginia in Charlottesville. He received his degree at the University of Delaware.

Kenneth L. Hoving is professor of psychology at Kent State University in Ohio. He received his degree from the University of Washington and has done research in cognitive development during childhood.

Leonard I. Jacobson has conducted studies in cognitive, social, and emotional development in childhood. He is a member of the psychology staff of the University of Miami at Coral Gables and received his training at the State University of New York at Buffalo.

Spencer Kagan has worked with Millard C. Madsen as a co-researcher at the Center for Research in Early Childhood Education, University of California at Los Angeles.

Patrick C. Lee is on the faculty of the Program for Early Childhood Education, Teachers College, Columbia University. He received his degree from Syracuse University.

Anna Leifer is a school psychologist with the Bethpage Schools in New York and is also a member of the faculty of Yeshiva University, where she received her degree.

Henry Clay Lindgren received his degree from Stanford University and is professor of psychology at San Francisco State University. He has published in the fields of developmental, social, educational, and counseling psychology.

Barbara Henry Long has conducted a number of studies on the social and personality development of children, with special emphasis on cross-cultural comparisons. She heads the Psychology Department at Goucher College in Baltimore, and received her degree from the University of Delaware.

Anne McIntyre is on the faculty of the Department of Human Development and Family Studies of Cornell University. She received training at Yale University and has shown special interest in children's emotional development, personality, and motivation.

John Paul McKinney received his doctorate at Ohio State University and is a member of the psychology faculty at Michigan State University. He has published in the field of social and cognitive development during childhood and adolescence.

Millard C. Madsen is on the psychology staff of the University of California at Los Angeles. He received his degree at the University of Oregon and has conducted cross-cultural research into the social and personality development in childhood.

Maria Jorgiza Mello is a consultant in educational psychology at the Demonstration School operated by the Regional Center for Educational Research in Bahia, Brazil. She was a Fulbright scholar at the University of Indiana and was also awarded a fellowship for the first UNESCO Seminar for the Training of Educational Researchers at the University of São Paulo, where she worked with Henry Clay Lindgren.

Albert Montare worked as a co-researcher with Mark Golden and Wagner Bridger when he was at Yeshiva University.

James Kenneth Morrison received his master's degree at the State University of New York at Albany and is on the staff of the Schenectady County Child Guidance Center in New York.

Tien-Ing Chyou Niem is a co-researcher with Roberta Randall Collard in the Department of Human Development, University of Massachusetts at Amherst.

Stephen P. Nowicki, Jr., received his doctorate from Purdue University and is a member of the psychology faculty at Mount St. Agnes College in Baltimore.

Susan Oldfield was formerly a co-researcher with Joy D. Osofsky at the New York State College of Human Ecology at Cornell University.

Anthony B. Oeljnik received his master's degree at Michigan State University. John P. McKinney was his thesis adviser and co-researcher.

Joy Doniger Osofsky is a member of the psychology faculty at Temple University in Philadelphia. She is also a consultant to the Department of Obstetrics and Gynecology and the Department of Neonatal Health of the Temple University Health Science Center. She received her degree from Cornell University and has been active in research dealing with child-parent interaction.

Donald R. Ottinger received his doctorate from Purdue University, where he is on the psychology staff. He is especially interested in the clinical problems of infancy and early childhood.

Paul Conrad Rosenblatt is a member of the Departments of Family Social Science and Psychology at the University of Minnesota. He received his degree from Northwestern University.

Sandra Wood Scarr-Salapatek has done research on cognition and behavior genetics in childhood. She received her training at Harvard University.

Elizabeth Skoogberg was formerly a co-researcher with Paul Conrad Rosenblatt in the Department of Family Social Science at the University of Minnesota.

Stephen J. Suomi is a researcher at the Primate Laboratory of the Psychology Department of the University of Wisconsin in Madison. He received his training at the University of Wisconsin and has done research in social and sexual behavior and in early experience of primates.

Ellis Paul Torrance is chairman of the Department of Educational Psychology, University of Georgia. He has done extensive research in the development of creativity in children and is the author of a widely used test of creativity.

Edward Tronick was formerly a researcher at the Center for Cognitive Studies, Harvard University.

Steven Robert Tulkin is a clinical and developmental psychologist who received his training at Harvard University. He is a member of the psychology faculty at the State University of New York at Buffalo.

Crane Walker and Timothy S. Walker are a husband-wife team of psychologists who received their training at the University of Georgia.

Emmy Elizabeth Werner has been active as a consultant and a research worker in India, Nepal, Thailand, and Indonesia as well as on the Island of Kauai, Hawaii. She received her training at the Universities of Mainz, California at Berkeley, and Nebraska; she is presently a staff member of the Department of Applied Behavioral Sciences, University of California at Davis.

Karen L. Westford is a social psychologist who is associated with the Psychology Department of the University of Washington.

John Delane Williams is professor of educational statistics at the University of North Dakota. He received his training at the University of Northern Colorado.

Pierre C. Woog received his doctorate at Hofstra University, Hempstead, Long Island, and is also a member of the Educational Psychology Department of that institution. In addition, he serves as a consultant to the Hempstead Schools.

Glossary

alleles A term used in genetics to refer to pairs of genes (the basic units of heredity) that affect the same traits.

analysis of variance (ANOVA) A statistical technique that enables an investigator to draw conclusions about differences between two or more groups or samples of subjects on a common measure. The performance differences between the samples are analyzed to determine the probability that they resulted from chance alone.

binomial test A test of statistical significance comparing the observed frequency of a binary event (such as heads versus tails, hits versus misses, or highs versus lows) against the frequencies predicted by chance.

biogenetics The science of the development of inherited traits in living organisms.

CA (chronological age) The number of years old an individual is; usually contrasted with MA (mental age), which represents a mental test score characteristic of the average child of a specified chronological age. A child has a mental age of 8 if his score is the same as that of an average eight-year-old child.

cathexis   A psychoanalytic term that refers to the affective or emotional value of an object, idea, or action.

chi square (χ^2)   A statistical test employed to compare observed frequencies of dichotomous or categorical events with hypothetical or expected frequencies. The chi square formula is used to obtain a ratio, which is then referred to a table of probability values arranged according to the number of *degrees of freedom* permitted by the number of categories into which the observations have been classified.

concrete operations period   The stage of cognitive development that occurs between the approximate ages of seven and twelve, during which a child typically acquires the ability to conserve, classify, and arrange objects in serial order.

conservation   A child's awareness that it is possible for one aspect of an object (shape, for example) to change without other aspects (weight or volume, for example) changing. Essentially, conservation refers to the ability to attend to relevant elements and to resist being distracted by irrelevant ones.

correlation   A statistical technique for measuring the degree of relationship between paired measures of each member of a set of individuals or cases (height and weight, for example). A correlational statistic that is frequently used is the Pearson product moment correlation, also termed Pearsonian *r*, or, simply, *r*.

degrees of freedom   In statistics, the number of observations (that is, subjects, test items, scores, trials, and so forth) less the number of prior calculations based on the sample or group. This reduction gives a more conservative basis for estimating the significance of the resulting statistic.

demographic   Refers to vital statistics, geographic distributions, and related measures of human populations.

dependent variable   The *variable* that is affected by and can be predicted from the *independent variable.*

dizygotic (DZ)   Refers to unlike or fraternal twins, who develop from separate fertilized eggs. Such twins are no more similar genetically than any other pair of siblings.

E   The experimenter or one of his assistants (*pl* Es).

eugenic   Relating to attempts to improve the inborn or inherited characteristics of the human race.

euthenic   Relating to scientific attempts to improve the human race by bringing about changes in the environment.

F ratio, or F value   A statistical index of the extent to which the means of samples or groups differ from one another. The most important difference between F ratio and the t test is that the t test is used to test differences between only two means, while F ratio reflects variations between two or more means.

Fisher exact probability test, or Fisher test   A technique like *chi square*, used to compare or contrast observed and categorized frequencies with expected or hypothetical frequencies. Usually employed with observations of small samples that can be categorized into two-by-two tables.

formal operations stage   The fourth stage of Piaget's theory, beginning at about age twelve. During this period, logical thinking develops, and the child takes the final steps toward abstract thinking and conceptualizing.

genotype   The hereditary factors that have a causative effect on development; the characteristics that are inherited and transmitted to offspring.

Gestalt traditions   Concepts emanating from a group of early twentieth century German and Austrian psychologists who emphasized the wholeness of experience, especially in perception.

h^2 Refers to heritability narrowly defined in terms of *correlations* between measures of traits (such as intelligence) in related individuals.

heterogeneous grouping   The educational practice of placing children of about the same age in the same class or grade without respect to differences in their ability.

homogeneous grouping   The educational practice of subdividing classes or groups of children into smaller groups of approximately equal ability, usually according to intelligence test scores.

independent variable   The *variable* that influences the *dependent variable* and can therefore be used to predict it.

intentionality   The degree to which an observer is aware of the intentions of another, especially of one who is misbehaving.

interaction (between variables)   Concurrent changes in two or more *variables*.

internalization   The process whereby one individual imitates the values, attitudes, standards, ideas, or actions of another and makes them his own.

interobserver (inter-O) reliability   The extent to which two or more observers are in agreement.

in utero   In a fetal stage; literally, "in the uterus."

IQ (intelligence quotient)   A ratio derived by dividing a child's mental age (MA) by his chronological age (CA) and multiplying the result by 100 to eliminate decimals. (Most intelligence test manuals today contain tables permitting the direct conversion of raw scores to IQs without going through this manipulation.)

latency period   In psychoanalytic theory, the period from about the fifth to the twelfth year of childhood, during which the child's sexual drives are presumed to be inactive.

learning tradition   Refers, in contrast with the Gestalt tradition, to the precise and rigorously controlled study by laboratory methods of highly specific responses to stimuli.

level of significance   An arbitrarily selected limit of the percentage of uncertainty or chance that an investigator will permit and still maintain confidence in his results. The usual limit accepted by psychologists is the 5% (.05) level, which is assumed to mean that the probability (p) is less than 5% ($p < .05$) that the observed difference or relationship is due to chance. The smaller the p value (for instance, $p < .02$ or even $p < .001$), the greater the likelihood that the observed difference or relationship is not due to chance. In some instances, investigators report p values larger than .05 (for instance, $p < .06$, or $p < .10$) if they feel that their findings are interesting or suggestive of further investigation or speculation. "Level of confidence" is sometimes used as a synonym for level of significance, although it actually has a somewhat different rationale.

Likert-type scale   A way of constructing attitude scales that permits the respondent to indicate a greater range or intensity of agreement or disagreement than is allowed by a yes-no answer. The investigator may provide, for example, a series of five-step choices ranging from "strongly agree" to "strongly disagree."

Lowenfeld Mosaic test, or mosaic test   A projective test of personality in which the subject is told to make anything he wishes out of 465 wooden tiles of different colors and shapes.

M, or mean   The arithmetical average, calculated by dividing the sum of all the observations or scores by the number (N) of observations.

MA (mental age)   See CA.

Mann-Whitney U test   An alternative to the t test, especially useful with small samples.

modal, mode   The most common value in a series or range of observations or scores.

monozygotic (MZ)   Refers to like or identical twins, who develop from the same fertilized egg. Pairs of such twins are always of the same sex and have identical genes.

moral judgment development   Progress through stages of judging the conduct of oneself and others with respect to some socially derived standard of behavior.

multivariate analysis of variance   An *analysis of variance* that includes a greater number of *independent variables* than a simple analysis of variance does.

N, or n   The number of cases, observations, or scores.

N.S., or n.s.   Not statistically significant; frequently used with reference to the arbitrarily selected limit of $p < .05$.

neonatal, neonate   Referring to a newborn infant.

O (observer)   Since all scores, ratings, and measures of performance are considered observations, every experimenter (E) is therefore an observer; however, the term *observer* is usually applied specifically to an experimenter who actually observes and notes the behavior of one or more subjects.

oedipal stage   In psychoanalytic theory, a stage during early childhood when a boy experiences an intense longing for his mother and a desire to replace his father in her affections.

one-tailed tests   A term used with reference to the level of significance or cut-off point beyond which the investigator will reject the hypothesis that his results are due to chance alone. Lower *correlations* and smaller differences will fall beyond the cut-off point and will therefore be significant, if the investigator's hypothesis makes a one-tailed test appropriate. If his hypothesis calls for a two-tailed test, correlations or differences must be greater in order to be considered statistically significant.

orienting response (reflex), or OR   A state of arousal in which the organism focuses its attention on the stimulus that alerted it.

p value   See *level of significance.*

Pearson *t* test   See *t test.*

perceptual cue   A specific portion or characteristic of a perceptual field or pattern of stimuli that leads to some consistent response.

person judgment   The way in which an individual is valued or appraised.

phenotype   The characteristics of an organism that can be observed or measured; often contrasted with *genotype.*

point biserial *r*   A statistic employed to describe the relationship between a continuous variable, such as height or IQ, and a dichotomous (either-or) variable, such as sex.

polygenic   Refers to traits that are influenced by more than one gene pair; also refers to a mingling of genes from more than one ancestral source.

postpartum   After childbirth.

prelatency period   The period of childhood just preceding the *latency period.*

preoperational thought period   The stage in development, according to Piaget, that occurs between about eighteen months and seven years of age, when the child is beginning to encounter reality on a representational level.

psychometric   Relating to the use of psychological tests.

psychopathology   Mental or behavioral disturbance or disorder.

r value   See *correlation.*

regression effects   The tendency for values to occur closer to the *mean* with repeated measurement or observation.

reinforcement   A process that increases the strength of a response or the frequency of its occurrence. The term is also applied to the stimulus employed to strengthen a response or to increase the rate of responding.

reliability coefficient   A *correlation* that indicates the extent to which a psychological measuring instrument or technique is dependable, stable, and internally consistent.

Rorschach test   The well-known "ink-blot" test. The subject or patient is encouraged to make free verbal interpretations of the blot. His responses are analyzed by the psychometrist in order to determine personality patterns or to identify problems of adjustment.

S   The subject in an experiment or investigation (*pl* Ss).

schizophrenia   A severe mental or behavioral disorder characterized by a group of symptoms involving fundamental disturbances in the individual's relationships with others, coupled with an inability to express hostility and aggressive feelings directly.

sensorimotor period   According to Piaget, the period from birth to about two years of age, when the infant is figuratively and literally coming to grips with his physical environment.

serological   Specifically relating to blood serum, but used to refer to studies of the characteristics of blood samples drawn from preselected donors.

Spearman-Brown formula   A formula employed in estimating the reliability of a test, using the split-half method.

split-half reliability or technique   A procedure whereby the responses made by a group of subjects to a test are divided, usually into two groups (for example, responses to odd items and responses to even items). The *correlation* between the scores of two sets of responses is usually modified by the *Spearman-Brown formula*, whereupon it serves as an estimate of the reliability of the test.

standard deviation (S.D.)   A measure of the dispersion or variation occurring within a collection of scores, measures, or observations.

stepwise multiple regression analysis   A complex type of analysis, usually performed with the aid of a computer program, that enables the investigator to analyze a great many more interactions among variables than would be possible by hand or even by machine calculations.

stimulus item   An arrangement of stimuli that is employed as an *independent variable* in an experiment.

Student's *t*   See *t* test.

t test   A ratio used to determine whether a *correlation* or a difference between *means* can be considered to be statistically significant.

transference   In psychoanalysis, the process whereby a patient transfers to his psychoanalyst the feelings he has toward another person.

variable   An event or measure that may be higher or lower in value. In experimental situations, the stimulus that is introduced by the experimenter becomes the *independent variable,* and the response that is thereby evoked becomes the *dependent variable.*

χ^2 See *chi square.*

z test   One type of test of statistical significance. See *level of significance.*

Index